DIGITAL
AFRICA

DIGITAL AFRICA

Technological Transformation for Jobs

Tania Begazo
Moussa P. Blimpo
Mark A. Dutz

WORLD BANK GROUP

Contents

CHAPTER 1

CHAPTER 2

CHAPTER 3

CHAPTER 4

TABLES

Foreword

As Africa's population grows, creating more and better jobs for youth will be essential for poverty reduction and shared prosperity. This report, *Digital Africa: Technological Transformation for Jobs*, makes the case for putting digital technologies at the center of a good-jobs strategy for the continent.

The report's overview of current challenges establishes that, although Africa's mobile internet availability has increased in recent years, its internet infrastructure and the quality of available services still lag behind other regions. Divides in the availability of quality digital services remain an issue in all countries, especially in remote and poorer subregions.

Additionally, Africa lags behind other regions in the use of internet services. Although 84 percent of country populations averaged across Sub-Saharan Africa live in areas where a minimal quality level of 3G or 4G mobile internet services is available, only 22 percent were actually using these services by the end of 2021.

A lack of *affordable* coverage partly explains this significant usage gap. Forty percent of Africans fall below the global extreme poverty line, and even basic mobile data plans alone can represent about one-third of their incomes. African small and medium businesses also face more expensive data plans than their counterparts in other regions.

Addressing these constraints will yield major dividends for development. The report offers robust evidence that internet availability can increase jobs and reduce poverty. Furthermore, new empirical data presented on Nigeria and Tanzania add to the rapidly growing literature about the direct impact of mobile internet availability (3G or 4G coverage) on jobs and welfare outcomes.

The new conceptual framework in this report focuses on policies that prioritize digital tools for *productive use* to generate inclusive, jobs-related spillover effects while expanding coverage of higher-quality broadband internet. These digital tools can create greater demand that, in turn, allows for increased investments in higher-quality digital and complementary technologies. Innovations are essential to attract people with fewer skills and boost their potential to generate higher earnings.

Strategic policies are critical to encourage the use of digital technologies. Interventions can include curbing excessive market power in order to drive down costs, undertaking complementary public investments, and supporting credit and demand-support programs to overcome affordability barriers and enable quality internet connectivity in underserved or remote areas. Specific data policies are also required to enable wider availability of relevant apps and to enhance trust in digital services. This report also recommends a new focus on developing more appropriate and accessible apps that support managers and lower-skilled workers so that they can learn as they work.

Digital technology is a necessary ingredient of economic transformation, and it plays a role in addressing multiple challenges from education to energy. As this report shows, it is imperative that policy makers scale up the availability and use of quality digital services across Africa to improve the lives of its citizens and unlock the potential of the continent to achieve inclusive development.

Guangzhe Chen
Vice President for Infrastructure
The World Bank

Ousmane Diagana
Regional Vice President for Western and Central Africa
The World Bank

Victoria Kwakwa
Regional Vice President for Eastern and Southern Africa
The World Bank

Acknowledgments

Digital Africa: Technological Transformation for Jobs is dedicated to Princeton University Professor Emeritus Robert (Bobby) Willig, in memory of his passion and excellence in developing and teaching microeconomics for improved public policies addressing social welfare. This book's focus on innovation-led productivity as a driver of inclusive jobs growth, supported by market competition in the provision of infrastructure services and grass-roots entrepreneurship, was deeply influenced by his work.

This report was prepared in support of the World Bank's Digital Economy for Africa Initiative (DE4A). It is the product of a collaboration across the World Bank's teams in the Africa; Infrastructure; and Equitable Growth, Finance and Institutions Vice Presidencies under the oversight of the Office of the Chief Economist of the Africa Region and the Office of the Chief Economist of the Infrastructure Vice Presidency. The preparation of this report was co-led by Tania Begazo, Moussa P. Blimpo, and Mark A. Dutz.

The main authors are as follows:

- *Chapters 1 and 2:* Mark Dutz, with contributions of original research for Africa from Carlos Rodríguez-Castelán and Takaaki Masaki on the effects of digital connectivity on household welfare; Xavier Cirera and Marcio Cruz on digital technology adoption by firms; İzak Atiyas on mobile internet availability and use as well as digital technology adoption by microenterprises; César Calderón and Catalina Cantú on the effects of digitalization on growth and poverty reduction; Georges Houngbonon, Justice Mensah, and Nouhoum Traoré on the effects of digital infrastructure availability on entrepreneurship and investment; Juni Zhu on digital business analysis; and Clara Stinshoff on Apptopia data analysis

- *Chapter 3:* Moussa Blimpo, with contributions from Ramaele Moshoeshoe and support from Henry Aviomoh and Tchapo Gbandi

- *Chapter 4:* Tania Begazo, with contributions from Clara Stinshoff, Estefania Vergara-Cobos, Xavier Decoster, Tim Kelly, Jerome Bezzina, and Aneliya Muller, and original research by Edward Oughton, Genaro Cruz, and Kalvin Bahia on geospatial data and broadband internet in Africa

The authors are especially appreciative of the various background research papers prepared for this report and cited throughout it.

The work commenced with an internal workshop on regional digital infrastructure regulation in Africa held at the World Bank on March 28, 2019, that benefited from the participation of Penny Goldberg, Paul Klemperer, and the late Robert Willig.

The book benefited from useful guidance and advice from Simon Andrews, Haroon Bhorat, Pablo Fajnzylber, Mary Hallward-Driemeier, Daniel Lederman, Aliou Maiga, and Deepak Mishra, among others present at the book's inception and decision meetings.

The team also incorporated feedback from members of the research program advisory committee including Daniel Björkegren, Ibrahim Elbadawi, Avi Goldfarb, Jonas Hjort, Ayhan Kose, Njuguna Ndung'u, Yaw Nyarko, and Davide Strusani. The team remains grateful for their helpful suggestions.

Finally, this flagship report was conducted under the general direction of Albert Zeufack and Vivien Foster, with contributions from Andrew Dabalen. The team is also grateful for the overarching guidance received from Hafez M. H. Ghanem, Riccardo Puliti, Boutheina Guermazi, Christine Qiang, Michel Rogy, and Isabel Neto.

Beatrice Berman, Flore Martinant de Preneuf, Kelly Alderson, and Breen Byrnes provided superb communications support. Justice Mensah helped oversee the finalization of the book from the Office of the Chief Economist of the Africa Region. Nora FitzGerald, Mary Anderson, and Nora Mara provided timely editorial assistance. The World Bank's formal publishing team included production editor Mark McClure, acquisitions editor Jewel McFadden, and print coordinator Orlando Mota.

About the Authors

Tania Begazo is a senior economist in the Markets and Technology unit of the World Bank's Trade, Investment and Competitiveness Practice Group. She leads analytical initiatives and provides technical guidance on competition policy. In a previous position at the Digital Development Global Practice, she oversaw major economic policy and research initiatives related to digital infrastructure and policy to inform thought leadership, corporate strategy, and operational engagements with clients, with an emphasis on Africa. She led the dissemination of knowledge on digital development and contributed to the formulation and implementation of country operations targeting reforms in the digital sector, building on collaboration within the World Bank Group and external partners. Formerly, she was the global lead of the World Bank Group's Markets and Competition Policy team, overseeing the competition policy portfolio covering more than 60 countries and key areas for thought leadership and external partnerships. She also worked for the International Telecommunication Union, APOYO Consultoría, and the Peruvian telecommunications regulator. She holds a master's degree in public administration in international development from Harvard University.

Moussa P. Blimpo is an assistant professor of economic inequality and societies at the University of Toronto's Munk School of Global Affairs and Public Policy. Earlier, he was a senior economist in the World Bank's Office of the Chief Economist for the Africa Region. He is primarily an applied economist interested in a range of research and policy issues in low- and middle-income economies, mainly in Africa. Before joining the World Bank, he served for three years as an assistant professor of economics and international studies at the University of Oklahoma. He is a senior fellow at the Clean Air Task Force's Energy and Climate Innovation Program in Africa and is a fellow at the Energy for Growth Hub; he was the founding director of the Center for Research and Opinion Polls, a think tank in Togo that he led between 2011 and 2015. He holds a doctorate in economics from New York University and spent two years as a postdoctoral fellow at Stanford University's Institute for Economic Policy Research.

Mark A. Dutz is a consultant in the Economic Policy Research department of the International Finance Corporation of the World Bank Group. He contributes to work on productivity growth and its interaction with poverty reduction and shared prosperity. He has worked at the World Bank since 1990 and has experience in all regions and in the Office of the Chief Economist, as well as most recently as lead economist in the Office of the Chief Economist for Africa. He also has worked as a senior consultant with Compass Lexecon LLC, as senior adviser to Türkiye's Minister of Economic Affairs and Treasury, as principal economist in the European Bank for Reconstruction and Development's Office of the Chief Economist, and as consultant to Organisation for Economic

Co-operation and Development, World Trade Organization, World Intellectual Property Organization, and Canada's Networks of Centers of Excellence. He has published journal articles and books on applied microeconomics, including on competition, innovation, digital technology adoption, productivity, climate change, and investment and trade issues, as well as their links to growth and inclusion. He has also taught at Princeton University, from which he holds a doctorate in economics and a master's degree in public affairs.

Main Messages

The promise of technological transformation for a growing African workforce

Digital technologies (DTs) have emerged as an essential element of a good-jobs strategy for African countries. *Digital Africa: Technological Transformation for Jobs* presents the best available evidence on the transformative effects of DTs—showing, for instance, that internet use significantly increases inclusive jobs on the continent, which is poised to have the *largest workforce in the world by 2100* relative to other regions.

The report's robust analysis provides strategies that can be adopted to capitalize on this growing evidence. For example, when high-quality internet (third- or fourth-generation mobile communications technology, 3G or 4G) was available for at least three years, *labor force participation increased by 3 percentage points in Nigeria and by 8 points in Tanzania.* In addition, poverty rates fell by 7 percentage points in each country. These welfare impacts were higher among poorer and less-educated households.

In highlighting results such as these, the report informs the digitalization and complementary technology adoption policies and programs that African governments can employ for *inclusive* impact—jobs that generate income growth for all, including faster per capita income growth for the bottom 40 percent of each country's population as well as for women and for lower-skilled workers more generally. It is especially intended for technical advisers who provide input for government policies on economic transformation and growth in Africa, although it should also be of interest to all people in the region. Government beneficiaries include ministries and regulators in charge of information and communications, finance, industry (agriculture, manufacturing, and services), competition, technology and innovation, and jobs and poverty reduction.

Africa's digital challenges and divides

The primary challenge for Africa is its low productive use of DTs. Enterprises and households alike need *greater ability to pay for* and *willingness to productively use* these technologies, as the following findings show.

- As a share of country populations averaged across Sub-Saharan Africa, 84 percent live in areas where mobile internet services are available, yet only 22 percent used them by the end of 2021. This usage rate is the lowest in the world.

- Enterprise digitalization is also low, and small and medium businesses in Africa pay more for data plans than those in other regions, while 70 percent of surveyed microenterprises do not perceive the need for internet-supported technologies.

- Forty percent of Africans fall below the global extreme poverty line, meaning the cost of even basic mobile data plans would represent about one-third of their incomes. Only about 5 percent of extremely poor households access the internet.

- Africa's lagging internet infrastructure and service quality constrain potential user willingness to use DTs. Although the region's mobile internet availability has increased in recent years, it still lags the world's other regions—especially regarding the quality of digital services, requiring support by reliable and resilient infrastructure.

Policies to boost DT use for more, and better, jobs

Africa needs more activist policies that promote the use of digital and complementary technologies, especially affordable, attractive skill-appropriate technologies that support productive and inclusive jobs. Such policies must target all potential users' ability to pay for these technologies as well as their willingness to productively use them.

Policies that ensure the ability to pay should address internet affordability, additional infrastructure availability, adequate data infrastructure, and availability of affordable complementary technologies. *Policies that support greater willingness to use* should focus on developing more attractive applications and building the awareness and education required for productive DT adoption. These policies include innovation policies, data policies and regulations, capability support programs, and national strategies for productive use of DTs.

- *Internet affordability policies* encompass effective pro-competition regulations to reduce investment costs, including rules on licensing and market dominance, infrastructure access and sharing, and spectrum availability and use, ideally through more integrated continental markets. Regulations to help drive down operational costs include rules on access to essential infrastructure controlled by state-owned enterprises, operation of open-access fiber networks, and progressive elimination of excise taxes.

- *Policies for better internet quality everywhere and for availability in areas that are not commercially viable* after implementing regulatory reforms require targeted interventions. Demand-side incentives and financing (through earmarked funds, obligations on operators, and universal service funds) can boost use, improve service quality, and support climate-resilient infrastructure development.

- *Policies for affordable availability of data infrastructure* include pro-competition rules for upgrading internet exchange points that can grow into regional data centers and cloud computing facilities to help drive down costs. Effective regional integration for cross-border digital connectivity and data markets is critical to gain economies of scale and to expand and upgrade data infrastructure.

- *Policies to support affordable access to complementary analog technologies* require broader interventions. Improvement of electricity, transportation, and agricultural (tractors and irrigation) systems would enhance the income-generation potential of DT use and strengthen potential users' ability to pay.

- *Innovation policies* can redirect technology development toward generating and scaling up skill-appropriate DTs. To enable enterprises and households to use DTs and learn as they work, Africa must provide sophisticated, inclusive, and attractive apps through touch-screen pictures, voice, and video in languages that local people speak. Development requires public-private investments in public goods, such as country-wide availability of digital addresses, geotagged land records, and local weather mapping, as well as public goods specific to value chains. More integrated continental markets will allow entrepreneurs to profitably design and scale attractive apps that are affordable and enhance people's earnings.

- *Data policies* are needed as both enablers and safeguards of data use and reuse to ensure the development of new, attractive, data-driven DTs, along with appropriate levels of trust in their use.

- *Capability support programs* to enhance the productive use of available DTs must be institutionalized for micro, small, and medium enterprises as well as for households. These programs include business advisory services, technology information and upgrading services, and manager and worker skills training, together with longer-term investments in high-quality secondary and tertiary education.

- *National strategies* are essential to support familiarity with and use of DTs to support higher earnings. They could include investments in common-access facilities at internet cafés, local schools, or community centers, especially for microentrepreneurs.

Overview

Africa's imperative: Better technology for better jobs

For Africa's large and growing youthful labor force to thrive, the continent urgently needs good jobs. Countries need business environments conducive to generating the kinds of jobs that enable productive learning as a basis for supporting growth in earnings over time.

Africa's jobs and technology challenges are immense and urgent. Its share of the global workforce is projected to become the largest in the world by the twenty-second century, rising from 16 percent in 2025 to over 41 percent by 2100. More than 22 million Africans between the ages of 15 and 64 join the workforce each year—almost 2 million people per month. This flow of workers is expected to increase to over 33 million per year by 2050 (UN DESA 2022). The imperative is to create good jobs for these millions of young entrants to the workforce and better jobs for today's workers. Greater adoption of improved and adequate technologies is a critical and underemphasized requirement to meet this goal. Moreover, the continent needs better technologies and products that all Africans want and can afford to buy.

Africa has the potential to generate more and better jobs through greater adoption of technologies that enable scaled-up production and hence generate good jobs in expanding medium and large firms, entrepreneurial start-ups, and informal microenterprises. Often, though, productive technologies are designed in higher-income countries for use by workers with higher skill levels or to replace tasks performed by people to reduce the workers required. Adoption of such technologies in Africa can lead larger local firms to become more productive and competitive but generate few additional jobs. Smaller firms rarely use these technologies, remaining at lower productivity and competitiveness, with jobs that pay too little. And these technologies are often not appropriate for more productive use by lower-skilled owners, managers, and workers in Africa's labor-abundant countries.

There are two ways to bridge the gap between technologies designed for use in higher-income economies and those needed in the low- and middle-income world, especially in African countries. The conventional strategy involves investment in longer-term upgrading of skills to match the level for which these technologies have been designed. The alternative is for entrepreneurs to design technologies—often requiring cutting-edge adaptations of existing products—to fit with current skill levels and needs, ensuring that the technologies are attractive and easy to use, labor-augmenting, and supportive of continuous learning and higher worker productivity.

African economies require a technological transformation that generates both productive learning and job growth. The challenge is to produce and promote the expanded use of affordable, attractive, skill-appropriate technologies that support jobs that are more productive and inclusive—that is, jobs that generate income growth for all, including faster income per capita growth for the bottom 40 percent of each country's population. Fortunately, Africa's demographic dynamics can positively affect the use of new technologies. Great potential lies in the continent's large and growing youth population, including tech-savvy entrepreneurs, managers, and workers likely to generate and use new digital and complementary technologies. By using better technologies, Africans can produce more goods and services for consumption in local markets and for export, thereby generating more good jobs for Africans.

Contributions of the *Digital Africa* report

New analyses to support job growth strategies

This overview and the full report provide new analyses to support improved efforts on the part of governments and the private sector to spur more inclusive job growth with appropriate technologies while narrowing the current digital divides. These findings can inform the implementation of the African Union's Digital Transformation Strategy for Africa (2020–2030) (AU 2020) and the Digital Economy for Africa initiative.[1]

The overview also summarizes the report's diagnostic review of current trends and drivers of digital and data infrastructure availability, and the use of digital technologies (DTs) in Africa. Broadly defined, DTs include not only digital and data infrastructure, broadband internet, smartphones, tablets, and computers but also a wide range of more specialized productivity-enhancing digital solutions—ranging from communications, management upgrading, and worker training to procurement, production, marketing, logistics, and financing and insurance.

DTs enable economywide productivity gains and job growth by catalyzing the uptake and use of complementary technologies, including many that are inaccessible without digital and data infrastructure. In general, taking advantage of Internet of Things technologies requires investments in the "internet" as well as the "things." In the agriculture sector, for example, precision agriculture requires internet coverage. Foremost, however, it requires the prerequisite of tractors and irrigation systems that can then be equipped with sensors, as well as smartphones to access weather forecasts and upload pictures of unusual plant diseases. Appropriate apps with video or voice interfaces enable farmers to integrate into formal value chains, learn from upstream seed providers and downstream buyers, and gain better access to financing and markets.

Complementary technologies also include critical infrastructure for services such as electricity, transportation, and logistics. Therefore, even though the report largely focuses on provision and adoption of broadband internet, it must be viewed as an entry point or gateway to a broader discussion of the role of technology adoption—or lack thereof—in the ability of African economies to meet their job creation challenges.

A new conceptual framework for policy directions

The report answers three primary policy questions:

1. What are the effects of digital and data infrastructure, and the use of DTs, on enterprise productivity, jobs, and household welfare?

2. What is the extent of digital and data infrastructure availability and use of DTs and complementary technologies, and what are the main barriers preventing broader and more intensive productive use by enterprises and households?

3. What are key areas where policy and regulatory interventions could be implemented to strengthen consumers' ability to pay and willingness to use DTs for productive purposes?

The report's conceptual framework lays the foundation for this policy analysis, emphasizing that the impact of DTs on inclusive job growth depends on two objectives: ensuring potential users' *ability to pay for* and *willingness to use* DTs (figure O.1). First, the affordable availability of digital and data infrastructure is a prerequisite for inclusive job growth. And the affordable availability of DTs, including broadband internet, depends on the affordable availability of electricity and transportation infrastructure. Second, inclusive job growth from DTs requires a willingness among all enterprises and individuals to *use* these technologies—meaning that these consumers find DTs attractive to use, understand how to use them, and believe that the DTs meet their productivity needs with opportunities to learn. A complementary requirement is that users possess sufficient capabilities to use the DTs productively.

DTs can lead to faster job growth, more inclusive jobs, and improved household welfare, primarily through (a) jobs and labor income, and (b) entrepreneurship and capital income (figure O.1). Through the first of these channels, productive use of DTs enables better, more inclusive jobs as well as higher earnings for more people. Through the second channel, productive use of DTs increases entrepreneurial jobs and capital income, including profits earned not only by entrepreneurs and owners of larger firms but also by owners of smaller formal and informal enterprises.

By focusing on *productive use* and *inclusive impacts*, the conceptual framework highlights the critical distinction between two views of digitalization policy. Traditional digitalization policy prioritizes *universal availability* of digital infrastructure, largely a

FIGURE O.1 Conceptual framework for policy analysis of DTs' impacts on job and income growth

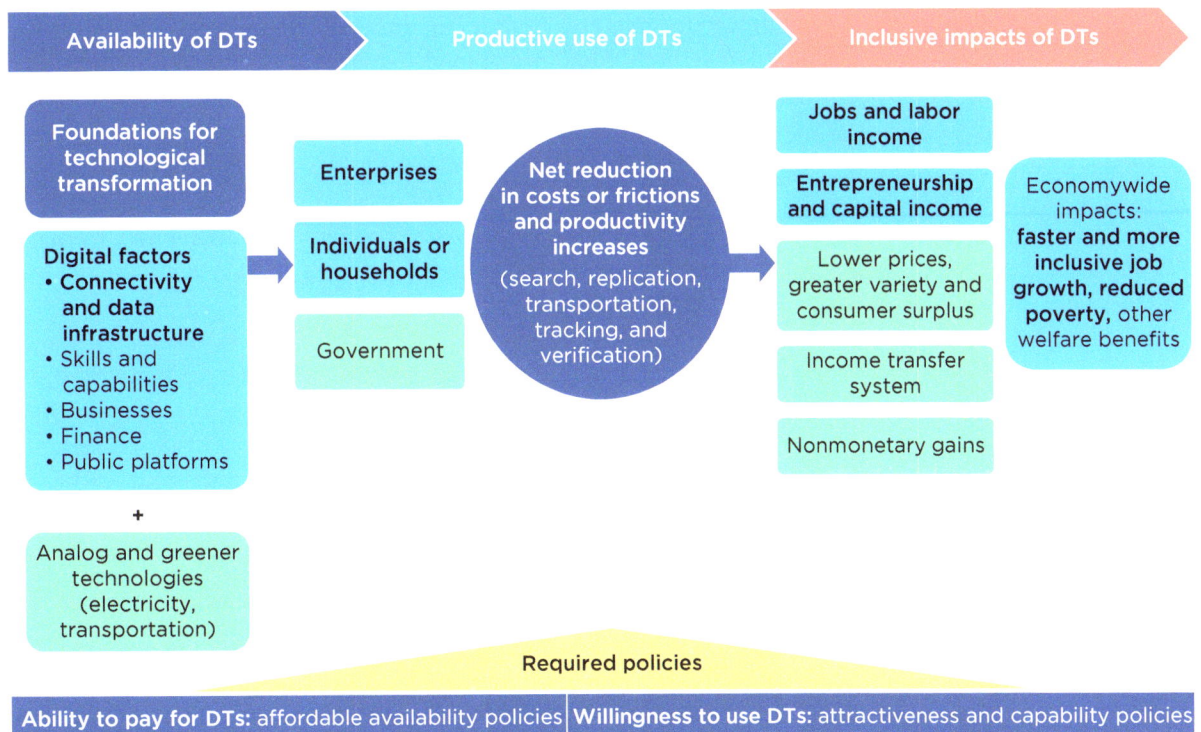

Source: Original figure for this publication.
Note: Bolded text indicates the primary focuses and themes of this report, emphasizing the production side of the economy (enterprises and workers). DTs = digital technologies.

supply-side view. This view underscores the internet's role as a general-purpose technology, through which widespread availability—and presumably usage—will raise overall economic productivity over time. However, in contexts of limited resources, formidable needs across sectors, low income, and countries that often lack scale, this approach faces daunting challenges on the financial front.

The new conceptual framework in this report focuses instead on a second view of digitalization policy—prioritizing *productive use* that generates large, inclusive, jobs-related spillover effects while also expanding coverage of quality broadband internet. Innovations are essential in technologies that will attract people with fewer digital skills and boost their capabilities to generate higher earnings. This nuanced view of digitalization policy emphasizes the interdependency between demand and supply: greater demand for productive use and the ability to pay for these services will enable increased investments in higher-quality DT services.

Technological transformation: A pathway to inclusive productivity growth

Two new empirical studies undertaken for the report have added to the rapidly growing positive evidence base by exploring the direct impact of mobile internet availability (third-generation [3G] or fourth-generation [4G] mobile communications technology coverage) on jobs and welfare. The studies examine geospatial information on the rollout of mobile internet towers over time, combined with at least two rounds of household data over six to seven years (Bahia et al. 2020; Bahia et al. 2021). Figure O.2 summarizes the main jobs and welfare (consumption and poverty) results for Nigeria and Tanzania.

Internet availability improved jobs and welfare outcomes in both Nigeria and Tanzania. In Nigeria, labor force participation and wage employment increased by 3 percentage points and 1 percentage point, respectively, in areas having three or more years of exposure to internet availability relative to those without coverage, after accounting for potential confounding factors.[2] Total consumption increased by about 9 percent, and the proportion of households below the extreme poverty line (US$1.90 per person per day) declined by 7 percent after three years. Poorer households and those living in rural areas benefited the most, perhaps reflecting the internet connectivity already available to most urban households over the period of analysis.

The job estimates for Tanzania are similarly significant. Working-age individuals (ages 15–64) living in areas with internet availability witnessed increases of 8 percentage points in labor force participation and 4 percentage points in wage employment after three or more years of exposure. Total consumption per capita among households residing in areas with 3G availability was about 10 percent higher than in areas without coverage. Moreover, the proportion of households falling below the national basic needs poverty line dropped by 7 percentage points.[3] Welfare gains were higher among households headed by women, those with lower incomes, and those with less education (not having completed primary school). Larger relative gains are observed in urban areas, reflecting an earlier rollout from zero to 3G coverage in the early 2010s.

Other empirical studies highlight the indirect impacts of internet availability on access to more and better jobs through effects on improving firm–worker matching and improving firm productivity through entrepreneurship, innovation, and foreign direct investment. A background study for this report has found evidence of internet-induced entrepreneurship in 10 African countries.[4] The probability that a household establishes a

FIGURE O.2 **Effects of mobile internet availability on job creation and household welfare, Nigeria and Tanzania**

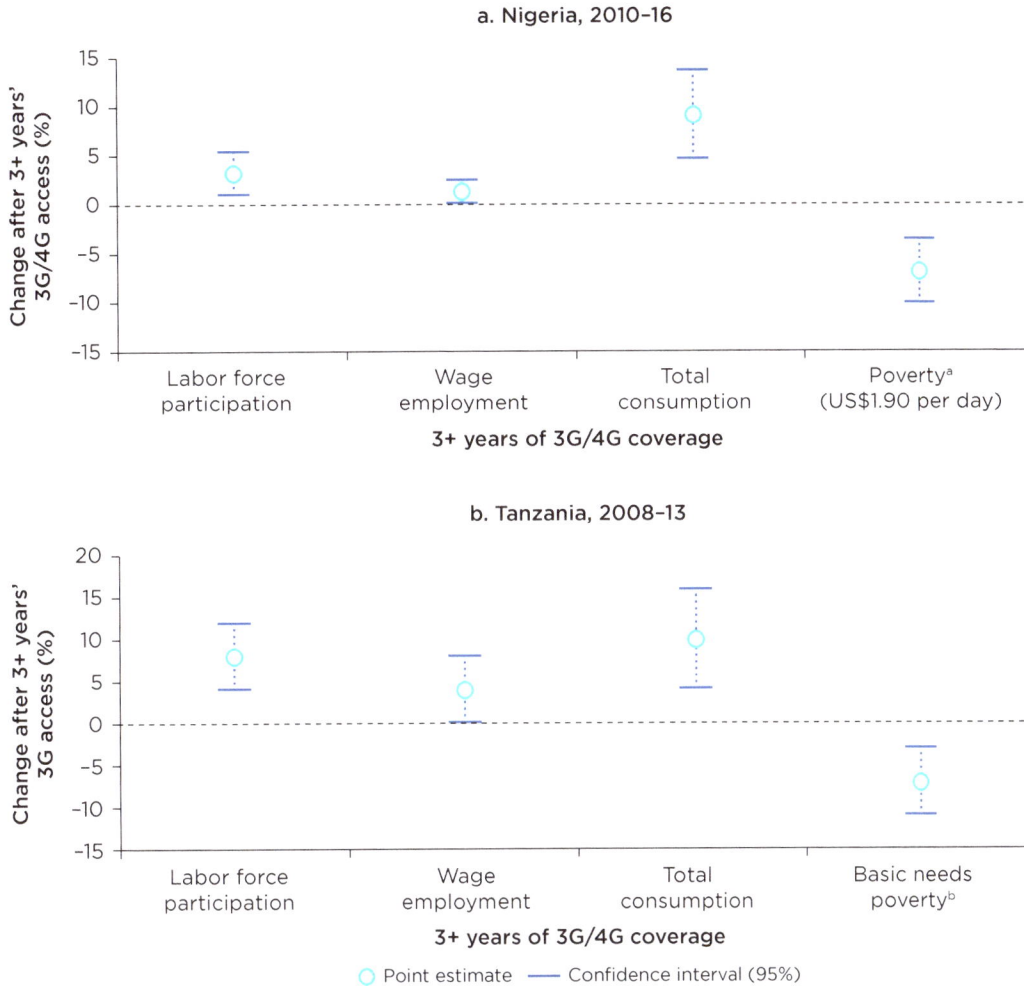

a. Nigeria, 2010–16

b. Tanzania, 2008–13

○ Point estimate —— Confidence interval (95%)

Source: Bahia et al. 2020; Bahia et al. 2021.
Note: The studies examine geospatial information on the rollout of mobile internet towers, combined with three rounds of household data over seven years for Nigeria and two rounds over six years for Tanzania. The estimates on poverty and consumption include all individuals or households, whereas labor outcomes include only working-age populations (ages 15–64). The results represent percentage changes in the covered locations after three or more years of high-quality internet exposure relative to those without such coverage after accounting for potential confounding factors. The figure shows difference-in-difference average value point estimates with 95 percent confidence intervals. 3G = third-generation mobile communications technology; 4G = fourth-generation mobile communications technology.
a. Nigeria's poverty status of households is calculated based on the international poverty line of US$1.90 per day (2011 purchasing power parity) and after applying the Consumer Price Index to adjust for both spatial and temporal inflation.
b. Tanzania's poverty status of households is calculated based on the cost of acquiring enough food to provide adequate daily nutrition per person (food line) plus the cost of some nonfood essentials (nonfood component).

nonfarm business is 17 percentage points higher in areas with internet availability. This increase in entrepreneurial activities is concentrated in the service sector, plausibly because of the low entry cost of establishing many service-related businesses relative to those in agribusiness and manufacturing (Houngbonon, Mensah, and Traore 2022).

The same study also found evidence of a positive impact of internet availability on innovation: internet availability increases the probability of a firm undertaking process and product innovation by 20 percentage points and 12 percentage points, respectively. The effect on process innovation stems largely from the adoption of DTs for business functions, such as sales, distribution, and marketing, and is boosted by the availability of digital skills within the firm.

Another new study for this report provides evidence that internet availability is associated with increases of 6 percentage points and 3 percentage points, respectively, in the probability of foreign direct investment in the financial and technology services sectors (Mensah and Traore 2022). The number of foreign direct investment projects in financial services increased by almost 20 percent following the arrival of submarine internet cables.

Internet availability also expands the demand side of production and boosts aggregate growth. Evidence from a background study of the rollout of 3G internet networks in Ethiopia (Abreha et al. 2021) suggests that internet availability can boost jobs by closing gaps in information between buyers and sellers. Enterprises operating in areas with 3G availability experienced an average 29 percent decline in markups, an 18 percent rise in firm productivity, and a 28 percent increase in jobs. These improvements are interpreted as resulting from increased competition as consumers become aware of price information and alternatives in nearby markets and as firms respond to increased competition and compressed profit margins by reducing costs—with increased productivity enabling output expansion and more jobs.

Finally, another study undertaken for this report indicates that internet availability boosts aggregate economic growth, with job expansion presumed from the output expansion accompanying faster growth. Aggregate country-level data show that increases in mobile internet subscriptions and the population share of internet users contribute to the growth of output per worker and reductions in poverty and income inequality (Calderón and Cantú 2021). Internet use has a significant effect in reducing poverty, and mobile connections are found to have a significant effect on reducing income inequality.

Digital transformation in Africa: Challenges and divides

Despite the good news on the positive causal inclusive impacts of internet availability on jobs and poverty, Africa faces the challenge of insufficient use. Too few people can truly access these benefits. Though mobile internet availability has increased, Africa's internet infrastructure coverage and the quality of available services still lag other regions. Divides in availability of quality digital services remain an issue in all countries, especially in remote and poorer subregions.

This divide is compounded by Africa's large usage gap (Atiyas and Dutz 2022). Although 84 percent of country populations averaged across Sub-Saharan Africa had at least some level of 3G mobile internet availability and 63 percent had some level of 4G mobile internet services, only 22 percent used mobile internet services as of the end of 2021 (figure O.3, panel a). These figures represent a usage gap of 62 percent as a share of total population. Africa's uptake gap, or internet users with internet availability, is 74 percent, almost three-quarters, on average across countries (figure O.3, panel b), the highest in the world.

Recent increases in digital infrastructure investment following the onset of the COVID-19 pandemic have not been accompanied by concomitant increases in use. Instead, there are growing digital divides in use between large formal and micro-size informal enterprises; between enterprises owned by young men and those owned by older women; and between richer, urban, and better educated households and poorer, rural, and less educated households.

FIGURE O.3 Gap between mobile internet coverage and usage, Sub-Saharan Africa and other regions, 2010–21

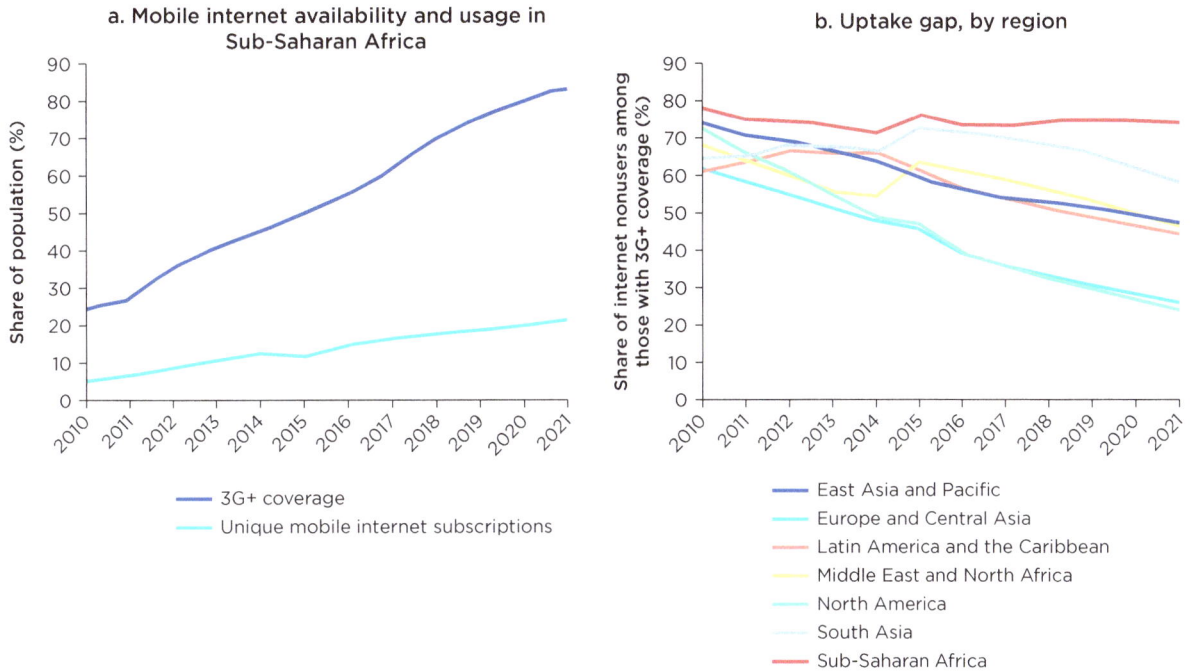

a. Mobile internet availability and usage in Sub-Saharan Africa

b. Uptake gap, by region

3G+ coverage
Unique mobile internet subscriptions

East Asia and Pacific
Europe and Central Asia
Latin America and the Caribbean
Middle East and North Africa
North America
South Asia
Sub-Saharan Africa

Source: Atiyas and Dutz 2022, based on Global System for Mobile Communications Association (GSMA) data.
Note: The figure incorporates updated 2016–21 data based on an improved 2022 methodology for calculating unique subscribers. In panel a, mobile internet availability (3G+ coverage) and use (unique mobile internet subscribers) are expressed as unweighted averages across countries, as a share of total country population. In panel b, the "uptake gap" is the percentage of people who live within the footprint of a mobile broadband network but who do not use mobile internet. "North America" comprises Bermuda, Canada, and the United States. 3G+ = third-generation (or later) mobile communications technology.

Enterprises: More jobs for more people

To increase the availability of jobs, African enterprises must invest to expand their technology frontier, which appears to be relatively stagnant. African and global entrepreneurs must also generate more digital and complementary technologies that align with Africa's current skills profile and production context (such as smaller-scale farms) and that evolve with workers as they increase capabilities. In addition, most enterprises must adopt and use DTs and complementary technologies more intensively. Such skill- and context-appropriate technologies would enable existing and newly entering workers, managers, and entrepreneur-owners to continuously raise productivity and generate higher earnings.

Productivity and job gains from sophisticated technologies

The use of more sophisticated DTs and related technologies is associated with higher productivity across African countries for enterprises employing five or more full-time employees (Cirera, Comin, and Cruz 2022). Firms with higher average technological sophistication have higher productivity on average, with varying degrees of responsiveness (figure O.4, panel a). Interestingly, the association between technology use and productivity

FIGURE O.4 Association between firms' use of more sophisticated DTs and productivity and job growth, selected countries, 2019–21

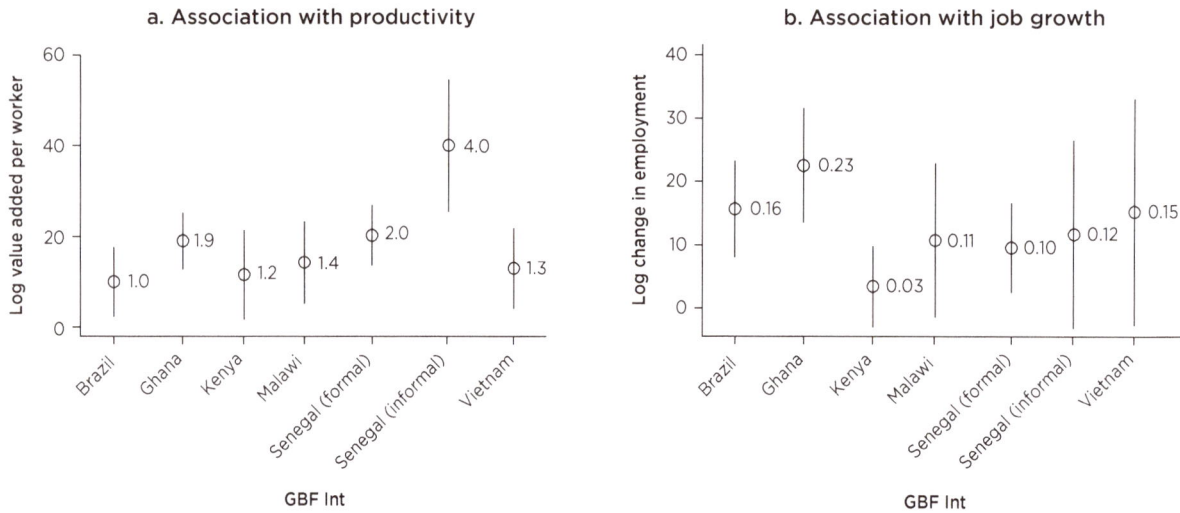

a. Association with productivity

b. Association with job growth

Source: Cirera, Comin, and Cruz 2022, based on 2019–21 FAT (Firm-level Adoption of Technology) survey data.
Note: The figure shows regression coefficients (circles) and 95 percent confidence intervals (vertical lines) from country-level regressions of a new technology sophistication index that averages the most intensively used technologies across general business functions (GBF Int) for each firm on productivity levels (panel a) and changes in full-time workers over the preceding three years (panel b), while controlling for sector, firm size, and region. Country samples are restricted to enterprises with five or more employees. Senegal is the only country that includes a representative subsample of informal as well as formal enterprises.

is stronger for informal than formal Senegalese firms. There is also a positive association between the use of more sophisticated technologies and job growth for Senegal (formal firms) and Ghana (figure O.4, panel b).

Findings for microenterprises show a positive progression in the number of more sophisticated DTs (figure O.5, light blue bars) associated in turn with higher productivity, sales, and job levels. Six internet-enabled and three non-internet-enabled DT uses (figure O.5, dark blue bars) are the only significant conditional correlates of higher job levels. So a greater range of more sophisticated DT uses based on internet-enabled computers or smartphones relative to DT uses based only on second-generation (2G) phones is associated with higher jobs levels.

Despite these beneficial associations, the average African enterprise with five or more full-time employees in Ghana, Kenya, Malawi, and Senegal lags in the use of computers relative to Brazil and in the use of smartphones for most enterprise size groupings. Informal enterprises (with Senegal being the only available country with nationally representative data) lag much more (figure O.6). Microenterprises lag even more, with large digital divides: only 7 percent of all microfirms and 3 percent of microfirms owned by older women (over 30 years of age) use a smartphone. The digital divide in computer use is even larger: only 2 percent of microfirms owned by young women (30 years of age or younger) use a computer, but four times as many (8 percent) microfirms owned by young men do (Atiyas and Dutz 2023).

Factors affecting productive use of DTs

The key DT-related issue for African enterprises is low productive use. The main factors affecting enterprise use of smartphones, computers, and the more-sophisticated DTs that rely on these access technologies are related to the ability to pay for them and the

FIGURE O.5 Association between microenterprises' use of technologies and higher productivity, sales, and jobs, 2017–18

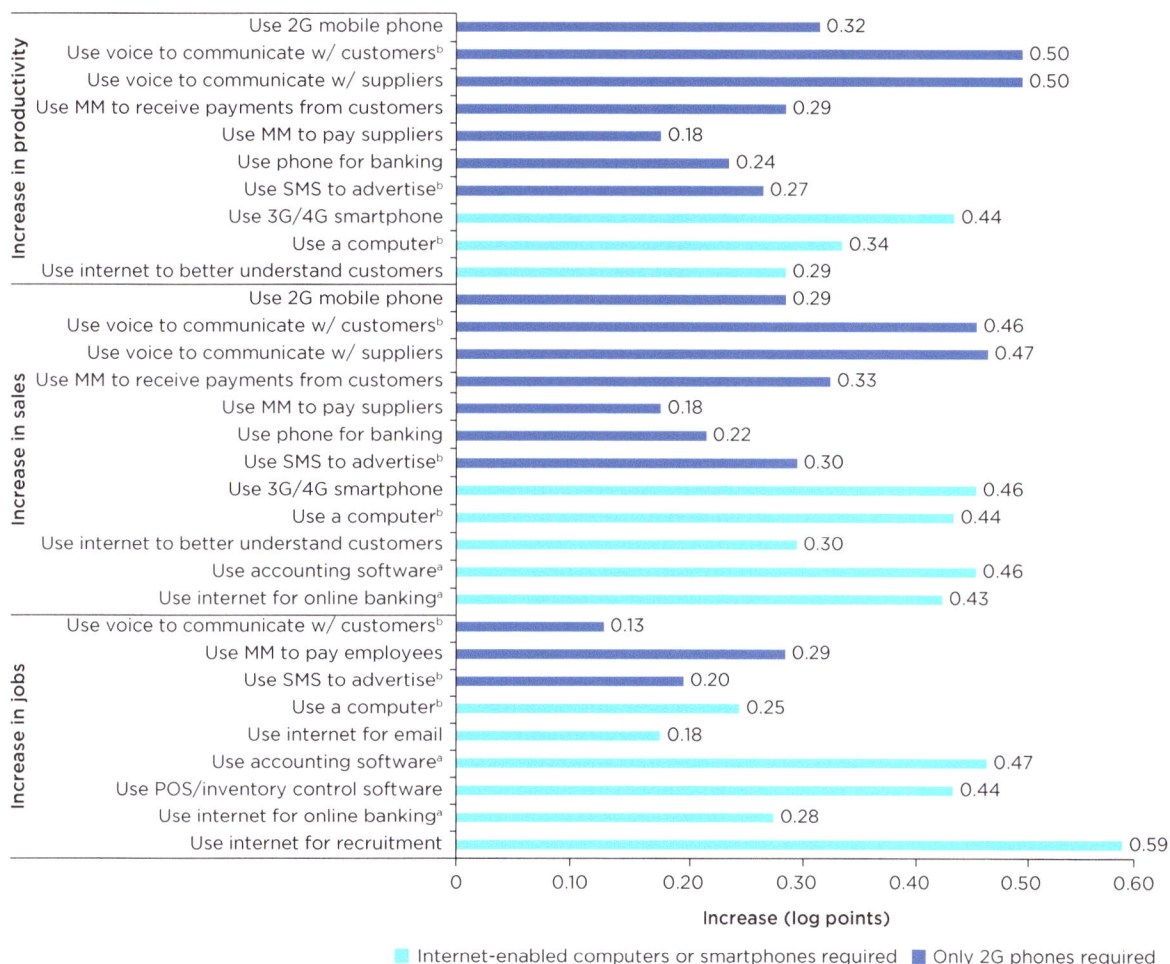

Source: Atiyas and Dutz 2023, based on 2017–18 Research ICT Africa (RIA) survey data.
Note: The figure shows the association between average firm use of selected digital technologies (DTs) and the percentage increase in three outcome variables: productivity, sales, and jobs. The included business-related uses of DTs—listed in order from simple-access technologies to more sophisticated uses—are those for which the conditional correlates are significant at least at the 5 percent level based on ordinary least squares with robust standard errors using unweighted data. Controls include whether the enterprise has ever had a loan, has access to electricity, is run by transformational entrepreneurs, and has links with more sophisticated upstream suppliers or downstream buyers, among others, together with country fixed effects. The data cover 3,325 formal and informal microenterprises (the median firm being informal and self-employed with no full-time workers) across seven African countries. Dark blue bars represent non-internet-enabled DTs; light blue bars represent internet-enabled DTs. 2G = second-generation mobile communications technology; 3G = third-generation; 4G = fourth-generation; MM = mobile money; POS = point of sale; SMS = short message service.
a. Variable is significant across all three performance outcomes: productivity, sales, and jobs.
b. Variable is significant across both sales and jobs.

willingness to use them (figure O.7). These factors are relatively similar across larger enterprises (with five or more workers) and microenterprises.

Ability to pay. Affordable availability of DTs is linked to the prices of quality internet services, access technologies, and apps relative to enterprise earnings, as well as access to financing to help pay for DTs. Small and medium enterprises in Africa face high prices and lack adequate business offerings in terms of speed and data allowances. Ability to pay is also linked to the affordable availability of complementary infrastructure, especially that of reliable electricity as well as transportation and logistics services.

FIGURE O.6 **Smartphone and computer use, by firm size, selected countries, 2019–21**

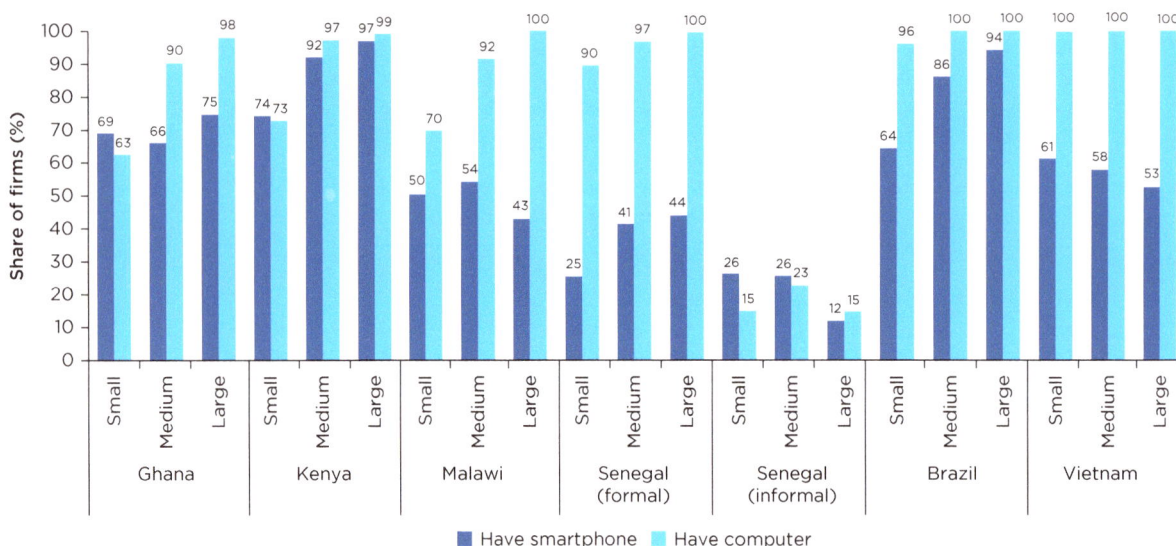

Source: Cirera, Comin, and Cruz 2022, based on 2019–21 Firm-level Adoption of Technology (FAT) survey data.
Note: Included enterprises are those employing at least five full-time workers. "Large" firms have 100 or more employees; "medium" firms, 20–99 employees; and "small" firms, 5–19 employees.

Affordability is influenced by whether enterprises, be they larger firms or microfirms, have loans; information is also available on whether microfirms have a credit line with suppliers, an indicator of their creditworthiness. Access to finance, as reflected by having a loan, is one of the largest correlates of use. Larger firms that have a loan are 12 percent more likely than those without loans to use smartphones and 9 percent less likely to use a 2G phone (Cirera, Comin, and Cruz 2022). Microenterprises that have a loan are 18 percent more likely to use smartphones and nearly 15 percent less likely to use a 2G phone; they are also over 9 percent more likely to use a computer (Atiyas and Dutz 2023). Having electricity and being in an urban location are associated with computer use for larger firms and with smartphone use for microenterprises.

Willingness to use. Willingness to use DTs is linked to both the firms' capabilities and the DTs' attractiveness—in turn related to both the availability of information about DTs and whether they meet the productive needs of users.

Regarding capabilities, skills (especially at the managerial level in larger firms) and vocational training (in microenterprises) are strongly associated with both smartphone and computer use (Atiyas and Dutz 2023; Cirera, Comin, and Cruz 2022). Enterprise technological capabilities are also affected by the firm's

- *Size,* with those employing five or more workers and microfirms that are larger (relative to other microfirms) being more likely to use computers;

- *Age,* with those that have been in operation longer being less likely to use a smartphone than younger firms; and

- *Formality status,* with formal firms of any size being more likely than informal firms to use computers.

FIGURE O.7 Correlates of smartphone and computer adoption by African firms, 2017–21

a. Adoption correlates for larger enterprises

b. Adoption correlates for microenterprises

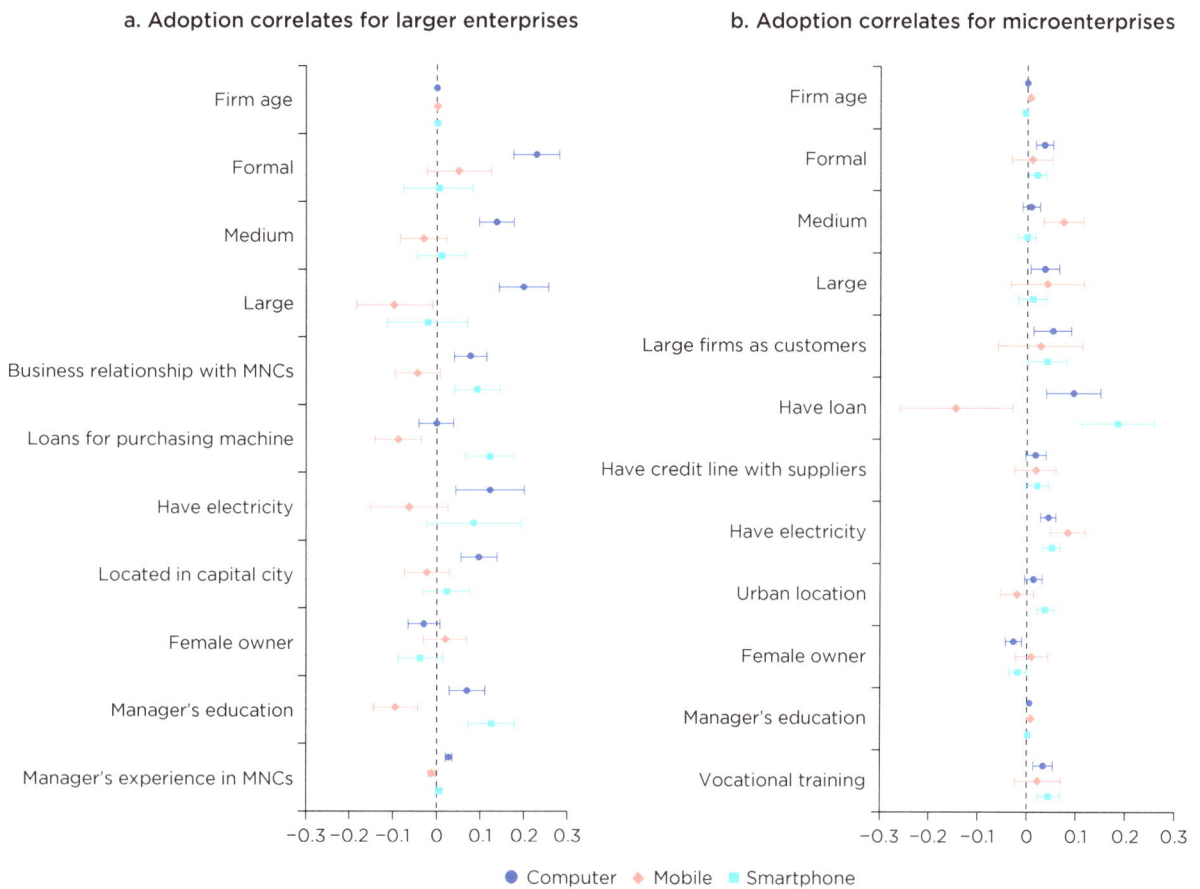

● Computer   ◆ Mobile   ■ Smartphone

Sources: Atiyas and Dutz 2023; Cirera, Comin, and Cruz 2022.
Note: Reported results are marginal effects based on probit regressions on enterprise characteristics, controlling for country fixed effects. Error bars indicate 95 percent confidence intervals. Panel a is based on 2019–21 FAT (Firm-level Adoption of Technology) survey data. "Larger" enterprises are those with at least five full-time employees. Panel b is based on 2017–18 Research ICT Africa (RIA) data. The median "microenterprise" is informal and self-employed with zero full-time employees. MNCs = multinational companies.

The attractiveness of DTs, and the consequent adoption of smartphones and computers, is likely driven by the need to adopt specific DTs when larger firms have business relationships with multinational companies and when microenterprises have large firms as customers.

Business and socioeconomic factors. Finally, specific elements of the business environment (linked to market access and competition-related incentives) and socioeconomic factors (whether social norms and rules make ownership of access devices difficult for women) also affect DT use. Among microenterprises, female-owned firms are less likely than male-owned firms to use either a smartphone or a computer (Atiyas and Dutz 2023). Because most microfirms are owned and managed by self-employed individuals with no full-time paid employees, this digital divide may reflect prevailing social norms and rules that make access to finance and ownership of access devices more difficult for women.

Public policies and investments are needed both to incentivize the creation of attractive apps—especially solutions that are simple to use and boost the productivity of enterprises with lower-skilled workers—and to stimulate use by enterprises, including through investments in capabilities. Three broad policy recommendations arise from these findings:

1. *Institutionalize technology upgrading* and worker and management capability support programs.

2. *Support start-up entrepreneurs* in developing more appropriate technologies for Africa's current and future asset base, including through incentives for creating skill-appropriate technologies, intellectual property rights protection, and regulations facilitating a more job-inclusive development of machine learning and other forms of artificial intelligence.

3. *Facilitate enterprise financing* for the generation and use of DTs as well as complementary technologies. Public financing support policies should include (a) targeted partial credit guarantees, matching grants, and vouchers for the adoption of technologies and needed capabilities; and (b) credit infrastructure with a focus on credit bureaus and secured transactions as well as mechanisms to access key data for credit ratings.

Households: Inclusive impact through productive use

Several factors could explain the low internet use and low intensity of use by African households. The latest evidence from seven West African Economic and Monetary Union (WAEMU) countries finds that three key factors correlate with low adoption (Rodriguez-Castelán et al. 2021):

1. *Affordable availability,* encompassing the ability to pay (influenced by household expenditure, the price of mobile services, and asset ownership); access to electricity; and urban location

2. *Attractiveness* of alternative modalities of internet access

3. *Capabilities,* including tertiary educational attainment, French language proficiency (in francophone countries), and sector of employment, together with socioeconomic factors

Constraints on the ability to pay and willingness to use

Many Africans do not use DTs because the costs appear to outweigh the benefits. Two main groups of factors underpin the low perceived benefits to costs: ability to pay for DTs and willingness to use them.

Ability to pay involves the availability of quality digital services and the price and affordability of access devices, data plans, and apps relative to purchasing power. A package that covers a few hours of basic daily use—1.5 gigabytes of data over 30 days—amounts to about a third of the income of the 40 percent of Africans who fall below the global extreme poverty line (US$1.90 per person per day at 2017 purchasing power parity). Low-consumption users face prices per unit of data that are more than double those for high-consumption users, holding back higher intensity of use among low-income users.

Attractiveness of DTs, and hence the willingness to use them, is linked to multiple factors: Do users have information about the existence of DTs and how to use them? Do DTs meet minimum speed and latency requirements for effective use? Do they meet users' productive (and other) needs? Are they designed for the users' skills level? Do they raise trust concerns related to data protection, cybercrime, or data surveillance? Do the expected benefits of using DTs outweigh the costs of devices, data plans, and other investments? Ultimately, household members' capabilities—their skills and technological sophistication—also affect their ability to extract value from DTs.

Policies to expand access to credit, better regulations, and market-induced price reductions can help address affordability. Policies that can induce the development of easy-to-use DTs and capability-enhancing content are also needed to meet the productive needs of households, especially among poor people, who face constraints on many fronts including skills gaps and a lack of information on how internet use could benefit them. Providing information to households on the variety of ways DTs can help people—through community-based associations, town hall meetings, religious organizations, and social networks—could help to address some of these constraints.

Policy routes to productive internet use by households

Given the low income levels and high inequality across Africa, broader internet adoption among households is financially sustainable only if adoption results in higher earnings. Policy makers can play a role in promoting and enabling productive uses.

Figure O.8 depicts a framework to increase internet use, offering two complementary approaches: Route 1 targets internet adoption as an end goal, while Route 2 views adoption as the means to enhance people's earnings and livelihood opportunities and achieve greater economic impact. Although Route 2 may close gaps at a slower pace, it would be more financially sustainable in the long term. The goal is to create a positively reinforcing cycle through which productive internet use enhances earnings, feeding back into more DT use.

FIGURE O.8 **Policy routes for increasing households' inclusive uptake and productive use of DTs**

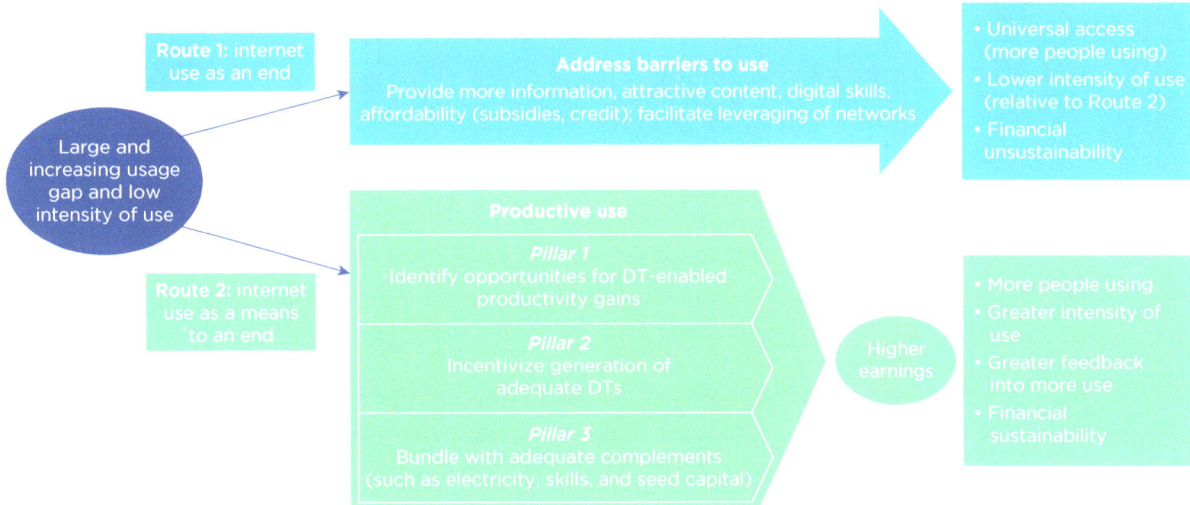

Source: Adapted from Blimpo and Cosgrove-Davies 2019.
Note: DTs = digital technologies.

Internet use as the end goal. Under Route 1, policies focus mainly on addressing the symptomatic barriers to use. These interventions will contribute to achieving the universal access goal faster, especially if countries support adoption and use with significant subsidies.

Via this route, increased internet use ideally would lead to increased productivity—which may happen in some households. However, without the presence of analog complements (such as electricity and skills), productive use and the returns that encourage further use are weaker. This strategy may thus be financially unsustainable because it requires sustained provision of credit or subsidies for adoption and use.

Internet use as a means to an end. Under Route 2, internet use is seen as the means to increasing household earnings and reducing poverty. The policy goal is to increase the productive use of the internet to increase household earnings, thereby strengthening the ability to pay and stimulating further internet use. This approach views the internet and related DTs as inputs and tools to enable technological transformation and higher earnings.

As with many other types of inputs, DTs are necessary, but insufficient, to generate income. Availability of electricity, adequate education and skills, road access, and attainable financing are all complements with varying degrees of relevance, depending on the context. (This policy alternative requires synergies among at least three types of interventions, shown as the three pillars in figure O.8.)

These policy interventions are expected to increase productive use, which will in turn boost household earnings. With higher earnings, households can afford to buy smartphones and mobile broadband data and increase the intensity of internet use.

Digital and data infrastructure: Policy reforms to increase availability and use

Two sets of complementary and mutually reinforcing policies are required for DTs to support inclusive job growth in Africa: those that ensure the ability to pay for DTs and those that elicit willingness to use DTs for productive purposes (as illustrated earlier in figure O.1). Downside risks include the potential for increased digital divides affecting low-income people displaced by the adoption of newer technologies and unable to adjust and adapt. The potential for misuse by business (data protection, cybersecurity, and consumer protection) and government (surveillance and misinformation) must also be managed.

Policies to ensure ability to pay

Policies to ensure all potential users' ability to pay must address internet affordability, additional infrastructure availability, adequate data infrastructure, and affordable availability of complementary technologies. The big problem in effectively addressing affordability issues is that prevailing market structures do not yet enable enough competition in Africa. Markets are concentrated (figure O.9). Monopolies and duopolies still exist in many African countries, including in key bottleneck markets such as international connectivity. State-owned enterprises remain important in the sector and have the potential to thwart competition.

Moreover, vertical integration of dominant firms in Africa creates risks to competition: 53 firms in 36 countries have at least 40 percent market share in mobile retail or fiber backbone and are vertically integrated into two other segments (World Bank, forthcoming).

Regulation of dominant operators is weak. Internet affordability requires effective pro-competition regulations to reduce investment costs—including rules on licensing and market dominance, infrastructure access and sharing, and radioelectric spectrum

FIGURE O.9 Extent of competitive constraints in market structures across the digital value chain in Africa, 2021

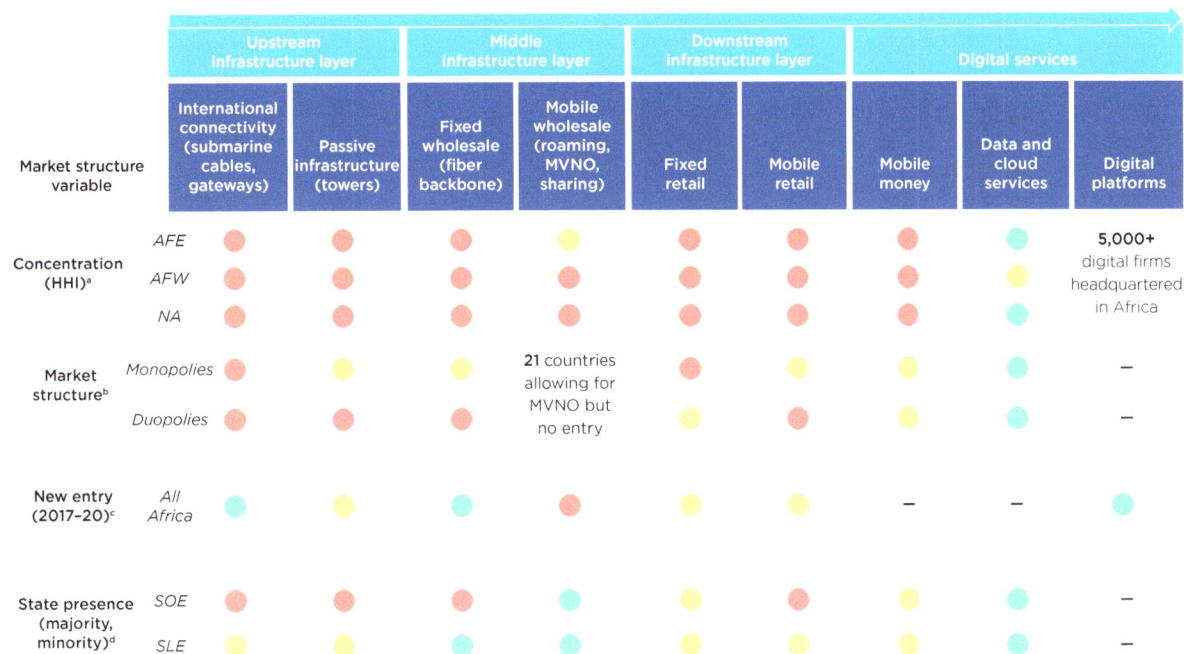

Market structure variable		International connectivity (submarine cables, gateways)	Passive infrastructure (towers)	Fixed wholesale (fiber backbone)	Mobile wholesale (roaming, MVNO, sharing)	Fixed retail	Mobile retail	Mobile money	Data and cloud services	Digital platforms
		Upstream infrastructure layer		Middle infrastructure layer		Downstream infrastructure layer		Digital services		
Concentration (HHI)[a]	AFE	orange	orange	orange	yellow	orange	orange	orange	green	5,000+ digital firms headquartered in Africa
	AFW	orange	orange	orange	orange	orange	orange	orange	yellow	
	NA	orange	orange	orange	orange	orange	orange	orange	green	
Market structure[b]	Monopolies	yellow	yellow	yellow	21 countries allowing for MVNO but no entry	orange	yellow	yellow	green	—
	Duopolies	orange	orange	orange		yellow	orange	yellow	green	—
New entry (2017–20)[c]	All Africa	green	yellow	green	orange	yellow	yellow	—	—	green
State presence (majority, minority)[d]	SOE	orange	orange	orange	green	yellow	orange	yellow	green	—
	SLE	yellow	yellow	green	green	yellow	yellow	yellow	green	—

Source: World Bank, Africa Digital Market Players Database (internal), 2021, built on data from numerous sources, including TeleGeography, Global System for Mobile Communications Association (GSMA), Africa Bandwidth Maps, Afterfibre.org, Policytracker, TowerXchange, PeeringDB, and Xalam Analytics.

Note: Red circles represent higher risk to competition, on average; orange circles, medium risk; and green circles, lower risk. The sample covers 54 African countries for mobile retail, 38 for fixed retail, 52 for fiber backbone, 26 for telecommunications towers, 35 for submarine cables, 25 for data centers, and 15 for mobile money. AFE = Eastern and Southern Africa; AFW = Western and Central Africa; HHI = Herfindahl-Hirschman index (market concentration measure); MVNO = mobile virtual network operator; NA = North Africa; SLE = state as minority shareholder; SOE = majority or fully state-owned enterprise; — = not available.
a. A market with HHI of less than 1,500 is considered to have a competitive market structure, HHI of 1,500 to 2,500 is moderately concentrated, and an HHI of 2,500 or greater is highly concentrated.
b. In terms of monopolies and duopolies, less than 5 percent of countries are monopolies/duopolies = green, 5–20 percent of countries = orange, above 20 percent of countries = red.
c. For new entry, new entry in less than 5 percent of countries = red, in 5–20 percent of countries = orange, in more than 20 percent of countries = green.
d. SOE presence in less than 10 percent of countries = green, in 10–50 percent of countries = orange, and in more than 50 percent of countries = red.

availability and use—within the context of more integrated continental markets. Regulations are also required to drive down operational costs, including rules on access to essential infrastructure controlled by state-owned enterprises, operation of open-access fiber networks, and minimization of excise taxes.

An empirical analysis of six countries conducted for this report shows that cost-reducing policy reforms (on spectrum, infrastructure sharing, and taxation) can save 10–20 percent of the cost required to achieve near-universal availability, resulting in over US$200 million in savings for governments across the countries included in the analysis (World Bank 2022). Increasing market competition can deliver additional benefits and could achieve levels of use similar to those spurred by supply-side subsidies, as simulations for Ghana show.

Infrastructure availability in areas that are not commercially viable after implementing regulatory reforms requires targeted subsidies and financing (through earmarked funds, obligations on operators, universal service funds, or alternative solutions) to incentivize universal access and service and to support climate-resilient development.

If demand-side policies were to increase potential 4G use above the current level in uncovered areas (currently less than 5 percent) to 40 percent for the six studied African countries, expansion would become commercially viable, and 4G availability would reach the same near-universal levels as it would under a pure supply subsidy. This finding highlights the importance of demand-side programs to not only expand use but also boost coverage. Furthermore, affordable availability of data infrastructure requires transparent, pro-competition rules for upgrading internet exchange points and for accessing data centers and cloud computing to help drive down costs.

Policies to increase willingness to use

Policies on attractiveness and capabilities are required to promote DT use for productive purposes. These include national strategies for productive use of DTs, innovation policies, data policies and regulations, and capability support programs. The implementation of these tailored strategies is essential to support familiarity with and use of DTs as well as to ensure productive gains by all enterprises. These strategies could include investments in common-access facilities and demonstrations at internet cafés, local schools, or community centers, especially for microentrepreneurs.

For DT use to be inclusive, Africa must provide sophisticated yet simple-to-use and attractive apps through touch-screen pictures, voice, and video in the languages people speak—enabling enterprises and households to want them, use them, and learn as they work. Africa must redirect technologies to the different contexts across its countries, particularly its differing skill compositions. To that end, entrepreneurs are needed to further develop existing DTs to enable productive use and learning by all people in the region. Development of new DTs by private entepreneurs may require prior public-private investments in public goods, such as countrywide availability of digital addresses, geotagged land records, and local weather mapping. Data policies are needed as both enablers and safeguards for data use and reuse to ensure the development of new, attractive, data-driven DTs along with appropriate levels of trust in their use.

Finally, capability support programs must be institutionalized for micro, small, and medium enterprises as well as for households, so that they know how to make productive use of available DTs. These programs include business advisory services, technology information and upgrading services, and manager and worker skills training, together with longer-term investments in high-quality secondary and tertiary education.

The role of regional cooperation

Looking ahead, African countries have the potential to benefit further from deeper regional integration and the adoption of environmentally friendly DTs to advance the continent's technological transformation. The African Union has developed and is implementing the Digital Transformation Strategy for Africa (2020–2030) to boost DT use and innovation to promote Africa's integration (AU 2020).

Creating a single continental market for both connectivity and data will require the harmonization and compatibility of national policy and regulatory frameworks. Integrated regional connectivity and data markets, in turn, can facilitate the scalability of DTs across the continent, boosting positive network effects, economies of scale and scope, and competition benefits. The operation of continental data infrastructure and cross-border connectivity infrastructure enabled by domestic and regional regulatory frameworks is fundamental for a single digital market. Table O.1 presents how national

TABLE O.1 Main policy recommendations for advancing the use of digital technologies to support inclusive job growth

	Goal	Policy area	Topic	Emerging sector[a]	Evolving between "emerging" and "transitioning"	Transitioning sector[b]
Policies to ensure ability to pay	Affordability of internet	Pro-competition regulation	Licensing and regulation of dominance	Entry liberalization: simpler licensing, no exclusivities, including for cross-border connectivity	Rules to allow ISPs to deploy infrastructure, elimination of voice over internet protocol (VoIP) restrictions	SMP rules: designation and remedies; control of license transfers/mergers
			Access and sharing of essential infrastructure	Interconnection rules for domestic networks	Infrastructure sharing/access to essential infrastructure, regulation of regional roaming and cross-border transportation	Rules for coinvestment and wholesale-only networks
			Management of radio frequencies	Spectrum policy; Published national spectrum frequency register	Spectrum rules: allocation, assignment, pricing, sharing/transfer, coordination at regional level	5G spectrum allocation and assignment; unlicensed spectrum and dynamic spectrum access
		Cost-reducing regulation	SOEs	SOEs open to private shareholding; Restructuring of SOEs for better governance	Open access to state fiber networks (energy); SOE accountability	PPPs for open-access fiber network, co-investments for uncovered areas
			Sectoral taxes and fees	Elimination of sector-specific (excise) taxes on telecommunications services	Revision of taxes on digital services; Cost-oriented regulatory fees	Harmonization of subnational fees for infrastructure deployment
	Availability of internet and complementary technologies (analog infrastructure)	Government interventions to complement markets	Universal access and service	Creation of USF; Transparent and more effective USF, focusing on availability of demand-responsive services and use	Redefine USF scope (DTs to pull internet demand) and contribution modality (capital expenditure versus contribution)	Focus on use and upgrading: targeted demand-side support, pricing rules for vulnerable groups
			Climate adaptation and resilience	Mandatory emergency preparedness plans	Policies for resilient and green design, construction, operation of digital infrastructure	E-waste management; incentives for energy-efficient and green digital infrastructure
	Affordable availability of data	Data infrastructure	IXPs, data centers, and cloud computing	Improved governance of IXPs to allow for growth, updated telecommunications rules for regional IXPs	Rules on cross-border data flows that allow for regional data hubs and edge computing	Neutral data centers, rules to facilitate switching between providers, including at regional level

(continued)

TABLE O.1 Main policy recommendations for advancing the use of digital technologies to support inclusive job growth (*continued*)

Goal	Policy area	Topic	Emerging sector[a]	Evolving between "emerging" and "transitioning"	Transitioning sector[b]
Policies to ensure willingness to use — **Attractiveness of and capabilities to use DTs**	Digital entrepreneurship	Reduction of barriers and support of drivers of entry and expansion	Elimination of administrative barriers; access to finance (partial credit guarantees, matching grants), incubators, and accelerators	Access to data and effective data portability, incentives to develop pro-poor DTs, creation of public-good data platforms, elimination of barriers to regional expansion	Appropriate taxation of digital services and effective competition enforcement (entry and exit, mergers, abuse of dominance), including regional approach
	Technology and innovation	DT generation and use by firms	Information to increase attractiveness of DTs, support for basic digitalization, government e-services to pull demand	Support to business advisory and technology extension services and to FDI and joint ventures for tech transfer, for generation and use of DTs	Test beds for generation and adoption of new DTs in specific industries, including low-skill-based DTs that enable learning over time
	Data policies and regulations	Enablers of new DTs and trust; safeguards for data use and reuse	Clear laws on data protection, cybersecurity, cybercrime, open data, e-transactions, and cross-border data flows, aligned at the regional and global levels	Effective enforcement by data protection authorities, cybersecurity agencies, and the like Compliance and awareness for start-ups and SMEs Regional interoperability of national laws	Data spaces, data sharing between government and private sector and across enterprises Regional convergence and harmonization of frameworks
	Social inclusion	DTs for productive use by individuals and households	Exposure to DTs through access in community centers, schools and health clinics, government programs, digital public service delivery	Comprehensive interventions complementing internet availability and affordability: skills and capabilities; attractiveness and information; affordability and access to finance, electricity, and transportation; social norms	Identification of productive DT uses by low-income, vulnerable, and underserved groups; programs to incentivize the generation and use of DTs targeting these segments

Source: Original table for this publication.

Note: 5G = fifth-generation mobile internet technology; DTs = digital technologies; FDI = foreign direct investment; ISPs = internet service providers; IXPs = internet exchange points; PPPs = public-private partnerships; SMEs = small and medium enterprises; SMP = significant market power; SOE = state-owned enterprise; USF = universal service fund.

a. An "emerging sector" refers to a digital sector where the digital economy is still emerging and internet use is low.

b. A "transitioning sector" refers to a digital sector transitioning toward universal internet use.

and regional policy actions are complements to ensure ability to pay and willingness to use DTs in Africa.

In addition, as African countries expand their data use, the deployment of a greener connectivity and data infrastructure that takes advantage of renewable energy and better e-waste management will become more important to support climate mitigation and adaptation while making DTs more environmentally sustainable.

Africa should embrace the adoption of jobs-enhancing technologies—including cloud computing, artificial intelligence, and robotics—in ways that enhance the learning and earning potential of each country's workforce. Positive impacts can materialize only if governments, enterprises, and households support bold policy actions to create an enabling environment. This report offers an evidence-based framework to spur action toward an even brighter future for the continent.

Notes

1. The Digital Economy for Africa (DE4A) flagship initiative is a partnership between the World Bank, African governments, the African Union, and other development partners. For more information, see the DE4A initiative website: https://www.worldbank.org/en/programs/all -africa-digital-transformation.
2. Because the regression specifications differ by type of outcome, some are expressed as percentage changes (when variables are in log such as for income) and others as percentage points (when variables are binary such as for poverty and labor outcomes).
3. Tanzania's household poverty rate is based on the national "basic needs" poverty line: the cost of acquiring enough food to provide adequate daily nutrition per person (food line) plus the cost of some nonfood essentials (nonfood component). The food line is derived from the cost of buying 2,200 calories per adult per day according to the food consumption patterns prevailing in the population whose per adult real consumption is below the median during a period of 28 days valued at prices faced by the reference population. The nonfood component of the basic needs poverty line uses the average nonfood consumption share of the population whose total consumption per adult is in the bottom 25 percent.
4. The countries studied included the Democratic Republic of Congo, Ghana, Kenya, Malawi, Namibia, Nigeria, Sudan, Tanzania, Uganda, and Zambia.

References

Abreha, Kaleb G., Jieun Choi, Woubet Kassa, Hyun Ju Kim, and Maurice Kugler. 2021. "Mobile Access Expansion and Price Information Diffusion: Firm Performance after Ethiopia's Transition to 3G in 2008." Policy Research Working Paper 9752, World Bank, Washington, DC.

Atiyas, İzak, and Mark A. Dutz. 2022. "Digitalization in MENA and Sub-Saharan Africa: A Comparative Analysis of Mobile Internet Uptake and Use in Sub-Saharan Africa and MENA Countries." Working Paper No. 1549, Economic Research Forum, Giza, Egypt.

Atiyas, İzak, and Mark A. Dutz. 2023. "Digital Technology Uses among Microenterprises: Why Is Productive Use So Low across Sub-Saharan Africa?" Policy Research Working Paper 10280, World Bank, Washington, DC.

AU (African Union). 2020. "The Digital Transformation Strategy for Africa (2020–2030)." Strategy document, AU, Addis Ababa, Ethiopia.

Bahia, Kalvin, Pau Castells, Genaro Cruz, Takaaki Masaki, Xavier Pedrós, Tobias Pfutze, Carlos Rodríguez-Castelán, and Hernan Winkler. 2020. "The Welfare Effects of Mobile Broadband Internet: Evidence from Nigeria." Policy Research Working Paper 9230, World Bank, Washington, DC.

Bahia, Kalvin, Pau Castells, Takaaki Masaki, Genaro Cruz, Carlos Rodríguez-Castelán, and Viviane Sanfelice. 2021. "Mobile Broadband Internet, Poverty and Labor Outcomes in Tanzania." Policy Research Working Paper 9749, World Bank, Washington, DC.

Blimpo, Moussa P., and Malcolm Cosgrove-Davies. 2019. *Electricity Access in Sub-Saharan Africa: Uptake, Reliability, and Complementary Factors for Economic Impact.* Africa Development Forum Series. Washington, DC: World Bank.

Calderón, César, and Catalina Cantú. 2021. "The Impact of Digital Infrastructure on African Development." Policy Research Working Paper 9853, World Bank, Washington, DC.

Cirera, Xavier, Diego Comin, and Marcio Cruz. 2022. *Bridging the Technological Divide: Technology Adoption by Firms in Developing Countries.* Washington, DC: World Bank.

Houngbonon, Georges V., Justice Tei Mensah, and Nouhoum Traore. 2022. "*The Impact of Internet Access on Innovation and Entrepreneurship in Africa.*" Policy Research Working Paper 9945, World Bank, Washington, DC.

Mensah, Justice Tei, and Nouhoum Traore. 2022. "*Infrastructure Quality and FDI Inflows: Evidence from the Arrival of High-Speed Internet in Africa.*" Policy Research Working Paper 9946, World Bank, Washington, DC.

Rodríguez-Castelán, Carlos, Rogelio Granguillhome Ochoa, Samantha Lach, and Takaaki Masaki. 2021. "Mobile Internet Adoption in West Africa." Policy Research Working Paper 9560, World Bank, Washington, DC.

UN DESA (United Nations Department of Economic and Social Affairs). 2019. *World Population Prospects 2019.* 2 vols. ST/ESA/SER.A/426. New York: United Nations.

World Bank. 2022. "Using Geospatial Analysis to Overhaul Connectivity Policies: How to Expand Mobile Internet Coverage and Adoption in Sub-Saharan Africa." Report No. 169437, World Bank, Washington, DC.

World Bank. Forthcoming. "Regulating the Digital Economy in Africa: Managing Old and New Risks to Economic Governance for Inclusive Opportunities." Report, World Bank, Washington, DC.

Abbreviations

2G	second-generation mobile communications technology
3G	third-generation mobile communications technology
4G	fourth-generation mobile communications technology
ABFs	all business functions
AI	artificial intelligence
BAS	business advisory services
B2B	business-to-business
DT	digital technology
ERP	enterprise resource planning
FAT	Firm-level Adoption of Technology
FDI	foreign direct investment
GBFs	general business functions
GDP	gross domestic product
GPS	Global Positioning System
GSMA	Global System for Mobile Communications Association
HIC	high-income country
IoT	Internet of Things
ME	mesa ejecutiva (Peru)
ML	machine learning
MNC	multinational company
MSMEs	micro, small, and medium enterprises
OECD	Organisation for Economic Co-operation and Development
POS	point-of-sale
RCT	randomized controlled trial
R&D	research and development
RIA	Research ICT Africa
SaaS	software as a service

SBFs	sector-specific business functions
SMEs	small and medium enterprises
SMS	short message system
TC	technology center
TES	technology extension services
SOE	state-owned enterprise
TFP	total factor productivity
USF	universal service fund

CHAPTER 1

Digital Technologies

Enabling Technological Transformation for Jobs

What are digital technologies?

Africa needs better and more jobs for its growing population. Digital technologies (DTs) can enable economic transformation for jobs. They do so by helping all people work better and learn as they work, catalyzing adoption and productivity of complementary technologies, and thereby boosting competitiveness, production, and jobs across the economy.

DTs are technologies that capture, generate, store, modify, and transmit data through binary digits,[1] encompassing

- The internet and internet-based databases, data tools, and other information services;

- All software, computers, and tablets;

- Internet-enabled smartphones (that is, using third-, fourth-, and fifth-generation mobile communications technology), which combine computing and telephone functions into one unit and progressively enable faster access to and processing of more data;

- Digital cameras and video;

- Geolocation systems; and

- Digital platforms—that is, software-based online marketplaces and intermediation systems that facilitate peer-to-peer transactions, match buyers and sellers of goods and services, and enable crowd-based transactions.

Computers, tablets, and smartphones enable critical access to the vast range of information and digital services available on the internet. In addition to linking data collected by sensors on a variety of production and household goods through the IoT (Internet of Things), productivity-enhancing DTs also include cloud computing, on-demand availability of data storage, and computing power so that enterprises and households, instead of buying the underlying software, can buy the associated online services on a per-use basis and discontinue use when no longer needed.

They also include artificial intelligence offerings, typically supported by machine learning, which are predictive analytic algorithms that improve their efficacy over time with the use of increasingly large amounts of data.

Other available DTs include blockchains (decentralized, distributed digital records linked together using cryptography to be tamper-proof and resistant to modification);

cryptocurrencies or digital money based on decentralized ledger technologies; and 3D printing or additive manufacturing—that is, the construction of objects from a digital 3D computer graphic.

DTs help reduce economic production and transaction costs, including search, replication, transportation, tracking, and verification costs.[2]

Africa's jobs and technology challenges

The jobs and technology imperative

Africa's jobs challenge is to put in place business environments conducive to sustainable "good jobs" for its growing workforce (box 1.1).[3]

Continental Africa's workforce is estimated to triple by the twenty-second century—from almost 875 million working-age people (ages 15–64) in 2025 to over 2.5 billion by 2100 (UN DESA 2022a). As a result, Africa's share of the global workforce would increase from 16 percent to over 41 percent, surpassing South Asia and East Asia and Pacific for the largest global share by 2100 (figure 1.1).

This increase is overwhelmingly led by Sub-Saharan Africa, whose workforce is projected to more than triple, from just over 700 million people in 2025 to 1.3 billion by 2050 and 2.3 billion by 2100. Meanwhile, North Africa's working-age population is projected to almost double, from 142 million to 203 million people.

BOX 1.1
What are "good jobs"?

This report defines "good jobs" as those that (a) generate sufficient income for anyone in the workforce and their household to be able to escape from and not fall back into poverty; and (b) enable productive learning—in enterprises that enable increased earnings over time.

However, various authors offer more expansive definitions. As Rodrik and Sabel (2022, 62) acknowledge, "The definition of a 'good job' is necessarily slippery." However, they continue:

> We have in mind in the first instance stable, formal-sector employment that comes with core labor protections such as safe working conditions, collective bargaining rights, and regulations against arbitrary dismissal. A good job allows at least a middle-class existence, by a region's standards, with enough income for housing, food, transportation, education, and other family expenses, as well as some saving. More broadly, good jobs provide workers with clear career paths, possibilities of self-development, flexibility, responsibility, and fulfillment. The depth and range of such characteristics may depend on context: the prevailing levels of productivity and economic development, costs of living, prevailing income gaps, and so on. Further, a good job need not imply classical full-time employment and could permit job sharing and work flexibility. We expect each community to set its own standards and aspirations, which will evolve over time.

Hovhannisyan et al. (2022) also define good jobs more broadly than the two-dimensional one adopted for this report (sufficient income and productive learning opportunities) based on four dimensions: sufficient income, access to employment benefits, job stability, and adequate working conditions. By this four-dimensional measure applied to wage employment, countries in Sub-Saharan Africa display the lowest levels of job quality.

a. 2025 b. 2050 c. 2100

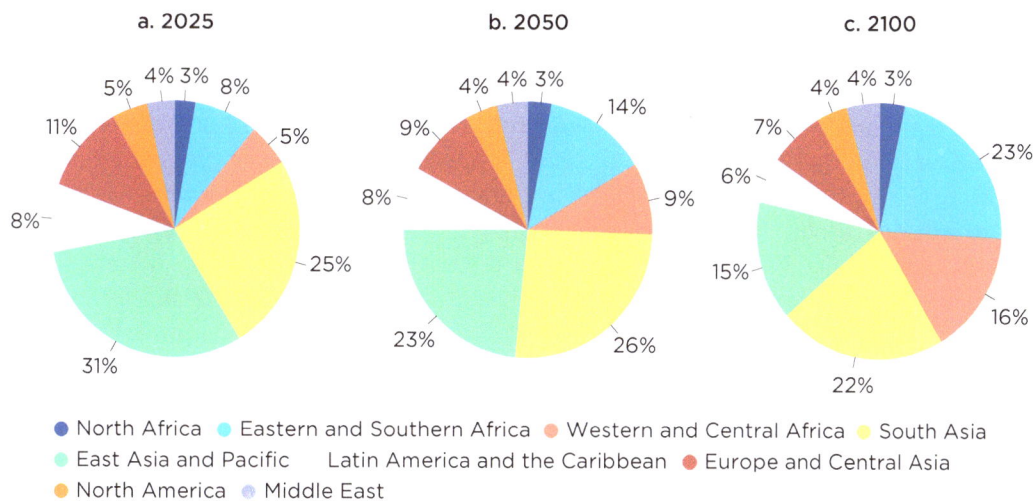

- North Africa ● Eastern and Southern Africa ● Western and Central Africa ● South Asia
- East Asia and Pacific Latin America and the Caribbean ● Europe and Central Asia
- North America ● Middle East

Source: UN DESA 2022a.
Note: Projections are based on the medium fertility rate variant, as described in UN DESA (2022b). "Workforce" comprises the number of people in the 15–64 age group, based on United Nations (UN) projections for 2025 (panel a), 2050 (panel b), and 2100 (panel c). Regions are defined according to World Bank classifications.

Africa's jobs and technology challenges over the coming years are immense—requiring greater use of better and more appropriate technologies in ways that support good local jobs. Good jobs require productive enterprises that can profitably expand production. The jobs challenge presents opportunities for enterprises, households, governments, and civil society at local, national, and regional levels to do things differently and better. Demographic, technological, and market developments provide prospects to design and implement productivity policies and investments that generate jobs-for-all growth and truly shared prosperity.

At the same time, appropriate government interventions are required because Africa's shortfall in good jobs can be viewed as a massive negative externality–type market failure. That is, enterprises often use existing, available technologies and adopt new ones to maximize profits without taking into account the negative effects of leaving workers unemployed or underemployed, which include the following (Rodrik and Sabel 2022; Rodrik and Stantcheva 2021):

- *Economic efficiency and growth costs*—that is, costs associated with producing less than the economy could produce if it were operating efficiently and from a slowdown of the dissemination of innovation from the more advanced sectors to the rest of the economy

- *Social costs,* such as crime and the persistence of poverty linked to undernourishment and low levels of education

- *Political costs,* which include fostering the rise of authoritarian and nativist populism

Such government interventions must be bold and context-specific, considering rapid technological change and uncertainty about the appropriateness of technologies within the context of each country's asset base.[4] Sustainable good jobs require a business environment that supports and stimulates technology adoption and increased productivity by enterprises as well as profitable expansion of the more-productive firms in ways that also generate good jobs for all.[5]

Promise and challenge of Africa's youthful workforce

Providing good jobs for the large number of young people entering the workforce is among the first tests for jobs-rich growth. The flow of net entrants per year into Sub-Saharan Africa's workforce (ages 15–64 years) in 2022 was more than 23 million people—almost 2 million per month. This flow is projected to rise to 27 million by 2030 and to over 33 million by 2050 (UN DESA 2022a). By 2033, the number of net entrants to the workforce (28.5 million) will exceed the number for the rest of the world combined (28.0 million), a total that is declining over time.[6]

This youth bulge is a potentially immense source of flexible, talented, and tech-savvy entrepreneurs and workers who could produce more for local markets and for exports and thereby generate more jobs. However, this challenge for jobs-rich growth requires significant new private investments, supported by public policies and investments that adequately support the education, skills, and upgrading of capabilities needed to nurture this talent. It also requires open, transparent, and enforceable business rules, centered on competition as well as trusted collaboration.

There are two pertinent questions for this report: Are Africa's entrepreneurs getting the chance to develop their talents? Where will they allocate their talents and investments over the coming years? Business rules must make it more profitable for enterprises to invest in innovation (by adopting better technologies and competing for customers in domestic and export markets) than to seek special favors from governments. Enterprise support policies and the actions of state-owned enterprises have unfortunately too often restricted private sector competition and impeded more inclusive growth. Wherever essential business services and other inputs are subject to local monopolization and foreclosure in ways that favor incumbents, younger entrepreneurs with talent but without connections are likely to leave for countries where growth options are better.[7]

Two complementary latent assets of African society provide rays of hope to help address the challenge presented to Africa's youth: First, Africa has experienced high levels of perceived and actual social mobility, and the typical way to get ahead has been through hard work.[8] Second, Africans are highly skeptical of authority and attuned to the abuse of power—presumably not only political power but also abuses of market power. These attitudes can be a critical basis for building better political and economic institutions.

Constraints and opportunity from lagging DT adoption

Another hindrance to jobs-rich growth arises from Africa's technological lag in a broad range of applications for businesses, households, and governments. Yet this lag could provide openings for entrepreneurs to adapt and create technologies specific to Africa's local context, including its rich linguistic heritage. Such tailored DTs could spur enterprise and household users to adopt and use them intensively.[9]

New technologies have the potential to accelerate jobs in agriculture and agribusiness, manufacturing, and services, including education, health, communications, power, transportation, logistics, and financial services (Nayyar, Hallward-Driemeier, and Davies 2021). All technologies need complementary capabilities and physical capital. DTs such as the IoT (physical objects that contain sensors and software to connect with other internet-enabled devices) need investments in and uptake of both the internet (digital infrastructure) and the "things"—complementary essential investments in hard and soft technologies such as tractors, irrigation systems, rural roads, and management capabilities.

However, Africa lags the rest of the world in adoption of many technologies, both digital and analog, which makes Africa the last and most critical frontier for investments in better technologies.[10] For example, Sub-Saharan Africa lags other low- and middle-income regions in the adoption and use of agricultural technologies such as tractors, irrigation systems, and fertilizer (figure 1.2)—with these gaps being larger than any regional differences in crops and land conditions would warrant.

Africa's technology lag in use of agricultural inputs has increased over time: although Africa had more tractors per 1,000 farm workers than East and South Asia in 1960 (0.7 versus 0.2), by 2015 it lagged significantly across technologies (Fuglie et al. 2020, table 4.1). Fuglie et al. (2020) emphasize that the emergence of new technologies especially suited for small farms—labor-intensive horticulture, solar-powered water pumps, minitractors combined with leasing markets—enable the introduction of highly productive farming on small plots of land. Intensification of precision agriculture applying rapidly emerging DTs is likely to further reduce any size-based advantages or disadvantages in crop management. Those authors conclude that, when overall input use is considered, it is not clear whether there are systematic differences in economic efficiency by farm size, and any differences may be diminishing with technological advances and movements into higher-value-added commodities.

Finally, jobs and technology challenges on the supply side of product markets require greater consumer demand to provide profitable outlets for the increased production that drives jobs—and the improved welfare of higher-consuming households. Africa's low consumption of many basic products, which is linked to high poverty rates, has depressed demand for local production as opposed to production for export markets. However, a modest increase in household income across African countries could generate high pent-up demand for low-priced but higher-quality goods and services—such as nutrition-rich fresh produce and processed foods as well as better-quality education, health, entertainment, transportation, and energy services.

FIGURE 1.2 **Use of selected agricultural technologies, by region, 2015**

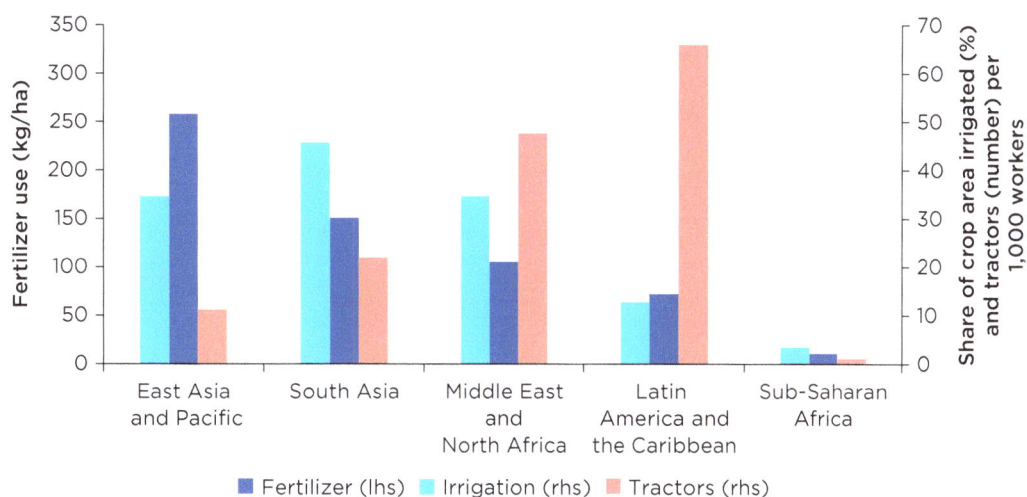

Source: Fuglie et al. 2020.
Note: Values are averages of each region's countries, based on regions defined by the World Bank. kg/ha = kilograms per hectare; lhs = left-hand side; rhs = right-hand side.

Enterprise adoption of better technologies in Africa has the potential to generate low-skill jobs as well, provided the productivity benefits of these technologies result in large enough output expansion. These expansion effects may be more likely in Africa than in other regions, given that demand for these products is significantly lower and therefore likely more elastic to productivity and price changes—provided production *takes place* in Africa. Thus, the region's situation contrasts with that of high-income countries, where demand for many of the same products is more satiated and inelastic in its response to any further productivity and price changes.[11]

Potential of skill-appropriate DTs for jobs-rich economic transformation

"Economic transformation for jobs" is a framework to turn the aforementioned challenges into opportunities over time (box 1.2). The term refers to pathways to inclusive productivity growth that generate more jobs and earnings for all. It is driven by three complementary underlying types of transformations—technological, sectoral, and spatial—that should be underpinned by public policy reforms and investments.

These reforms and investments should directly promote inclusive productivity growth across three support pillars:

1. *Skills,* including investments in basic education as well as vocational or activity-specific training oriented toward the needs of prospective employers as well as on-the-job learning

2. *Infrastructure,* including investments in soft infrastructure (such as finance) and hard infrastructure (such as electricity and digital) across sectors

3. *Institutions,* including macroeconomic stability as well as transparency and accountabilty for good governance

This report emphasizes technological transformation driven by innovation. Technological transformation, as a pathway to more inclusive productivity growth, occurs when enterprises and households adopt and more intensively use better currently available technologies or modify and create appropriate new technologies—generating more jobs and income for all people.[12] Recent World Bank reports on Africa focus on productivity policies to improve resource allocation (Abreha et al. 2021; Calderón and Cantú 2021). The premise underlying this report is that investments in upgrading

---

BOX 1.2
The World Bank's "economic transformation for jobs" framework

Economic transformation for jobs is referred to as the "JET" (jobs and economic transformation) framework within the World Bank Group.

Within this framework, economic transformation is viewed as a radically different economic development strategy from "trickle-down" growth policies. Rather, it postulates that *inclusive* jobs policies and investments must explicitly support productivity growth among lower-income, lower-skilled entrepreneurs and workers, enabling them to learn as they work and thereby to improve their ability to generate higher earnings.

The design of inclusive productivity growth policies presumes that there will at times be trade-offs between faster aggregate growth and more inclusive, jobs-rich growth and that policy choices should be made in favor of the latter.

technologies and associated capabilities in all economic activities in which African enterprises have the potential to be competitive are as essential, if not more so, than improving resource allocation across enterprises and economic activities.

Across all geographic regions for low- and middle-income countries as well as for high-income countries, at least two-thirds of labor productivity growth between 1995 and 2018 is explained by increases *within* sectors rather than *between* sectors—such as between agriculture and manufacturing or between manufacturing and services (Nayyar, Hallward-Driemeier, and Davies 2021, figure 1.5).[13] The finding that within-enterprise technology upgrading accounted for the largest share of China's and Ethiopia's physical productivity growth from 2000 to 2007 suggests that technology upgrading can be the most important driver of productivity growth in countries where most enterprises are in a position to take advantage of technological catchup (Cusolito and Maloney 2018).[14]

The extremely low levels of average managerial practices found by Bloom et al. (2016) in African enterprises, based on Bloom and van Reenen (2007, 2010), highlight another barrier facing technology upgrading in Africa. However, they also show the upside potential of simple technologies that facilitate management upgrading—such as point-of-sale solutions allowing managers to compare inventory levels and offer enticing deals to expand sales and jobs. Management upgrading through DTs arguably is a natural entry point for the subsequent upgrading of other enterprise technologies.[15]

The world is undergoing a significant technological transformation that is already reshaping how and where businesses and households buy, make, sell, and consume goods and services, as well as where more and better jobs are created. Internet-enabled DTs reduce costs or frictions across the economy and allow for better data-driven decision-making.[16] They can be transformed through productive use into increased economic opportunities for all enterprises and households, including for the large number of lower-skilled people living in Africa. Although the use of DTs also supports sectoral and spatial transformations as additional, complementary pathways toward better jobs for more people, the main contribution of DTs is to directly support technological transformation.

The challenge of skill-biased technological change

Low- and middle-income countries seeking a more inclusive jobs growth path through DT adoption have additional obstacles because many better technologies that could be adopted and used by local enterprises are skill-biased.[17] This problem is particularly stark for African countries given the number of people already in the workforce and the large number of less educated youth entering the workforce. The preponderance of skill-biased technologies is related to the abundance of skilled labor in high-income countries and the fact that most technologies are still produced there.[18]

Generating more lower-skill jobs through the adoption of skill-biased technologies requires sufficiently larger volumes of production and sales by both existing and new firms. Most adopted technologies allow businesses to reduce their unit production costs or improve quality. Greater sales are driven by the lower prices that the cost reductions enable. It is the output expansion and the new tasks associated with increased output that generate the demand for more employment that includes lower-skilled workers.[19]

These advances require (a) competition in input and output markets for more efficient firms to expand; (b) sufficient responsiveness of consumer demand to the lower prices stimulated by technologies and product competition; and (c) sufficient complementariness between the adopted technologies and lower-skilled workers so their jobs are enhanced rather than eliminated. For inclusive productivity growth, generated and adopted technologies must be focused toward lower-skilled workers so that DTs enhance communities and bring jobs rather than replacing people and jobs.

The potential of skill-appropriate technologies

A complementary technology-driven path is the creation, adoption, and intensive use by enterprise workers and managers, as well as by households involved in informal economic activities, of skill-appropriate DTs. Technological change has been largely higher-skill-biased for most of the twentieth century in high-income countries because the rapid increase in the supply of higher-skilled workers induced the development of such technologies.[20]

In contrast to *skill-biased* technologies, *skill-appropriate* technologies are directed at the productive use and learning needs of lower-skilled people and thus directly favor lower-skilled rather than higher-skilled workers by increasing their relative productivity. They also support higher-skilled workers through the jobs created in generating these technologies, which require sophisticated software engineers to build on existing apps to make them easier and more intuitive to use, such as through video activation and response in a range of local languages and dialects.

Higher-skill jobs also are stimulated through the higher production volumes and the more sophisticated tasks that these technologies enable. Acemoglu and Restrepo (2020, 25) have argued:

> Recent technological change has been biased towards automation, with insufficient focus on creating new tasks where labor can be productively employed. The consequences of this choice have been stagnating labor demand, declining labor shares in national income, rising inequality, and the lowering of productivity growth.

Trajtenberg (2019, 185) has posed the policy-related question as follows:

> It would seem that AI-based human-enhancing innovations (HEIs) have the potential to unleash a new wave of human creativity and productivity, particularly in services, whereas human-replacing innovations (HRIs) either decrease employment or create unworthy jobs. Is it possible to design strategies to affect the direction of technical change, in the sense of stimulating HEIs versus HRIs? It is hard to say, but it is certainly worthwhile investigating such possibility, given the large impact that a change in direction may have on the economy. . . . Some attention to the "direction" [of technological change rather than the rate] may bring much larger returns.

And Rodrik and Stantcheva (2021, 832) argue:

> As a matter of logic, the gap between skills and technology can be closed in one of two ways: either by increasing education to match the demands of new technologies, or by redirecting innovation to match the skills of the current (and prospective) labour force. The second strategy, which gets practically no attention in policy discussions, is worth taking seriously.

For lower-skilled people in Africa, there is a critical added benefit of designing skill-appropriate DTs that enable learning as people work. It transforms what would be a one-time productivity increase—namely adoption of a new DT—into dynamic growth in productivity. It enables people to continuously boost the productivity of their tasks or move to higher-skilled tasks as they develop new skills over time.

A conceptual framework—from DT availability to inclusive jobs

This report provides new data and analyses to better understand the extent of DT use in Africa—and how inclusive jobs outcomes can be associated with the use of DTs and complementary technologies to a greater extent. To that end, this chapter presents the

FIGURE 1.3 Conceptual framework for policy analysis of DTs' impacts on job and income growth

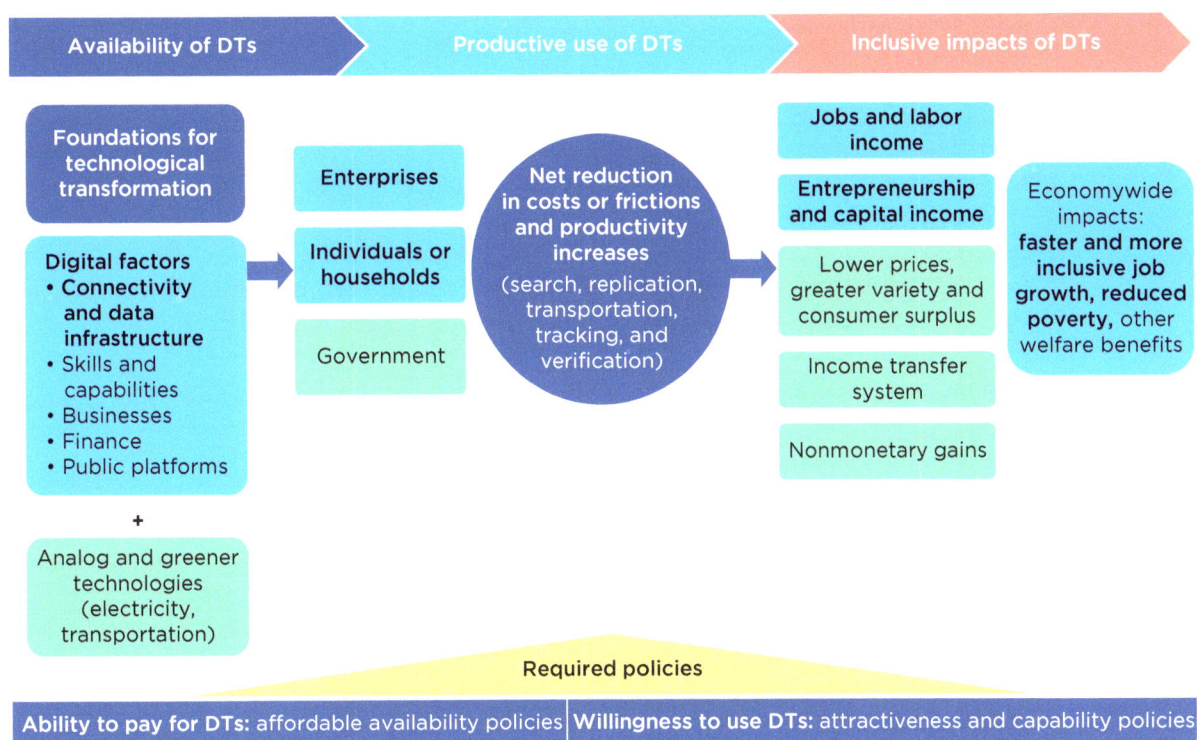

Availability of DTs ▸ **Productive use of DTs** ▸ **Inclusive impacts of DTs**

Foundations for technological transformation

Digital factors
• Connectivity and data infrastructure
• Skills and capabilities
• Businesses
• Finance
• Public platforms

+

Analog and greener technologies (electricity, transportation)

Enterprises

Individuals or households

Government

Net reduction in costs or frictions and productivity increases (search, replication, transportation, tracking, and verification)

Jobs and labor income

Entrepreneurship and capital income

Lower prices, greater variety and consumer surplus

Income transfer system

Nonmonetary gains

Economywide impacts: **faster and more inclusive job growth, reduced poverty,** other welfare benefits

Required policies

Ability to pay for DTs: affordable availability policies | **Willingness to use DTs:** attractiveness and capability policies

Source: World Bank.
Note: Bolded text (in the blue boxes) indicates the primary areas and themes covered by this report, with a focus on the production side of the economy (enterprises and workers). "Inclusive impacts" are those that generate income growth for all, including faster income per capita growth for the bottom 40 percent of each country's population. DTs = digital technologies.

report's conceptual framework (figure 1.3). The framework links availability of DTs and their use to inclusive jobs growth and reduced poverty through various channels, including better jobs for more people.

The framework builds on the theory of change proposed in the World Bank's Digital Economy for Africa (DE4A) initiative.[21] It includes five enablers of DT availability that facilitate use and impact of DTs: connectivity and data infrastructure, skills, digital businesses (the main providers of digital solutions), digital finance, and digital public platforms.

Components of the basic framework

Availability of DTs. Within the conceptual framework shown in figure 1.3, the left column pertains to *availability of DTs*. Affordable availability of both connectivity (broadband internet) and data infrastructure, as well as complementary electricity and transportation infrastructure, are necessary conditions as economywide enablers.

Productive use of DTs. The framework's middle column covers *productive use of DTs* by enterprises, individuals and households, and governments. Drivers of use by enterprises and individuals relate to the *ability to pay* for them—in turn, contingent on the affordability of internet connectivity, access technologies (smartphones, computers, and tablets), and electricity as well as on having sufficient disposable income or access to finance. Ability to pay is facilitated by cost-reflective prices, stimulated by

(a) investments in new infrastructure-related technologies and (b) competition for available digital infrastructure connections.

Drivers affecting *willingness to use* DTs include attractiveness to users, stemming from available information about the DTs, their relevance to the local context, and their ease of use.

Inclusive impacts of DTs. As highlighted in the framework's right column, the inclusive impacts of DTs on jobs depend on how intensively people use DTs that increase productivity. The prevailing business environment, including intensity of product market competition, also affects the intensity of productive use and the outcomes arising from DTs—whether by providing incentives for enterprise and household use and expansion of use, or by impeding sufficient gains from their use, such that uptake becomes unattractive.

The framework clarifies how cost reductions and productivity increases have inclusive impacts on people across five channels:

1. *Jobs and labor income* arising from productive use by enterprises and individuals as managers and workers

2. *Entrepreneurship and capital income* earned by owners of larger firms and household enterprises

3. *Consumer surplus,* arising from the consumption of goods and services at lower prices, of higher quality, or of wider variety[22]

4. *The income transfer system* via taxes and various forms of income support

5. *Nonmonetary gains* such as the intrinsic benefits of better health and education for civil society, of human dignity and individual empowerment, and other nonpecuniary aspects of quality of life

This cost-centric framework and its components highlight how DT use increases opportunities to access local and global product, labor, land, and financial markets by enterprises and individuals, as these costs include searching, job matching, transportation, and other transaction costs. The framework also clarifies that it is through the reduction of various costs that the use of DTs facilitates business continuity when face-to-face or close-contact production of goods and services would otherwise be disrupted by COVID-19 or similar health risks.[23]

Within figure 1.3, the text in bold represents areas that receive greater emphasis in this report, namely enterprises and households that make productive use of DTs for impacts on jobs and poverty-reducing earnings. The roles of complementary technologies and complementary or foundational factors that support DT availability—such as skills, digital businesses (including start-ups as well as larger global private digital platforms), digital finance, and public platforms—are examined only insofar as they support the focus of the report.[24]

An expanded framework: Policies to address digital divides

Figure 1.4 expands on the basic conceptual framework by clarifying the challenges posed by various types of digital divides across enterprises and individuals. For example, larger, formal enterprises typically are quicker to more intensively use various DTs. Smaller and especially informal microenterprises with fewer than five full-time employees—including self-employed household enterprises with no full-time paid employees—are less

FIGURE 1.4 Expanded conceptual framework for policy analysis of DTs' job and income impacts through the lens of digital divides

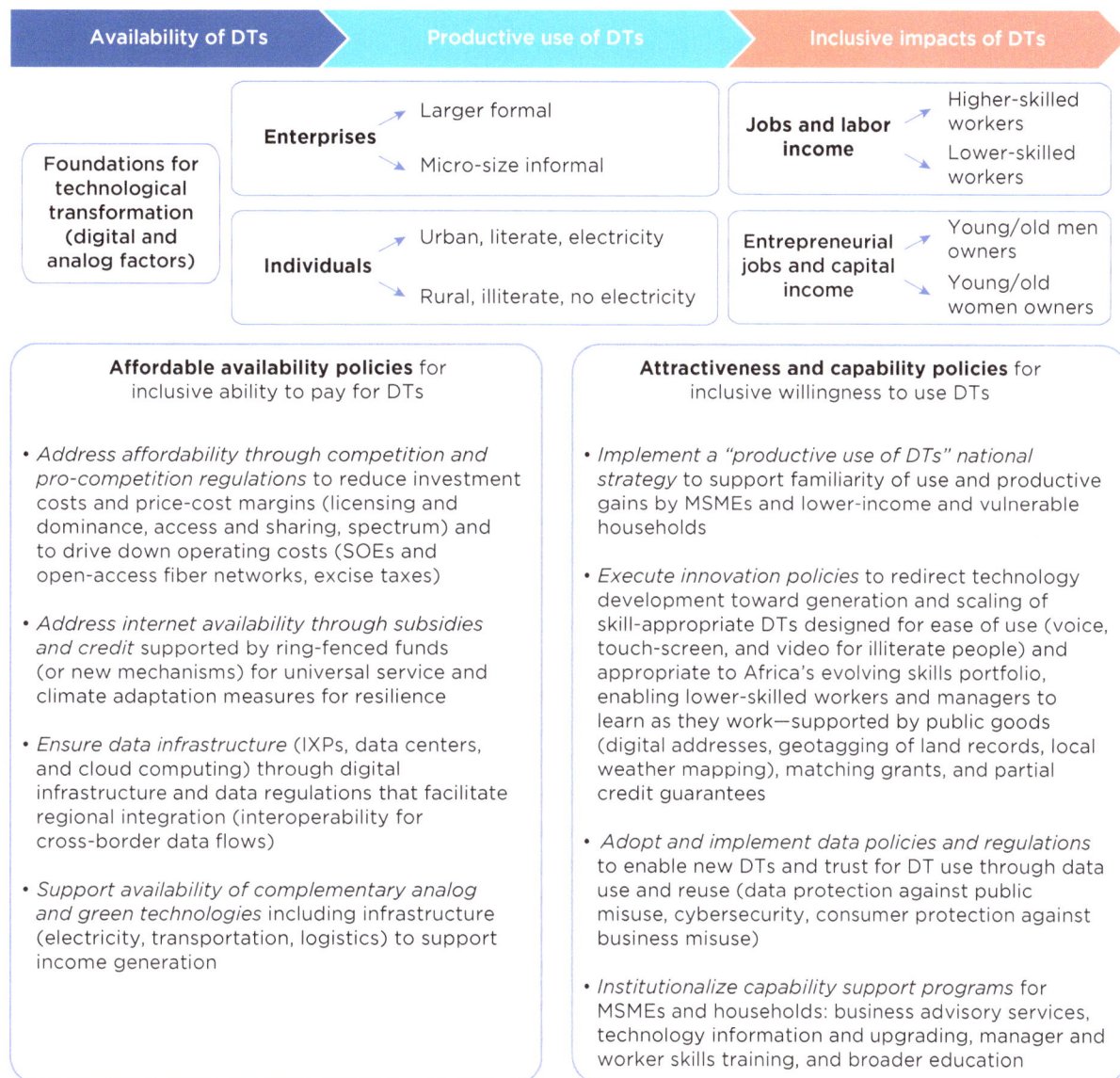

Availability of DTs	Productive use of DTs	Inclusive impacts of DTs

Foundations for technological transformation (digital and analog factors)

Enterprises
→ Larger formal
↘ Micro-size informal

Individuals
→ Urban, literate, electricity
↘ Rural, illiterate, no electricity

Jobs and labor income
→ Higher-skilled workers
↘ Lower-skilled workers

Entrepreneurial jobs and capital income
→ Young/old men owners
↘ Young/old women owners

Affordable availability policies for inclusive ability to pay for DTs

- *Address affordability through competition and pro-competition regulations* to reduce investment costs and price-cost margins (licensing and dominance, access and sharing, spectrum) and to drive down operating costs (SOEs and open-access fiber networks, excise taxes)

- *Address internet availability through subsidies and credit* supported by ring-fenced funds (or new mechanisms) for universal service and climate adaptation measures for resilience

- *Ensure data infrastructure* (IXPs, data centers, and cloud computing) through digital infrastructure and data regulations that facilitate regional integration (interoperability for cross-border data flows)

- *Support availability of complementary analog and green technologies* including infrastructure (electricity, transportation, logistics) to support income generation

Attractiveness and capability policies for inclusive willingness to use DTs

- *Implement a "productive use of DTs" national strategy* to support familiarity of use and productive gains by MSMEs and lower-income and vulnerable households

- *Execute innovation policies* to redirect technology development toward generation and scaling of skill-appropriate DTs designed for ease of use (voice, touch-screen, and video for illiterate people) and appropriate to Africa's evolving skills portfolio, enabling lower-skilled workers and managers to learn as they work—supported by public goods (digital addresses, geotagging of land records, local weather mapping), matching grants, and partial credit guarantees

- *Adopt and implement data policies and regulations* to enable new DTs and trust for DT use through data use and reuse (data protection against public misuse, cybersecurity, consumer protection against business misuse)

- *Institutionalize capability support programs* for MSMEs and households: business advisory services, technology information and upgrading, manager and worker skills training, and broader education

Source: World Bank.
Note: "Inclusive" refers to policy impacts or jobs that generate income growth for all, including faster income per capita growth for the bottom 40 percent of each country's population. DTs = digital technologies; IXPs = internet exchange points; MSMEs = micro, small, and medium enterprises; SOEs = state-owned enterprises.

likely to use DTs that provide internet access. Similarly, literate households in urban locations with electricity are more likely to use DTs than illiterate households in rural locations with no electricity or no reliable supply.

In terms of inclusive impacts, to the extent that DTs are skill-biased, higher-skilled workers are more likely than lower-skilled workers to benefit in terms of better jobs and higher labor income earnings from enterprises using these technologies. Male business owners are similarly more likely than female owners to use DTs and benefit in terms of higher capital income. Gender divides include not only social norms and rules favoring male ownership of DTs but also discrimination in the workplace, resulting in lower business success for female-owned enterprises using DTs.

The potential digital divides and how they can be narrowed by using better technologies, as figure 1.4 highlights, are further illuminated by a recent analysis of the mechanisms through which DTs affect poorer households' income-earning choices. Porto (2021) uses household data from Kenya and Senegal to investigate, through simulations, the implications of lower consumer prices for rice and of higher producer prices and lower input prices for groundnuts—price changes enabled by the adoption of specific DTs.[25] A DT upgrade that lowers the consumer prices of rice benefits the average *poor* household twice as much as the average household, and the rural household more than the urban household. It does so because rice is consumed more in poor households, and most rural rice-producing households are also net buyers of rice. The welfare effects of a productivity improvement in groundnut production are significantly larger than those of a price increase at the farm gate (the price received by the producer from direct sales at the farm), but differences in magnitudes will depend on the access to technologies.

The expanded framework in figure 1.4 also summarizes policy responses for availability, use, and inclusive impacts. Policies for affordable availability of connectivity and data infrastructure and data policies to enhance DT attractiveness are covered in chapter 4. Policies to increase enterprises' and households' willingness to use DTs that ride on the connectivity and data infrastructure are mainly covered in chapters 2 and 3.

In general, to be effective, policies and institutional design across all areas should adhere to three principles:

1. *Competition in markets,* which is a critical incentive to enable availability, use, and impact of DTs

2. *Coordination,* including (a) the bundling of complementary technology, skills, capabilities, and financing support in ways that overcome the combined obstacles to DT use by enterprises and households; and (b) coordination across different public support entities and between government and business

3. *Contestability of policies,* namely that their objectives, including the market failures that they seek to address, are transparent and accompanied by rigorous monitoring and evaluation yielding evidence of impact that allows only the most effective policies to stay operational. Policy experimentation, together with impact evaluation, is essential to learn more about what specific types and combinations of public policies and investments are most effective in different local, national, and subregional contexts.

Impacts of digital technology use on jobs and poverty

This section presents empirical evidence of the impact of DTs on jobs and poverty reduction, with a focus on recent findings from Africa. As highlighted in the conceptual framework earlier, DTs can sustainably reduce poverty and increase consumption among lower-income households, largely through their impact on generating better jobs for more people as well as by reducing prices and improving the quality of products consumed by poorer households.

The connection between DT use and more and better jobs is through the output expansion that adoption of DTs generates and the consequent need for more workers, through either (a) *the supply side* of production (by directly increasing labor productivity or other aspects of enterprise performance) or (b) *the demand side* (by directly expanding enterprises' and consumers' market access and by addressing information frictions).[26]

Impacts of internet use and availability

The good news is that there is increasingly robust evidence that internet availability has a causal inclusive impact on more jobs and reduced poverty in selected African countries.[27] The bad news, as highlighted in the next section ("Africa's large internet uptake gap"), is that too few people are taking advantage of these benefits, as shown by the low internet uptake relative to availability.

Regionwide impacts on jobs

Faster internet in Sub-Saharan Africa was facilitated by the gradual arrival of submarine cables over the past two decades, which greatly increased the speed and capacity of terrestrial networks. For the enterprises and households near these networks in Sub-Saharan Africa, relative to those in unconnected areas, the probability that an individual is employed increases by an average of 6.9 percent for the eight countries in a Demographic and Health Survey sample, by 13.2 percent in an Afrobarometer sample across nine countries, and by 3.1 percent in a separate South Africa survey (Hjort and Poulsen 2019).[28] These impacts attributable to faster internet are net positive job increases and sizable in magnitude, rather than displacement of jobs from unconnected areas.[29]

Faster internet adoption is skill-biased—that is, internet adoption complements more-skilled jobs, as has been shown in high-income countries.[30] Less educated workers benefit, though workers who did not complete primary education are disadvantaged: the percentage change in the probability of employment is significantly positive—in the range of 6 percent for workers with primary, secondary, and higher education levels—but not statistically significant for workers who did not complete primary education.

Some of the increase in jobs is explained by net firm entry (about 23 percent in South Africa), including a large increase in firm entry and a decrease in firm exit of similar magnitude. Another part of the jobs increase appears to be due to increased productivity in existing manufacturing firms (in Ethiopia). Enterprises in Ghana, Kenya, Mauritania, Nigeria, Senegal, and Tanzania export more when they have access to faster internet, communicate with clients more, and train employees more, according to World Bank Enterprise Survey data.[31] The productivity of less educated workers (those who completed only primary education) may have benefited from provision by employers of targeted on-the-job training.

Country case studies: Impacts on jobs, household welfare, and poverty

Three subsequent country case studies (on Nigeria, Senegal, and Tanzania) strengthen this rapidly growing evidence base by exploring the impact of mobile internet availability (third-generation [3G] or fourth-generation [4G] coverage)—instead of fixed terrestrial broadband—on jobs and welfare. The studies take advantage of geospatial information on the rollout of mobile internet towers over time, combined with at least two rounds of household data over a six-year period (Tanzania) and a seven-year period (Nigeria).

Figure 1.5 summarizes the main jobs and welfare (consumption and poverty) results for Nigeria and Tanzania.

Nigeria. The job estimates from Nigeria show that internet availability has positive impacts: labor force participation and wage employment increase by 3 percentage points and 1 percentage point, respectively, after three or more years of exposure in areas with internet availability relative to those with no coverage (Bahia et al. 2020).[32] The internet-induced improvement in labor market outcomes is especially large for women. The internet availability leading to these jobs effects also causes large and positive increases in household consumption levels: households with at least one year of mobile broadband availability increase total consumption by about 6 percent. These effects increase to about 9 percent after three or more years of mobile internet coverage.

Mobile internet availability also reduces the proportion of households below the poverty line—a reduction driven by higher food and nonfood consumption in rural households. The proportion of households below the extreme poverty line decreases by 4 percentage points after one year of gaining mobile internet availability and by 7 percent after three years.[33] The welfare results are higher among poorer and rural households, with results for urban households mostly statistically insignificant, perhaps reflecting the

FIGURE 1.5 Impacts of mobile internet availability on job creation and household welfare, Nigeria and Tanzania

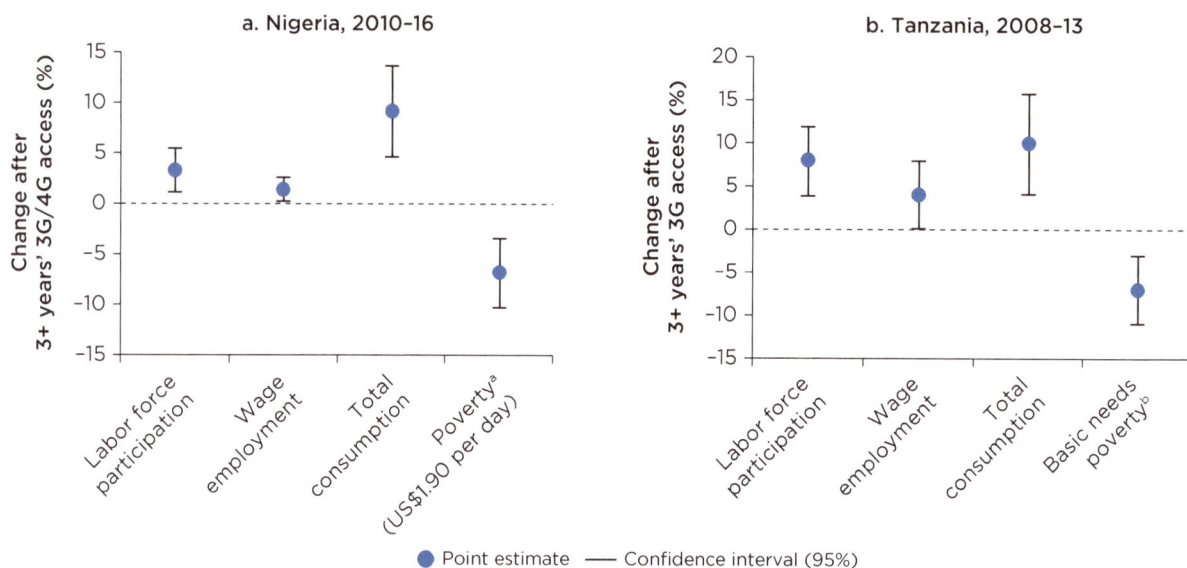

a. Nigeria, 2010–16

b. Tanzania, 2008–13

● Point estimate —— Confidence interval (95%)

Sources: Bahia et al. 2020; Bahia et al., forthcoming.
Note: The studies examine geospatial information on the rollout of mobile internet towers, combined with three rounds of household data over seven years for Nigeria and two rounds over six years for Tanzania. The estimates on poverty and consumption include all individuals or households, whereas labor outcomes include only working-age populations (ages 15–64). The results represent percentage changes in the covered locations after three or more years of high-quality internet exposure relative to those without such coverage after accounting for potential confounding factors. Each point represents the estimated impact of mobile internet coverage on labor and welfare outcomes using difference-in-difference estimates with 95 percent confidence intervals. The reported effects on poverty in the graph are not comparable. 3G = third-generation mobile communications technology; 4G = fourth-generation mobile communications technology.
a. Nigeria's poverty status of households is calculated using the international poverty line of US$1.90 per day (2011 purchasing power parity) and after applying the Consumer Price Index to adjust for both spatial and temporal inflation.
b. Tanzania's poverty status of households is calculated using the cost of acquiring enough food to provide adequate daily nutrition per person (food line) plus the cost of some nonfood essentials (nonfood component).

fact that over the period of analysis most households in urban areas had already been living in connected areas.

Tanzania. The job estimates for Tanzania are similarly significant, with richer jobs data allowing for a more detailed exploration (Bahia et al., forthcoming).[34] Internet availability facilitates a transition out of farm jobs into wage and nonfarm self-employment. Living in areas covered by mobile internet reduces farm self-employment by 7 percentage points after three or more years of coverage. Correspondingly, working-age individuals living in areas with internet availability witness increases in labor force participation, wage employment, and nonfarm self-employment of 8, 4, and 4 percentage points, respectively, after three or more years of exposure.

Younger (less than 30 years of age) and more educated (more than primary education) individuals, and males benefit the most through higher labor force participation and wage employment. Mobile internet availability has no effect on overall female labor force participation or wage employment. However, women who are higher-skilled, are literate, and have completed primary education do benefit from shifts out of farm work into non-farm self-employment and family enterprises.[35]

The internet availability leading to these jobs effects also causes large and positive increases in household consumption levels: per capita total consumption among households residing in areas with 3G availability is about 10 percent higher than in those without coverage after three or more years of exposure. The proportion of households below the national basic needs poverty line is reduced by 7 percentage points after three or more years of coverage.[36] There are higher welfare gains among households whose heads are female, poorer, or less-educated (not having completed primary).[37]

Senegal. The estimated job impacts in Senegal are also positive for some job categories: 3G availability is associated with 5 percent higher formal employment than in uncovered areas, though availability does not have a significant impact on overall employment (Masaki, Ochoa, and Rodríguez-Castelán 2020).[38]

The welfare estimates for Senegal also align with the findings for Nigeria and Tanzania—namely, large effects on household consumption and poverty reduction.[39] Total consumption among households with 3G availability is 14 percent greater than among noncovered households, and the average nonfood consumption of households with 3G availability is 26 percent greater than that of noncovered households. Households with 3G availability also exhibit a 10 percent lower extreme poverty rate than households without coverage.[40]

Availability of 3G is significantly and positively correlated with total consumption and negatively associated with poverty only for urban households; however, this correlation is particularly pronounced for *food* consumption among urban households, whereas 3G availability is significantly and positively correlated with *nonfood* consumption for rural households as well as for poorer households. The positive effects of 3G availability on nonfood consumption are particularly pronounced among male-headed households. Splitting the sample by age (using age 50 as a threshold, roughly the median age of household heads), the positive welfare effects of 3G availability are also more evident among households headed by younger people.

Channels of indirect impact

Other empirical studies on Africa explore indirect impacts on more and better jobs through the effects of internet availability on improving firm-worker matching, improving firm productivity through entrepreneurship, spurring innovation and foreign investments, increasing market access, reducing informational frictions, and boosting aggregate economic growth. The link between jobs and poverty reduction, which the Nigeria, Senegal, and Tanzania studies emphasize, is not explicitly explored in most of these other studies. Given appropriate data on individuals, the effects on poverty could also be explored through the impact of internet availability on consumer surplus gains to lower-income and less educated people.[41]

Firm-worker matching. One channel through which the internet can increase labor productivity and better jobs is through better firm-worker matching. Search and match-making frictions are likely to be particularly important in African countries.[42] DTs that reduce job application costs can enable employers to attract more talented applicants. Decreasing job application costs, by using the internet and precluding the need to apply in person, has been shown to enable employers to attract higher-ability applicants by incentivizing a pool of higher-ability female, inexperienced, unemployed job seekers who are unlikely to quickly secure good positions otherwise. The results are driven by the fact that job application costs are typically large and heterogeneous and that high-ability candidates face, on average, higher application costs (Abebe, Caria, and Ortiz-Ospina 2021).[43] The potential dynamic gains from relaxing these frictions could be large if worker ability is complementary to capital and technology.

Even non-internet-linked DTs can reduce search costs, including for farmers to find workers and for workers to find jobs on farms in rural labor markets. A short message system (SMS)–based messaging app designed to connect agriculture workers and employers increases the size of the labor market, facilitating employers' consideration of a new set of workers whom they had not hired in the past. The app decreases within-village wage dispersion by 16–40 percent, inducing initially higher-paying employers to reduce the wage and lower-paying employers to increase the wage (Jeong 2020).[44] The app has helped employers and workers better connect and thereby improved the efficiency of localized rural labor markets.

Firm productivity, entrepreneurship, and foreign investment. Internet availability can also improve firm productivity and lead to better jobs through increased entrepreneurship, adoption of other complementary technologies, and foreign investments. With the staggered arrival of submarine cables and the subsequent rollout of terrestrial fiber networks across Africa, there is evidence of associated internet-induced entrepreneurship: the probability that a household establishes a nonfarm business is 17 percentage points higher in areas with internet availability than in areas without availability (Houngbonon, Mensah, and Traore 2022). However, this increase in entrepreneurial activities is largely concentrated in the service sector. The low entry cost of establishing many service-related businesses relative to agribusiness and manufacturing is a plausible explanation for this result.

There is also evidence that internet availability spurs both process and product innovation: it increases the probability of a firm undertaking process and product innovation by 20 and 12 percentage points, respectively. The effect on process innovation largely stems from the adoption of DTs for business functions such as sales, distribution, and marketing, and the effect is boosted by the availability of digital skills within the firm (Houngbonon, Mensah, and Traore 2022).[45]

As for foreign investments, there is evidence that internet availability plays a role in stimulating foreign direct investment (FDI) in the banking and technology sectors: it is associated with increases of 6 and 3 percentage points, respectively, in the probability of FDI in the financial and technology services sectors (Mensah and Traore 2022).

As well, the number of FDI projects in financial services increased by 20 percent following the arrival of the submarine internet cables, with the value (size) of FDI also increasing. However, the effect is largely concentrated in countries with a reliable supply of electricity—largely because access to electricity is essential in powering access devices such as computers and mobile phones that use the internet.[46]

Market access. In addition to its direct impact on jobs through labor and broader firm productivity on the supply side of production, internet availability also expands the demand side of production. A positive relationship between internet usage and exports has been found across African countries (Hinson and Adjasi 2009).[47] This finding is attributed to internet usage reducing the market entry and search costs associated with exporting.

Internet availability can also increase access to markets by reducing informational frictions associated with selling to bigger corporations, governments, and other large buyers. Supporting this statement is evidence that smaller firms taking part in a program teaching them how to sell to larger buyers win about three times as many contracts as nonparticipants, but only if they have internet access (Hjort, Iyer, and de Rochambeau 2020).[48]

Informational frictions. Internet availability can also expand the demand side by reducing informational frictions. A now-classic illustration of the benefits of pre-internet DTs is the reduction in price dispersion associated with the adoption of second-generation (2G) mobile phones by fishermen and wholesalers in the Indian state of Kerala (Jensen 2007).[49] Related evidence is available for Africa—for instance, a reduction of 10–16 percent in millet consumer price dispersion in Niger (Aker 2010) and a reduction of 6 percent in the spatial producer price dispersion of cowpea, a semiperishable commodity, also in Niger (Aker and Fafchamps 2014). Both of these results were linked to the rollout of 2G mobile phone coverage.

Suggestive evidence of how internet availability can boost jobs by closing information asymmetry gaps between buyers and sellers is provided by the rollout of 3G internet networks in Ethiopia (Abreha et al. 2021).[50] Enterprises operating in areas with 3G availability experience a 29 percent decline in markups, an 18 percent rise in firm productivity, and a 28 percent increase in jobs. These outcomes are interpreted as resulting from increased competition as consumers become aware of price information and more alternatives in nearby markets, and as firms respond to increased competition and compressed profit margins by reducing costs—with increased productivity enabling output expansion and more jobs.

Aggregate economic growth. Finally, there is evidence that internet availability boosts aggregate economic growth, with jobs expansion presumed from the output expansion accompanying faster growth. A causal connection is shown between internet availability and economic growth, which increases by an average of 2 percentage points in towns across 10 Sub-Saharan African countries that benefited from the arrival of submarine cable connections, relative to similar towns not yet connected (Goldbeck and Lindlacher 2021).[51] Regions that get connected earlier find themselves with stronger decreasing shares of agriculture and stronger increasing shares of manufacturing and services than regions that become connected relatively later, suggesting the increase in economic activity comes from changing industry shares induced by the arrival of internet availability.

A complementary empirical approach, based on aggregate, country-level data on mobile internet subscriptions and the population share of internet users, also finds a causal impact on increasing the growth of output per worker as well as reducing poverty and income inequality (Calderón and Cantú 2021).[52] The growth returns of investing in digital infrastructure appear to be larger when considering the 3G and 4G connections jointly rather than individually. Moreover, the growth returns of expanding the digital infrastructure network are higher for countries with greater human capital and electricity access rates. The combination of 3G and 4G connections per capita has an impact on economic growth primarily through the total factor productivity growth channel, while internet users expand the economy via the capital accumulation channel. Finally, while internet use is found to have a significant effect in reducing poverty, mobile connections are found to also have a significant effect on reducing income inequality.

Impacts of finance- and agriculture-related DTs

Across African countries, poverty is overwhelmingly a rural phenomenon: 82 percent of Africa's poor people are rural, earning their living primarily in farming or, when working off the farm, in agriculture-related activities (Beegle and Christiaensen 2019). Informal microenterprises are the main source of nonagricultural employment and income for poor and near-poor people. Strikingly, rural poverty is higher in areas with better agro-ecological potential. This situation indicates a policy entry point, either to reinforce the income-earning opportunities of poor people where they are located or to help them connect with income-earning opportunities elsewhere. Therefore, skill-appropriate DTs that are simple to use could potentially both increase productivity of those people remaining in agricultural jobs and help those seeking jobs elsewhere to connect to them.

Financial services

Mobile money applications. Mobile money is the most prominent and best-known African DT that adds value to a digital phone. It is simple to adopt and use, is used widely by lower-income households and individuals as well as enterprises and governments to make and receive payments, and can yield visibly immediate benefits.

Launched in 2007 by Safaricom, the M-Pesa mobile money application could be found in 97 percent of Kenyan households as of 2014.[53] Robust causal evidence exists that better access to mobile money has led to better jobs and a reduction in poverty over time. In Kenya, the longer-term impacts of M-Pesa include significant changes in occupation choice, largely among women; for example, 185,000 women moved away from agriculture as their main occupation to business and retail—activities with higher earnings potential (Suri and Jack 2016).

Better access to mobile money services also has increased financial resilience, with significant increases in total savings. Both labor market outcomes and increased financial resilience, in turn, are associated with increased household consumption and reduced poverty rates in Kenya: poverty rates declined by 2 percentage points, with 196,000 households moving out of extreme poverty and with larger reductions among female-headed households (Suri and Jack 2016).[54] In rural northern Uganda, rollout of mobile money agents nearly doubled the nonfarm self-employment rate, from 3.4 percent to 6.4 percent, and reduced the fraction of households with very low food security from 62.9 percent to 47.2 percent in areas far from a bank branch (Wieser et al. 2019).[55]

In addition, M-Pesa has facilitated Kilimo Salama, a weather index and crop insurance scheme, by serving as a payment gateway. Kilimo Salama helps farmers to better manage natural hazards such as drought or excessive rainfall by relying on data from automated weather stations. Farmers can hedge against production uncertainties, because they are compensated if they suffer losses. Thus, households are incentivized to increase their input use for higher crop productivity (Sibiko and Qaim 2020). Annual insurance uptake by households increased sharply from 1.3–3.5 percent in 2009, when Kilimo Salama was launched in Kenya, to about 34 percent in 2012 (Kirimi, Njue, and Mathenge 2015). It became ACRE (Agriculture and Climate Risk Enterprise Ltd.) in 2014, with projects providing risk management solutions to reduce agricultural and climate risks in Ghana, Kenya, Malawi, Mozambique, Tanzania, and Uganda.

Access to mobile money services also has been shown to increase broad local economic activity. For example, access increases the intensity of evening lights by about 9 percent (Fabregas and Yokossi 2022).[56] The positive effects are more pronounced in areas that are initially richer, urban, and connected to roads and banks. These results suggest that the presence of complementary infrastructure can strengthen the economic potential of mobile money. They are consistent with the idea that mobile money affects overall economic growth rather than just the redistribution of income from wealthier to impoverished areas—enabling lower-income people to connect, trade, and allocate investments within their networks.

Access to credit. A more recent DT innovation is the use of scoring rules or algorithms based on user transaction records to allocate financial credit. In 2011, Kenya's Safaricom partnered with the Commercial Bank of Africa to create M-Shwari, a microcredit and microsavings product that has become one of the most popular digital loan products in the world.[57] Robust evidence exists that such digital loans can dramatically lower the costs associated with lending and borrowing, leading to high uptake and improvements in household resilience to shocks, thereby reducing poverty (Suri, Bharadwaj, and Jack 2021).[58]

M-Shwari has an overall uptake of nearly 34 percent among the eligible population studied, and within two years those who initially qualified have 37 percent more loans. The uptake in household credit is entirely due to M-Shwari truly expanding credit access.[59] The loans improve household resilience and have the potential to reduce poverty by enabling an increase in household education expenditures: beneficiary households are 6.3 percentage points less likely to forgo such expenses because of negative shocks.[60]

Insurance. One of the most potentially transformational applications of digital financial services in Africa is to insurance, particularly agricultural insurance. A failed crop due to climate change–related rain patterns, drought, or other volatile weather events, without proper risk protection, can be calamitous for any one of the estimated 65 million smallholder farmers. Diminished savings or resources could lead to lower quantities of seed, lower farm sizes, and lower appetite for adopting higher-yield varieties.

Pula, a microinsurance firm based in Nairobi founded in 2015, has created a new market by providing insurance protection for low-income individuals who lack access to conventional coverage. Pula designs and delivers yield index insurance products to protect farmers by offering their products to insurance companies and other intermediaries that offer insurance to farmers. Pula serves more than 6 million smallholder farms across more than 15 countries in Africa and Asia through such intermediaries.[61]

Information and knowledge resources

Beyond facilitating access to finance and customized insurance products that can help farmers purchase and adopt better agricultural technologies, DTs can directly raise agricultural productivity of individual farmers and support better jobs by providing science-based, tailored information to target agricultural inputs and increase yields. This information is especially crucial in the face of environmental stress and climate change affecting soil, water, and weather conditions for different crops.[62]

Simple, SMS-based agricultural extension messages are found to have modest impacts overall; however, given the low cost of text messages, these programs can be cost-effective in changing farmer behavior. Repeating the same messages has a statistically significant impact on the adoption of inputs (Fabregas, Kremer, Lowes et al. 2019).[63]

More specialized text messages have the potential to have larger impacts, especially for the lowest-skilled farmers. For example, sending SMS messages to smallholder contract sugarcane farmers about when to perform specific agricultural tasks increased yields by 11.5 percent relative to a control group with no messages (Casaburi et al. 2019). These effects are concentrated among farmers who had no agronomy training and had little interaction with sugarcane company staff at the baseline.[64] The findings provide evidence that DTs can affect efficiency in agricultural supply chains.

Local-language videos on tablet computers and a decision-support-tool app on a smartphone, used by extension agents to provide personalized advice to individual farmers, increased crop yields and profits of lower-income farmers. Smallholder maize farmers in Uganda shown a short video on improved maize practices perform significantly better on a knowledge test, are more likely to apply recommended practices, and are more likely to use fertilizer than farmers who did not view the video. These farmers also had maize yields about 10.5 percent higher than those who did not view the video (Campenhout, Spielman, and Lecoutere 2021).[65] In Ethiopia, a decentralized extension-only service and extension service combined with video both increase integrated soil fertility management practices across major cereal crops for smallholder farmers. The additional video intervention had a significant complementary effect among farmers in treatment communities that did not actively participate in the extension activities (Hörner et al. 2019).[66]

Rice-farming households in Nigeria that received personalized nutrient management advice from a smartphone-based, decision-support-tool app increased their yields by an average of about 7 percent and increased their profit from rice by about 10 percent. As illustrated in figure 1.6, households that received the personalized advice in combination with a grant that financed the recommended level of fertilizer increased their yield by about 20 percent and their profit by about 23 percent (Arouna et al. 2021).[67] Use of the app tends to decrease the average amount of fertilizer used. The authors conclude that personalized recommendations delivered at lower cost by DTs could improve productivity and livelihoods in Africa without necessarily increasing the overall amount of chemical fertilizer used and the corresponding negative effects on the environment.

Mechanization services. Another skill-appropriate DT application involves the rental of tractors and other high-cost agricultural machinery to enable smaller farmers to hire mechanization services. The findings to date suggest limited effects on reducing transaction costs for farmers, because the major provider, Hello Tractor, has not yet offered a digital interface for farmers (Daum et al. 2021).[68] Transaction cost effects are also limited for service providers owning only a few tractors, because they rely on conventional provision of mechanization services, reducing transaction costs and risks by focusing on trusted customers. However, such DTs seem to reduce the supervision and marketing costs of large-scale migratory tractor service providers that operate across large distances and with unknown customers. If Hello Tractor contributes to creating a

a. Rice yields

b. Rice farm profits

Control [C] — — — RiceAdvice [T1] ·········· RiceAdvice + subsidy [T2]

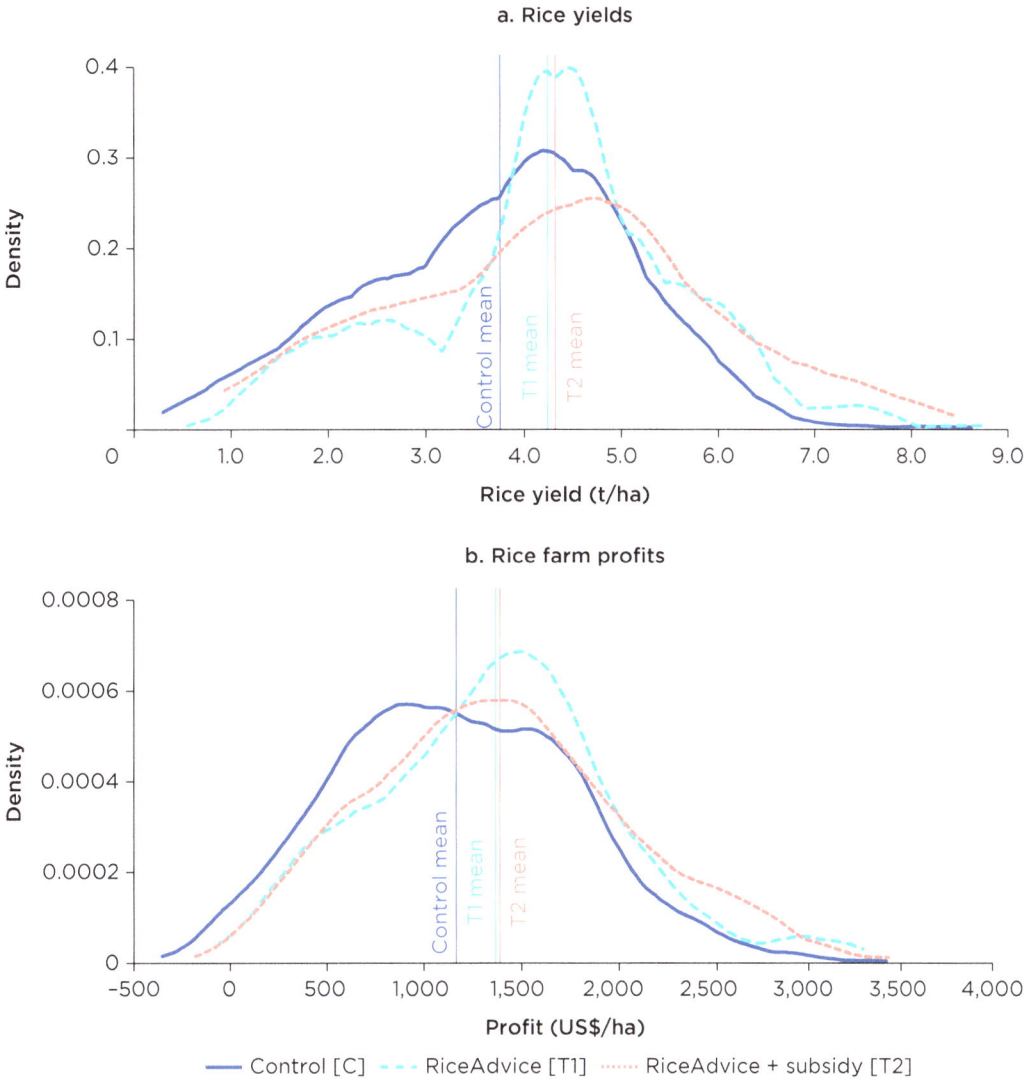

Source: Arouna et al. 2021, figure 3.
Note: The distributions of postexperiment (2016 and 2017 pooled) values are shown for rice yields and profits by treatment group. Vertical lines mark the mean values by treatment group. ha = hectares; t/ha = tons per hectare.

larger supply of tractor services, it may indirectly benefit smallholder farmers. Another benefit is that booking agents are more likely to accept requests from female farmers.[69]

Africa's large internet uptake gap

Africa's uptake gap has remained intractably large relative both to the continent's internet availability and to uptake in other regions. Sub-Saharan Africa has the largest uptake gap in the world as a share of its country populations with internet availability, which was 74 percent at the end of 2021. This figure means that, on average across countries, almost three-quarters of Africa's people with 3G+ coverage are not users.

Gaps between Africa and other regions

Internet availability gaps

Expansion of internet-enabled (3G and 4G) networks has increased availability, but Africa still lags other regions (Atiyas and Dutz 2022). Figure 1.7 shows the evolution of internet-enabled mobile service networks in different regions of the world. In the case of 3G networks (panel a), the figure shows that a major convergence has occurred in availability in all regions over the past decade—with a major convergence by Sub-Saharan Africa over recent years, likely driven at least in part by increased investments in response to demand following the onset of the COVID-19 pandemic. By the end of 2021, 3G networks were available to at least 90 percent of populations in all regions (89.4 percent of the population in South Asia) except Sub-Saharan Africa, where availability was still only at 84 percent—despite the notable increase from 62.9 percent at the end of 2017.

As for availability of 4G networks (panel b), all other regions have converged more quickly to the North American level over the past decade, with Sub-Saharan Africa having only 62.5 percent availability by 2021. The region had 4G coverage of 8.8 percent in 2012, ahead of South Asia (3.1 percent), but by 2021, availability in South Asia was 25 percentage points higher (87.2 percent versus 62.5 percent).

Internet usage and uptake gaps

Africa's uptake and use of mobile internet technology have also increased over the past decade, but the gap with other regions has widened (Atiyas and Dutz 2022). Sub-Saharan Africa has made progress in 3G+ mobile unique internet subscriptions in the past decade,

FIGURE 1.7 **Availability of internet-enabled (3G and 4G) networks, by region, 2010–21**

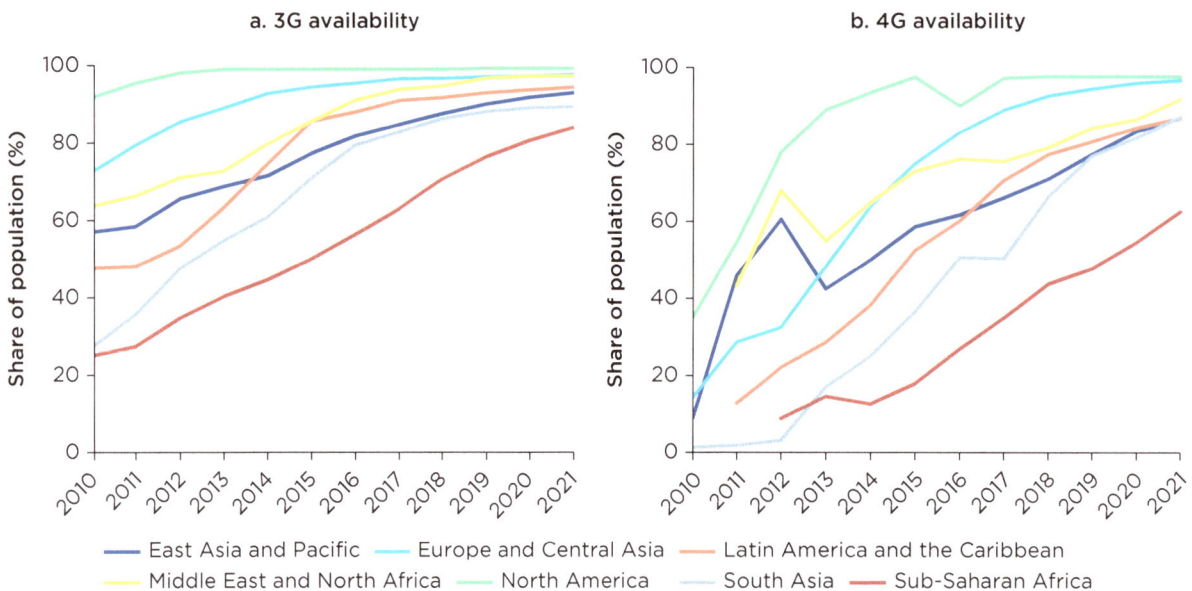

Source: Atiyas and Dutz 2022, based on Global System for Mobile Communications Association (GSMA) data.
Note: The figure incorporates updated 2015–21 data based on an improved 2022 methodology for calculating unique subscribers. Mobile internet availability (the percentage of population living in areas covered by third-generation [3G] or fourth-generation [4G] technology signals) is expressed as unweighted averages of countries in each region, as a share of total country populations. By giving equal importance to each country, heterogeneity across countries is highlighted. Regions are defined according to World Bank classifications. "North America" includes Bermuda, Canada, and the United States.

FIGURE 1.8 Unique 3G+ mobile internet usage, by region, 2010–21

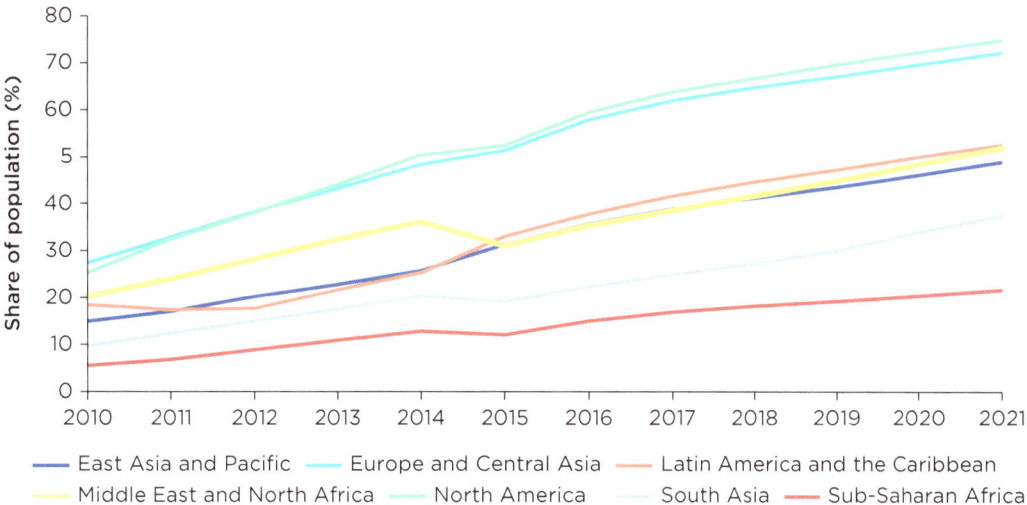

Source: Atiyas and Dutz 2022, based on Global System for Mobile Communications Association (GSMA) data.
Note: The figure incorporates updated 2015–21 data based on an improved 2022 methodology for calculating unique subscribers. Usage (unique mobile internet subscribers) is expressed as unweighted averages of countries in each region, as a share of total country populations. By giving equal importance to each country, heterogeneity across countries is highlighted. There is a discontinuity in 2015 due to a methodological change, but general trends remain unaffected. Regions are defined according to World Bank classifications. "North America" comprises Bermuda, Canada, and the United States.

reaching 22 percent of its population by the end of 2021 (figure 1.8). However, an increasing gap remains as other regions increased uptake and use more rapidly.

Most alarmingly, mobile internet usage has been significantly slower than increases in availability (Atiyas and Dutz 2022). Figure 1.9 shows the evolution of the availability of 3G (or better) internet *coverage* relative to mobile internet *usage*, defined as unique mobile internet subscriptions as a percentage of Sub-Saharan Africa's country-by-country population. The figure shows that the rate of increase of availability (the slope of the coverage curve) has been higher than that of usage: the usage gap as a share of total population, defined as the distance between both lines, was significantly larger in 2021 than in 2010. By 2021, availability of 3G networks reached 84 percent of the regional population but use was only 22 percent, a usage gap of 62 percentage points.

Sub-Saharan Africa has the world's highest uptake gap—the share of unconnected users of total covered people—because of the region's low increase in uptake of mobile internet service relative to availability in recent years. It has the highest usage gap as a share of population, at 62 percent (figure 1.10, panel a), as well as the largest uptake gap of any world region, at 74 percent (figure 1.10, panel b). Almost three-quarters of Africa's people with 3G+ coverage are unconnected without subscriptions (Atiyas and Dutz 2022). In contrast, the uptake gap of other regions has continued to decline.

Despite the increased investments in infrastructure over recent years, the region had no commensurate increases in uptake and use. This discrepancy suggests that low uptake and use are not primarily due to the physical availability of networks, though they are linked to affordability and may be at least partly linked to uneven quality of services, which often do not meet minimum speed and latency requirements for effective use.

FIGURE 1.9 Gap between mobile internet coverage and usage, Sub-Saharan Africa, 2010–21

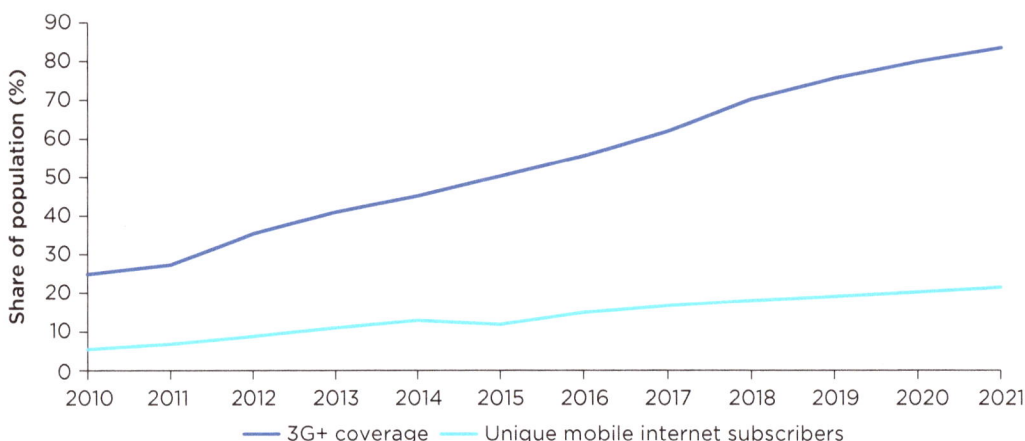

Source: Atiyas and Dutz 2022, based on Global System for Mobile Communications Association (GSMA) data.
Note: The figure incorporates updated 2015–21 data based on an improved 2022 methodology for calculating unique subscribers. Mobile internet availability (3G+ coverage) and use (unique mobile internet subscribers) are expressed as unweighted averages of across Sub-Saharan African countries, as a share of total country populations. By giving equal importance to each country, heterogeneity across countries is highlighted. Eritrea is not included for lack of coverage data. 3G+ = third-generation (or later) mobile internet technology.

FIGURE 1.10 Internet usage and gaps, by region

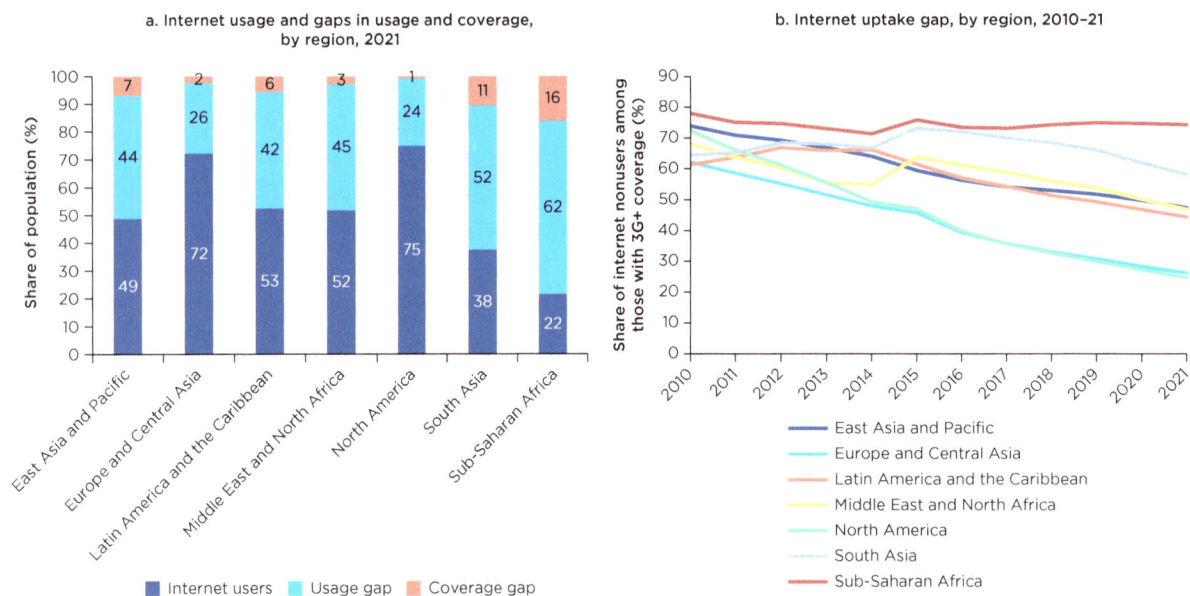

Source: Atiyas and Dutz 2022, based on Global System for Mobile Communications Association (GSMA) data.
Note: The figure incorporates updated 2015–21 data based on an improved 2022 methodology for calculating unique subscribers. They are calculated as 1–(unique mobile subscriptions/3G+ coverage) percent. The figure excludes Eritrea for lack of coverage data. Usage and coverage gaps are defined as a share of total regional population. Uptake gaps are defined as the share of all people with internet availability who have not taken up internet use. Uptake gaps are expressed as unweighted regional averages across countries (by giving equal importance to each country, heterogeneity across countries is highlighted). Regions are defined according to World Bank classifications. "North America" comprises Bermuda, Canada, and the United States. 3G+ = third-generation (or later) mobile internet technology.

Gaps across country income groups

The relatively low levels of availability and uptake of mobile internet services could simply reflect that countries are poorer, with less income to spend on mobile internet services. To explore this possibility, figure 1.11 compares availability and uptake data for different countries grouped by income levels in 2022: low income (28 countries, of which 24 are in Sub-Saharan Africa); lower-middle income (54 countries, 17 in Sub-Saharan Africa); and upper-middle income (54 countries, 6 in Sub-Saharan Africa). For each group, the figure shows average 3G and 4G availability, unique mobile subscribers (including 2G and 2.5G feature phones), and unique mobile internet subscribers for Sub-Saharan African and countries outside the region for the years 2010 and 2019.

The figure shows that Sub-Saharan Africa lags across all income groups. The largest gaps are observed for unique mobile internet subscribers in middle-income countries and 4G coverage across all income categories. The expansion of both availability and uptake of mobile and mobile internet services in Sub-Saharan Africa lags peer countries across most income groups. Moreover, gaps have not decreased over time. Importantly, this comparative analysis highlights that the relative lower availability and uptake in Sub-Saharan Africa are not solely a reflection of lower income levels, with other factors playing an important role.[70]

FIGURE 1.11 Average mobile internet availability and usage, by technology type, Sub-Saharan Africa versus other regions, 2010 and 2021

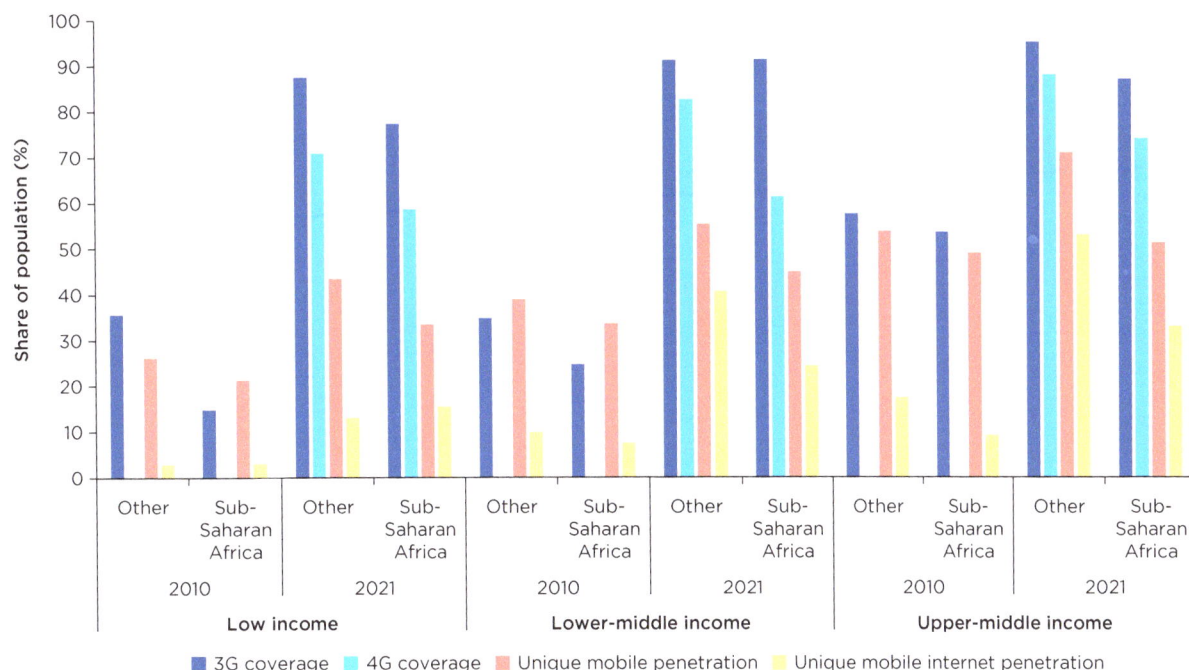

Source: Global System for Mobile Communications Association (GSMA) and World Development Indicators databases.
Note: The figure excludes 2010 data on 4G coverage because of its low availability at the time and missing values for some countries. Income categories follow World Bank Group income classification in 2022. 3G = third-generation mobile communications technology; 4G = fourth-generation mobile communications technology.

Gaps within and across Africa

Uptake gaps, almost all above 50 percent, vary widely across countries in Africa. The uptake gaps vary from 47 percent and 51 percent for South Africa and Seychelles to 90 percent for South Sudan and 89 percent for the Central African Republic and Ethiopia (figure 1.12). They all reflect non-use of an infrastructure asset that has become available.

Addressing uptake gaps requires policies and investments stimulating uptake and use but not necessarily additional investments in telecommunications infrastructure—except to the extent that additional investments increase market competition as a driver of price reductions and quality improvements. However, uptake gap measures also hide the extent to which countries have improved infrastructure availability. Benin, Guinea-Bissau, and Ethiopia all have uptake gaps higher than 85 percent, but almost their entire populations are covered by 3G. In contrast, uptake gaps are similar in the Central African Republic, Democratic Republic of Congo, and Equatorial Guinea, but in those countries less than two-thirds of the population lives in areas with 3G coverage. The solutions to address usage and coverage gaps, of course, are multidimensional, requiring additional investments in telecommunications infrastructure as well as policies and investments stimulating uptake and use.

Assuming that poverty reduction is a key goal, an analysis of the demographic and socioeconomic characteristics of internet users is helpful to understand the complementarity of telecommunications infrastructure availability and affordability to stimulate uptake and use. The coverage-based uptake gaps and population-based usage gaps in Nigeria and Senegal are relatively similar—65 percent versus 62 percent for uptake, 51 percent versus 58 percent for usage (table 1.1).[71]

The lower usage gap in Nigeria reflects in part the larger outstanding availability challenge relative to Senegal: 22 versus 6 percent of people lack access to internet service. In both countries, lack of availability is largely a rural issue: more than 95 percent of the noncovered people live in rural areas. It is vital to extend coverage to the noncovered as well as stimulate uptake of already-covered people. In Senegal, of those below the US$3.20 a day poverty line, 13 percent are noncovered, whereas this rate drops to only 3 percent for

FIGURE 1.12 **Mobile internet uptake gaps, by country, Sub-Saharan Africa, 2021**

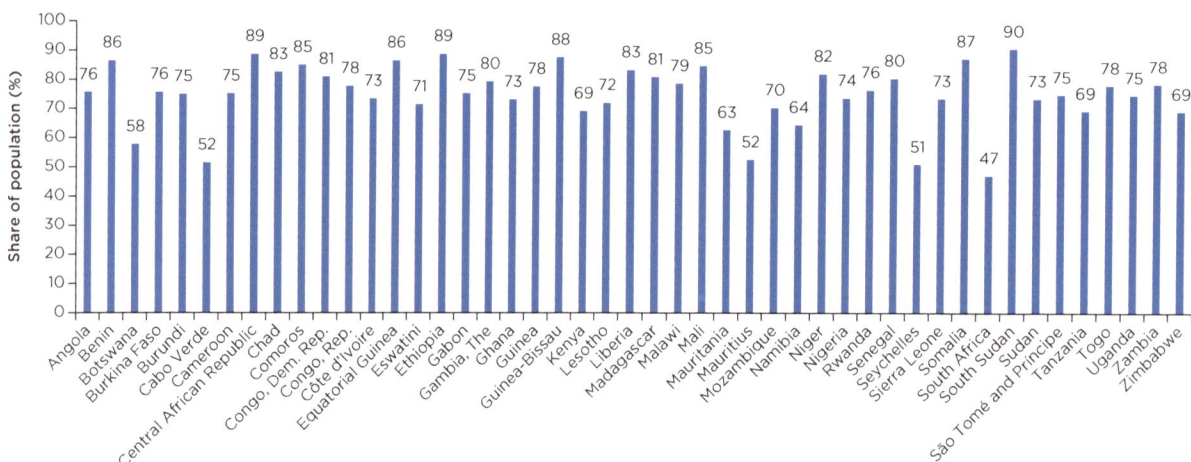

Source: Global System for Mobile Communications Association (GSMA) Intelligence data for 2021.
Note: Uptake gaps are defined as the share of all people with internet availability who have not taken up internet use. They are calculated as 1–(unique mobile internet subscriptions/population with 3G+ coverage) percent. The figure excludes Eritrea for lack of coverage data. 3G+ = third-generation (or later) mobile internet technology.

TABLE 1.1 Coverage, usage, and uptake gaps, by user characteristic, Nigeria and Senegal, 2018/19

Percent

Distribution groups	Nigeria					Senegal				
	Uncovered (3G)	Usage gap (as share of pop.)	Uptake gap (as share of covered)	3G covered, connected	Population average	Uncovered (3G)	Usage gap (as share of pop.)	Uptake gap (as share of covered)	3G covered, connected	Population average
Population share	21.9	50.9	65.2	27.2	100*	5.9	58.3	61.9	35.8	100.0
Income threshold										
Below	34.1	51.6	78.4	14.2	44.3	8.6	69.0	75.5	22.4	58.3
Above	12.2	50.3	57.4	37.4	55.7	2.2	43.0	44.0	54.8	41.7
Poverty line (US$3.20)										
Below						13.0	74.1	85.2	12.9	27.9
Above						3.2	52.1	53.8	44.8	72.1
Urban	1.1	50.1	50.7	48.8	29.2	0.7	47.8	48.1	51.6	52.6
Rural	30.5	51.2	73.9	18.1	70.8	11.7	69.8	79.1	18.4	47.4
Men	22.0	45.6	58.3	32.6	48.5	6.1	52.6	56.0	41.3	44.3
Women	21.8	55.9	71.8	22.0	51.5	5.8	62.7	66.6	31.5	56.2
Age										
15 to 24 years old	21.8	47.5	60.6	30.9	34.0	5.7	58.0	61.6	36.2	35.9
25 to 40 years old	21.9	48.8	62.8	29.0	37.9	5.7	49.9	52.9	44.4	35.9
41 and older	22.0	57.3	73.5	20.6	28.1	6.5	69.3	74.1	24.3	28.2
Education										
Literate	17.5	49.5	60.1	32.9	77.7	3.1	46.6	48.1	50.3	53.8
Illiterate	37.3	55.4	87.8	7.7	22.3	9.2	71.8	79.1	19.0	46.2
Labor force status										
In labor force	21.0	51.3	64.9	27.8	63.0	5.4	54.4	57.4	40.3	57.9
Not in labor force	23.5	50.2	65.8	26.1	37.0	5.6	61.9	65.6	32.5	42.1
Household assets										
Computer owner	4.4	22.3	23.2	74.0	4.8	1.1	31.7	32.0	67.2	12.4
TV ownership	9.5	49.0	54.1	41.6	46.1	1.5	48.9	49.7	49.6	61.7
Complementary infrastructure										
Access to electricity	5.9	53.3	56.6	40.8	54.7	1.1	49.7	50.2	49.3	62.7

Source: Nigeria General Household Survey (GHS) 2018/2019 Wave 4; Senegal Harmonized Survey on Household Living Conditions (EHCVM) 2018/2019.

Note: Whereas "usage gaps" refer to those who are 3G covered but unconnected as a share of the total population, "uptake gaps" are 3G unconnected as a share of those covered by 3G. The poverty line is US$3.20 per day (2011 purchasing power parity). Statistics are based on individuals 15–64 years old. Columns headed "Uncovered (3G)" indicate the percentage of people living in areas uncovered by 3G. Columns headed "3G covered, unconnected" indicate the percentage of individuals living in 3G coverage areas who indicated not using the internet (uptake gap), and columns headed "3G covered, connected" indicate the percentage of individuals covered by 3G who indicated actually using the internet. Because of the design of Nigeria's GHS survey, it is not possible to know how many individuals accessed the internet. Thus, "connectivity" for Nigeria is defined as using the internet in general, which includes both fixed and mobile broadband internet even if the device or internet connection belongs to somebody else; whereas for Senegal, "connectivity" is defined exclusively as using the internet through mobile phones. Each tabulation is carried out at the individual level adjusting for sampling weights. For Nigeria, coverage columns may not add up to 100 percent because of missing values in the access to internet variable (5.4 percent missing). The uncovered includes all individuals from the sample, whereas the covered includes only a subsample of individuals for whom data on connectivity or usage are available. In addition to the survey data sources, coverage data were provided by GSMA intelligence for Nigeria and by major mobile service providers for Senegal.

those above the poverty line, indicating that poor people are much more likely to live in noncovered areas. Furthermore, of poor people living in covered areas, only 13 percent indicated using the internet[72]—attesting to high usage and uptake gaps among those below the poverty line—whereas 45 percent of nonpoor people indicated using the internet.

The availability and uptake of mobile internet is correlated with educational outcomes in Senegal. Although a higher proportion of illiterate people (9 percent) than literate people (3 percent) lives in noncovered areas, the former are also much less likely to use the internet even when they live in covered areas. Only 19 percent of illiterate people living in coverage areas indicated using the internet, which is strikingly lower than the corresponding percentage for literate people (50 percent).

A similar pattern exists for Nigeria: a lack of 3G coverage is much more common among poorer people or those below the median of the income or consumption distribution (34 percent) and also among illiterate people (37 percent) compared with those above the income or consumption median (12 percent) and literate people (18 percent). By the same token, poorer or illiterate people are much less likely to use the internet[73] even when they live in 3G coverage areas. Only 14 percent of poorer people and 8 percent of illiterate people living in 3G coverage areas indicated using the internet.

In summary, both availability and usage or uptake gaps are strongly correlated with welfare and other socioeconomic characteristics like education. Importantly, even though 3G coverage is available for a predominant share of the overall population in both countries, internet uptake is still low, particularly among poor and illiterate people. Thus, complementary policies must be in place to address uptake constraints, particularly facing poor people, beyond investing in the physical expansion of the mobile broadband infrastructure.

Gaps between Africa and other regions in key drivers of uptake

An aggregate-level comparison of Sub-Saharan Africa with other regions provides insights into the critical nature of capabilities, affordability, infrastructure regulatory policy, and availability of complementary assets to explain the internet uptake gap (table 1.2).

Capabilities. In table 1.2, the first three rows of data show that Sub-Saharan Africa suffers from a large gap regarding capabilities. Capabilities determine the extent to which people can use the internet productively; thus, they are major determinants of DT attractiveness. The capabilities gap is especially important when there is a dearth of internet applications appropriate for productive use by lower-skilled users.

Adult literacy and especially youth literacy are much lower in Sub-Saharan Africa than in other regions: the average literacy rate among young people is only 78 percent in Sub-Saharan Africa, whereas in South Asia, the region with the second-lowest rate of youth literacy, the rate is 88 percent. In all other regions, it is higher than 97 percent.

Affordability. The table's second set of data reveals another major constraint to internet uptake in Africa: affordability. A comparison of average prices, in US dollars, of mobile data and voice packages suggests that, in absolute terms, prices in Sub-Saharan Africa are not that high relative to the regions of East Asia and Pacific and Latin America and the Caribbean, although they are much higher than in South Asia. However, comparisons of prices as percentage of gross national income—which reflect the share of mobile costs in relation to incomes—show that prices in Sub-Saharan Africa are incomparably high relative to other regions. Mobile data and voice packages cost 10–20 percent of gross national income, yet the cost is lower than 6 percent in other regions. This disparity reflects the very low incomes in Sub-Saharan Africa as well as how serious a constraint income is to uptake and more intensive use.

Drivers, by category	East Asia and Pacific	Latin American and the Caribbean	Middle East and North Africa	South Asia	Sub-Saharan Africa
Capabilities					
Learning-adjusted years of schooling (HCI, 2020)	8.3	7.8	7.6	6.5	5.0
Adult literacy (%) (WDI, 2018)	93.6	94.7	92.2	70.2	67.2
Youth literacy (%, ages 15–24) (WDI, 2018)	97.5	98.8	98.9	88.3	77.6
Affordability					
Mobile data and voice high usage package (US$) (ITU, 2020)	22.7	28.1	18.4	7.1	16.9
Mobile data and voice low usage package (US$) (ITU, 2020)	15.5	24.3	12.2	4.2	9.9
Mobile data and voice high usage package (% of GNI) (ITU, 2020)	5.9	4.5	3.0	5.5	20.4
Mobile data and voice low usage package (% of GNI) (ITU, 2020)	3.4	3.5	1.9	3.5	12.3
Regulatory policy					
ITU index of overall ICT regulation (2018)	60.0	72.3	63.4	70.6	69.3
Mobile termination rate (US$) (TeleG, 2020)	0.027	0.013	0.010	0.002	0.018
HHI (from TeleG market shares of subscribers, 2020)	0.50	0.45	0.43	0.37	0.49
Complementary assets: Electricity					
Electricity access overall (%) (WDI, 2019)	93.7	97.3	94.8	93.9	49.4

Source: Calculated from World Bank's World Development Indicators (WDI), World Bank's Human Capital Index (HCI), International Telecommunication Union (ITU) data, and TeleGeography (TeleG) data.
Note: Figures are unweighted regional averages across countries (by giving equal importance to each country, heterogeneity across countries is highlighted). GNI = gross national income; HHI = Hirschman-Herfindahl concentration index; ICT= information and communication technology.

Regulatory policy. The table's third set of data shows another source of constraints to both the availability and affordability of internet service: regulatory policy toward mobile network operators and other internet service providers. On the average of an index of overall information and communication technology regulation, Sub-Saharan Africa does not appear to perform badly: the region's index is higher than for the East Asia and Pacific and the Middle East and North Africa regions. This index is based on a de jure assessment of the existence of relevant laws and regulations but does not consider the extent to which these laws and regulations are effectively enforced.

The next two variables somewhat better capture the degree to which regulatory authorities adopt a pro-competitive stance. The average mobile termination rate is the tariff that mobile operators charge to their competitors when a subscriber of a competitor calls a subscriber of the receiving or the terminating operator. The higher the mobile termination rate, the easier it is for incumbents to prevent the entry and expansion of smaller competitors. The mobile termination rate in Sub-Saharan Africa is higher than other regions except for East Asia and Pacific. The Herfindahl-Hirschman index (HHI) is the sum of squared market shares of mobile operators. A high HHI denotes a more concentrated market and generally reflects a lower degree of competition. The HHI in Sub-Saharan Africa is quite high, though it is also high in other regions, except for South Asia.

Complementary assets. Finally, electricity access is a critical complementary asset. In Sub-Saharan Africa, only about half of the population has access to electricity, whereas this ratio is above 90 percent in the rest of the regions.

When explored in a cross-country regression framework that combines these variables with income per capita, quantitatively the most important variable that is conditionally correlated with internet uptake is affordability, followed by skills and electricity. Next is regulatory stance: market concentration remains significant whereas mobile termination rates do not, plausibly suggesting that regulatory actions and timing, including how they affect the nature and sequencing of entry, may be more important than policies specifically focusing on mobile termination rates (Atiyas and Dutz 2022; also see chapter 3, figure 3.14b, which highlights the high level of prices relative to income in Africa and especially for low-income countries).

Data and knowledge gaps for future work

A key priority for improved policy formulation is to gather better data on DT availability and usage over time that allow causal impact on jobs and earnings to be inferred, including distributional impacts on lower-income, lower-skilled people as well as women. Systematic collection of data through household and enterprise surveys is necessary.

The types of data collected by the World Bank's FAT (Firm-level Adoption of Technology) survey are a good starting point for enterprises (Cirera, Comin, and Cruz 2022). The FAT collects data on the sophistication of technologies—manual processes, simple DTs that access the internet, or more complex DTs that generate predictions based on artifical intelligence and machine learning techniques—and whether these technologies are used. Importantly, the FAT also collects data on how DTs are used, whether for general business functions like accounting and other management practices or for sector-specific business functions like livestock herd management (ranging from manual monitoring to digital tracking devices attached to each animal).

Such data should ideally be collected by all national statistical agencies across Africa for as large a sample of both formal and informal enterprises as possible, based on nationally representative censuses. Although the FAT survey currently limits its coverage to enterprises with five or more full-time employees, most enterprises across Africa are smaller in size. A representative sample of smaller informal enterprises also should be included in future FAT surveys.

A useful complementary survey effort has been undertaken by Research ICT Africa (RIA), which asks related questions of microenterprises.[74] It should be continued, strengthened, and ideally administered by national statistical agencies, and it should include those questions from FAT that are appropriate for microenterprises. World Bank Enterprise Surveys for all firms, including microenterprises and informal firms, should integrate questions related to use of DTs and other technologies and be administered by national statistical agencies. Complementary enterprise data collection should be consolidated to ensure a common set of questions across countries. By requiring all enterprises (including household enterprises) that are beneficiaries of any publicly funded technology support to fill out a questionnaire with FAT questions, the impact of public technology support programs could be better assessed. As well, enterprises would be able to benchmark themselves against other enterprises in their economic activity and size grouping, both in their country and across all countries where such surveys have been implemented.

Data must be collected every two to five years, constituting a time-series cross-section panel data set of enterprises, with replenishment for enterprises that have exited. These collection initiatives are indispensable to examine barriers of technology adoption as well as the impacts of DTs on productivity, production and sales, and jobs and earnings. They should also enable a representative understanding of new enterprise entry, investment and production expansion, exits of nonprofitable enterprises, and the impacts of DTs on jobs and earnings for all types of enterprises and workers. National household surveys such as the Living Standards Measurement Study (LSMS) should also integrate key questions on use of DTs to create nationally matched employer-employee data sets. The DT module in the World Bank's COVID-19 high-frequency survey could be a starting point. Reliable data over time can help identify potential spatial gaps in the use of DTs and how these gaps change, allowing for a better understanding of the economic and welfare implications of digital divides.

Several crucial policy questions linking DTs to enterprise performance and household welfare should be the subject of future research:[75]

- What is the relative contribution of different factors that explain the effect of DTs on welfare and poverty, including synergies with complementary technologies?

- What is the current and future role of greater youth and women participation, at the owner or entrepreneur, managerial, and worker levels across sectors?

- How do education levels and skills affect the degree to which individuals benefit from access to the internet and associated DTs?

- What are the critical complements that enhance the gains from DT adoption?

- How does the use of digital platforms related to e-commerce and e-finance affect efficiency and equity?

- Who would benefit most from a fast rollout of digitalization of government functions, particularly delivery of services such as the World Bank's ID4D (digital identification for development) initiative, asset registries, and social protection services that mitigate various risks by providing insurance?

- What are the business functions that are most relevant for inclusive productivity growth?

- What is the relative importance for jobs and poverty reduction of different DTs (such as availability of digital finance services apps, insurance services, and management applications such as inventory control and point-of-sale software)?

The implementation of a Public Expenditure Review (PER) of business support policies and programs is a priority. Such business-support PERs can be divided into three phases: (a) a mapping of policy instruments supporting technology adoption as well as generation of new technologies and digital entrepreneurship; (b) a functional analysis of existing programs and policy instruments; and (c) an efficiency analysis.

Close collaboration with responsible line ministries is required to obtain details on programs supporting businesses, with a focus on technology adoption and entrepreneurship. This exercise has typically been more effective when implemented in collaboration with the national government unit responsible for budget prioritization and allocation (typically ministries of finance). Ultimately, a PER of business support policies and programs should be an ongoing activity that helps policy makers understand the impact of expenditures and improve policies and programs over time, making use of complementary insights from enterprise panel data.[76] These PERs should be supported by a transparent process of "diagnostic monitoring," with new programs benefiting from structured experiments that are subject to monitoring in the form of diagnostics, namely, to learn what works and what does not, and to constantly raise each program's benefits by using new learning.[77]

Some knowledge gaps need to be filled by country-specific policy and regulatory experiments that go beyond data-based diagnostics. Such experimentation is needed to provide implementation-related insights based on small-scale pilot projects and regulatory sandboxes, adapted to varied national and subregional contexts.[78] Those that yield positive impact can then be scaled nationally and subregionally to have significant economywide effects across Africa on productivity, production and sales, and jobs.

Robust data for effective policy support are essential to boost the productivity, jobs and earnings, and upgrading needs of lower-skilled, lower-income workers, managers, and owner-enterprises. As mentioned earlier, there are only two ways to narrow the skills gap in the use of DTs. The first is to provide training to upgrade the capabilities of lower-skilled people. The second is to redirect technological change toward the level of skills that most people actually have through the design of simpler-to-use DTs that support learning. The latter approach has not been sufficiently explored. Experimentation is needed to examine the potential of simpler-to-use DTs as a lower-cost, more effective strategy than investing significant resources in digital skills training. Currently, training may be too generic for the productive needs of lower-income people. In addition, the prevailing approach is to rely on intermediaries to use the more sophisticated available smartphones and tablets with internet-enabled apps, to enter business-related data, and to gain insights that are then shared with intended beneficiaries. This approach does not allow the beneficiaries themselves to learn by doing. Experimentation is needed to better understand

- Whether sufficiently simple DTs could enable intended beneficiaries to directly use them and whether such direct use is likely to generate higher learning, productivity, and jobs-related benefits;

- The benefits and costs of supporting the productivity upgrading of lower-skilled owner-entrepreneurs who are operating informal enterprises, relative to supporting higher-productivity formal firms that self-select into enterprise productivity support programs, or whether both types of program are desirable; and[79]

- The extent to which productivity-enhancing management skills can be acquired through the use of simple apps, such as point-of-sale and inventory control solutions. The use of intuitive-to-use apps that monitor which products a retailer is selling more quickly and which inventory levels are too low relative to sales can be a first step toward management capabilities upgrading and enhancing enterprise productivity and profitability.

In summary, hypotheses that could benefit from further learning through on-the-ground experimentation in different country contexts include the following:

- *That digital skill requirements are not a fundamental barrier to use of DTs by lower-skilled people.* Of the two complementary approaches to address skill-related challenges in the use of DTs, simplifying the apps so that lower-skilled people can use them and learn as they do so is likely a lower-cost and more effective strategy than investing significant resources in digital skills training.

- *That learning and productivity gains are possible by simplifying internet-enabled apps accessible on smartphones and other low-cost devices so that lower-skilled people can directly use them.* More learning by intended beneficiaries is probably possible through direct use rather than through intermediaries.

- *That the largest productivity gains are likely possible by those informal firms that can learn but are lagging the most in productivity terms.* Supporting productivity improvements, and thereby demonstrating the benefits of formalization, is probably a priority before requiring these enterprises to become formal.

- *That the introduction of simple-to-use digital apps that teach simple management skills is a cost-efficient and effective approach to begin to acquire such skills by microenterprise and small firm owner-entrepreneurs.* Introducing such apps could be a first step toward more systematic management capabilities upgrading.

Another complementary area for more applied research work is exploring policy questions at the interface between agriculture, greater use of DTs, and sustainable adaptation to climate change and other environmental problems. A first set of issues involves the interface between agriculture and greater use of DTs, especially given that most poor people in Africa earn their living primarily in agriculture-related activities and stand to benefit greatly from skill-appropriate DTs that enable on-the-job learning. Questions remain about how farmers can best benefit from productivity upgrading. There also are questions regarding how digital agriculture can best address supply chain problems such as limited competition and high markups as well as adulteration and counterfeiting of inputs. Studying the distributional effects of different interventions remains a fruitful area for investigation (Fabregas, Kremer, and Schilbach 2017).

The increasing climate and environmental challenges present an additional set of questions that explore how digital and complementary technologies can help Africa most effectively boost its food system to meet its growing population. Rising and more variable temperatures, unpredictable precipitation, floods and droughts, and sea level rises are mainly driven by excess carbon consumption and greenhouse gas emissions in the rest of the world. Africa has contributed the least to climate change but is the most affected. Still, additional environment-related problems are locally generated, including air pollution from burning forests to clear land and burning of crop residues, deforestation and associated biodiversity loss, agricultural chemical residues and live waste, and excessive water withdrawals.

Most of these problems require locally generated knowledge to address, which can all be facilitated by DTs as well as investments in complementary technologies. Three related sets of policy research avenues (Barrett, Ortiz-Bobea, and Pham 2021) are centered around

1. *Adaptive agriculture research and extension services,* including postharvest research and development services based on advances in genomics and synthetic biology needed to fine-tune varietal characteristics to changing local conditions;

2. *De-agrarianization,* referring to the replacement of land by physical capital, including controlled-environment agriculture, such as indoor agriculture and vertical farming to produce high-quality fruits and vegetables; and

3. *Rural infrastructure services*, including not only increased use of the internet but also more cost-effective provision and use of electricity and rural roads to stimulate agricultural productivity growth as well as facilitate complementary nonfarm markets.

All three related areas will require policy research and experimentation to generate and scale locally appropriate, efficient, and sustainable solutions.

Finally, a key open empirical question is the extent to which communication networks can gather valuable information from farmers and other users to be shared. The spread of GPS (Global Positioning System)–enabled smartphones with skill-appropriate apps should increase these benefits by enabling customized information, two-way video communication, and other solutions that incentivize farmers to contribute data to the system both by being remunerated and by benefiting from its aggregation and value-added feedback. In the United States, the Farmers Business Network (https://fbn.com) applies machine learning to hundreds of thousands of acre-years of data to provide high-quality yield predictions for seed varieties. Mobile phone systems could potentially be used across Africa to collect data to serve as inputs in machine learning applications, learn from farmers' experiences with specific agricultural technologies, and facilitate networking among farmers in ways that best meet their interest.

On the policy side regarding digital infrastructure, more systematic understanding of the characteristics of the regulatory environment, its implementation, and successful practices—including at the regional level—would be useful to build evidence of adoption of good practices in Africa. The International Telecommunications Union's regulatory tracker provides a first view of the regulatory landscape based on self-reported information by country authorities. It is a useful starting point. The World Bank's Regulatory Watch Initiative aims to systematize both information on regulations on the books and implementation based on an expert judgment methodology. It covers about half of the African countries and selected areas. This initiative could be expanded, and information could be collected every two to three years to understand the evolution of regulatory practices. These indicators can help countries identify areas for improvement and peer-to-peer learning, and also facilitate analysis of the effects of the policies adopted.

The implementation of demand-side interventions to increase internet adoption and usage begs for research on the most successful interventions in the context of low- and middle-income economies. Impact assessments of interventions to increase affordability would be useful to inform policy decisions. They include subsidies or financing of access devices; vouchers to targeted households and micro, small, and medium enterprises to reduce internet prices; and social plans targeting low-income consumers. Similarly, the impact of programs to increase the attractiveness of internet usage should be assessed—including capacity building, development of DTs that cater specifically to lower-skilled users, internet access at schools and public spaces to increase familiarity with DTs, and use of digital means to deliver social transfers. More detailed understanding of consumer behavior, especially for low-income consumers and in rural areas, regarding the adoption of smartphones and consumption of data as well as their responsiveness to prices is also essential to fine-tune demand-side interventions for affordability. Such understanding can be gained using detailed consumer-level data gathered by mobile operators.[80]

Systematic information on the status of country data policies and the effects of certain data rules is essential. For *World Development Report 2021: Data for Better Lives*, the World Bank collected information on the features of data policy covering 20 countries in Africa (World Bank 2021). This work could be broadened to include data on implementation and enabling rules for the development of productivity- and jobs-enhancing DTs. Vital research includes cross-border data flows: What are the best mechanisms to balance data protection and free flow of data, and what are the effects of the different approaches to cross-border data flows in Africa? Finally, on the intersection of climate change and digital and data infrastructure, a baseline and analysis of effects are required to understand the implications of the growth of data consumption in terms of both costs and climate cobenefits across sectors.

Notes

1. Whereas radio signals on the initial first-generation (1G) cellular networks were analog and converted data into electric rhythms of multiple amplitudes, radio signals on second-generation (2G) and later-generation networks are digital; 2G phones also enable basic data services such as short message service (SMS) text and picture messages. However, even 2.5G "feature phones" are typically too slow to enable productive internet use beyond simple payments using short codes and limited browsing—for which third-generation (3G) and later-generation devices are required.

2. Goldfarb and Tucker (2019) explore how standard economic models change as these costs fall substantially and approach zero. Monitoring costs are reduced by the joint fall in tracking and verification costs.

3. This chapter and the entire report build on the arguments and findings presented in Choi, Dutz, and Usman (2020) for Africa as a whole, and in Cruz, Dutz, and Rodríguez-Castelán (2021) for Senegal. The current report provides a richer conceptual framework, more supporting empirical findings, and a more specific set of policy recommendations for enterprises, households, and digital infrastructure.

4. Tõnurist and Hanson (2020) outline an emerging framework to guide policy making in complex and uncertain contexts and set out some questions for further research in the area of anticipatory innovation governance.

5. See Cirera and Maloney (2017) on the challenges facing governments in formulating and implementing the policy mix required to help enterprises build the complementary physical and human capital factors—particularly firms' managerial capabilities—needed to reap the returns to technological catchup.

6. The projections are based on UN DESA (2022a) medium fertility assumptions, as described in UN DESA 2022b. Whereas the stock figures underlying figure 1.1 are derived from the population data file POP/03-1 by broad age group, the annual flow figures are derived from the single-age data file POP/01-1. To calculate net entrant flows, the number of people who are 65 years old (exiters) are subtracted from those who are 15 years old (new entrants). Most other countries not only have fewer entrants but also more exiters.

7. See Baumol (1990) and Murphy, Shleifer, and Vishny (1991) for early expositions of the notion that changes in the rules of the game that specify the relative payoffs to different entrepreneurial activities can play a key role in determining where entrepreneurial talent will be allocated. See also Dutz, Ordover, and Willig (2000).

8. Africans on average perceive significantly more social mobility than do Asians or Latin Americans, and they anticipate significantly more social mobility for their children than in either other region. Observed mobility in Africa is higher than in either South Asia, the Middle East and North Africa, or Latin America and the Caribbean, though it is lower than in high-income countries, East Asia and Pacific, or Europe and Central Asia, based on social mobility in education data from the World Bank's Global Database on Intergenerational Mobility (https://datacatalog.worldbank.org /search/dataset/0050771/global-database-on-intergenerational-mobility). Africans also are significantly more likely to believe that hard work is more important than luck and connections for getting ahead (Henn and Robinson 2021, section 3 and table A1).

9. A third "latent asset" of African society that Henn and Robinson (2021) highlight is "cosmopolitanness," namely that Africans are the most multilingual people in the world (significantly more likely to speak more than one language than people in any other part of the world); have high levels of religious tolerance; and are welcoming to strangers. The experience of navigating this linguistic and cultural diversity, Henn and Robinson argue, sets Africans up for success in a globalized world. The multilingual challenge presents an opportunity to develop a new generation of DT apps that more easily allow productive learning in any language.

10. Regarding agriculture, Fuglie et al. (2020) conclude that the potential gains in terms of productivity growth from reallocation are likely to be less than previously expected. Achieving faster economic transformation instead requires focusing on achieving productivity growth through technological progress both on and off the farm.

11. Bessen (2019) analyzes the productivity and jobs growth dynamics in the cotton cloth, steel, and motor vehicles industries in the United States, highlighting how, when demand was elastic and not yet relatively satiated for these products, large increases in productivity were accompanied by even larger increases in employment, followed by declines in employment in more recent stages of maturity. He interprets this pattern through a model of heterogeneous final demand that changes over time: price declines in the initial stages of productivity growth make formerly prohibitively expensive products affordable for mass consumption, yielding a large positive demand response. Once large unmet needs become saturated and demand becomes less elastic, further productivity gains in these industries may bring reduced employment.

12. For a complementary exposition of policies for technological transformation driven by jobs-enhancing innovation, see Breznitz (2021). He argues that policy makers need to understand the changed structure of the global system of production and use those insights to enable communities to recognize their own advantages and foster innovation that can lead to good jobs for all.

13. For similar findings based on earlier data, for most high-income and transition economies, and for growth accelerations in Latin American, Asian, and Sub-Saharan African countries, respectively, see also Herrendorf, Rogerson, and Valentinyi (2014) and McMillan, Rodrik, and Verduzco-Gallo (2014). Aligned with these findings, Midrigan and Xu (2014) find that the bulk of total factor productivity (TFP) and output losses from financial frictions based on establishment-level data from China, Colombia, and the Republic of Korea come from distortions in enterprises' entry and technology adoption decisions, with only small losses coming from misallocation of capital across producers.

14. In Cusolito and Maloney (2018), figure 1.11 offers the first decompositions for a sample of low- and middle-income countries and emerging markets of technical efficiency based on *physical* TFP, wherein mark-ups (an element of traditionally measured *revenue* TFP) have been removed. The within-enterprise component is relatively more important than the between-enterprise component in four of the six cases examined, explaining roughly half or more of efficiency growth in these economies, especially in China and Ethiopia (the others being India 2000–08 and Malaysia 2005–10).

15. The lowest average management practices of all surveyed countries in the world are in Sub-Saharan Africa, including Ethiopia, Ghana, Mozambique, Tanzania, and Zambia (Cusolito and Maloney 2018, figure 2.12).

16. General purpose technologies (GPTs) are transformational technologies. They include the steam engine at the time of the Industrial Revolution in the late eighteenth century, the electric motor in the late nineteenth century, and the internet. GPTs are characterized by pervasiveness (used as inputs by many downstream industries), inherent potential for technical improvements, and the ability to enable many positive spillovers. As GPTs are adopted across the economy, they generate economywide productivity gains. For a seminal article, see Bresnahan and Trajtenberg (1995).

17. Skill-biased technological change (SBTC) is a shift in the enterprise's production technology, typically due to adoption of a new technology (including a change in production methods or in the organization of work) that favors (is complementary to) more-skilled workers over less-skilled workers in the required composition of tasks that must be performed. SBTC increases higher-skilled workers' relative productivity, and therefore their relative demand, at fixed relative wages. For this definition of SBTC and an application to US labor markets, see Autor, Katz, and Kearney (2008).

18. Diao, McMillan, and Rodrik (2021) argue, based on firm-level data, that African firms that are either productive or rapidly increasing their productivity cannot generate commensurate numerical levels of jobs because of inappropriate technology choices—namely, manufacturing production modes that are excessively physical capital–intensive and skill-intensive. They claim that manufacturing technologies available on world markets have moved steadily away from the factor proportions of African labor-abundant countries and toward greater skill and automation biases. Specifically, they show that the consequent increase in capital intensity in large manufacturing firms in both Ethiopia and Tanzania has far outstripped economywide capital deepening and led to less price-responsive labor supply curves.

19. For a graphical illustration of the output expansion effect from the adoption of skill-biased technologies generating more high-skill and low-skill jobs alike, see Choi, Dutz, and Usman (2020, figure B1.2.1 and box 1.2).

20. Acemoglu (2002) argues that the early nineteenth century was characterized by higher-skill-replacing (lower-skill-appropriate) technological change because the increased supply of lower-skilled workers in the English cities (resulting from migration from rural areas and from Ireland) made the introduction of these technologies profitable.

21. The Digital Economy for Africa (DE4A) flagship initiative is a partnership between the World Bank, African governments, the African Union, and other development partners. For more information, see the DE4A website: https://www.worldbank.org/en/programs/all-africa-digital-transformation. Also see World Bank (2020) for a more detailed description of the proposed digital enablers.

22. "Consumer surplus" refers to the benefit obtained by all those consumers who purchase a product for a price that is less than the highest hypothetical price that they would be *willing to pay* to purchase the product. It increases as prices are reduced—a gain both to existing consumers and to new consumers who were not willing or able to purchase the product at higher prices.

23. The cost reductions are both explicit and implicit relative to traditional non-DT production. For instance, uptake of DTs increased during the COVID-19 pandemic, at least partly *not* because of a low explicit cost of use relative to purchasing from a traditional local brick-and-mortar shop (avoiding the cost of shipping from online retailers) but rather because the associated implicit cost of going into a normal shop could be to expose the purchaser to COVID-19.

24. Other impacts of DTs that are not examined in this report include the impact of DT use on economywide lower prices, greater variety and consumer surplus, government digital services on taxation, the provision of health and education services, social assistance income transfers, public institution building, and the strengthening of government accountability and trust. Nor does the report explore the impact of DTs on nonmonetary effects such as the intrinsic benefits of better health and education for civil society, of human dignity and individual empowerment, and other nonpecuniary aspects of quality of life.

25. The Kenya case study complements the Senegal explorations to illustrate the effect on nonfarm enterprises, many of which are informal businesses. Nonfarm enterprises could not be explored in the Senegal case because of lack of detailed data.

26. This section, especially the first subsection, benefits from a useful recent literature review that divides available research on internet connectivity into supply-side and demand-side impacts (Hjort and Tian 2021).

27. The research focus on internet network availability rather than uptake and use is empirically more robust because it is independent of or external to individual household decisions. Having availability as the variable of interest also captures not only direct impact but also spillover effects. To circumvent the concern that internet service has been rolled out in a nonrandom manner, with operators tending to target the more prosperous areas first, tests are conducted to ensure that the assumption of similar pretreatment trends for the treated (those with coverage) and nontreated (noncovered) holds, among other techniques to ensure robust unbiased findings.

28. The Demographic and Health Survey sample covers Benin, the Democratic Republic of Congo, Ghana, Kenya, Namibia, Nigeria, Tanzania, and Togo. The Afrobarometer sample covers Benin, Ghana, Kenya, Madagascar, Mozambique, Nigeria, Senegal, South Africa, and Tanzania. South Africa's Quarterly Labour Force Survey covers a nationally representative cross-section every quarter. The three data sets together cover 12 countries with a combined population of roughly half a billion people.

29. Additional robustness checks include sensitivity analysis on the definition of connectivity by altering the radius from the backbone network, measuring the impact of other infrastructure, and labor displacement effects arising from commuting, all resulting in indiscernible changes in the reported outcomes. The response in jobs did not appear to arise from formalization of "preexisting informal jobs," nor did the surveys find evidence of jobs rising in connected areas before the arrival of submarine cables.

30. A key mechanism that likely underlies the inclusive jobs outcome of skill-biased internet availability found by Hjort and Poulsen (2019) is the output expansion effect highlighted by

Dutz, Almeida, and Packard (2018) in Latin American countries. In separate complementary empirical studies on Argentina, Brazil, Chile, Colombia, and Mexico summarized therein, low-skilled workers also benefit from the more intensive use of the internet as firm productivity and output increase sufficiently to overcome the substitution of lower-skilled workers for higher-skilled workers combined with DTs at initial output levels.

31. In earlier related work based on a sample of 26,000 manufacturing firms including 15 African countries from World Bank Enterprise Survey data, Dutz et al. (2012) were the first to find that reported innovation activity in products and processes at the enterprise level is linked to capabilities and internet use, that this innovation activity in turn is linked to jobs growth, and that jobs growth is linked to inclusive impacts because low-skilled and female-filled jobs grew at a faster pace than overall employment.

32. The identifying assumption of causal effects is linked to the gradual deployment of mobile broadband over a seven-year period (2010–16), based on Global System for Mobile Communications Association (GSMA) coverage maps combined with three rounds of General Household Survey panel data. Controls include access to electricity, ownership of dwelling, household size, and an index related to wealth measuring dwelling characteristics. In addition to testing for similarity of pretreatment trends, additional specifications are run that exploit the fact that some households get "unintentional" mobile broadband coverage, which is potentially quasi-random. Labor force participation is defined as those working-age (ages 15–64) individuals who were employed or unemployed (looking for a job) in the past seven days. Working-age individuals who worked for someone who was not their family member during the last seven days were considered to be salaried or wage workers. Main results are robust to specifications including self-reported access to internet as controls.

33. The "extreme" and "moderate" poverty lines are, respectively, US$1.90 per person per day and US$3.20 per person per day. Impacts on moderate poverty are not statistically significant.

34. The identifying assumption of causal effects is again linked to the gradual deployment of mobile broadband—this time over a six-year period (2008–13)—based on GSMA coverage maps, combined with three rounds of the National Panel Survey.

35. As reported in Bahia et al. (forthcoming), these findings are consistent with previous studies, which suggest that, although women can benefit from DTs, they often face greater difficulties in leveraging the use of DTs owing to a mix of social norms, intrahousehold dynamics, lack of access to productive assets, and being less likely than men to use the internet.

36. Impacts on the international "extreme" and "moderate" poverty lines (US$1.90 per person per day and US$3.20 per person per day, respectively) are negative but statistically insignificant. Tanzania's "national basic needs poverty line" is calculated on the basis of households' cost of acquiring enough food to provide adequate daily nutrition per person (food line) plus the cost of some nonfood essentials (nonfood component).

37. On the one hand, in contrast to the findings in Nigeria, Tanzania has higher welfare gains in urban areas because the data reflect an earlier rollout from zero to 3G coverage in urban areas in the early 2010s. On the other hand, in contrast to the consumption and poverty levels of female-headed households being statistically significant in Tanzania, they are not statistically significant in Nigeria. One suggested reason is that in Nigeria women can face significant barriers relative to men in using mobile internet. Such barriers might prevent women from reaping associated benefits: for example, women were 32 percent less likely than men to use mobile internet technology in 2017.

38. The Senegal findings are based on integrating two household budget surveys—the 2011 Deuxième Enquête de Suivi de la Pauvreté au Sénégal (Second Poverty Monitoring Survey, ESPS-II) and the 2017–18 Enquête Légère Expérimentale sur la Pauvreté (2017–18 Light Experimental Poverty Assessment Survey, ELEPS)—with data on the expansion of mobile broadband coverage combining the Mobile Coverage Maps database by Collins Bartholomew (https://www.collinsbartholomew.com/mobile-coverage-maps/mobile-coverage-explorer/) and 2G–3G coverage information collected directly from the three major mobile operators in Senegal. The results are robust to controlling for household demographics and other spatial characteristics, including region fixed effects, road density, nighttime lights, and elevation above sea level, as well as for access to complementary digital infrastructure.

39. The welfare findings are also robust to an instrumental variable approach that relies on distance to 3G coverage in neighboring areas.

40. Although 3G availability is also correlated negatively with moderate poverty (based on the international poverty line of US$3.20 per day), its effect is not robust to the inclusion of the additional set of controls.

41. Dutz, Orszag, and Willig (2012) estimate a nested logit demand system with instrumental variables and allowing preferences to vary depending on the share of rural households in each US metropolitan statistical area. They find net US consumer benefits from home broadband in 2008 on the order of US$32 billion per year. Additional willingness to pay for broadband is significantly higher among higher-income, younger, and more-educated (bachelors degree of more relative to high school diploma or less) households, suggesting that lower tariffs for lower-income, older, and less-educated households could yield higher uptake by these demographic groups.

42. Based on international data from 2000–17, Lederman and Zouaidi (2020) document a robust, negative partial correlation between long-term national unemployment rates (frictional unemployment) and internet use, proxied by the share of the adult population that reports using the internet to pay bills.

43. These findings come from a randomized controlled trial (RCT) studying an employer that wanted to attract talented workers for a clerical position in an urban setting in Addis Ababa, Ethiopia. All job applicants were offered a monetary incentive of US$4.50, calibrated to reimburse them for both transportation costs (an in-person application was required for this position) and their opportunity cost of time. Abebe, Caria, and Ortiz-Ospina (2021) found that the application incentive improves the quality of the applicant pool: the number of top applicants doubles.

44. The findings are based on an RCT implemented in 70 rural villages in Kilimanjaro and Manyara, two northern regions of Tanzania, in February–March 2019. The app was designed to mimic an online job portal, except that ads are announced over feature phones without internet data. No effects are found on job creation or the average wage.

45. As in Hjort and Poulsen (2019), the identification strategy of Houngbonon, Mensah, and Traore (2022) exploits plausibly exogenous spatial and time variations in high-speed internet availability in a difference-in-difference design as well as an instrumental variable approach. They match spatial data on the rollout of high-speed internet with georeferenced data on households and firms. The data on entrepreneurship come from the Living Standards Measurement Study–Integrated Surveys on Agriculture (LSMS-ISA) for Ethiopia, Malawi, Nigeria, Tanzania, and Uganda; the data on innovation come from the World Bank Enterprise Survey–Innovation Follow-up Survey (WBES-IFS) conducted between 2011 and 2015 for the Democratic Republic of Congo, Ghana, Kenya, Malawi, Namibia, Nigeria, Sudan, Tanzania, Uganda, and Zambia.

46. An identification strategy is used like that of Houngbonon, Mensah, and Traore (2022), based on project-level data on FDI from fDiMarkets 2003–18 for all countries on the African continent.

47. A 1.0 percent increase in internet use is associated with a 2.2 percent increase in exports, based on data from 43 African countries for 1996–2006 (Hinson and Adjasi 2009). The dependent variable is the export value of goods and services; "internet use" is the proportion of internet users per 1,000 people. Control variables include gross domestic product (GDP) per capita, population, land area, and the exchange rate. The model is estimated with random effects. As mentioned earlier, Hjort and Poulsen (2019) also find that enterprises with internet availability export more.

48. These findings are based on a 2016 RCT in Monrovia, Liberia. Treated formally registered firms with 14 employees on average received a seven-day training on how to bid on tenders from larger buyers. The training raises the number of tenders firms bid on, total contracts won, nontender contracts won, and revenue from contracts only among firms that used the internet for business purposes at baseline. The benefits of the training are concentrated among firms with internet access not only when online demand is high but even when online demand is low. This result supports the view that internet use converts marketing to sales not only through directly expanded online market access (some contracts are publicized only online) but also by reducing search and communications frictions—by facilitating suppliers' ability to search for information about, to be found by, and to communicate with buyers, whether or not the contracts are publicized online.

49. The findings are based on microlevel survey data spanning 1997 (when 2G phone service was introduced) to 2001 (when over 60 percent of fishing boats and most wholesale and retail traders were using mobile phones to coordinate sales). The fisheries sector was transformed from a collection of essentially autarkic fishing markets to a state of nearly perfect spatial arbitrage. The mean coefficient of variation of price across markets (the standard deviation divided by the mean) declined from 60–70 percent to 15 percent or less (Jensen 2007). Further, waste, averaging 5–8 percent of daily catch before mobile phones, was eliminated. In addition, fishermen's profits increased on average by 8 percent while the consumer price declined by 4 percent and consumer surplus in sardine consumption increased by 6 percent.

50. The exogenous shock to identify impacts is the transition from 2G to 3G broadband networks in 2008 and the induced changes in the geographic variation across districts of data plan availability for households. Ethiopia's Large and Medium Manufacturing Industries (LMMI) annual census data from 2000–14—covering all public and private manufacturing firms that have more than 10 employees and use electricity for production—is combined with the nationally representative Household Income, Consumption and Expenditure Surveys (HCES) in 2004–05 and 2010–11, which include expenditures on mobile cards; average expenditure levels are used to designate treated and untreated districts.

51. Building on Hjort and Poulsen (2019), the focus of Goldbeck and Lindlacher (2021) is on local economic growth in "incidentally connected towns"—namely, towns close to an access point that are not endogenously connected nodal cities across 10 African countries: Angola, Benin, Botswana, Ethiopia, Mali, Sudan, Senegal, Togo, Zambia, and Zimbabwe. Access points were constructed along other potentially confounding infrastructure, such as roads, railroads, and the electricity grid. They find that internet availability, on average, leads to a 7 percent increase in nighttime satellite luminosity of towns in the years after connection, which approximately translates into 2-percentage-point higher economic growth, applying the GDP-to-light elasticity by Henderson, Storeygard, and Weil (2011). The Goldbeck and Lindlacher (2021) finding is relatively close to the Hjort and Poulsen (2019) estimate of a 3.3 percent increase in average incomes. Mensah (2021) provides related subnational impact findings at the global level across 3,419 regions in 201 countries.

52. Economic growth (real GDP per worker), TFP, and capital per worker growth (as measured by annual average growth over a nonoverlapping five-year period from 1990 to 2019) as well as the poverty headcount and the Gini index, respectively, are regressed on total mobile internet subscriptions per capita (from a GSMA Intelligence database) and the population share of internet users (from the World Development Indicators database, based on International Telecommunication Union data), for 46 Sub-Saharan African countries. Generalized method of moments for instrumental variables (GMM-IV) system estimators are used to deal with unobserved time effects through the inclusion of period-specific intercepts. The method then uses differencing and instrumentation to control for unobserved country effects and likely endogeneity and reserve causality.

53. Mobile money is distinct from mobile banking, which allows access to existing bank accounts via a smartphone. It is an app that operates via software installed on a subscriber identity module (SIM) card and is typically used on 2G or 2.5G feature phones, though mobile money agents require an internet connection to be considered. It is a financial service that does not require a banking account and is typically provided by mobile network operators. Its use remains mostly limited to digital person-to-person digital payments, largely for transfers over large distances or as an alternative payment where holding cash is risky. See Suri (2017) for an overview of the operations, regulations, and impacts of mobile money in low- and middle-income countries.

54. Between 2008 and 2014, five rounds of a household panel survey were conducted (Suri and Jack 2016). To identify the causal effects of M-Pesa on the economic well-being of households, changes in access to mobile money, not adoption itself, was used. Access to the service was measured by the geographic proximity of households to mobile money agents.

55. The underlying question in the Uganda study (Wieser et al. 2019) is whether the sample areas are too remote and poor to benefit from mobile money (because they receive few remittances and may not have enough income to save). To measure the effect of mobile money in poor and remote areas, the International Finance Corporation collaborated with Airtel Uganda to implement this RCT in

Northern Uganda where none of the areas had Airtel Money agents at baseline. In the treatment group, Airtel Money agents were rolled out in 2017, with 46 percent of areas receiving at least one agent. The authors conclude that mobile money services can improve livelihoods even in very poor and remote areas, even though the analysis finds no direct effect on savings, agricultural outcomes, or poverty.

56. Data are combined from the expansion of the mobile agent network in Kenya for the period 2000–13, with a local-level measure of economic performance proxied by the intensity of nighttime lights.

57. To make a lending decision, the DT asks for permission to scrape the applicant's phone for data on handset details, Global Positioning System (GPS) info, call and SMS logs (including airtime purchases and mobile money transactions), social network data from Facebook, and contact lists. A machine learning algorithm then uses these data to create a credit score and make a lending decision. Increased use results in lower interest fees and larger loans. See Suri (2017).

58. The identification strategy relies on a regression discontinuity design of individuals around the cutoff point where they are just eligible or ineligible for the digital loan product, based on administrative data from the bank for customers who opened their accounts between January and March 2015. These data are combined with survey data conducted in September 2016–January 2017, and administrative data on a random sample of 10,000 M-Shwari customers who opened their accounts between January and March 2016 where the entire evolution of their loan histories and credit limits can be followed.

59. This is important because households in the sample have extremely poor access to any form of formal credit, as they comprise poor and vulnerable individuals: only 6 percent have had a bank loan over the two years before the survey; only 2 percent have had a microfinance loan; only 5 percent have had a loan from a savings and credit cooperative; and only 6 percent have borrowed from a rotating savings and credit association (ROSCA), an informal peer-to-peer lending arrangement.

60. Roughly 68 percent of the control group reports having had to forgo some expenses in response to a negative shock. Even though households may spend the actual loan money on, say, medication, the marginal dollars from the loan get spent on education—the item they would have adjusted had they not had access to the loan.

61. For more information, see the Pula website, https://www.pula-advisors.com.

62. That information on optimal local agricultural practices is valuable to farmers is confirmed by four trials that estimate farmers' willingness to pay (WTP) for such local agricultural information. The mean WTP for local soil test results is between US$0.20 and US$4.80; for results from local experimental plots, it is US$2.30. The aggregate WTP for soil information in an area exceeds the costs of generating and delivering such information under plausible assumptions: at scale, soil information is estimated to be generated and delivered at less than US$0.15 per farmer (for 150 farmers per test), which is less than the US$0.20 WTP per farmer in the conservative scenario in which farmers were asked to use their own money to acquire the information. See Fabregas, Kremer, Robinson, and Schilbach (2019).

63. The odds ratio estimates for the effects of the programs on purchases of agricultural lime is 1.21—in other words, there is a 1.21 times greater likelihood of applying lime to reduce soil acidity and increase yields relative to the control group of farmers not receiving the SMS messages. Results are based on six RCTs implemented between 2015 and 2017 with farmers in Kenya and Rwanda by three organizations: the Kenya Agriculture and Livestock Research Organization (KALRO), a public agency with the mandate to promote agricultural research and dissemination; Precision for Development (PxD), jointly with Innovations for Poverty Action (IPA), a research nonprofit; and the One Acre Fund (OAF), a nonprofit social enterprise for smallholder farmers. A back-of-the-envelope calculation shows a benefit of US$0.41 per farmer treated. Considering that the programs' cost averaged US$0.04 per farmer, the benefit-cost ratio is 10. However, at scale, with a unit cost of US$0.001 per SMS, the implied benefit-cost ratio would be 100.

64. The findings are based on an SMS intervention in 2011–13 in a large sugarcane contract farming scheme owned by one of the largest agribusiness companies in East Africa. The increase in yields generated increases of about US$43 in company profits and about US$54 in farmer earnings, and

the per-farmer cost of the program is about US$0.30 per farmer. However, a follow-up RCT of the same intervention has had no significant impact on yields. Possible explanations for the different findings include differences in season, farmer characteristics, and other features of the underlying environment.

65. The field experiment involved approximately 4,000 farm households sampled from the population of households cultivating maize across five districts of eastern Uganda. The videos were of farmer-actors speaking in the local language in a manner relatable to low-skilled, including illiterate, farmers. They were shown on 10-inch Android tablet computers and screened by a trained field enumerator during one-to-one meetings with either an individual farmer or the male and female coheads of the household. Videos were screened twice with the households in the sample, once before maize planting (August 2017) and once at planting time (September 2017).

66. The RCT was implemented in three highland regions within the Integrated Soil Fertility Management Project of the German Agency for International Cooperation (GIZ) in 2015–18. The main characters for the video were carefully chosen to be as much as possible representative of the target audience in terms of socioeconomic status and living environment: given the cultural, linguistic, and agroecological differences between Tigray, Amhara, and Oromia, three different farmer couples were selected and featured in the version for each respective region. The video was shown in public spaces such as farmer training centers, health posts, or schools, and was followed by group discussions facilitated by extension agents. Despite larger effect sizes of the combined over the extension-only treatment, there is no evidence of a significant complementary effect of the video on adoption of the integrated package or any individual component.

67. The field experiment involved 700 households sampled across 75 villages in five irrigated rice production areas in Kano state, the major rice-producing region in Nigeria in 2016–17. The RiceAdvice app, developed by AfricaRice in conjunction with national partners, is an Android-based decision support tool that extension agents use to provide farming households with preseason, field-specific management guidelines for rice production. The extension advice includes a nutrient management plan, a suggested crop calendar, and information regarding best practices for rice cultivation. To generate this advice, farmers provide information on the geographic location of the plot, descriptive soil quality measures, local rice-growing conditions, seed variety, typical management practices, expected sowing date, availability of fertilizers, market prices for inputs, and expected production costs.

68. A mixed-methods approach was applied involving approximately 400 respondents and comprising a participatory mapping tool, focus group discussions, interviews with tractor owners and other stakeholders, and a survey among farmers in October 2018 in the Federal Capital Territory of Nigeria. The average land size served by both Hello Tractor (4.6 hectares) and the conventional service providers (5.3 hectares) in the sample was well above the level of two hectares that is often used as a threshold to define smallholder farming. Tractor hiring requires the recording of data such as plot sizes, type of equipment required, and land conditions, some of which cannot easily be aided by visual tools. As well, few smallholder farmers trust mobile services sufficiently to make business transactions if those transactions include an up-front payment. So farmers engage with Hello Tractor indirectly through booking agents and phone calls rather than through a smartphone app.

69. Among the farmers accessing services and interviewed for this study, 11 percent of those who relied on the Hello Tractor model were female, whereas the farmers using existing traditional methods were all male, a highly statistically significant difference in means. The authors (Daum et al. 2021) surmise that, because booking agents come from outside the communities, often from urban areas, they are less constrained by social norms and rules favoring male farmers.

70. Cross-country regressions over 2010–20 highlight that, although income is a key driver, the mobile internet uptake gap between Sub-Saharan Africa and the rest of the world is not explained by income alone (Atiyas and Dutz 2022). Unique mobile internet uptake is regressed on GDP per capita, squared and cubed (to allow for the possibility that the association between uptake and income is nonlinear). Income alone explains a little more than half of the variation in uptake across all countries and years. When a dummy for Sub-Saharan Africa is added, its coefficient is negative and statistically highly significant, suggesting that, even controlling for income, mobile internet uptake is about 5.6 percentage points lower than the rest of the world.

71. These figures differ from those based exclusively on GSMA data because they rely on individual responses on uptake based on household surveys.

72. For Senegal, usage is based on individuals who report accessing the internet through their mobile phones.

73. For Nigeria, "usage" is based on individuals who report accessing the internet in general, which includes both fixed and mobile broadband internet even if the device or internet connection belongs to somebody else. It is not possible to distinguish the type of device used to connect to the internet.

74. Because RIA did not have independent information on the distribution of informal firms, sampling for the business survey was done in parallel to the sampling for the complementary RIA household survey. Specifically, the national census sample frames were split into urban and rural Enumerator Areas (EAs). Then EAs were sampled for each stratum using probability proportional to size. For each EA, two listings were compiled, one for households and one for firms; these listings served as the sampling frames. Twenty-four households and 10 firms were selected randomly from each EA. Application of sampling weights yield EA-level representative data for the RIA microenterprise survey. See Mothobi, Gillwald, and Aguera (2020) for a descriptive analysis of these data.

75. See Suri (2017) for a list of outstanding research questions related to mobile money.

76. Investments in the analysis of administrative government data and impact evaluation can unlock great potential for the improvement of public service delivery in low- and middle-income countries. This finding is based, among others, on an empirical analysis of the spread of a phone-based agricultural extension system in Ethiopia by Figueiredo Walter et al. (2021). They show how small changes in the design of the interactive voice response system can have substantial effects on the amount of agricultural advice accessed by farmers. Their work suggests that system development was not held back by lack of political will but rather by lack of government capacity to identify beneficial system changes. The forgone potential for system improvement appears to have been due to passive rather than active government failure.

77. On the concept of diagnostic monitoring or "learning by monitoring," see Sabel (1994).

78. Campenhout, Spielman, and Lecoutere (2021) encourage replication of similar studies in different country contexts—alongside variations in the choice of DTs and the experimental designs in which they are introduced to farmers—across multiple agroecological, social, and economic contexts.

79. In a recent RCT experiment, a training program involving mentoring offered randomly to people of different abilities and willingness to join yielded significantly better outcomes than the same program offered to those who self-selected to participate: individuals in the former group outperformed those in the latter group by 18 percent in the subsequent six months on the job. Sandvik et al. (2021) conclude as follows: "Formal mentorship program treatment effects are largest for workers who would otherwise opt out of these programs. Demographic and personality characteristics are relatively weak predictors of selection into the training program, suggesting broad-based programs are likely more effective than alternative targeting rules."

80. Using transaction data from nearly the entire network of Rwandan mobile phone subscribers over 4.5 years, Björkegren (2019) estimates that shifting from handset to usage taxes would have increased the surplus of poorer users by at least 26 percent.

References

Abebe, Girum, A. Stefano Caria, and Esteban Ortiz-Ospina. 2021. "The Selection of Talent: Experimental and Structural Evidence from Ethiopia." *American Economic Review* 111 (6): 1757–806.

Abreha, Kaleb G., Jieun Choi, Woubet Kassa, Hyun Ju Kim, and Maurice Kugler. 2021. "Mobile Access Expansion and Price Information Diffusion: Firm Performance after Ethiopia's Transition to 3G in 2008." Policy Research Working Paper 9752, World Bank, Washington, DC.

Acemoglu, Daron. 2002. "Technical Change, Inequality, and the Labor Market." *Journal of Economic Literature* 40 (1): 7–72.

Acemoglu, Daron, and Pascal Restrepo. 2020. "The Wrong Kind of AI? Artificial Intelligence and the Future of Labor Demand." *Cambridge Journal of Regions, Economy and Society* 13 (1): 25–35.

Aker, Jenny C. 2010. "Information from Markets Near and Far: Mobile Phones and Agricultural Markets in Niger." *American Economic Journal: Applied Economics* 2 (3): 46–59.

Aker, Jenny C., and Marcel Fafchamps. 2014. "Mobile Phone Coverage and Producer Markets: Evidence from West Africa." *World Bank Economic Review* 29 (2): 262–92.

Arouna, Aminou, Jeffrey D. Michler, Wilfried G. Yergo, and Kazuki Saito. 2021. "One Size Fits All? Experimental Evidence on the Digital Delivery of Personalized Extension Advice in Nigeria." *American Journal of Agricultural Economics* 103 (2): 596–619.

Atiyas, İzak, and Mark A. Dutz. 2022. "Digitalization in MENA and Sub-Saharan Africa: A Comparative Analysis of Mobile Internet Uptake and Use in Sub-Saharan Africa and MENA Countries." Working Paper No. 1549, Economic Research Forum, Giza, Egypt.

Autor, David, Lawrence Katz, and Melissa Kearney. 2008. "Trends in US Wage Inequality: Revising the Revisionists." *Review of Economics and Statistics* 90 (2): 300–23.

Bahia, Kalvin, Pau Castells, Genaro Cruz, Takaaki Masaki, Xavier Pedrós, Tobias Pfutze, Carlos Rodríguez-Castelán, and Hernan Winkler. 2020. "The Welfare Effects of Mobile Broadband Internet: Evidence from Nigeria." Policy Research Working Paper 9230, World Bank, Washington, DC.

Bahia, Kalvin, Pau Castells, Takaaki Masaki, Genaro Cruz, Carlos Rodríguez-Castelán, and Viviane Sanfelice. Forthcoming. "Mobile Broadband Internet, Poverty and Labor Outcomes in Tanzania." *World Bank Economic Review*.

Barrett, Christopher B., Ariel Ortiz-Bobea, and Trinh Pham. 2021. "Structural Transformation, Agriculture, Climate, and the Environment." Applied Economics and Policy Working Paper Series, Cornell University, Ithaca, NY.

Baumol, William J. 1990. "Entrepreneurship: Productive, Unproductive, and Destructive." *Journal of Political Economy* 98 (5): 893–921.

Beegle, Kathleen, and Luc Christiaensen, eds. 2019. *Accelerating Poverty Reduction in Africa.* Washington, DC: World Bank.

Bessen, James. 2019. "Artificial Intelligence and Jobs: The Role of Demand." In *The Economics of Artificial Intelligence: An Agenda*, edited by Ajay Agrawal, Joshua Gans, and Avi Goldfarb, 291–307. Chicago: University of Chicago Press.

Björkegren, Daniel. 2019. "The Adoption of Network Goods: Evidence from the Spread of Mobile Phones in Rwanda." *Review of Economic Studies* 86 (3): 1033–60.

Bloom, Nicholas, Renata Lemos, Raffaella Sadun, Daniela Scur, and John Van Reenen. 2016. "International Data on Measuring Management Practices." *American Economic Review* 106 (5): 152–56.

Bloom, Nicholas, and John Van Reenen. 2007. "Measuring and Explaining Management Practices across Firms and Countries." *Quarterly Journal of Economics* 122 (4): 1351–408.

Bloom, Nicholas, and John Van Reenen. 2010. "Why Do Management Practices Differ across Firms and Countries?" *Journal of Economic Perspectives* 24 (1): 203–24.

Bresnahan, Timothy F., and Manuel Trajtenberg. 1995. "General Purpose Technologies: 'Engines of Growth'?" *Journal of Econometrics* 65 (1): 83–108.

Breznitz, Daniel. 2021. *Innovation in Real Places: Strategies for Prosperity in an Unforgiving World.* Oxford: Oxford University Press.

Calderón, César, and Catalina Cantú. 2021. "The Impact of Digital Infrastructure on African Development." Policy Research Working Paper 9853, World Bank, Washington, DC.

Campenhout, Bjorn van, David J. Spielman, and Els Lecoutere. 2021. "Information and Communication Technologies to Provide Agricultural Advice to Smallholder Farmers: Experimental Evidence from Uganda." *American Journal of Agricultural Economics* 103 (1): 317–37.

Casaburi, Lorenzo, Michael Kremer, Sendhil Mullainathan, and Ravindra Ramrattan. 2019. "Harnessing ICT to Increase Agricultural Production: Evidence from Kenya." Working paper, Innovations for Poverty Action and Abdul Latif Jameel Poverty Action Lab, Cambridge, MA.

Choi, Jieun, Mark A. Dutz, and Zainab Usman. 2020. *The Future of Work in Africa: Harnessing the Potential of Digital Technologies for All*. Africa Development Forum Series. Washington, DC: World Bank.

Cirera, Xavier, Diego Comin, and Marcio Cruz. 2022. *Bridging the Technological Divide: Technology Adoption by Firms in Developing Countries*. Washington, DC: World Bank.

Cirera, Xavier, and William Maloney. 2017. *The Innovation Paradox : Developing-Country Capabilities and the Unrealized Promise of Technological Catch-Up*. Washington, DC: World Bank.

Cruz, Marcio, Mark A. Dutz, and Carlos Rodríguez-Castelán. 2021. *Digital Senegal for Inclusive Growth: Technological Transformation for Better and More Jobs*. Washington, DC: World Bank.

Cusolito, Ana Paula, and William F. Maloney. 2018. *Productivity Revisited: Shifting Paradigms in Analysis and Policy*. Washington, DC: World Bank.

Daum, Thomas, Roberto Villalba, Oluwakayode Anidi, Sharon Masakhwe Mayienga, Saurabh Gupta, and Regina Birner. 2021. "Uber for Tractors? Opportunities and Challenges of Digital Tools for Tractor Hire in India and Nigeria." *World Development* 144: 105480.

Diao, Xinshen, Mia Ellis, Margaret S. McMillan, and Dani Rodrik. 2021. "Africa's Manufacturing Puzzle: Evidence from Tanzanian and Ethiopian Firms." Working Paper No. 28344, National Bureau of Economic Research, Cambridge, MA.

Dutz, Mark A., Rita K. Almeida, and Truman G. Packard. 2018. *The Jobs of Tomorrow: Technology, Productivity, and Prosperity in Latin America and the Caribbean*. Directions in Development Series. Washington, DC: World Bank.

Dutz, Mark A., Ioannis N. Kessides, Stephen D. O'Connell, and Robert D. Willig. 2012. "Competition and Innovation-Driven Inclusive Growth." In *Promoting Inclusive Growth: Challenges and Policies*, edited by Luiz de Mello and Mark A. Dutz, 221–77. Paris: OECD Publishing.

Dutz, Mark A., Janusz Ordover, and Robert D. Willig. 2000. "Entrepreneurship, Access Policy and Economic Development: Lessons from Industrial Organization." *European Economic Review* 44 (4–6): 739–47.

Dutz, Mark A., Jonathan M. Orszag, and Robert D. Willig. 2012. "The Liftoff of Consumer Benefits from the Broadband Revolution." *Review of Network Economics* 11 (4): 1–34.

Fabregas, Raissa, Michael Kremer, Matthew Lowes, Robert On, and Giulia Zane. 2019. "SMS-Extension and Farmer Behavior: Lessons from Six RCTs in East Africa." Working paper, Agricultural Technology Adoption Initiative (ATAI), Cambridge, MA.

Fabregas, Raissa, Michael Kremer, Jonathan Robinson, and Frank Schilbach. 2019. "The Value of Local Agricultural Information: Evidence from Kenya." Working paper, Agricultural Technology Adoption Initiative (ATAI), Cambridge, MA.

Fabregas, Raissa, Michael Kremer, and Frank Schilbach. 2017. "Realizing the Potential of Digital Development: The Case of Agricultural Advice." *Science* 366 (6471): eeay3038.

Fabregas, Raissa, and Tite Yokossi. 2022. "Mobile Money and Economic Activity: Evidence from Kenya." *World Bank Economic Review* 36 (3): 734–56.

Figueiredo Walter, Torsten, Michael Kremer, Ofir Reich, Zhengyun Sun, Sam van Herwaardenk, and Habtamu Yesigat. 2021. "Using Data for Development: Evidence from a Phone System for Agricultural Advice." Working paper, Precision Agriculture for Development, Boston.

Fuglie, Keith, Madhur Gautam, Aparajita Goyal, and William F. Maloney. 2020. *Harvesting Prosperity: Technology and Productivity Growth in Agriculture*. Washington, DC: World Bank.

Goldbeck, Moritz, and Valentin Lindlacher. 2021. "Digital Infrastructure and Local Economic Growth: Early Internet in Sub-Saharan Africa." Job market paper, ifo Institute for Economic Research, University of Munich.

Goldfarb, Avi, and Catherine Tucker. 2019. "Digital Economics." *Journal of Economic Literature* 57 (1): 3–43.

Henderson, Vernon, Adam Storeygard, and David N. Weil. 2011. "A Bright Idea for Measuring Economic Growth." *American Economic Review* 101 (3): 194–99.

Henn, Soeren J., and James A. Robinson. 2021. "Africa's Latent Assets." Working Paper No. 28603, National Bureau of Economic Research, Cambridge, MA.

Herrendorf, Berthold, Richard Rogerson, and Ákos Valentinyi. 2014. "Growth and Structural Transformation." In *Handbook of Economic Growth*, Volume 2A, edited by Philippe Aghion and Steven N. Durlauf, 855–941. Oxford and San Diego: North Holland.

Hinson, Robert E., and Charles K. D. Adjasi. 2009. "The Internet and Export: Some Cross-Country Evidence from Selected African Countries." *Journal of Internet Commerce* 8 (3–4): 309–24.

Hjort, Jonas, Vinayak Iyer, and Golvine de Rochambeau. 2020. "Informational Barriers to Market Access: Experimental Evidence from Liberian Firms." Working Paper No. 27662, National Bureau of Economic Research, Cambridge, MA.

Hjort, Jonas, and Jonas Poulsen. 2019. "The Arrival of Fast Internet and Employment in Africa." *American Economic Review* 109 (3): 1032–79.

Hjort, Jonas, and Lin Tian. 2021. "The Economic Impact of Internet Connectivity in Developing Countries." Synthesis Paper No. 6, Private Enterprise Development in Low-Income Countries (PEDL), London.

Hörner, Denise, Adrien Bouguen, Markus Frölich, and Meike Wollni. 2019. "The Effects of Decentralized and Video-Based Extension on the Adoption of Integrated Soil Fertility Management: Experimental Evidence from Ethiopia." Working Paper No. 26052, National Bureau of Economic Research, Cambridge, MA.

Houngbonon, Georges V., Justice Tei Mensah, and Nouhoum Traore. 2022. "The Impact of Internet Access on Innovation and Entrepreneurship in Africa." Policy Research Working Paper 9945, World Bank, Washington, DC.

Hovhannisyan, Shoghik, Veronica Montalva-Talledo, Tyler Remick, Carlos Rodríguez-Castelán, and Kersten Stamm. 2022. "Global Job Quality: Evidence from Wage Employment across Developing Countries." Policy Research Working Paper 10134 , World Bank, Washington, DC.

Jensen, Robert. 2007. "The Digital Provide: Information (Technology), Market Performance, and Welfare in the South Indian Fisheries Sector." *Quarterly Journal of Economics* 122 (3): 879–924.

Jeong, Dahyeon. 2020. "Creating (Digital) Labor Markets in Rural Tanzania." Unpublished manuscript, University of California, Santa Cruz.

Kirimi, Lilian, Eric Njue, and Mary Mathenge. 2015. "Uptake of Crop Insurance in Kenya in the Face of Climate Change." Policy Brief No. 15, Tegembo Institute of Agricultural Policy and Development, Egerton University, Njoro, Kenya.

Lederman, Daniel, and Marwane Zouaidi. 2020. "Incidence of the Digital Economy and Frictional Unemployment: International Evidence." Policy Research Working Paper 9170, World Bank, Washington, DC.

Masaki, Takaaki, Rogelio Granguillhome Ochoa, and Carlos Rodríguez-Castelán. 2020. "Broadband Internet and Household Welfare in Senegal." Policy Research Working Paper 9386, World Bank, Washington, DC.

McMillan, Margaret, Dani Rodrik, and Íñigo Verduzco-Gallo. 2014. "Globalization, Structural Change, and Productivity Growth, with an Update on Africa." *World Development* 63: 11–32.

Mensah, Justice Tei. 2021. "Mobile Phones and Local Economic Development: A Global Evidence." Working Paper, International Finance Corporation, Washington, DC.

Mensah, Justice Tei, and Nouhoum Traore. 2022. "Infrastructure Quality and FDI Inflows: Evidence from the Arrival of High-Speed Internet in Africa." Policy Research Working Paper 9946, World Bank, Washington, DC.

Midrigan, Virgiliu, and Daniel Yi Xu. 2014. "Finance and Misallocation: Evidence from Plant-Level Data." *American Economic Review* 104 (2): 422–58.

Mothobi, Onkokame, Alison Gillwald, and Pablo Aguera. 2020. "A Demand Side View of Informality and Financial Inclusion." Policy Paper No. 9, Series 5: After Access, Research ICT Africa, Cape Town, South Africa.

Murphy, Kevin M., Andrei Shleifer, and Robert W. Vishny. 1991. "The Allocation of Talent: Implications for Growth." *Quarterly Journal of Economics* 106 (2): 503–30.

Nayyar, Gaurav, Mary Hallward-Driemeier, and Elwyn Davies. 2021. *At Your Service? The Promise of Services-Led Development*. Washington, DC: World Bank.

Porto, Guido. 2021. "Digital Technologies and Poorer Households' Income Earning Choices in Sub-Saharan Africa: Analytical Framework and a Case Study for Senegal and Kenya." Background study for *Digital Senegal for Inclusive Growth: Technological Transformation for Better and More Jobs*, by Marcio Cruz, Mark A. Dutz, and Carlos Rodríguez-Castelán. Washington, DC: World Bank.

Rodrik, Dani, and Charles Sabel. 2022. "Building a Good Jobs Economy." In *A Political Economy of Justice*, edited by Danielle Allen, Yochai Benkler, Leah Downey, Rebecca Henderson, and Josh Simons, 61–95. Chicago: University of Chicago Press.

Rodrik, Dani, and Stefanie Stantcheva. 2021. "Fixing Capitalism's Good Jobs Problem." *Oxford Review of Economic Policy* 37 (4): 824–37.

Sabel, Charles F. 1994. "Learning by Monitoring: The Institutions of Economic Development." In *Handbook of Economic Sociology*, edited by Neil Smelser and Richard Swedberg, 137–65. Princeton, NJ: Princeton University Press and Russell Sage Foundation.

Sandvik, Jason, Richard Saouma, Nathan Seegert, and Christopher T. Stanton. 2021. "Treatment and Selection Effects of Formal Workplace Mentorship Programs." Working Paper No. 29148, National Bureau of Economic Research, Cambridge, MA.

Sibiko, Kenneth W., and Matin Qaim. 2020. "Weather Index Insurance, Agricultural Input Use, and Crop Productivity in Kenya." *Food Security* 12 (1): 151–67.

Suri, Tavneet. 2017. "Mobile Money." *Annual Review of Economics* 9: 497–520.

Suri, Tavneet, Prashant Bharadwaj, and William Jack. 2021. "Fintech and Household Resilience to Shocks: Evidence from Digital Loans in Kenya." *Journal of Development Economics* 153: 102697.

Suri, Tavneet, and William Jack. 2016. "The Long-Run Poverty and Gender Impacts of Mobile Money." *Science* 354 (6317): 1288–92.

Tõnurist, P., and A. Hanson. 2020. "Anticipatory Innovation Governance: Shaping the Future through Proactive Policy Making." Working Papers on Public Governance No. 44, Organisation for Economic Co-operation and Development, OECD Publishing, Paris.

Trajtenberg, Manuel. 2019. "Artificial Intelligence as the Next GPT: A Political-Economy Perspective." In *The Economics of Artificial Intelligence: An Agenda*, edited by Ajay Agrawal, Joshua Gans, and Avi Goldfarb, 175–86. Chicago: University of Chicago Press.

UN DESA (United Nations Department of Economic and Social Affairs). 2022a. *World Population Prospects 2022*. Population data files. New York: United Nations. https://population.un.org/wpp /Download/Standard/Population/.

UN DESA (United Nations Department of Economic and Social Affairs). 2022b. *World Population Prospects 2022: Methodology of the United Nations Population Estimates and Projections*. UN DESA/POP/2022/DC/No.6. New York: United Nations.

Wieser, Christina, Miriam Bruhn, Johannes Kinzinger, Christian Ruckteschler, and Soren Heitmann. 2019. "The Impact of Mobile Money on Poor Rural Households: Experimental Evidence from Uganda." Policy Research Working Paper 8913, World Bank, Washington, DC.

World Bank. 2020. "Digital Economy for Africa Country Diagnostic Tool and Guidelines for Task Teams." Version 2.0. Digital Economy for Africa (DE4A) Initiative, World Bank, Washington, DC.

World Bank. 2021. *World Development Report 2021: Data for Better Lives*. Washington, DC: World Bank.

CHAPTER 2

Enterprises

Creating Better Jobs for More People through Innovation

Digital technology use by African enterprises

Digital technologies (DTs) and complementary technologies are associated with higher productivity, higher production and sales, and better jobs for more people. But African enterprises lag in DT use relative to peer countries. To narrow their technology gap with the rest of the world and achieve inclusive jobs benefits, they must generate and adopt DTs and complementary technologies—especially those technologies aligned with Africa's current comparative advantage of a large and growing number of lower-skilled workers. And African enterprises must adopt and use these technologies more intensively. The aim is to enable existing and newly entering entrepreneur-owners, managers, and workers to learn as they work, thereby enabling them to raise their productivity and generate higher earnings as well as to create more jobs over time.

Association with higher productivity and jobs

Two complementary surveys provide new findings on use of technologies and associated productivity, sales, jobs, and earnings outcomes: The World Bank's Firm-level Adoption of Technology (FAT) survey is restricted to enterprises with five or more employees for this report across four African countries—Ghana, Kenya, Malawi, and Senegal—together with Brazil and Vietnam as available peer countries.[1] The Research ICT Africa (RIA) After Access business survey is focused on micro-size enterprises (the median being a self-employed household enterprise with no full-time employees) in seven countries: Ghana, Kenya, Mozambique, Nigeria, Senegal, South Africa, and Tanzania.[2]

A new finding from the FAT survey is the significant within-firm variation in technological sophistication for general business functions (GBFs): while a firm may be using more sophisticated DTs for accounting and marketing, it simultaneously may be using manual nondigital technologies for quality control (Cirera et al. 2021).

Productivity gains

The intensive use of more sophisticated DTs and related technologies is associated with higher productivity across enterprises in Africa. An important finding is that a higher average sophistication of the most intensively used technologies across all business functions (ABFs)—covering both GBFs and sector-specific business functions (SBFs)—is positively and significantly associated with higher labor productivity.[3] Firms with higher average levels of technological sophistication have higher productivity (figure 2.1).

FIGURE 2.1 Association of higher technological sophistication with higher enterprise productivity, selected African countries, 2019–21

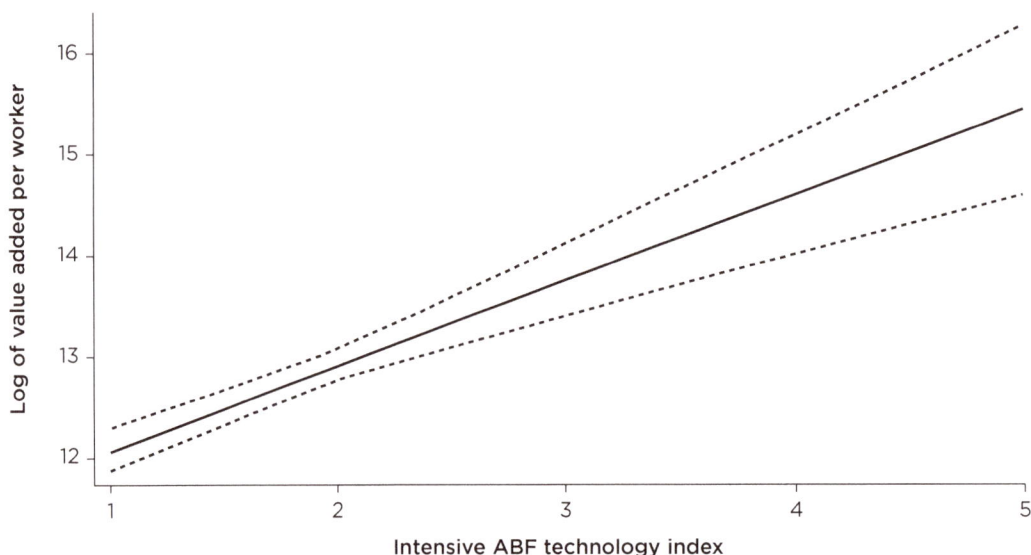

Source: Cirera, Comin, and Cruz 2022 (figure 4.2), restricted to four available African countries.
Note: The figure summarizes data from 4,835 enterprises (with at least five employees) across Ghana, Kenya, Malawi, and Senegal. Only in Senegal was it possible to draw a representative sample of informal firms; thus, the Senegal sample encompasses representative subsamples of both formal and informal firms. The technology index for intensive use of all business functions (ABFs) refers to the sophistication of each enterprise's most intensively used technologies, averaged across all its business functions (general and sector-specific business functions). "Value added per worker" is nominal value added (in US dollars, at 2019 purchasing power parity). Dotted lines represent the 95 percent confidence interval, with higher productivity dispersion at higher values of technological sophistication due to fewer observations and greater variation in availability of complementary inputs.

This finding, based exclusively on data from Africa, implies that the relationship between technology intensity and productivity is larger across African countries than across other studied countries. That is, a given increase in enterprises' average technological sophistication is associated with higher labor productivity increases in African countries than across all countries with available data.[4] This association suggests that increases in technological sophistication are likely to have even higher productivity premiums in Africa than in the rest of the world.

The use of more sophisticated DTs and related technologies is also associated with higher productivity country by country across Africa, especially among informal firms. At the country level, firms with higher average technological sophistication have higher productivity on average, with varying degrees of responsiveness: formal firms with a 1 point higher score in the technology adoption index for technologies used most intensively for GBF tasks are associated with labor productivity increases of 1.9 percent, 1.2 percent, 1.4 percent, and 2.0 percent in Ghana, Kenya, Malawi, and Senegal, respectively (figure 2.2, panel a).[5]

Interestingly, the association between technology use and productivity is significantly higher for informal than formal Senegalese firms, with the average informal firm having double the value added per worker from more sophisticated technology use than formal firms, a 4 percent relative to 2 percent higher level of labor productivity. The average firm in Ghana, Malawi, and Senegal also has a higher productivity level associated with an increase in technological sophistication than the average firm in Brazil and Vietnam.[6]

FIGURE 2.2 **Association between firms' use of sophisticated technologies and growth of productivity and jobs, selected African and comparator countries, 2019–21**

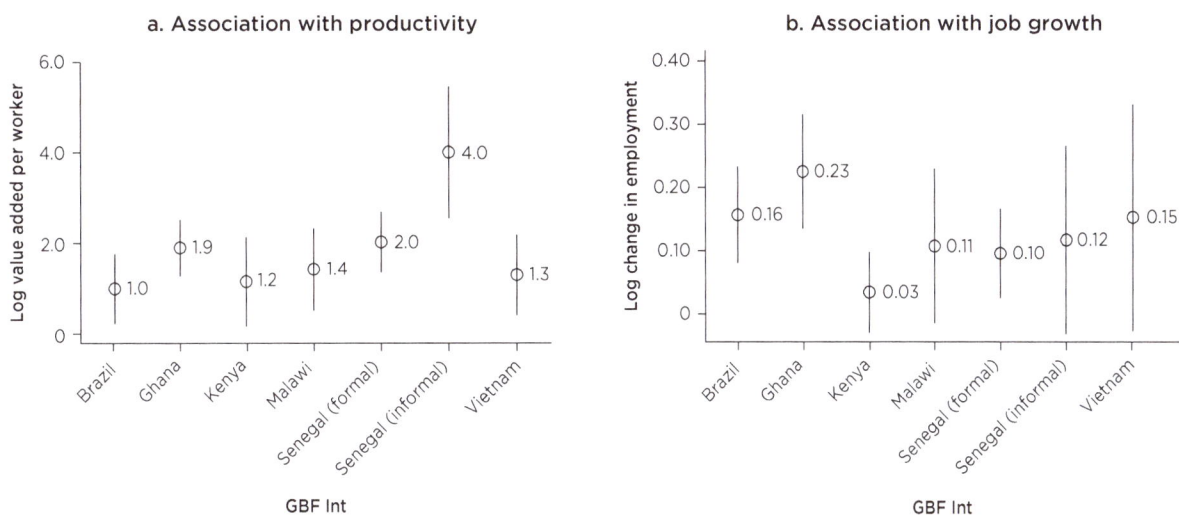

a. Association with productivity

b. Association with job growth

Source: Cirera, Comin, and Cruz 2022, based on 2019–21 FAT (Firm-level Adoption of Technology) survey data.
Note: The figure shows regression coefficients (circles) and 95 percent confidence intervals (vertical lines) from country-level regressions of a new technology sophistication index—averaging the most intensively used technologies across general business functions (GBF Int)—for each firm on labor productivity levels (panel a) and changes in full-time workers over the preceding three years (panel b), while controlling for sector, firm size, and region. GBF Int values range from 1 to 5 for each GBF, with 1 representing the most basic level of technology (nondigital) and 5 representing the most sophisticated level being used in the world. Country samples are restricted to enterprises with five or more employees. Only in Senegal was it possible to draw a representative sample of informal firms; thus, the Senegal sample includes representative subsamples of both informal and formal firms.

More, and more inclusive, jobs

The more intensive use of DTs and other sophisticated technologies is also prominently associated both with more jobs and with more inclusive jobs. At the country level, a 1 point increase in the technology adoption index for the technologies used most intensively for GBF tasks is associated with statistically significant increases of approximately 23 percent and 10 percent, respectively, in the number of workers in the average firm in Ghana and Senegal (figure 2.2, panel b).[7] The average Ghanaian firm also has a higher increase in jobs associated with an increase in technological sophistication than the average firm in Brazil and Vietnam.

Moreover, Senegalese firms (across both formal and informal subsamples) are more likely to increase the share of lower-skilled workers. Even if some new DTs may be labor saving, Senegalese firms disproportionally increase the share of lower-skilled workers as they expand total jobs: an increase of 1 point in the technology adoption index for the technologies used most intensively for GBF tasks is associated with a 7 percent decrease in the share of high-skilled workers in total employment.[8]

These country-level findings of both more jobs and more inclusive jobs also hold for a larger cross-country sample of firms across Bangladesh, Brazil, Ghana, India, Kenya, the Republic of Korea, Senegal, and Vietnam: an increase of 1 point in the technology index for GBFs at the intensive margin is associated with an increase of 8.9 percent in the number of workers in the average firm and a reduction of 0.8 percentage point in the share of high-skilled workers.[9] These associations do not allow causal relationships to be inferred between technology, productivity, jobs, and lower-skill-intensity jobs. However, aligned with the findings summarized in chapter 1, they support the view that, on average, enterprises with greater intensive use of more sophisticated DTs and complementary technologies generate more jobs while increasing the share of lower-skilled workers.

Gains in microenterprise performance outcomes

Complementary findings for microenterprises are based on the RIA After Access business survey. The data enable comparisons between users and nonusers of DTs on three performance outcomes: labor productivity, total sales, and jobs. In terms of access technologies, differences in performance outcomes associated with the use of non-internet-enabled (second-generation [2G or 2.5G]) phones relative to computers and internet-enabled (third- or fourth-generation [3G or 4G]) smartphones are explored. Additional performance benefits from using these access technologies for specific purposes and with additional DTs also are explored.

Moreover, the basic use of mobile phones to communicate with customers and to advertise using short message service (SMS) text messages (enabled by 2G phones) is compared with the more sophisticated use of accounting software, inventory control, and point-of-sale (POS) software enabled by 3G or higher technology accessed through computers. This advanced technology also has specific applications, through the internet, to find suppliers, to better understand customers, and to enable online banking. An assessment of statistically significant associations between these uses of DTs and firm performance—both unconditional and conditional (controlling for other correlates of DT use)—provides valuable insights to enrich the understanding of the microentrepreneurial business environment in African countries.

Unconditional outcomes. Micro-size enterprises that use DTs with internet-enabled computers or smartphones have higher unconditional productivity, sales, and jobs outcomes than nonusers, as well as higher outcomes than those enterprises using only 2G phones (figure 2.3). Microenterprises using smartphones have 2.8 times higher productivity, 6.0 times higher sales, and 1.9 times the number of jobs than nonusers. Computer users have 2.4 times higher productivity, 7.5 times higher sales, and 2.5 times higher jobs.

Across all DTs, the highest increase in sales from DTs is for the use of accounting software (13.7 times higher than nonusers) and the use of internet for online banking. The uses of accounting software and inventory control and POS software are associated with some of the highest jobs increases (3.8 times and 3.5 times higher than nonusers, respectively).

Conditional outcomes. Microenterprises that use DTs with internet-enabled computers or smartphones also have higher conditional job outcomes than nonusers as well as higher conditional outcomes than those enterprises using only 2G phones. Figure 2.4 reports findings of associations between DT use and microenterprise performance that explicitly control for whether the enterprise has ever had a loan, has access to electricity, is run by "transformational" entrepreneurs,[10] or has links with more sophisticated upstream suppliers and/or downstream buyers, among other available relevant variables; country fixed effects also are included.

Findings show that a greater range of more sophisticated DT uses by microenterprises based on internet-enabled computers or smartphones (light blue bars) relative to DT uses based on only 2G phones (dark blue bars) are conditionally associated with higher job levels. There is a positive progression in the number of more sophisticated DTs associated with higher productivity, sales, and job levels. Six internet-enabled and three non-internet-enabled DT uses are significant conditional correlates of higher job levels—as

FIGURE 2.3 Unconditional performance improvements among microenterprises using DTs relative to nonusers, selected African countries, 2017–18

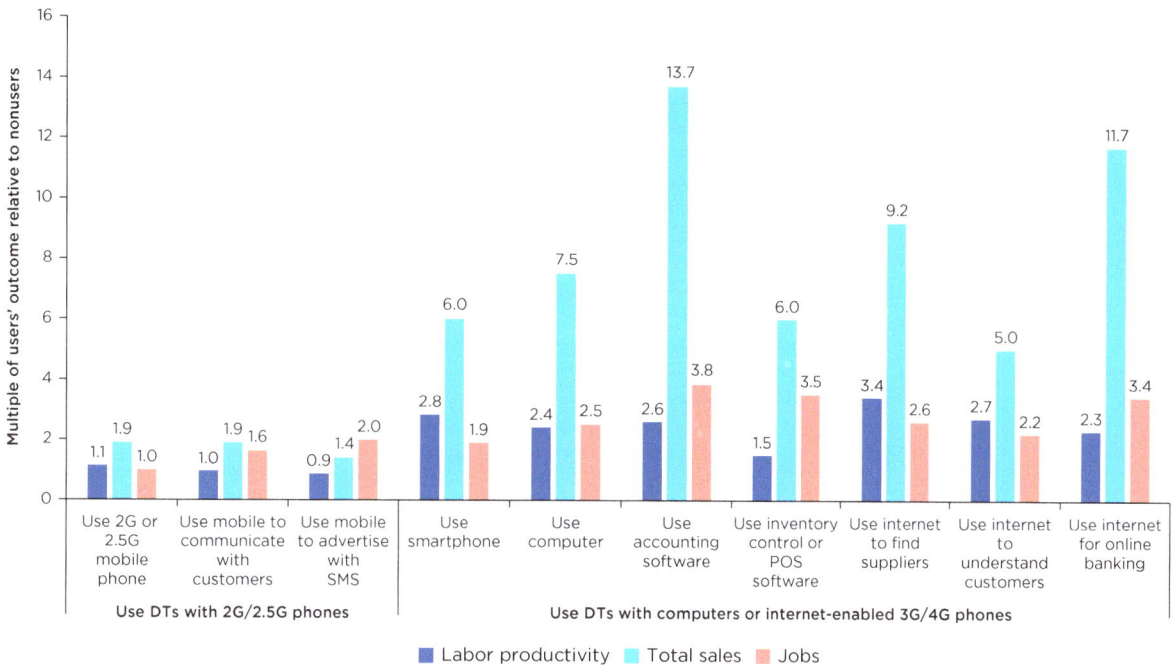

Source: Atiyas and Dutz 2023, based on 2017–18 Research ICT Africa (RIA) survey data.
Note: "Unconditional" refers to assessment of users relative to nonusers (nonusers = 1.0) for each specified digital technology (DT) across Ghana, Kenya, Mozambique, Nigeria, Senegal, South Africa, and Tanzania during 2017–18—without controlling for other correlates of DT use. Labor productivity is measured as value added (total sales minus raw materials and intermediate inputs plus water and electricity used in production) divided by the sum of full-time workers and the number of owners. 2G or 2.5G = second-generation mobile communications technology; 3G = third-generation; 4G = fourth-generation; POS = point of sale; SMS = short message service.

well as gender and age of the manager (being male and younger), the manager having vocational training, the owner being a transformational entrepreneur, and the enterprise having sophisticated upstream and/or downstream links with suppliers and customers. Other significant correlates for enterprises include the age and formality of the firms as well as whether the firm has ever had a loan and has electricity. The level of schooling of the manager is also a significant positive conditional correlate of productivity, sales, and wages per worker.

The more sophisticated DT uses that are conditionally associated, at statistical significance, with some performance outcomes include using a 3G/4G smartphone; using a computer; using the internet for email, to better understand customers, for online banking, and for recruitment; and using accounting and inventory control or POS software. More specifically, the largest positive significant conditional correlates of higher job levels are using the internet for recruitment, using accounting software, and using inventory control or POS software. Importantly, use of DTs for these simple management functions is more strongly associated with jobs than are most other uses of DTs reported by microenterprises: firms using accounting and inventory control or POS software are associated with a roughly 1.6-person larger firm size (0.47 and 0.44 log points, respectively) than those not using them.

FIGURE 2.4 Association between microenterprises' use of technologies and higher productivity, sales, and jobs, selected African countries, 2017–18

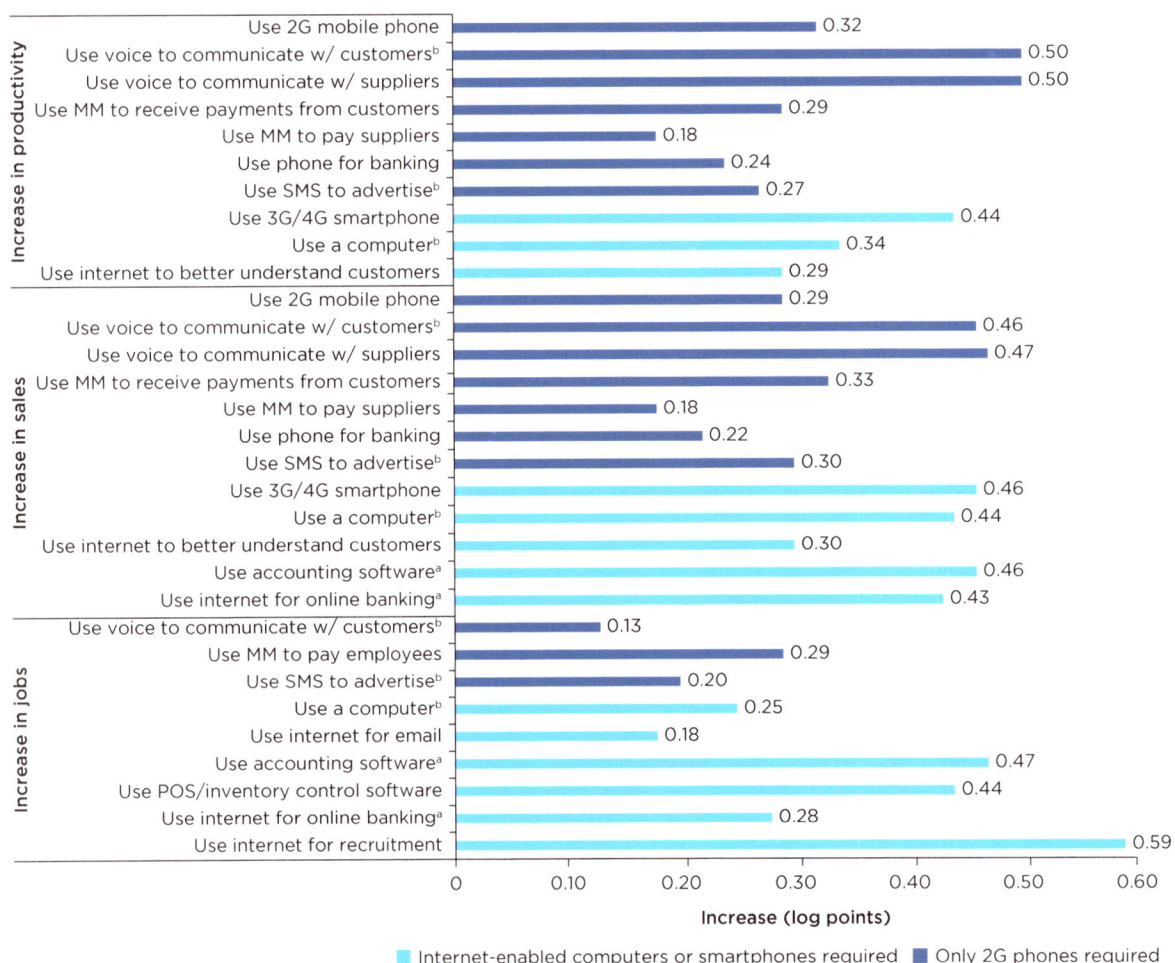

Source: Atiyas and Dutz 2023, based on 2017–18 Research ICT Africa (RIA) survey data.

Note: The figure shows the association between average microenterprise use of selected digital technologies (DTs) and productivity, sales, and jobs. The included business-related uses of DTs—listed in order from simple-access technologies to more sophisticated uses—are those for which the conditional correlates are significant at least at the 5 percent level based on ordinary least squares regressions (with robust standard errors) of the respective performance variable in logs on dummy variables representing the use of individual DTs by each enterprise. Light blue bars represent those DTs with computers or smartphones; dark blue bars represent those with non-internet-enabled DTs. Each number indicates how many log points higher the respective performance variable is, on average, for microenterprises using the DT relative to nonuser microenterprises. Controls include manager age and gender of owner(s), schooling and vocational training, firm age and age squared, having electricity, having had a loan and having a line of credit/credit facility with suppliers, whether the owner is transformational, links with more sophisticated upstream suppliers or downstream customers, informal and urban/rural status, and sector, plus country fixed effects. The data cover 3,325 firms, 73 percent of which are informal, across Ghana, Kenya, Mozambique, Nigeria, Senegal, South Africa, and Tanzania during 2017–18. The median microenterprise is self-employed with no full-time workers. Productivity is measured as value added (total sales minus raw materials and intermediate inputs plus water and electricity used in production) divided by the sum of full-time workers and the number of owners. Employment is the number of full-time employees plus owners. 2G = second-generation mobile communications technology; 3G = third-generation; 4G = fourth-generation; MM = mobile money; POS = point of sale; SMS = short message service.

a. Variable is significant across all three performance outcomes: productivity, sales, and jobs.
b. Variable is significant across both sales and jobs.

Overall benefits of DT use for firms and job growth

The large, statistically significant associations between use of internet-enabled DTs and more productive firms that generate more jobs suggest that DT use could also lead to more competitive firms, even among informal microenterprises. As firms create more jobs, they likely benefit significantly more from these technologies.

As the next subsection emphasizes, these findings also highlight how few firms take advantage of these benefits. The findings suggest that the adoption of relatively simple DTs together with smartphones and computers to improve basic management functions—as well as communications, learning, recruitment, and banking—should be a critical component of a more inclusive job growth agenda.

Lag in DT use by small enterprises

A large technological gap persists across enterprises in Africa. Despite the large benefits of DT adoption and use in terms of productivity and inclusive jobs growth, enterprises have low uptake and use, including in agriculture relative to manufacturing and service firms, smaller relative to larger firms, informal relative to formal firms, and most firms in African countries relative to global peer countries.

Average lag across all African enterprises

African enterprises on average lag in the use of DTs and complementary technologies. Based on the novel FAT technological sophistication index introduced earlier (figures 2.1 and 2.2), table 2.1 presents the average level of technological sophistication of enterprises with at least five full-time workers, by available countries, across three measures: the enterprises' average level of technological sophistication across ABFs, average sophistication across GBFs that are common across all firms, and average sophistication across SBFs.

TABLE 2.1 Comparison of enterprises' average technological sophistication, by business function type, selected African and comparator countries, 2019–21

Country	ABFs	GBFs	SBFs
Brazil	2.3	2.5	1.9
Vietnam	1.9	1.9	1.8
Ghana	1.6	1.5	1.7
Kenya	1.6	1.6	1.5
Senegal[a]	1.3	1.3	1.3
Formal	1.6	1.7	1.6
Informal	1.2	1.2	1.2

Source: Based on data from Cirera, Comin, and Cruz 2022, using 2019–21 FAT (Firm-level Adoption of Technology) survey data.
Note: The table presents the average level of technological sophistication of enterprises (with five or more full-time workers) by country across three measures: the average technological sophistication across all business functions (ABFs); average sophistication across general business functions (GBFs) that are common across all firms; and average sophistication across sector-specific business functions (SBFs), covering the agricultural crops, food processing, apparel, and retail sectors. Estimated means are calculated using sampling weights. Enterprises included in the FAT surveys are those employing at least five full-time workers.
a. Senegal data are summarized countrywide and then disaggregated into formal and informal firms (the latter being those without a formal accounting system according to SYSCOA [accounting standards of the West African Economic Union] or an alternate formal harmonized accounting system).

The table shows that most firms across all countries listed in the table are far from the global technological frontier (a maximum level of 5 across each business function). It also shows that African countries have an average technological sophistication across ABFs that is lower than comparator countries for which data are available. The average firm across all African countries is below the level of 2 (the level at which DTs start to be used for most business functions), indicating that most African enterprises are still using largely nondigital analog technologies for most business functions. The table also shows the large gap in technological sophistication between the average formal and informal enterprise in Senegal across ABFs, GBFs, and SBFs.

Relatively greater lags in the agriculture sector

The largest gap in technological sophistication across countries is in the agriculture sector rather than the manufacturing or services sectors. Both the highest and next-to-lowest of all country-level technological sophistication indexes across ABFs across enterprises in specific sectors are in agriculture (figure 2.5).

FIGURE 2.5 **Technological sophistication of enterprises, by broad sector, selected African and comparator countries, 2019–21**

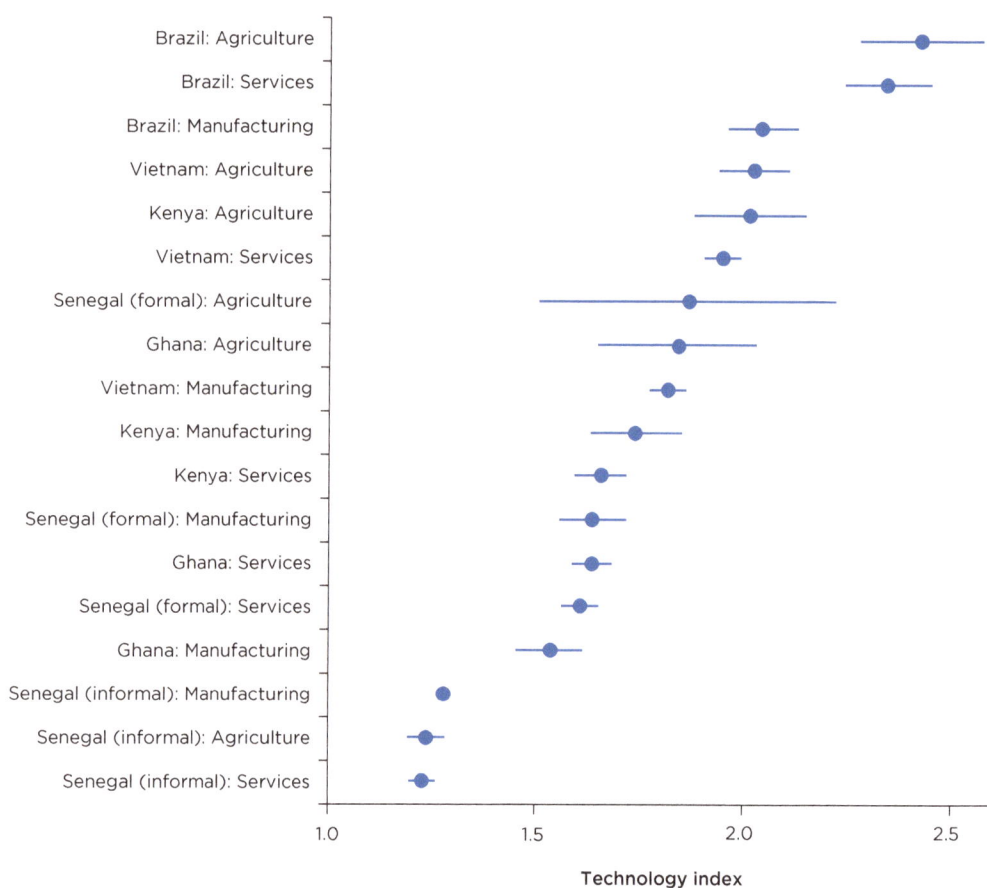

Source: Based on Cirera, Comin, and Cruz 2022, using 2019–21 FAT (Firm-level Adoption of Technology) survey data.
Note: "Technology index" values are the estimated all business function (ABF) averages, using sampling weights, controlling for differences across each country in the size composition of enterprises. Index values are shown in order of highest (top) to lowest (bottom). The confidence interval (– to +) reflects a 95 percent confidence level. Enterprises included in the FAT surveys are those employing at least five full-time workers. Senegal data are disaggregated into formal and informal firms, the latter being those without a formal accounting system according to SYSCOA (accounting standards of the West African Economic Union) or an alternate formal harmonized accounting system.

That Brazilian agriculture has the highest overall index indicates that its agriculture sector is quite technologically sophisticated, more so than its manufacturing and services sectors—incorporating the use of DT sensors for precision agriculture irrigation and fertilizing; drones controlled by advanced software for pest detection; tractors with integrated computer systems for training, pruning, and harvesting; and modified atmosphere postharvest packaging (adding a particular gas atmosphere to extend shelf life within sealed packages) digitally linked to the harvesting process. Soybeans are the most important crop in Brazil based on production value, with cultivation of corn, sugarcane, coffee, cotton, rice, cassava, and citrus also important, among others. So Brazilian agricultural technological sophistication has not developed solely because of a few technologically demanding specialty niche products.

That Senegal's informal agriculture has the next-to-lowest overall index is no doubt representative of informal agriculture across Africa, even among informal farms with five or more workers. And Senegal's average technological sophistication index—less than 1.5—indicates that most Senegalese firms use analog, predigital technologies for most business functions.

Relatively greater lags among small enterprises

Africa's small enterprises lag in the use of DTs and complementary technologies relative to larger enterprises. Figure 2.6 shows that, in each country, small formal firms (5–19 workers) lag large formal firms (100 workers or more) in the average technological sophistication index across ABFs. It also shows that large firms in Kenya and Senegal have lower technological sophistication, on average, than small firms in Brazil. Interestingly, while small and medium informal firms in Senegal have some of the lowest average technological sophistication indexes, large informal enterprises have the absolute lowest average technological sophistication index—suggesting that at least some large informal firms may face lower market competition, are protected because of ethnic or political links, or are functioning for non-profit-maximizing objectives.[11]

That the average technological sophistication indexes for small and large informal enterprises as well as for small firms in African countries are all less than or approximately 1.5 indicates that most small firms use analog, predigital technologies for most business functions.

Lags in use of basic DTs for GBFs. Small African firms lag especially relative to larger African firms and global peers in the use of even the most basic DTs for GBFs. GBFs such as business administration, marketing, and quality control are the functions for which the FAT technology adoption index maps most directly with DT use. That is, the technology options beyond the nondigital analog processes for GBFs—say, on the handwritten or face-to-face level (technology index level 1)—are all DTs with increasing levels of sophistication, from the simplest Excel spreadsheet to ERP (enterprise resource planning) software integrated with production planning for business administration.

On average, no small firm in any African country with data available surpasses level 2 of the technology sophistication index for any of the seven GBFs identified as common across all enterprises: all of the dark blue lines (designating small firms) remain inside level 2 for Ghana, Kenya, Malawi, and Senegal (figure 2.7). In contrast, the average medium and large firms across African countries typically use DTs (beyond level 2) for at least one or more of the seven GBFs. Similarly, the average small firms in both Brazil and Vietnam use DTs (beyond level 2) for at least one or more of the seven GBFs.

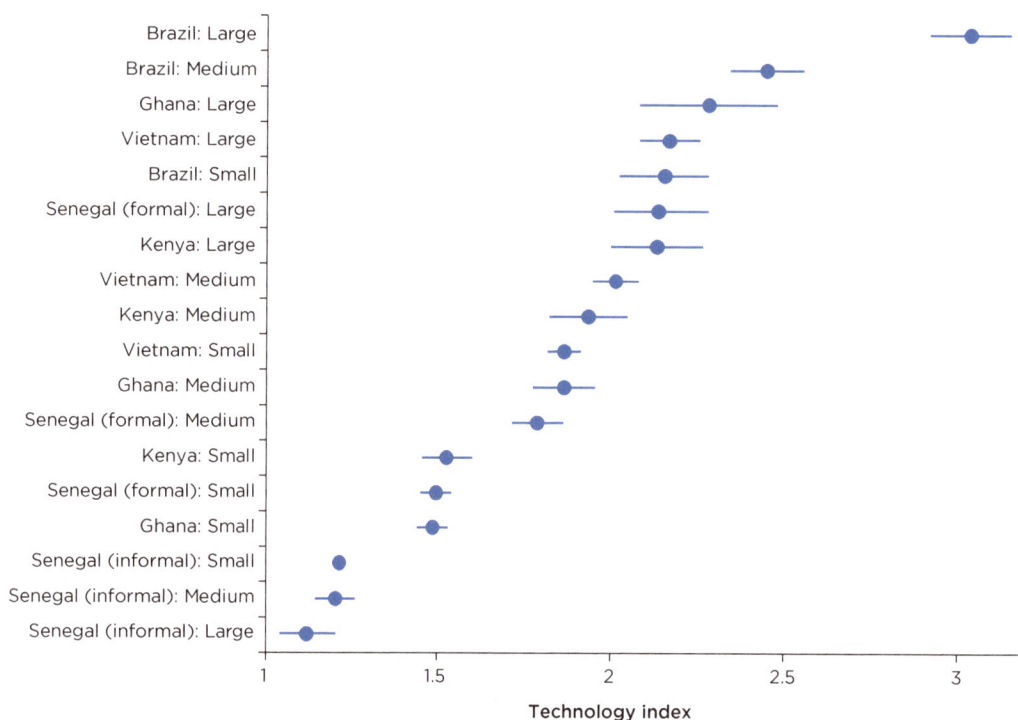

Source: Based on Cirera, Comin, and Cruz 2022, using 2019–21 FAT (Firm-level Adoption of Technology) survey data.
Note: "Technology index" values are the estimated averages of technological sophistication across all business functions (ABFs), using sampling weights, controlling for differences across each country in the sector composition of enterprises. The confidence interval (– to +) reflects a 95 percent confidence level. Enterprises included in the FAT surveys are those employing at least five full-time workers. "Large" firms have 100 or more employees; "medium" firms, 20–99 employees; and "small" firms, 5–19 employees. Senegal data are disaggregated into formal and informal firms, the latter being those without a formal accounting system according to SYSCOA (accounting standards of the West African Economic Union) or an alternate formal harmonized accounting system.

Lags in basic access technologies. Small African firms also lag relative to larger African firms and global peers in the use of key access technologies for other internet-enabled DTs—namely, smartphones and computers. In Senegal, 25–26 percent of small firms use smartphones (a similar share for both formal and informal enterprises), whereas 50 percent of small firms in Malawi use them, roughly 70 percent in Ghana and Kenya, and about 60 percent in Brazil and Vietnam (figure 2.8).

Typically, larger firms are more frequent users of smartphones, including in Ghana, Kenya, and among formal firms in Senegal, as well as in Brazil. In Malawi and Vietnam, however, large firms are lower users of smartphones than small firms. The lowest use of smartphones is by large informal firms in Senegal, mirroring their low levels on the technology sophistication index (as shown in figure 2.6).

As for computer use by formal firms, small African firms invariably lag larger firms: 63 percent of small firms in Ghana, 73 percent in Kenya, 70 percent in Malawi, and 90 percent in Senegal use computers, relative to 98–100 percent of large firms. In contrast, in Brazil and Vietnam, almost all small firms—96 percent and 100 percent, respectively—are also already using computers. This disparity indicates a significant lag among smaller

FIGURE 2.7 Use of DTs by enterprises, by firm size and general business function, selected African and comparator countries, 2019–21

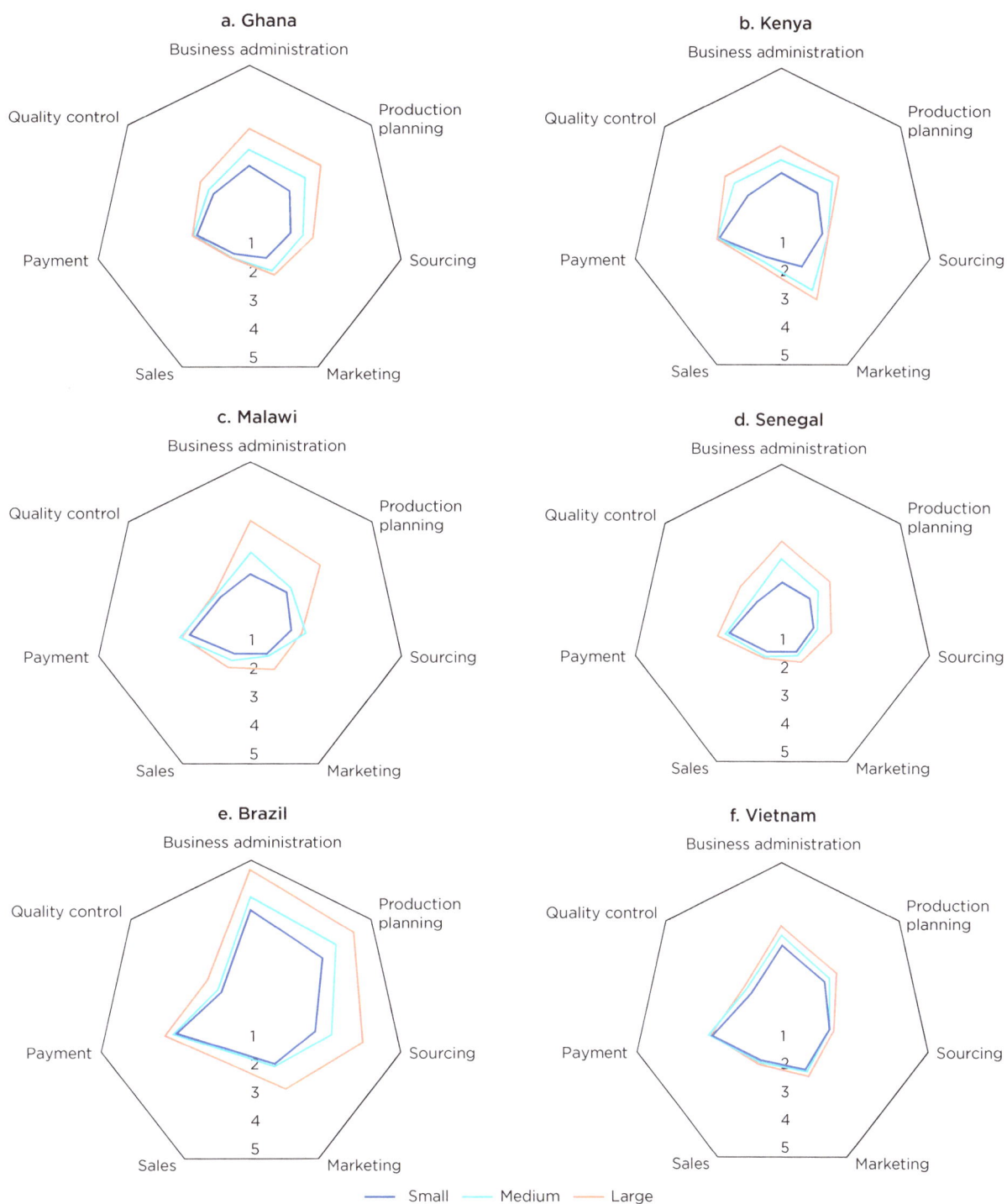

a. Ghana

b. Kenya

c. Malawi

d. Senegal

e. Brazil

f. Vietnam

— Small — Medium — Large

Source: Based on Cirera, Comin, and Cruz 2022, using 2019–21 FAT (Firm-level Adoption of Technology) survey data.
Note: The radar diagrams show the relative levels (1–5) on the index of technology used most intensively by each firm for each of seven general business functions (GBFs), averaged across all firms. Level 1 represents analog, nondigital technologies, and levels 2 and higher represent increasingly more sophisticated digital technologies (DTs). Enterprises included in the FAT surveys are those employing at least five full-time workers. "Large" firms have 100 or more employees; "medium" firms, 20–99 employees; and "small" firms, 5–19 employees. Only in Senegal was it possible to draw a representative sample of informal firms; hence, the Senegal sample encompasses representative subsamples of both formal and informal firms.

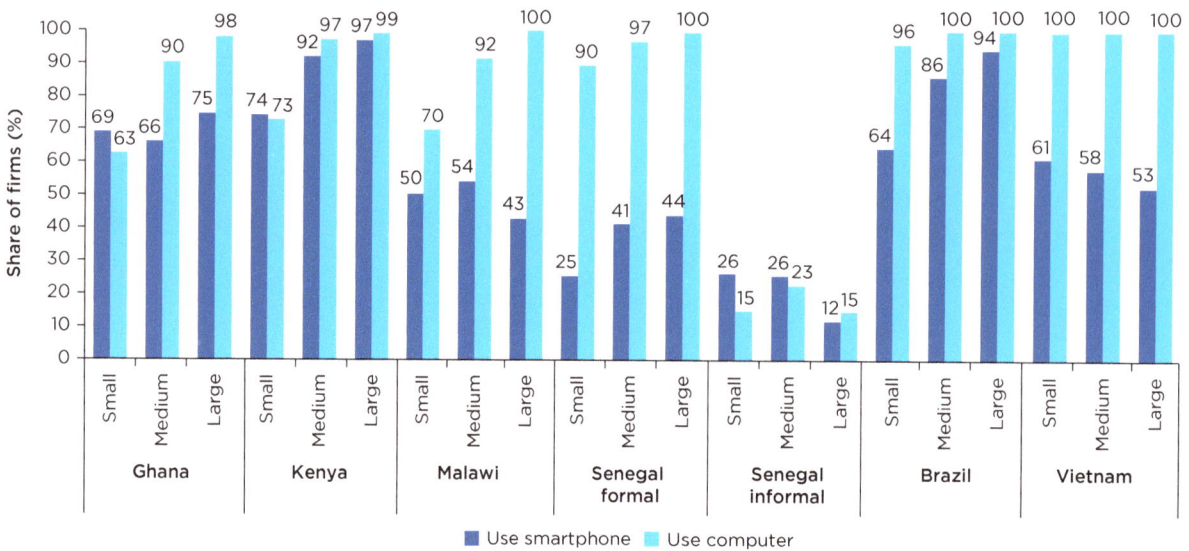

Source: Based on Cirera, Comin, and Cruz 2022, using 2019–21 FAT (Firm-level Adoption of Technology) survey data.
Note: Included enterprises are those employing at least five full-time workers. "Large" firms have 100 or more employees; "medium" firms, 20–99 employees; and "small" firms, 5–19 employees. Senegal data are disaggregated into formal and informal firms, the latter being those without a formal accounting system according to SYSCOA (accounting standards of the West African Economic Union) or an alternate formal harmonized accounting system.

African firms in the use of a DT that has already become essential and ubiquitous for small firms in available global peer countries. Again, the low use of computers by informal firms in Senegal is striking, with only 15 percent of both small and large informal firms using a computer.

Lags in more sophisticated DTs. As for the use of more sophisticated DTs that must be accessed through internet-enabled smartphones or computers, small firms also lag relative to larger firms, and African firms lag relative to Brazil. The average small firm lags the average large firm across the board—in African countries as well as global comparators Brazil and Vietnam—in both the use of ERP software for business purposes and the use of big data supported by artificial intelligence (AI)–based machine learning (ML) algorithms (figure 2.9).

Small firms are typically expected to have less complex management challenges than larger firms. However, ERP software, typically a suite of business applications, allows even small enterprises to track business resources—cash, raw materials, production capacity, and sales—and the status of business commitments such as delivery orders, purchase orders, and payroll, and thereby facilitates a more efficient management of any firm.

Even relatively simpler versions of ERP are typically offered as software-as-a-service (SaaS) products supported by downloads from the cloud. SaaS products generate significant cost savings for businesses by eliminating the need for in-house, fixed-cost investments in the acquisition and regular upgrade of these business tools. By converting what traditionally were high fixed costs into lower variable costs, they also facilitate entry and experimentation, including by young start-up enterprises—because, if the initial business plan does not work out, the entrepreneur can flexibly try a new idea with

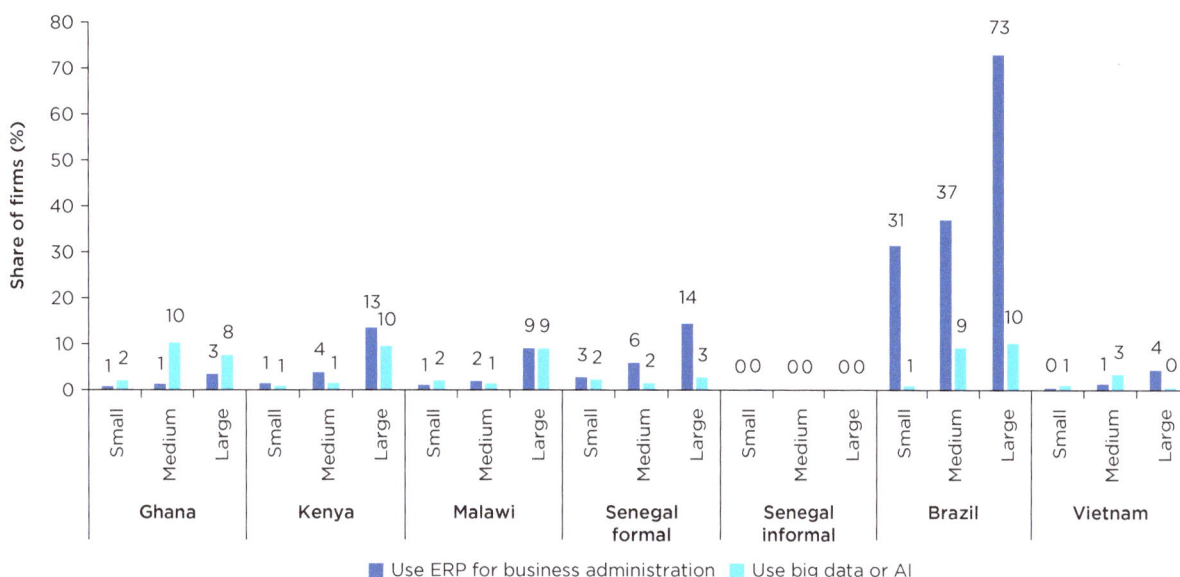

Source: Based on Cirera, Comin, and Cruz 2022, using 2019–21 FAT (Firm-level Adoption of Technology) survey data.
Note: Senegal data are disaggregated into formal and informal firms, the latter being those without a formal accounting system according to SYSCOA (accounting standards of the West African Economic Union) or an alternate formal harmonized accounting system. AI = artificial intelligence; ERP = enterprise resource planning.

different SaaS business tools at low cost. Already one in three small firms in Brazil uses such ERP services (figure 2.9). And big-data-supported digital services such as weather prediction and insurance pricing models can help offer better services even to small firms.

Although it may not be surprising that not a single informal Senegal enterprise uses ERP—given that these data define "informal" as not using a formal accounting system—in principle, even informal enterprises could benefit from the production- and sales-related insights that big data now enable. However, even among large African firms, a much smaller percentage of firms uses ERP than in Brazil: 3 percent of large firms in Ghana, 13 percent in Kenya, 9 percent in Malawi, and 14 percent of large formal firms in Senegal use ERP software, versus 73 percent of large firms in Brazil.

Regarding use of big data in AI-based ML algorithms, 8 percent of large firms in Ghana, 10 percent in Kenya, 9 percent in Malawi, and 3 percent of formal large firms in Senegal report using these DTs—in most of the African countries, comparable to large formal firms in Brazil (also 10 percent).

Particular lags among microenterprises. Microenterprises lag even more in the use of DTs, with large digital divides within gender and age subgroups of owners (figure 2.10). Among these groups, microenterprises owned by young men (30 years old or younger) are consistently the largest users of internet-enabled DTs. Whereas 13 percent of micro-size firms owned by younger men use a smartphone, only 3 percent of those owned by older women use one. The digital divide in computer use is even larger: only 2 percent of firms owned by young women use a computer, whereas 4 times the share of firms owned by younger men (8 percent) use one.

FIGURE 2.10 Average microenterprise uptake and use of DTs, by owner age and gender subgroup, selected African countries, 2017–18

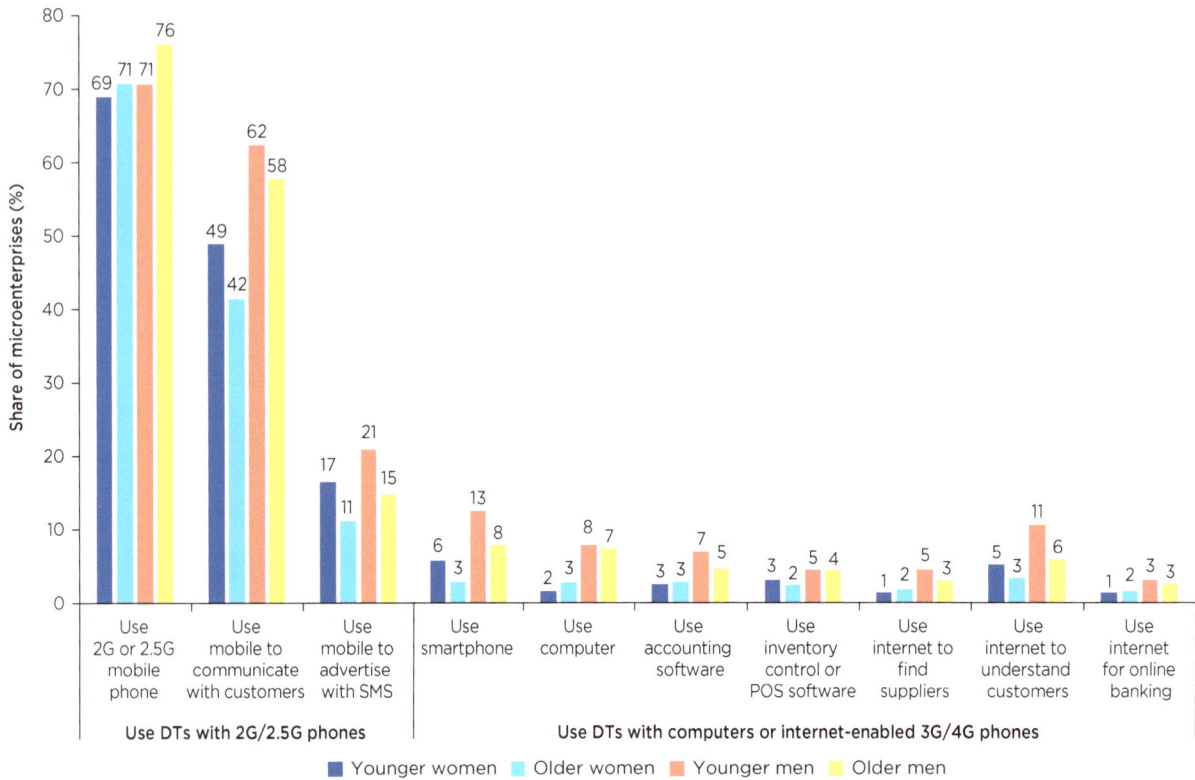

Source: Atiyas and Dutz 2023, based on 2017–18 Research ICT Africa (RIA) survey data.
Note: The RIA After Access 2017–18 business survey covered 2,174 formal and informal microenterprises that responded to owner gender and age (youth = 30 years and younger) questions across Ghana, Kenya, Mozambique, Nigeria, Senegal, South Africa, and Tanzania. The median microenterprise is informal and self-employed with no full-time workers. 2G or 2.5G = second-generation mobile communications technology; 3G = third-generation; 4G = fourth-generation; POS = point of sale; SMS = short message service.

How digital-solution businesses can support enterprise use of DTs

Digital-solution businesses in Africa have so far located most densely and received the most total investment in larger anglophone markets (Zhu et al. 2022). Nigeria, Kenya, and South Africa (in that order) are the African countries with the highest digital business densities and total investments, after controlling for per capita income (figure 2.11).

These three countries are also among the top 15 worldwide in digital business density and total investments, controlling for per capita income.[12] These findings suggest that market size and purchasing power are important determinants in the initial setup location and headquarters decisions of digital-solution businesses.

Sub-Saharan Africa is the only lower-income region whose top digital-solution business subsectors are all linked to productivity-enhancing services—a promising configuration to support inclusive growth and stimulate greater uptake by user enterprises. It is also the only lower-income region, in addition to high-income countries, in which all top five digital business subsectors (by total investments) provide business-to-business (B2B) digital solutions directly linked to supporting enterprise productivity growth (table 2.2).

FIGURE 2.11 **Top Sub-Saharan African countries in digital-solution business density and total investment, 2020**

a. Top 20 by digital business density

Nigeria	0.191
Kenya	0.175
South Africa	0.139
Uganda	0.093
Ghana	0.049
Rwanda	0.040
Tanzania	0.039
Ethiopia	0.025
Senegal	0.022
Zambia	0.020
Mozambique	0.020
Zimbabwe	0.017
Malawi	0.012
Sudan	0.011
Côte d'Ivoire	0.007
Cameroon	0.007
Mali	0.006
Angola	0.003
Namibia	0.002
Botswana	0.001

Number of digital businesses
(GDP per capita ratio)

b. Top 15 by total investments

Nigeria	1.683
Kenya	1.122
South Africa	0.759
Angola	0.358
Ghana	0.270
Tanzania	0.181
Zambia	0.086
Ethiopia	0.039
Senegal	0.015
Uganda	0.014
Zimbabwe	0.009
Rwanda	0.005
Botswana	0.004
Namibia	0.003
Côte d'Ivoire	0.001

Total funding
(GDP per capita ratio)

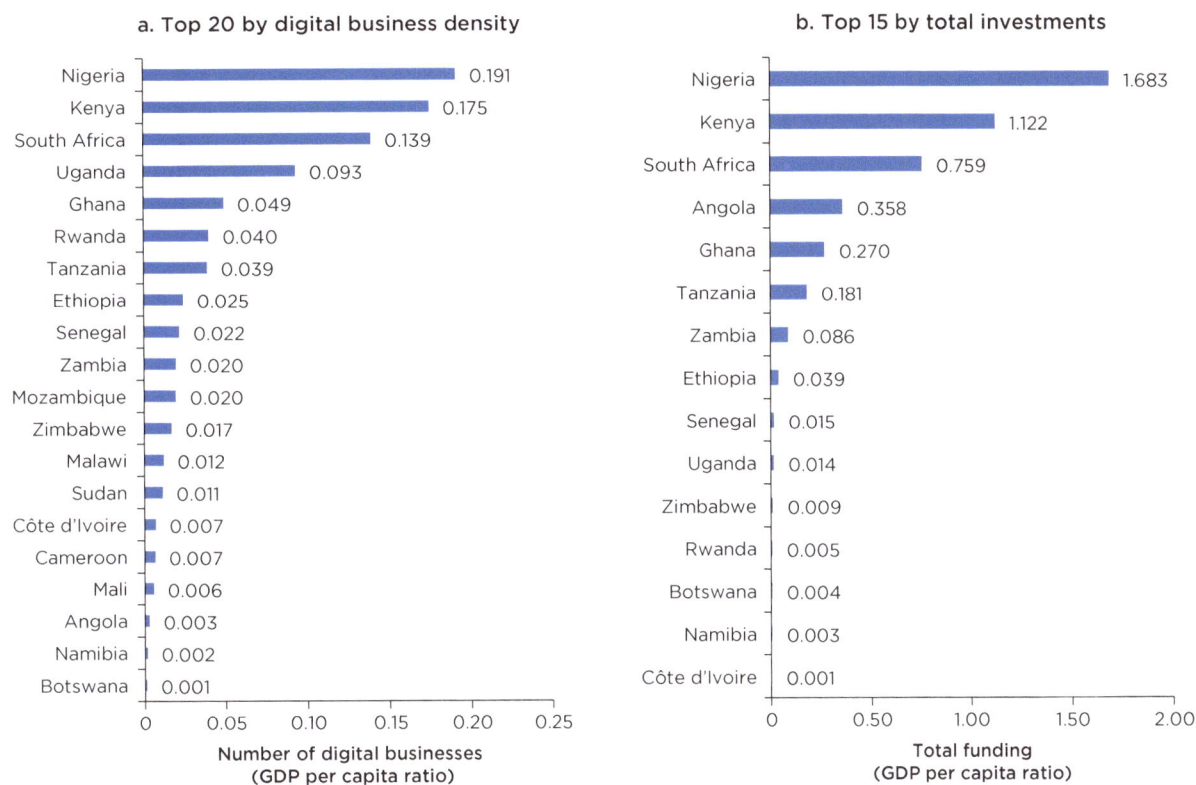

Source: Digital Business Database (as of 2020) of the World Bank's Finance, Competitiveness & Innovation Global Practice (FCI GP).
Note: The number of digital businesses per unit of gross domestic product (GDP) per capita (panel a) and total funding (in US dollars, millions) per unit of GDP per capita (panel b)—both in 2019 current US dollars—are based on the the World Bank's Digital Business 2020 Database, which includes 184,000 digital businesses extracted from CB Insights, Pitchbook, and Briterbridges by the World Bank's Global Markets and Technology Unit of the FCI GP. Countries with five or more digital businesses that operate and are headquartered in the country are included.

TABLE 2.2 **Top five digital business subsectors, ranked by share of total investment in B2B productivity solutions, by region, 2020**

Sub-Saharan Africa	East Asia and Pacific	Europe and Central Asia	Latin America and the Caribbean	Middle East and North Africa	South Asia	High-income countries
Telecom (17%)	Mobility tech (10%)	E-commerce (22%)	Fintech (17%)	E-commerce (25%)	E-commerce (22%)	Fintech (10%)
Fintech (15%)	E-commerce (10%)	Travel tech (8%)	Logistics tech (10%)	Telecom (14%)	Fintech (14%)	Health tech (8%)
E-commerce (11%)	Fintech (7%)	Fintech (7%)	E-commerce (9%)	Mobility tech (7%)	Business management tech (10%)	E-commerce (7%)
Logistics tech (8%)	Travel tech (6%)	Digital media (6%)	Entertainment tech (9%)	Digital media (5%)	Telecom (10%)	Business management tech (6%)
Health tech (4%)	Tech hardware (6%)	Entertainment tech (4%)	Food tech (7%)	Business management tech (5%)	Travel tech (10%)	Big data and analytics (5%)

Source: Digital Business Database (as of 2020) of the World Bank's Finance, Competitiveness & Innovation Global Practice.
Note: The table ranks the top five digital business subsectors in each region by share of total investment (shown in parentheses). "High-income countries" are those with gross national income per capita of US$12,536 or more. B2B = business-to-business.

Moreover, Sub-Saharan Africa is unique in having the most total investment in its telecommunications subsector. And it is the only region, in addition to the Middle East and North Africa and South Asia, with telecommunications in its top five digital business subsectors—linked to its ongoing sizable investments in digital infrastructure.[13]

The other top five digital business subsectors for Sub-Saharan Africa are financial technology (fintech), e-commerce, logistics tech, and health tech. In contrast, travel tech, mobility tech, entertainment tech, food tech, and digital media—which all appear in the top five subsectors of other low- and middle-income regions—are all business-to-consumer (B2C) subsectors that are more focused on selling directly to and profiting from consumer sales than on selling B2B digital solutions to businesses while supporting enterprise productivity upgrading.[14]

Notably, the concentration of investments in the top three subsectors in Sub-Saharan Africa—telecomunications, fintech, and e-commerce—jointly accounts for over 40 percent of total business-solution investments in the region. This pattern of investment concentration also exists in the Middle East and North Africa and South Asia regions. High-income countries, in contrast, have a much more diverse distribution of investments, with the top five subsectors accounting for only 36 percent of total investments in those countries.

Africa has huge potential for digital-solution business providers to expand across the continent. Only 3 percent of digital businesses headquartered in Sub-Saharan Africa (accounting for 4 percent of total investments) are regional businesses that operate in two or more countries in the region (figure 2.12, panels a and b). These regional digital businesses are mainly concentrated in fintech and e-commerce (figure 2.12, panels c and d). They also include other B2B productivity-enhancing, digital-solution business subsectors such as telecommunications, logistics tech, insure tech, big data and analytics, and business management tech. Interestingly, some regional digital businesses also offering B2C services that use a platform-based business model (in addition to e-commerce and fintech) include digital media, insure tech, health tech, and mobility tech—demonstrating the scalability of platform-driven digital business models in regional expansion and regional integration.

These trends indicate significant opportunities for large B2B digital businesses in Sub-Saharan Africa to expand services to other countries in the region, potentially helping to put these countries on a faster digital uptake trajectory with lower marginal uptake costs. Greater regional expansion and integration also would enable the continuous scaling and maturing of larger digital-solution provider businesses. It will be vital, as this expansion takes place, for policy makers and regulators to carefully monitor the risks of "winners take most" market dominance with possible anticompetitive business practices or acquisitions to avoid the stifling of local digital start-ups.

Regional digital-solution businesses are concentrated in major digital hubs. By far, Africa's largest hub for regional digital businesses is Kenya, accounting for 28 percent of the total number of regional firms (figure 2.13, panel a), followed by Ghana, Nigeria, and South Africa. Figure 2.13 (panels b and c) also shows the relative importance of regional businesses in Ghana, Kenya, and South Africa. Physical proximity is a possible factor partly explaining regional integration, but the unique role of a vibrant national digital business ecosystem also likely explains this uneven economic geography (Zhu et al. 2022).

FIGURE 2.12 **Local and regional shares, and top regional subsectors, of digital-solution providers,
Sub-Saharan Africa, 2020**

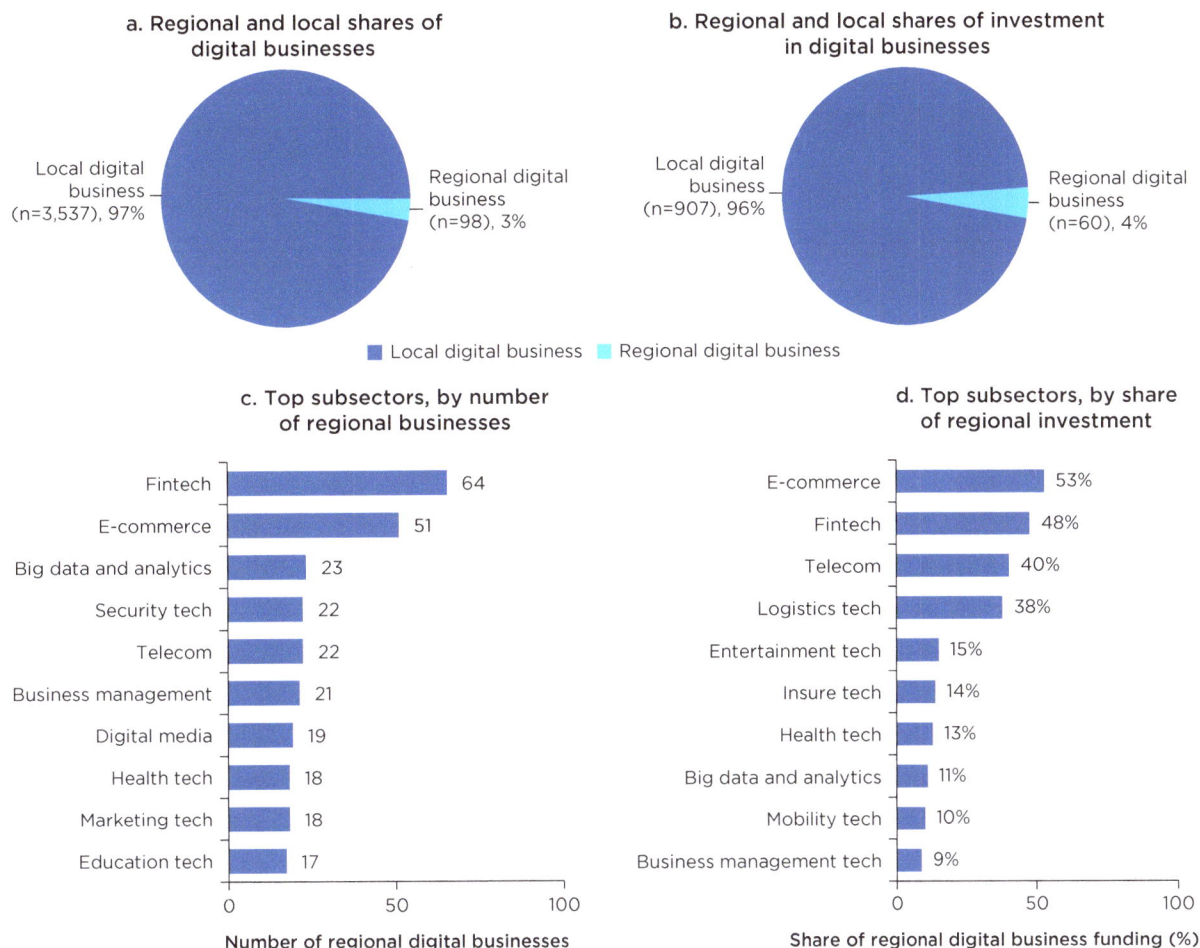

**a. Regional and local shares of
digital businesses**

Local digital
business
(n=3,537), 97%

Regional digital
business
(n=98), 3%

**b. Regional and local shares of investment
in digital businesses**

Local digital
business
(n=907), 96%

Regional digital
business
(n=60), 4%

■ Local digital business ■ Regional digital business

**c. Top subsectors, by number
of regional businesses**

Subsector	Number
Fintech	64
E-commerce	51
Big data and analytics	23
Security tech	22
Telecom	22
Business management	21
Digital media	19
Health tech	18
Marketing tech	18
Education tech	17

Number of regional digital businesses

**d. Top subsectors, by share
of regional investment**

Subsector	Share
E-commerce	53%
Fintech	48%
Telecom	40%
Logistics tech	38%
Entertainment tech	15%
Insure tech	14%
Health tech	13%
Big data and analytics	11%
Mobility tech	10%
Business management tech	9%

Share of regional digital business funding (%)

Source: Digital Business Database (as of 2020) of the World Bank's Finance, Competitiveness & Innovation Global Practice.
Note: Regional businesses are digital-solution providers headquartered in Sub-Saharan Africa that operate in two or more countries in the region. The pie chart in panel a shows the relative share of local and regional digital businesses based on number of enterprises. The bar charts in panels c and d present the top 10 digital business subsectors by number of enterprises and regional share of investment, respectively. Fintech = financial technology.

Many Kenyan regional firms operate in neighboring countries. However, both Kenyan and Ghanaian regional firms have been expanding in countries regardless of proximity: Kenyan firms also operate in Ghana, Nigeria, and South Africa, while Ghanaian firms also operate in Kenya, South Africa, and Tanzania. This suggests that vibrant national digital business ecosystems can serve as key test beds for solutions and facilitate regional expansions—likely, at least partly, because of their favorable digital start-up and capital market policies. Neighboring countries may benefit from positive spillover effects from increased regional integration and lower uptake costs, whereas smaller countries less connected to the hubs may experience a larger digital divide.

FIGURE 2.13 Major hubs of regional digital-solution businesses, Sub-Saharan Africa, 2020

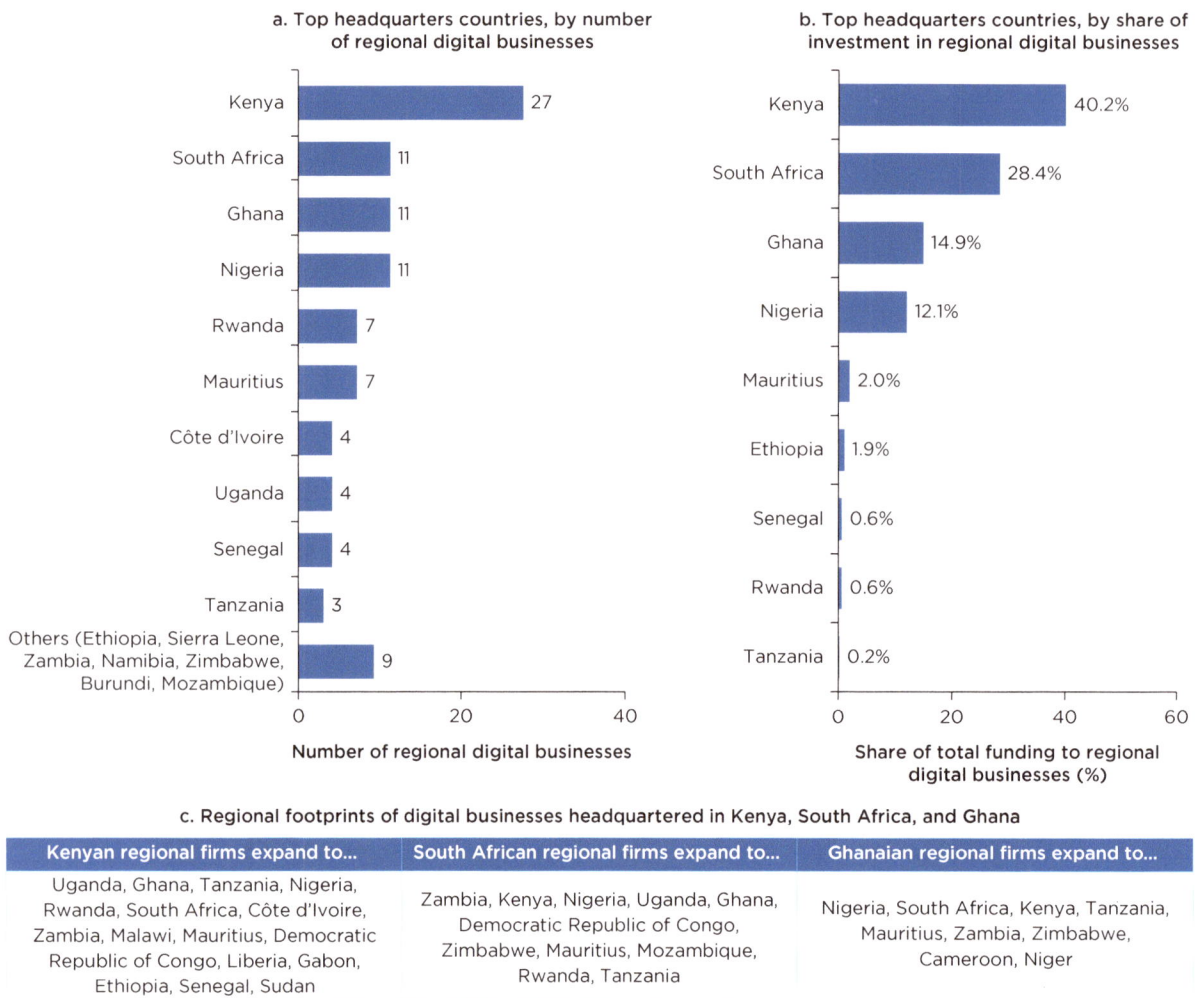

a. Top headquarters countries, by number of regional digital businesses

Country	Number
Kenya	27
South Africa	11
Ghana	11
Nigeria	11
Rwanda	7
Mauritius	7
Côte d'Ivoire	4
Uganda	4
Senegal	4
Tanzania	3
Others (Ethiopia, Sierra Leone, Zambia, Namibia, Zimbabwe, Burundi, Mozambique)	9

Number of regional digital businesses

b. Top headquarters countries, by share of investment in regional digital businesses

Country	Share
Kenya	40.2%
South Africa	28.4%
Ghana	14.9%
Nigeria	12.1%
Mauritius	2.0%
Ethiopia	1.9%
Senegal	0.6%
Rwanda	0.6%
Tanzania	0.2%

Share of total funding to regional digital businesses (%)

c. Regional footprints of digital businesses headquartered in Kenya, South Africa, and Ghana

Kenyan regional firms expand to...	South African regional firms expand to...	Ghanaian regional firms expand to...
Uganda, Ghana, Tanzania, Nigeria, Rwanda, South Africa, Côte d'Ivoire, Zambia, Malawi, Mauritius, Democratic Republic of Congo, Liberia, Gabon, Ethiopia, Senegal, Sudan	Zambia, Kenya, Nigeria, Uganda, Ghana, Democratic Republic of Congo, Zimbabwe, Mauritius, Mozambique, Rwanda, Tanzania	Nigeria, South Africa, Kenya, Tanzania, Mauritius, Zambia, Zimbabwe, Cameroon, Niger

Source: Digital Business Database (as of 2020) of the World Bank's Finance, Competitiveness & Innovation Global Practice.
Note: Regional businesses are digital-solution providers headquartered in Sub-Saharan Africa that operate in two or more countries in the region. Panels a and b present the number of enterprises and the total share of investment in those enterprises, respectively. Panel c lists the operating countries from the highest to the lowest number of regional businesses present.

COVID-19 and digital divides

Acceleration of DT uptake and use as digital divides increased

Enterprise responses to the COVID-19 pandemic have led to an overall faster increase in DT uptake and use although the responses have been uneven, with digital divides across countries and types of firms increasing because of the pandemic. The COVID-19 shock and attendant lockdown and social distancing measures implemented in many countries generated additional incentives for firms to adopt or increase the use of DTs. They did so because DTs can enable firms to change work, procurement, financing, production, sales, and payment patterns more easily and to better adjust when social distancing requirements limit face-to-face production and consumption interactions and when input bottlenecks and changing consumption patterns arise (box 2.1).

Rapid diffusion of website technology during COVID-19

The COVID-19 pandemic accelerated the pace of digitalization globally, yet little is known about the dynamics of relevant technology adoption across countries during the crisis. Evidence from a new database (BuiltWith)—comprising data on nearly the universe of websites and over 30,000 technologies embedded within them—shows a rapid growth of three types of technologies related to online transactions in 2020: e-commerce, online payments, and digital advertising. More important, their growth appears to have narrowed preexisting digital divides across countries: those countries with the fastest growth during 2020 had less intensive use of these technologies in 2019.[a]

Sub-Saharan African websites lag in technology use relative to other low- and middle-income regions and high-income economies. At the onset of the pandemic, for example, only 31 percent of African websites had embedded some form of analytics as opposed to 45 percent in low- and middle-income countries elsewhere, and 7 percent had technology for e-payments relative to double-digit shares in other regions.[b]

Adoption accelerated considerably during the COVID-19 pandemic. Globally, new websites during 2020 were almost twice as likely as the 2019 entrants had been to use e-commerce or online payments. And growth has been considerably faster in Sub-Saharan Africa, exceeding the world average in nearly every category and partially closing gaps relative to other regions. As in other regions, those countries with the lowest initial technology levels experienced the fastest growth (figure B2.1.1). The pandemic shifted the trend in digital development, taking advantage of increasingly accessible technologies for online transactions, such as off-the-shelf e-commerce websites, as well as digital financial services like mobile money.

FIGURE B2.1.1 Growth of e-payment use in websites, Sub-Saharan African countries versus other regions, 2019–20

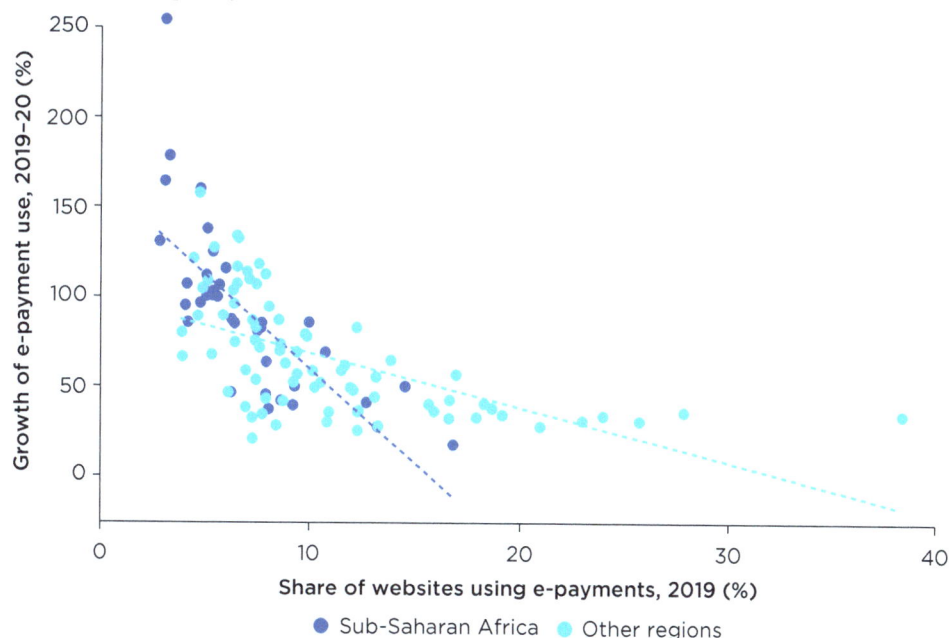

Source: Ragoussis and Timmis 2022.
Note: The chart includes data on website use of e-payments in 119 low- and middle-income countries, of which 41 are in Sub-Saharan Africa. Dashed lines are linear best-fit lines. The full source paper analyzes a sample of 185 countries across all regions and income groups.

(continued)

BOX 2.1
Rapid diffusion of website technology during COVID-19 *(continued)*

Although the technological *sophistication* of the average website has improved, BuiltWith and World Development Indicators data show that the *density* of websites in Sub-Saharan Africa remains the lowest in the world: on average, 8 websites per 10,000 people. Most countries in the continent count fewer than 1 website per 10,000 people, with South Africa being a notable outlier (121 websites per 10,000 people). The distance is huge relative to high-income economies, which typically record over 300 websites per 10,000 people, as well as to more advanced low- and middle-income regions like East Asia and Pacific and Latin America and the Caribbean, with an average of 50 websites per 10,000 people.

The rise of new websites in Sub-Saharan Africa, although not clearly attributable to the synchronized lockdowns, suggests that the region has been catching up during the pandemic. Its website growth has been higher than in any other region—double the average rate observed in high-income economies. But, at this low level of website *density*, meaningful progress would require significant investment in infrastructure, skills, and access for digital markets to flourish. Africa has much to gain from this prospect.

a. We consider cross-country differences, but the data do not allow us to examine divides between firms within a country.
b. The data do not capture e-commerce via social media platforms, so are likely to represent a lower bound of all technology diffusion.

Comparing Sub-Saharan African countries with lower-income countries in other regions, the pandemic has led to a roughly similar increase in uptake and use of DTs, though the uptake gap between small and large firms is greater and the share of firms investing in DTs is lower. In the World Bank's COVID-19 Business Pulse Surveys (BPS), across enterprise size groups, roughly 50 percent of interviewed firms across Africa as well as in low- to middle-income countries elsewhere increased their uptake and use of DTs. However, the gap between large and small firms is significantly greater in Africa (figure 2.14, panel a).[15]

Regarding increased investments, the shares of firms investing in new DTs are significantly lower across size groups for Africa: 25 percent of interviewed firms invested in new DTs versus 32 percent across other available low- and middle-income countries (figure 2.14, panel b).[16]

Significant heterogeneity exists across African countries, with the pandemic accelerating uptake and use in all countries while increasing divides between small and large enterprises. Up to 88 percent and 86 percent of interviewed firms increased uptake and use of DTs in South Africa and Kenya, respectively, with significant variation across countries and size groups. Only 22 percent of Ghanaian and 23 percent of Tanzanian small firms increased uptake and use of DTs (figure 2.15, panel a).

Regarding new investments, a significantly greater share of large firms has invested in new DTs than small firms: 66 percent of large firms invested in new DTs in Tanzania but only 7 percent of small firms, almost 10 times less. In Kenya, 59 percent of large firms invested in new DTs but only 27 percent of small firms (figure 2.15, panel b).

Complementary information on mobile app downloads—which captures the behavior of individuals and may track more closely the behavior of informal and individual enterprises—shows that, one year after the pandemic's onset, the number of active users of mobile apps on categories such as finance, business,[17] shopping, and travel has declined

FIGURE 2.14 **Increases in enterprise uptake, use, and investment in digital solutions after COVID-19 outbreak, by firm size, Sub-Saharan African versus comparator countries, 2020–21**

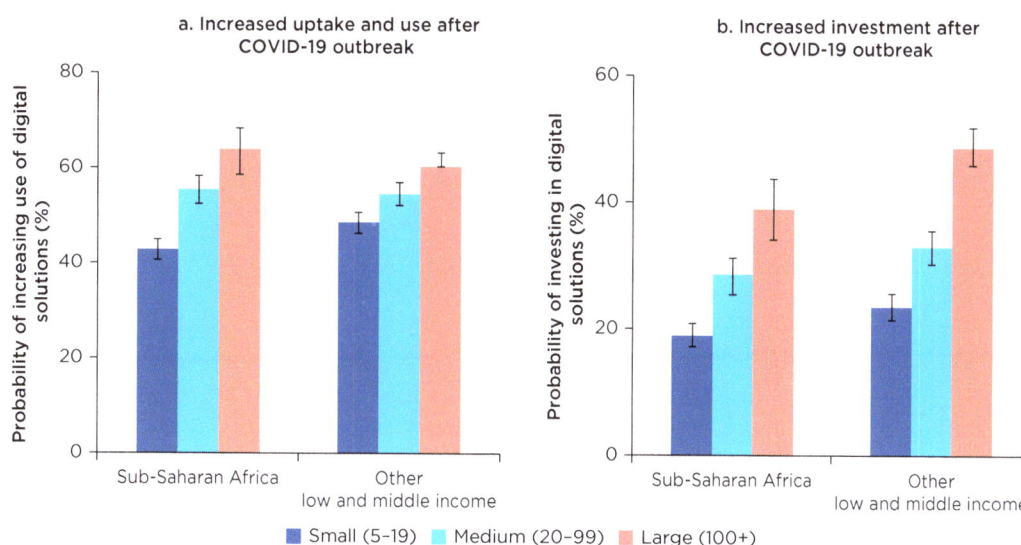

a. Increased uptake and use after COVID-19 outbreak

b. Increased investment after COVID-19 outbreak

■ Small (5–19) ■ Medium (20–99) ■ Large (100+)

Source: World Bank COVID-19 Business Pulse Surveys.

Note: Surveys of enterprises employing five or more full-time workers were implemented September 2020– February 2021. The charts present conditional average probabilities of starting or increasing the use of digital solutions (panel a) and investing in digital solutions (panel b), controlling for size, sector, and country. Enterprise size is based on values before the pandemic. All country weights are equal to one. Unweighted samples within countries. Error bars represent 95 percent confidence intervals. The Sub-Saharan African sample includes Benin, Ghana, Kenya, Madagascar, Malawi, Senegal, South Africa, Tanzania, and Zambia (total of 5,819 observations). The "other low and middle income" sample includes Brazil, Bulgaria, Cambodia, El Salvador, Georgia, Guatemala, Honduras, Indonesia, Malaysia, Moldova, Morocco, Nicaragua, Türkiye, and Vietnam (7,698 observations). Panel a shows responses to the question, "Has this establishment started using or increased the use of internet, online social media, specialized apps, or digital platforms in response to the COVID-19 outbreak?" Panel b shows responses to the question, "Has this establishment invested in any new equipment, software, or digital solution in response to COVID-19?"

on average (box 2.2). These trends, if unaddressed, risk widening productivity, sales, and owner and worker income gaps over time.

Technological readiness for unexpected shocks

Enterprises with higher pre-COVID-19 levels of technological sophistication had higher "technological readiness" that enabled them to have higher sales amid the COVID-19 crisis than did enterprises with less technological sophistication (Cirera, Comin, and Cruz 2022; Comin et al. 2022). The total average effect on sales from pre-COVID-19 technological sophistication amounted to 6.5 percentage points (figure 2.16).[18] It ranges from 5.5 percentage points for enterprises in the second quintile (relative to those in the bottom 20 percent of the technology sophistication distribution) to almost 14 percentage points for those in the top quintile.

This total effect combines (a) a relatively large *direct* effect related to firms' higher DT uptake before the pandemic's onset, which enabled them to quickly increase their share of online sales and to more quickly shift to home-based work for workers with

FIGURE 2.15 **Increases in enterprise use of and investment in DTs after COVID-19 outbreak, by firm size, selected African countries, 2020–21**

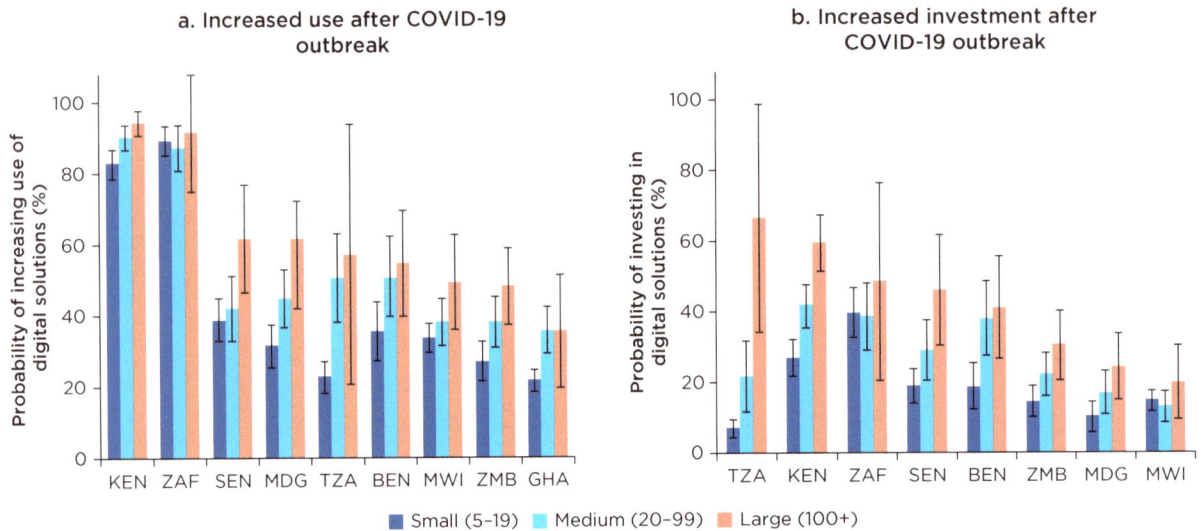

a. Increased use after COVID-19 outbreak

b. Increased investment after COVID-19 outbreak

■ Small (5–19)   ■ Medium (20–99)   ■ Large (100+)

Source: World Bank COVID-19 Business Pulse Surveys.
Note: Surveys of enterprises employing five or more full-time workers were implemented September 2020–February 2021. The charts present conditional average probabilities of starting or increasing the use of digital solutions (panel a) and investing in digital solutions (panel b), controlling for size, sector, and country. Enterprise size is based on values before the pandemic. All country weights are equal to one. Unweighted samples within countries. Error bars represent 95 percent confidence intervals. In terms of countries and number of observations, BEN = Benin (981), GHA = Ghana (979), KEN = Kenya (816), MDG = Madagascar (490), MWI = Malawi (789), SEN = Senegal (425), TZA = Tanzania (457), ZAF = South Africa (363), and ZMB = Zambia (507). Panel a shows responses to the question, "Has this establishment started using or increased the use of internet, online social media, specialized apps, or digital platforms in response to the COVID-19 outbreak?" Panel b shows responses to the question, "Has this establishment invested in any new equipment, software, or digital solution in response to COVID-19?"

BOX 2.2

Impact of the COVID-19 pandemic on mobile app use in Africa

The COVID-19 pandemic upended daily life around the world, including how, and how often, enterprises and people use digital technologies. App intelligence data allow an analysis of how the pandemic affected people's use of mobile apps globally, which can provide insights into the effect of the pandemic on the use of mobile data more broadly and the ability of Africans to adapt to the challenges posed by the pandemic and lockdown policies.

The initial shock of the spread of the virus and ensuing restrictions to travel and domestic lockdowns became visible in mobile internet app usage in the following months. Between April and May 2020, the number of apps that individuals downloaded on a monthly basis increased by 46.2 percent on average globally.

Similarly, the number of total app sessions grew by about 10 percent between April and May 2020. By the end of 2021, that number remained 8.6 percent higher globally than before the onset of the pandemic. However, the initial positive effects of the pandemic on app downloads and app sessions were smaller in Sub-Saharan Africa than in other regions. In addition, only Sub-Saharan Africa experienced a *decline* of downloads and total app sessions since the onset of the pandemic (–11.3 percent and –1.1 percent, respectively, between February 2020 and December 2021).

(continued)

Impact of the COVID-19 pandemic on mobile app use in Africa *(continued)*

Across four key app categories—business, finance, shopping, and travel and local—the total number of monthly active users of the top 50 ranked apps[a] per 100,000 in population decreased by 1.5 percent on average in the first year of the COVID-19 pandemic in Africa, compared with a 0.2 percent increase in a sample of other low- and middle-income countries (LMICs) (figure B2.2.1).

FIGURE B2.2.1 Change in number of monthly average users of digital apps, selected African and comparator countries, April 2020 to March 2021

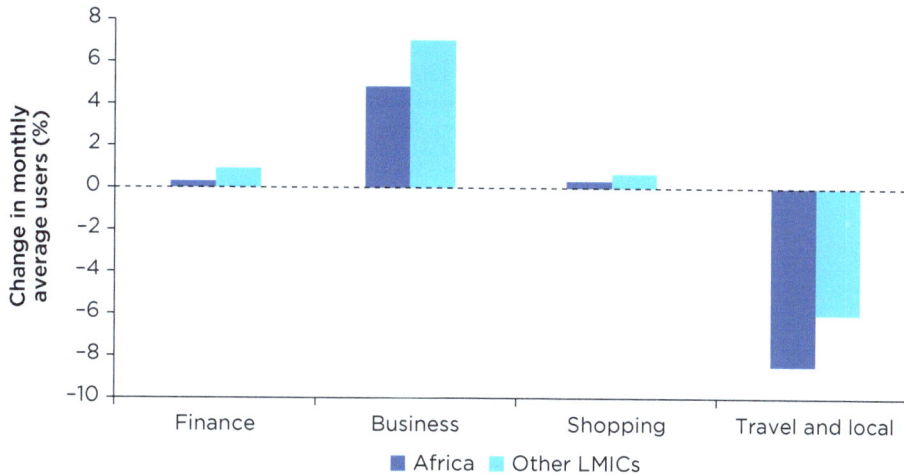

Source: Elaboration based on data from Apptopia.
Note: The African sample includes Burkina Faso, Arab Republic of Egypt, Ghana, Kenya, Malawi, Nigeria, Senegal, South Africa, and Tunisia. "Other LMICs" (low- and middle-income countries) include Argentina, Brazil, Bulgaria, Colombia, India, Indonesia, Malaysia, Mexico, Pakistan, Peru, the Philippines, Romania, the Russian Federation, Thailand, Türkiye, Ukraine, República Bolivariana de Venezuela, and Vietnam.

The impact of the pandemic and ensuing lockdowns on individual app usage (measured by monthly active users) appears slightly less pronounced in Africa than in other LMIC markets in the finance and business categories, whereas the opposite is true for the travel and local category. Although the use of finance apps in African countries increased more strongly in 2020 than in other LMICs, the growth stalled in 2021, at only 0.3 percent, compared with 1.0 percent in other LMICs. Among African countries, Senegal, Burkina Faso, and South Africa (in this order) saw monthly users of finance apps grow the most in 2020, but only Nigeria grew its user base of finance apps in 2021 relative to 2020.

a. Focusing on a sample of apps with high download and engagement figures improves the reliability of the estimation-based data.

computers; with (b) a more modest *indirect* effect linked to increasing investments in and uptake of additional DTs in response to the crisis. This indirect effect is also larger for more technologically sophisticated firms. Although, on average, a 1 unit increase in technological sophistication is associated with an increase of 17 percentage points in the likelihood of starting or increasing the use of different types of DTs, the additional likelihood for businesses in the top 60 percent is at least 35 percentage points.

FIGURE 2.16 Effects of higher pre-COVID-19 technological readiness on enterprises' post-COVID-19 sales, by technology sophistication quintile, 2021

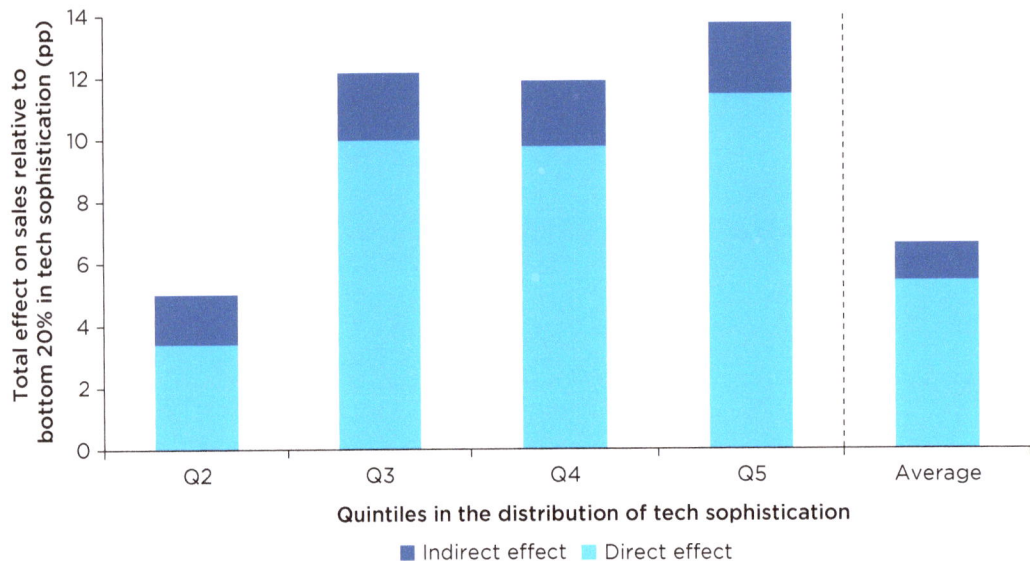

Source: Cirera, Comin, and Cruz 2022, figure 5.14.
Note: The estimated coefficients are based on combined data from three countries (Brazil, Senegal, and Vietnam) on both (a) measures of technological readiness before COVID-19 from the 2019–21 Firm-level Adoption of Technology (FAT) survey; and (b) information on digital response and firm performance after the COVID-19 outbreak from the World Bank's COVID-19 Business Pulse Surveys (BPS) of enterprises employing five or more full-time workers, implemented September 2020–February 2021. "Total effect" includes both direct and indirect effects of higher digital technology uptake and investments before and after pandemic onset. pp = percentage points.

Drivers of enterprise use

Of all the regions with available internet service, Africa has the highest share of unconnected users in the world. But enterprises are more likely than households to use smartphones and computers. Because the business use of DTs is associated with higher productivity and more jobs, as discussed earlier, why is use of these technologies (wherever available) not universal by all enterprises? This section presents novel data from both the FAT and RIA surveys to identify the main drivers of enterprise use. It is important to understand what drives enterprises to use DTs, starting with access technologies such as smartphones and computers, to formulate effective public policies to reduce the barriers and enhance the positive drivers of productive use.

Primary drivers of DT use

Main factors affecting the use of smartphones and computers by enterprises, as well as the use of more sophisticated DTs relying on these access technologies, are related to *ability to pay* and *willingness to use* as well as other factors.[19]

Ability to pay. Affordability, namely the ability to pay for DTs, is linked to both costs (relative to expected enhanced returns to enterprise revenues) and access to finance, including the extent to which local financial systems enable financing of the underlying equipment and software.

Affordability of complementary infrastructure can be interpreted as part of users' ability to pay, because the affordable availability of internet service is facilitated by that of complementary nondigital infrastructure. It includes the cost, availability, and reliability of electricity as well as roads and logistics for those apps requiring associated transportation services.

Willingness to use. Attractiveness—namely the underlying demand and willingness to use DTs (beyond issues of affordability)—is affected by the availability of information on the existence of DTs, how easy it is to use them, and whether they meet the productive needs of users. These variables are affected by whether DTs are designed for the user's skill level, are available in the language that the user speaks, and facilitate on-the-job learning. Attractiveness also is affected by internet connectivity requirements, such as sufficiently high speed (how fast data move), low latency (no discernible lag in requested items to appear), and reliability (always stable). Importantly, attractiveness is also affected by the uncertainty of the economic benefits of adoption associated with individual users' risk- or loss-aversion preferences and biases, including factors such as over- or underconfidence, status quo bias, misinformation, and trust.

Enterprises' willingness to use DTs is also affected by their capabilities, including both people skills and enterprise technological capabilities. People skills include the ability of workers, managers, and owners to extract value from DTs, and this ability is affected by levels and quality of basic education and follow-on technical and vocational education and training as well as experiential know-how.

Enterprise capabilities include the need and ability of firms to use DTs. Such capabilities are linked to the complexity of inputs, production processes, and quality of outputs required by markets, including managerial and organizational practice, as well as the extent of technology use, search, and research and development (R&D) activities undertaken (enabling the enterprise to accumulate relevant know-how assets beyond those that can be bought through markets). Given the low average literacy coupled with the low average quality of education across most African countries, DTs can serve as a means of knowledge diffusion to improve the quality of education and bridge skill shortages in Africa to facilitate higher productivity growth and job creation.

Business and socioeconomic factors. Other elements of the business environment— including the relative availability and cost of skilled labor and specific types of capital as well as competition incentives to spur technology adoption and the generation of new technologies—are linked to access to wider domestic and international markets and to government regulations that level the playing field. Such regulations, for example, aim to avoid favoring incumbents or impeding entry or expansion. They instead aim to enable any start-up to enter and experiment, expand rapidly, and exit and reenter if the initial business idea was not well executed and did not sufficiently respond to market needs.

Other socioeconomic factors include whether social norms and rules make ownership of access devices difficult for women.

Network effects. Smartphones, computers, and several other DTs, including platforms, have network effects. That is, the value of the DT increases with the number of users, including those users accessed through digital platforms. With network effects come additional factors affecting the uptake and use of DTs, including

- *Coordination issues,* including wait-and-see behavior relative to others in the network, and either weak or lack of interoperability and equal access across markets (linked to standards and regulation); and

- *Trust issues,* linked to possible shortcomings at the government legal and regulatory levels (such as lack of appropriate liability laws, online consumer protection, e-signature, personal data protection, and cybersecurity) and at the platform operator level (such as lack of third-party certifications and simple dispute resolution procedures).

Perceived barriers to DT use

The main reported barriers to enterprise use of new technologies including DTs are lack of capabilities, lack of demand and uncertainty (that is, lack of attractiveness), and lack of finance. These findings are based on the FAT survey, which directly asks enterprises with five or more full-time workers to identify the top three obstacles to adoption of new technologies including DTs. The findings across all African countries with available data (Ghana, Kenya, Malawi, and Senegal) are ranked by the largest share of responses from small firms (figure 2.17).

There is consensus that the top two obstacles across African enterprises are lack of capabilities and lack of attractiveness of technologies. For small firms, the most-reported obstacle is lack of capabilities, with 78 percent of small firms reporting it as one of their three main obstacles, followed by lack of demand and attractiveness of technologies

FIGURE 2.17 Reported barriers to enterprise use of technology, by firm size, selected African countries, 2019–21

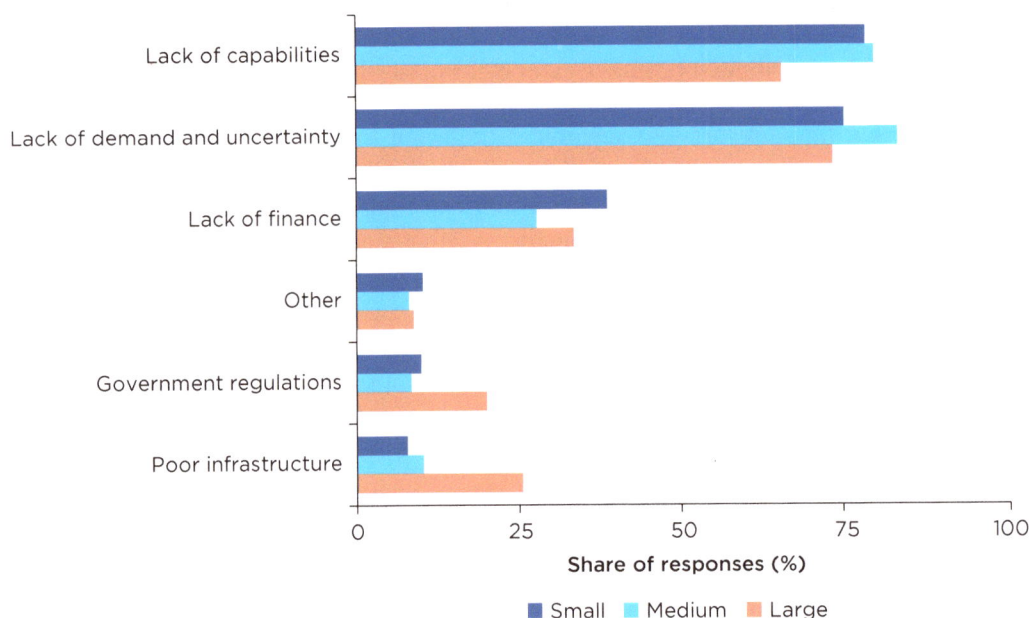

Share of responses (%)

■ Small ■ Medium ■ Large

Source: Based on Cirera, Comin, and Cruz 2022, using 2019–21 FAT (Firm-level Adoption of Technology) survey data.
Note: Each enterprise selected the three most important obstacles it faced "to adopt new equipment, machines, software, or processes to improve its performance." "Lack of capabilities" covers both individual skills and enterprise technological capabilities. "Lack of demand and uncertainty" reduce the attractiveness of the technologies. "Lack of finance" relates to affordability issues. The figure reports the share of all surveyed African enterprises in Ghana, Kenya, Malawi, and Senegal for each top response, by enterprise size. "Small" enterprises have 5–19 full-time employees; "medium" enterprises, 20–99; and "large" enterprises, 100 or more. Barriers are ranked by the largest share of responses from small firms. Only in Senegal was it possible to draw a representative sample of informal firms; thus, the Senegal sample encompasses both formal and informal firms.

(which includes uncertainty), with 75 percent of small firms giving that response. Lack of finance and affordability is a more distant third main reported obstacle, with 38 percent of small firms selecting it. Government regulations and poor infrastructure are perceived as relatively less critical obstacles, with 10 percent and 8 percent of small firms selecting those responses, respectively.

Among medium and large firms, the most-reported obstacle is lack of demand and attractiveness of technologies, with 82 percent and 73 percent of medium and large firms selecting that response, respectively, followed by lack of capabilities, selected by 79 percent of medium firms and 65 percent of large firms. Lack of finance and affordability again ranks as a more distant third as a main reported obstacle, with 28 percent and 33 percent of medium and large firms selecting it, respectively. Poor infrastructure is perceived as more important for large firms than for medium firms: 25 percent of large firms and 10 percent of medium firms report it as a major obstacle, followed by 20 percent of large and 8 percent of medium firms selecting government regulations as a major obstacle.

Among microenterprises' self-reported reasons for not using the internet, lack of attractiveness is the most important constraint, cited by 7 out of 10 nonusers (Atiyas and Dutz 2023). Availability of internet service is not a main constraint, with less than 20 percent of the RIA survey respondents citing it as a constraint.[20] And affordability is a major constraint for roughly one-third (35 percent) of the microenterprise respondents—likely linked to the inability to pay for a smartphone, a computer, or internet service, or lack of access to, or inability to pay for, electricity.

However, affordability alone does not explain why the majority of microenterprises lack a smartphone or a computer to access the internet. As noted above, by far the largest share of nonuser respondents—more than 70 percent—indicated that lack of *attractiveness* ("no need") is the main constraint, presumably either because (a) no apps are available that are useful to them in their local language that meet their productive needs; (b) their general skill level does not enable them to understand how they could productively use available apps; or (c) the available quality of service is so poor (with no or limited download availability of useful information when it is needed) that it is not useful to them.

Finally, roughly one-third of nonusers (34 percent) indicated that there is a capability or skill gap, likely because the apps are not designed with the level of digital skills of the users in mind and are not sufficiently intuitive and easy to use.

Conditional correlates of enterprise use of smartphones and computers

The main factual drivers of smartphone and computer use are associated with the *ability to pay* for internet (linked to affordability and availability of complementary infrastructure) and the *willingness to use* DTs (linked to attractiveness of and capabilities to use DTs).[21] The drivers of use are relatively similar across both larger firms (with five or more workers) and microenterprises (figure 2.18). These findings are based on objective data collected through the FAT and RIA surveys (Atiyas and Dutz 2023; Cirera, Comin, and Cruz 2022), which allow the conditional correlates of enterprise use to be explored along the full range of drivers of enterprise use.[22]

Loans and credit lines. Affordability is proxied by whether larger firms have loans to purchase machinery and equipment and whether micro-size firms have a loan. Information is also available on whether micro-size firms have a credit line with

FIGURE 2.18 Correlates of smartphone and computer adoption by African firms, 2017–21

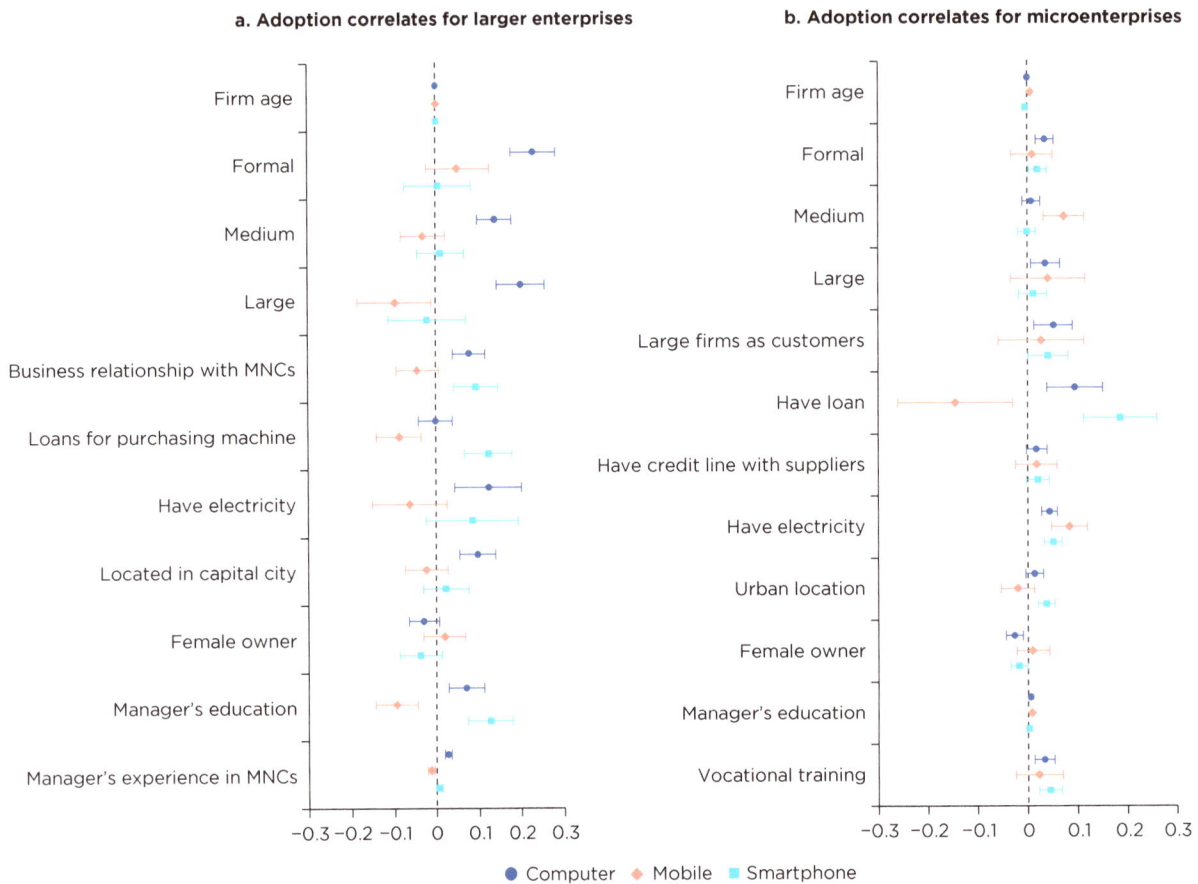

a. Adoption correlates for larger enterprises

b. Adoption correlates for microenterprises

● Computer   ◆ Mobile   ■ Smartphone

Sources: Atiyas and Dutz 2023; Cirera, Comin, and Cruz 2022.
Note: Reported results are marginal effects based on probit regressions on enterprise characteristics, controlling for country fixed effects. Error bars indicate 95 percent confidence intervals. Panel a is based on 2019–21 FAT (Firm-level Adoption of Technology) survey data of firms employing at least five full-time workers in four African countries with available data: Ghana, Kenya, Malawi, and Senegal. "Large" firms (with 100 or more employees) and "medium" firms (20–99 employees) are compared with the "small" firm group (5–19 employees). Only in Senegal was it possible to draw a representative sample of informal firms; thus, the Senegal sample includes both formal and informal firms. Panel b is based on 2017–18 Research ICT Africa (RIA) data on microenterprises across Ghana, Kenya, Mozambique, Nigeria, Senegal, South Africa, and Tanzania. "Large" microenterprises (with three or more full-time employees) and "medium" microenterprises (1–2 full-time employees) are compared with the "small" microenterprise group (0 full-time employees). MNCs = multinational companies.

suppliers, which could also be an indicator of the creditworthiness of these firms. Access to finance as reflected by extended loans is one of the largest correlates of uptake in addition to skills and the sectoral nature of the industrial activity for larger firms (that is, manufacturing and services relative to agriculture).

Larger firms that have a loan are 12 percentage points more likely to use smartphones and 9 points less likely to use a 2G phone; there is no statistically significant association between computer use and having a loan. Micro-size firms that have a loan are 18 percentage points more likely to use smartphones and almost 15 points less likely to use a 2G phone; they are also over 9 points more likely to use a computer.

Electricity and urban location. Reliable electricity and urban living are associated with computer use for larger firms and with smartphone use for microenterprises.

Data on complementary infrastructure are limited to enterprises' own responses about electricity. Whether enterprises are located in an urban or capital city is used as a proxy for availability of other complementary infrastructure, including access to better roads and logistics services.

Larger firms with access to electricity are 12 percentage points more likely to use a computer, while larger firms in the capital city are almost 10 points more likely to use one; the relationships between electricity access and urban location and smartphone use are not statistically significant.[23] Micro-size firms with electricity are 5 percentage points more likely to use a smartphone and 4 points more likely to use a computer. Micro-size firms in urban locations are 4 points more likely to use a smartphone.

Business relationships. Attractiveness of DTs—likely driven by requirements to adopt specific DTs when firms have business relationships with multinational companies (MNCs) and when microenterprises have large firms as customers—is also strongly associated with both smartphone and computer use. Attractiveness together with capabilities jointly affect the underlying demand and willingness to use specific DTs.

Attractiveness is affected by availability of information on the existence of DTs and whether they meet the productive needs of user firms. It is here proxied by whether larger firms have business relationships with MNCs and by whether micro-size firms have large enterprises as customers—with MNCs and larger firms likely requiring use of certain DTs for their interactions. Both are highly significantly and positively associated with smartphone and computer uptake.

Larger firms that have business relationships with MNCs are 9 percentage points more likely to use smartphones and are almost 8 points less likely not to use any phone for business purposes; they are almost 8 points more likely to use computers. Microenterprises that have large firms as customers are 4 percentage points more likely to use smartphones and are over 5 points more likely to use computers.

Manager's education. People skills are strongly associated with both smartphone and computer use. This is especially true of the level of *education* for managers of larger firms and the level of *vocational training* for microenterprises. Capabilities affect the willingness to use DTs largely by enabling understanding of how to use and extract productive value from the DTs.

The skills dimension of capabilities is proxied by (a) the highest year of schooling attained by the enterprise's manager for both larger firms and microenterprises; (b) technical training in the form of the manager's experience in MNCs for larger firms; and (c) vocational training certificates held by the manager for microenterprises.

The manager's education level is highly statistically significant, associated with both smartphone and computer uptake. Firms with managers that have one more year of schooling than other managers in similar firms are associated with 12 percent and 0.2 percent higher likelihoods (in larger firms and microenterprises, respectively) of adopting a smartphone and a 7 percent higher likelihood of adopting a computer.[24] These are big numbers for larger firms because they are marginal effects that should be scaled up in magnitude to the extent that some managers may have *several* more years of schooling than their counterparts in other firms if they have continued beyond primary to finish secondary schooling. Among managers of microenterprises, vocational training is associated with a 4-percentage-point higher likelihood of adopting a smartphone and a lower likelihood of not adopting any mobile phone.

Larger firm managers' experience with MNCs is, as expected, negatively associated with owning a 2G phone but positively associated with not owning *any* phone (albeit by a very small magnitude). Firms whose manager has MNC experience have a 2.7-percentage-point higher likelihood of adopting a computer.

Firm's size, age, formality, and sector. Enterprise technological capabilities are linked to the complexity of inputs, production, and quality of outputs required by markets. They are proxied by firm size, firm age, formality status, and sector of industrial activity, with the presumption that larger, younger, and formal firms, as well as firms in manufacturing and services, are likely to have more know-how assets and a greater need to use smartphones and computers.[25]

Firms with five or more workers ("5+worker firms") are more likely to use computers: large (100+ employees) and medium (20–99 employees) firms are 20 percentage points and roughly 14 points more likely, respectively, to use a computer than small (5–19 employees) firms. Micro-size firms that have 3 or more employees are 3.5 percentage points more likely to use a computer than those with fewer employees. The relationship between firm size and smartphone use is not statistically significant.

Regarding firm age, 5+worker firms and micro-size older firms (the median microenterprise being four years old across all countries) are less likely to use a smartphone than younger firms. Formal 5+worker firms as well as formal micro-size firms are more likely to use computers than their informal counterparts—formal 5+worker firms are roughly 23 percentage points more likely to use computers, while micro-size formal firms are roughly 3 points more likely to use them.[26] The relationship between formality and smartphone use is not statistically significant for 5+worker firms; for micro-size firms, formal firms are 2 percentage points more likely to use a smartphone.

Regarding sectors of enterprise activity, 5+worker firms in manufacturing as well as wholesale and retail trade are 22 percentage points more likely to use a smartphone than those in agriculture, while those in other services are 16 points more likely to do so. Also, 5+worker firms in wholesale and retail trade, and in "other services," are 18 percentage points and 16 percentage points more likely to use a computer, respectively, than those in agriculture.

Female ownership. The only other available socioeconomic variable is whether the enterprise is female-owned.[27] For 5+worker firms, the relationship between female ownership and smartphone and computer use is not statistically significant. Presumably in these firms, whose owners typically are removed from the day-to-day management of the firms, the gender of the owners is not as relevant for technology adoption decisions as it is for micro-size firms.

However, among the micro-size firms, female-owned firms are less likely to use either a smartphone or a computer. They are 2 percentage points and 3 percentage points less likely to use a smartphone and computer, respectively, than male-owned firms. Because most of these micro-size firms are self-employed enterprises with no full-time paid employees, and their owner is also the manager, this digital divide may reflect prevailing social norms and rules that make ownership of these access devices relatively more difficult for women.

More evidence on attractiveness, capabilities, and infrastructure as drivers of enterprise use

Attractiveness of new and better DTs as a driver of uptake is vitally linked to the uncertainty of the economic benefits of adoption—an uncertainty associated with behavioral biases, including overconfidence, status quo bias, and exposure to misinformation.

To address this question, the FAT survey asks enterprise respondents about their self-assessment of the technologies they are using relative to their perception of use of technologies by other firms in their sector and country.

Almost all firms are overconfident that they are using more sophisticated technologies than they actually are, relative to other national firms (figure 2.19). The average African enterprise's wider divergence between self-assessments and actual technological sophistication than among enterprises in other regions may be linked to generally lower technological sophistication across Africa than in other regions and therefore lower opportunities for African enterprises to benchmark themselves against other nearby enterprises using more sophisticated technologies. This overconfidence is likely to be a critical deterrent to adoption if enterprises have a low perceived need to upgrade relative to their national competitors.

Worker and management skills affect the ability to extract value from DTs and related technologies. Enterprises with a greater share of workers with technical and vocational education and training, and especially with a greater share of workers with college degrees, are significantly more likely to use more sophisticated technologies including DTs across business functions (figure 2.20, panel a). African enterprises with a larger share of secondary-educated workers are not associated with any technological sophistication premium for sector-specific technologies, in contrast to the data across all available countries, which suggests that the quality of secondary schooling may not adequately prepare workers for effective uses of such technologies.

Managers with high school degrees, who have studied abroad, and especially those with postcollege degrees are also more likely to work in enterprises using more sophisticated technologies including DTs (figure 2.20, panel b). The reported findings, based

FIGURE 2.19 **African enterprises' perceptions of own technology use relative to other firms within country, 2019–21**

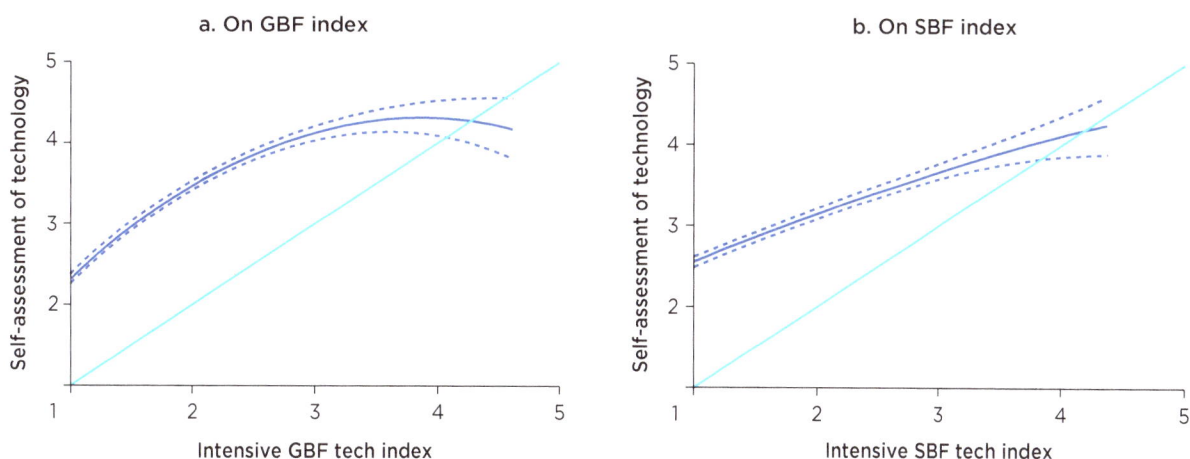

Source: Cirera, Comin, and Cruz 2022, figure 6.10, using 2019–21 FAT (Firm-level Adoption of Technology) survey data restricted to available African countries.
Note: The 45-degree line shows the point at which self-assessments and actuals coincide. The dark blue line shows the quadratic fit with 95 percent confidence interval. Each firm's general business function (GBF) technology index (panel a) and sector-specific business function (SBF) technology index (panel b) are regressed on its self-assessment relative to other firms in the country, while controlling for country, sector, size, and regions. Responses are to the question, "On a scale from 1 to 10, where 10 means that the establishment is using the most advanced production processes available in its sector, where do you think this establishment stands with respect to other firms in your country?" The self-assessments are rescaled to 1–5. Data were available from firms employing at least five full-time workers in four African countries responding to the FAT survey: Ghana, Kenya, Malawi, and Senegal.

FIGURE 2.20 Correlation of worker and manager skills with use of better technologies, selected African countries, 2019–21

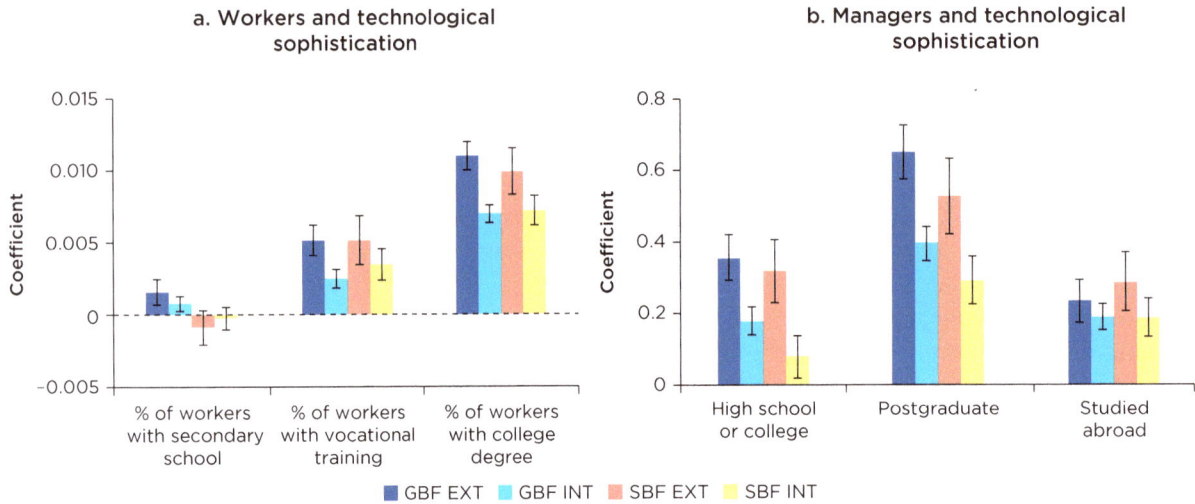

a. Workers and technological sophistication

b. Managers and technological sophistication

GBF EXT   GBF INT   SBF EXT   SBF INT

Source: Cirera, Comin, and Cruz 2022, figures 6.14 and 6.12, using 2019–21 FAT (Firm-level Adoption of Technology) survey data, restricted to available African countries.
Note: Each enterprise technology index (at both the extensive and intensive margins) is regressed on a dummy for (in panel a) the percentage of workers with different education levels (secondary school, vocational training, and college degree); and (in panel b) the top manager's education (high school or college, BA+, and study abroad) while controlling for country, sector, size, and regions. All estimates are weighted by sampling and country weights. Shaded bars indicate the coefficients, and error bars the 95 percent confidence intervals from regressions. Data were available from firms employing at least five full-time workers in four African countries responding to the FAT survey: Ghana, Kenya, Malawi, and Senegal. EXT = extensive margin (whether a technology is used at all); GBF = general business function; INT = intensive margin (the technology used most intensively); SBF = sector-specific business function.

exclusively on data from Africa, show that across all available countries managers with postgraduate degrees are almost twice as likely as those holding high school or college degrees to work in enterprises with more sophisticated technologies. This finding suggests that African countries have a relative scarcity of better-trained managers and that enterprises with more sophisticated technologies have a higher demand for managers with advanced degrees.

Enterprise management capabilities and organizational practices also affect the uptake of DTs and complementary technologies. Enterprises using formal worker incentives for better ways to produce goods or provide services (figure 2.21, panel a), and enterprises monitoring performance through a greater number of key performance indicators (KPIs) (figure 2.21, panel b) are significantly more likely to use more sophisticated technologies including DTs, for both GBFs and SBFs. Regarding the use of a large number (10 or more) of KPIs, the findings show that such enterprises monitoring performance across a broader range of indicators are again almost twice as likely to use more sophisticated technologies than enterprises across all available countries. The statistical significance of the findings across both panels suggests that improved management capabilities and organizational practices are complementary to the uptake of better DTs and other technologies.

Regarding digital infrastructure, geographic proximity to internet nodes in Senegal causally explains uptake by firms of more sophisticated technologies that include DTs for GBFs (Berkes et al., forthcoming).[28] However, digital infrastructure alone cannot causally explain, with statistical significance, which of the technologies will be used most

FIGURE 2.21 **Correlation of better management capabilities and organizational practices with enterprise use of better technologies, selected African countries, 2019–21**

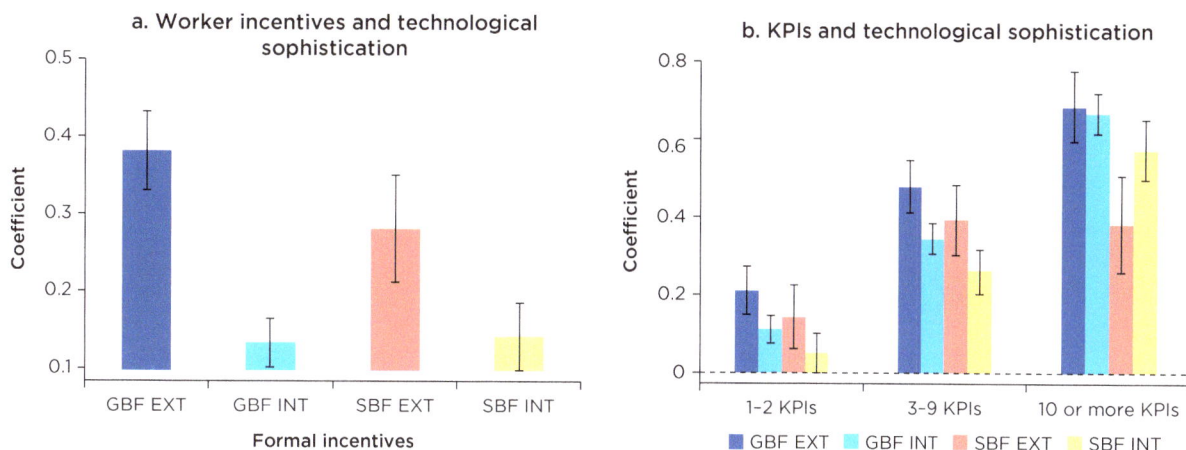

a. Worker incentives and technological sophistication

b. KPIs and technological sophistication

Source: Cirera, Comin, and Cruz 2022, figure 6.12, using 2019–21 FAT (Firm-level Adoption of Technology) survey data, restricted to available African countries.

Note: Each enterprise technology index (at both the extensive and intensive margins) is regressed on a dummy for (in panel a) providing formal incentives and (in panel b) key performance indicators (KPIs) while controlling for country, sector, size, and regions. All estimates are weighted by sampling and country weights. Shaded bars indicate the coefficients, and error bars the 95 percent confidence intervals from regressions. Data were available from firms employing at least five full-time workers in four African countries responding to the FAT survey: Ghana, Kenya, Malawi, and Senegal. Panel a shows yes/no responses to the question, "Does this establishment provide formal incentives for workers in the form of money, gift, or recognition to suggest and/or use better ways to produce goods or provide services?" Panel b shows the number of key performance indicators (KPIs) survey respondents reported that they monitored—providing, as examples, "metrics on production, cost, waste, quality, inventory, energy, absenteeism, and deliveries on time." EXT = extensive margin (whether a technology is used at all); GBF = general business function; INT = intensive margin (the technology used most intensively); SBF = sector-specific business function.

intensively for the various GBFs, nor can digital infrastructure alone explain the uptake and use of different levels of sophistication of technologies for SBFs.

This finding confirms the importance of digital infrastructure as an enabler of adoption of DTs by firms. It also highlights that many other factors jointly explain the uptake and intensive use of different levels of technological sophistication across enterprises and that the uptake and intensive use of more sophisticated technologies for SBFs, particularly for agriculture and manufacturing, are not just related to DTs but also are typically embedded in relatively sophisticated and expensive complementary technologies, including different types of machinery and equipment.

Technology policies for more and better firms

Public policies are needed to stimulate uptake of available DTs by user enterprises across each African country by addressing the identified drivers of adoption, including by disseminating information about DTs, upgrading people skills and enterprise capabilities, and providing financing support. Public policies also are needed to affect the direction of technological change by incentivizing the generation of more appropriate DTs for the jobs-related needs of lower-income countries, especially lower-skill-appropriate solutions that are easy to use and that boost the productivity of lower-income, lower-skilled owner-entrepreneurs, managers, and workers.

Three policy areas to support these objectives are

1. Technology upgrading and worker and management capability support programs;

2. Policies to support the generation of more appropriate technologies for Africa's current and future asset base, including supplier and intellectual property rights protection and regulations facilitating the appropriate development of ML and other forms of AI; and

3. Financing support, including targeted partial credit guarantees; matching grants and vouchers for adoption of technologies and the acquisition of needed capabilities; and credit infrastructure with a focus on credit bureaus, secured transactions, ethical use of data for creditworthiness assessment, and open banking rules.

To be effective, the more specific policies addressing these three areas should be supported by broader business environment policies that promote market competition while facilitating associated economic and social adjustment. Market competition is a critical incentive but often requires adjustment, including retraining, by workers in less productive enterprises.

In addition to promoting market competition, two other principles of effective policy and institutional design are coordination of complementary support activities and evidence-based contestability of policies. Coordination includes bundling of complementary technology, skills, capabilities, and financing support in ways that overcome the combination of obstacles to broader uptake of DTs explored in the previous section. It also includes coordination across different public support entities, between government and business, and regional harmonization to facilitate regional scalability. For policies to be contestable, their objectives, including the market failures that they seek to address, must be transparent and complemented by monitoring and evaluation with evidence of impact that allows those programs that are working to be strengthened and those that are not to be closed.[29] The application of agile regulation principles for participatory policy making, experimentation, and flexibility for course correction become more important in the context of digital transformation.

Accelerating technology adoption

Accelerating adoption of DTs and complementary technologies is one part of a broader set of support policies that also include technology generation and financing. Figure 2.22 summarizes the range of policy instruments that are typically used to support technology adoption and generation.[30] These policy instruments mainly apply to micro, small, and medium enterprises (MSMEs).

The most common instrument to support firms in the use of DTs is business advisory services (BAS). BAS support the types of GBFs that are the focus of many DTs, including general enterprise management capabilities as well as more specific marketing, sales, and e-commerce platforms. Together with technology extension services (TES) and technology centers (TCs), which support SBFs, they are the focus of this subsection, typically providing both services and financial support.

Public support for digital upgrading for GBFs is typically provided through existing or more focused BAS programs. General BAS programs include access to or the direct provision of specialist advice in areas such as financial and accounting services, human resource management, marketing and advertising, pricing strategies, supply chain

FIGURE 2.22 **Instruments to support generation and adoption of DTs for GBFs and SBFs**

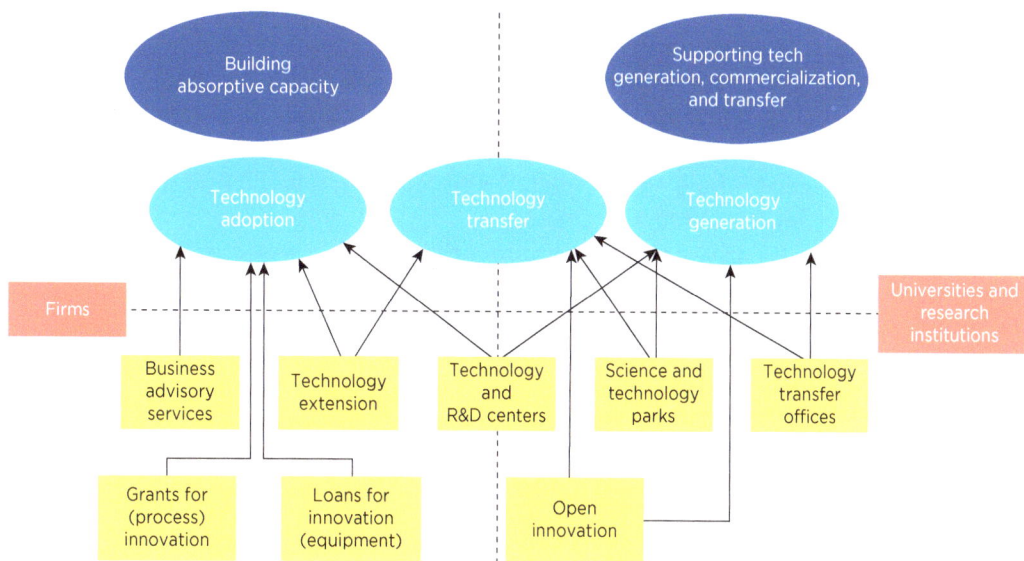

Source: Cirera et al. 2020, figure 4.5.
Note: In addition to grants for soft technologies and subsidized loans for hard technologies (equipment), public financing support may also be required to help address other barriers related to capabilities, attractiveness, and affordability-related drivers of DT use, as well as for new technology generation (including altering the direction of technology change)—either combined with BAS (business advisory), TES (technology extension), and TC (technology center) services or separately. Financing options are covered in the subsection on facilitating enterprise financing. DTs = digital technologies; GBFs = general business functions; R&D = research and development; SBFs = sector-specific business functions.

management, and quality management. They address shortcomings in private markets regarding access to information by small and microenterprises, including smaller enterprises having overconfidence in their capabilities, a problem that is more prevalent among enterprises using less sophisticated technologies. They also address shortcomings in private markets with coordination issues, incentivizing groups of MSMEs to jointly procure advisory services.

Elements of good BAS design include

- An initial diagnostic of enterprise capabilities that can provide benchmarking and function as a screening device for additional public support;

- A subsequent action plan with individual or joint support;

- A vetted list of providers that have a record valued by other enterprises; and

- A delivery model (either through individual vouchers or grants to purchase private services or through direct provision) that is aligned with prevailing needs.

Interestingly, more general BAS programs were a key policy instrument in Japan and Singapore (Cirera and Maloney 2017). A review of digital upgrading programs in Organisation for Economic Co-operation and Development (OECD) countries highlights that at least 40 percent of countries use BAS as the main instrument, with 36 percent using financial vouchers and 27 percent using direct grants. Most programs emphasize that the technical assistance must be complemented with additional investments (Balbontin at al. 2021).[31]

Public support for digital upgrading regarding SBFs is generally provided through TES and TCs. TES are direct on-site technology assistance and skills training services to small and medium enterprises (SMEs) through extension staff. They focus on supporting specific production technologies and include support for the adoption and use of DTs—such as digital sensors for agricultural production; for manufacturing production and quality control; and for services like tracking location, temperature, and speed of transport-related shipments—as well as complementary analog technology improvements.

BAS and TES are often offered sequentially.[32] TCs are sector-specific physical locations that typically offer BAS and TES as well as additional services including workforce training on the use of more complex technologies. TCs often include the shared use among SMEs of more expensive manufacturing equipment, product design and fabrication facilities (increasingly using 3D printers), technology development and demonstration initiatives to adapt technologies to local context, and certification services.[33] TCs can be either fully government owned or implemented as public-private partnerships with industry associations. Most TCs operate with at least some level of public subsidy, which is often initially large but declines over time with increasing enterprise contributions in the form of user fees. Another important channel for digital upgrading is through technology transfer, often facilitated through larger domestic and international supplier or buyer firms through the specific value chains in which the recipient enterprise is operating.

Supporting jobs-appropriate technology generation

Some DTs designed in higher-income countries are not appropriate to meet the needs for good jobs in lower-skilled, relatively labor-abundant African countries. As defined in chapter 1, "good" jobs enable learning in addition to generating sufficient earnings to help households to sustainably exit poverty.

Many DTs, including automation and AI technologies, have been designed for use by people in higher-income countries with relatively higher levels of skills and greater quantities of physical capital relative to the size of the workforce. However, even in the United States and other high-income countries, the automation of routine tasks (robotization) has been having adverse impacts on the labor share, with a decline in middle-class jobs and real wages for lower-skilled workers, and consequent increases in inequality (Acemoglu 2021a).[34] If the global development of AI technologies continues to be deployed along its current trajectory and remains unregulated, it may produce even more accentuated economic harms, including even more excessively automating work and further displacing lower-skilled workers undertaking routine tasks, fueling further inequality, inefficiently further pushing down real wages of lower-skilled workers, and failing to improve worker productivity (Acemoglu 2021b).

Global value chains (GVCs) are a key mechanism through which these technologies are being transferred to lower-income countries, from large global buyer firms to local supplier enterprises. As a result, African enterprises participating in these GVCs end up being much more intensive in the use of physical capital and in higher-skilled workers than the capital and skill endowments of the rest of the country. As a result, those enterprises linked to GVCs and able to compete globally cannot absorb the bulk of each country's lower-skilled workforce; conversely, the bulk of enterprises that *can* absorb each country's workforce cannot compete globally (Diao et al. 2021). Further automation in the high-income world risks changing the international division of labor, leading to faster deindustrialization in lower-income countries.

Many DTs have the potential to be adapted and redirected as low-skill-appropriate technologies. DTs can be human enhancing rather than excessively automating. This is because specific DTs can incorporate images on tactile screens, voice-activated commands, and instructional videos—in any local language dialect—in ways that are particularly appropriate to facilitate learning. It is also because of the possibility of existing DTs to be modified and simplified to become intuitive, easy-to-use applications, ideally requiring no prior digital skills to use, to empower lower-skilled workers to perform higher-skill tasks and learn as they work.[35]

In principle, the recording, tracking, and verification features of DTs can enable rural farmers and other local producers who possess valuable localized data to upload these data so that they can be aggregated in ways that enhance their value as well as in ways that allow the workers to be remunerated and benefit fairly and equitably from these data flows across input, production, and logistics markets. A similar approach is possible from tagged data indicating where, how, and by whom food and other products were produced, to the extent that these data are valued by end-use consumers.

Specific DTs also can enable workers who lack the ability to do basic arithmetic to accept payments for goods or services rendered, as has been done successfully with Uber-type mobility apps. In health care, AI tools can enhance the diagnostic and treatment capabilities of nurses, physicians' aides, and other medical technicians, allowing lower-skilled practitioners to perform tasks that only physicians with many more years of professional education have traditionally undertaken (see Acemoglu and Restrepo 2020). In education, AI can be directed to augment teacher capabilities rather than replacing teachers. In finance, AI can enable workers who lack traditional forms of collateral to gain access to credit and insurance services by demonstrating over time the ability both to make small purchases and to put aside small savings within their budget.

Policies to incentivize the generation of more attractive DTs for the jobs-related needs of lower-income African countries will need to build on complementary policies addressing availability, capabilities, attractiveness, and affordability of existing DTs. The creation and profitable commercialization of new low-skill-appropriate DTs requires a business environment that sufficiently rewards start-up entrepreneurs as well as global buyers and input provider corporations to design local solutions for lower-income people in ways that allow them to aggregate the relatively small-value purchases (dictated by ability to pay) of many disparate low-income users. These potential users in turn need to find the DTs sufficiently attractive and also be able to afford the costs of digital connectivity and the underlying smartphones, tablet computers, or other access technologies.[36]

Possible prerequisites for local start-up entrepreneurs as well as global corporations to build viable business models and invest in designing such new, low-skill-appropriate DTs may include public investments in public data systems and open data policies. Public data systems, including in partnerships with private companies, could provide spatial mapping including digital addresses for all geographic locations, geotagging of land records, and local weather mapping so that these are available as a set of common resource public goods. The common availability of such public goods, accessible through user fees, seems to be a preferred alternative to competing corporations, each investing in spatial digital mapping for the areas where they operate, thereby creating private rights for these data and preventing access by all entrepreneurs and other users seeking to add value to these data. Key areas for further policy experimentation and learning include (a) the extent to which innovation, including the creation and scaling of DTs by digital businesses, can be redirected by public policies and investments in favor of lower-skilled entrepreneurs and workers; and (b) the extent to which lower-skilled entrepreneurs and workers will adopt and intensively use these DTs.

Broader policies to enable innovation and development of productive and job-enhancing DTs that respond to Africa's demands are necessary too. Digital entrepreneurs need an environment in which they can appropriate the benefits of the development of new DTs and digital business models. Such an environment must adequately protect not only innovations, through effective intellectual property rights frameworks, but also access to these innovations through licensing of standard essential patents at fair, reasonable, and nondiscriminatory (FRAND) terms. More clarity on whether computational algorithms (such as for ML or AI) are patentable would create more certainty.

The regulatory burden for the deployment of new DTs can also affect the development of DTs, including complex business registration requirements, unclear sector-specific authorizations, and taxation matters. Furthermore, the ability of digital entrepreneurs to grow can be thwarted by weak competition frameworks that do not prevent exclusionary practices or envelopment practices by larger DT providers.[37]

Facilitating enterprise financing

DTs are powerful tools to facilitate enterprise access to finance for both technology adoption and technology generation, including through better measurement and management of financing-related risks. Investments in technology adoption by enterprises and technology generation by start-up entrepreneurs and other firms need to be enabled by financing.

Among the uncertainties caused by new technologies are whether these investments will be sufficiently productive and profitable to warrant extending financing both to user firms (in their adoption and any required buildup of needed new skills and capabilities) and to DT-generating firms. Information asymmetries between financiers and entrepreneurs make it even more difficult for financiers to assess the viability of entrepreneurs' untested ideas. These uncertainties have been further compounded by the COVID-19 pandemic; the risks of new, more virulent, and vaccine-resistant strains; and related local and global supply and demand disruptions.

Such uncertainties typically result in reduced financing, especially for MSMEs and start-ups that lack access to the alternate sources of financing and the types of collateral available to larger, more established firms.

Data provision to improve financiers' visibility and recourse

The inability of MSMEs to use alternate forms of collateral such as movable assets because of inefficient or nonexistent secured transactions regimes further inhibits the supply of financing. Financial service–related DTs, supported by better data and capabilities and by appropriate financial infrastructure and regulations, can enable enterprise financing by improving visibility and enhancing recourse.[38]

Visibility refers to the ability of financiers to access and use timely information to predict the ability and willingness of recipients to meet their repayment obligations. Improved visibility enables lenders to better predict each borrower's probability of default. DTs help make recipients of finance less informationally opaque.

Digital Africa

Recourse refers to the ability of financiers to act if repayment obligations are not met. Improved recourse enables lenders to better predict and minimize the anticipated loss given default. DTs help strengthen financiers' recourse options. Enhanced recourse enables lenders to broaden the market for collateral and the validity of guarantees that can mitigate any loss given default.

Both improved visibility and enhanced recourse help mitigate financing risks and thereby facilitate underserved enterprises to be financed. In addition to supporting the better functioning of private financial markets through the promotion of DT-driven fintech solutions by new and existing financial service providers, public financial support policies include targeted partial credit guarantees, matching grants and vouchers for adoption of technologies and needed capabilities, and credit infrastructure with a focus on credit bureaus and secured transactions.

DT-enabled approaches to improve visibility and recourse include alternate data and new risk modeling tools. In the context of increased digitalization of economic activities, a broad range of transactional data have become available that allow financiers to better understand the risks of extending financing, including the monitoring of current business activity and cash flows as well as real-time changes in profitability in response to technology adoption and investments associated with technology generation.

Relevant transactional data include histories of mobile money transfers,[39] deposits and withdrawals and past financing obtained, loan servicing, utility payments, payroll, rent, input orders and deliveries, sales orders and invoices, and tax information. They can be combined with personal data of the owner and manager(s) of the enterprise, including age, gender, education, wealth-related assets, household size and location, contacts, geo-location and satellite imagery data, and a range of other information based on the use of DTs, including the mobile phone operating system, calling patterns, history of charging and top-ups, social media and e-commerce footprints, and psychometrics. Credit scoring models based on ML and AI techniques can integrate these real-time, high-frequency data in ways that can be retuned as the economic context evolves.

Smaller enterprises and those located in less-developed cities and rural areas often benefit more than larger firms and those in urban areas from fintech lenders' use of these proprietary data by mobile operators, digital payments providers, and big tech firms when available—enabling them to compensate for the lack of traditional data for credit assessments.[40] These models are still nascent in most markets, representing in 2019 roughly 6 percent of the overall stock of credit to the private sector in Kenya, 2 percent in China, 1 percent in Indonesia, and less than 1 percent in other major markets (Cornelli et al. 2020). Open bank data initiatives also facilitate information sharing of transactions and other financial data from banks and nonbank financial institutions, providing key data for fintech developers. Open banking could support financial inclusion and innovation in Africa.[41]

Financial product changes for risk reduction

Financiers can also manage the greater risks in financing technology generation and adoption by changing the tenor and characteristics of their financing products. DTs decrease the costs of extending shorter-term financing by automating credit underwriting, monitoring, and collections and by enabling low-cost digital disbursement and repayment processes, thereby making shorter-term loans to MSMEs more viable. They have the potential to help unbanked enterprises build or rebuild their credit history and then gain access to larger and longer-term loans and other forms of financing. In 2019, for instance, 14 percent of adults had borrowed through short-term digital loans in Kenya, relative to only 9 percent of adults who had access to traditional sources of bank and non-bank credit (Gubbins 2019).

Contextual and embedded financing products, such as through e-commerce platforms and supply chain relationships, facilitated by DTs, enable a broader range of financing opportunities for more types of businesses. For example, MSME truck drivers and small fleet operators in Ghana, Kenya, Nigeria, Togo, and Uganda that use Kobo-360, an African e-logistics platform, can access vehicle financing via the platform. Kobo-360 under-writes working capital loans using proprietary data on the trip and income history for the driver or small fleet operator, with direct visibility into supply, demand, and book-ings. The platform also has insights into a significant portion of the truck operator's cash flow, which also offers the ability to automate loan repayments (Amosun and Unger 2020; Maylie 2020).

As digital order, inventory, and payments systems become more widely used, as end-to-end supply chain processes become fully digitalized, and as the track record of smaller borrowers and supply chain instruments is established, the receivables assets can be bundled and transferred, so that funding will be able to move from corporate balance sheets to bank balance sheets, to the capital markets, or to other investment vehicles.

Credit guarantees, subsidies, and other support

Partial credit guarantees are a useful credit enhancement tool to incentivize private lend-ers to offer more credit for higher-risk financing of technology adoption and generation. They give lenders recourse to the guarantor in case of borrower default, absorbing part of the loss to lenders and thereby boosting lenders' risk tolerance—which is typically insuf-ficient from a social perspective given the positive social externalities associated with technology adoption and generation.[42] The guarantors are typically governments or donors, though there are private guarantees such as credit insurance for trade finance. The contingent liability is direct when the guarantees are issued and administered by the central government, and indirect when the guarantees are channeled through public independent entities, such as in Morocco.

Support programs must be financially sustainable and designed so that well-run enter-prises that need support benefit from them.[43] DTs can help here, too, through the easier collection and analysis of data to transparently monitor and assess the performance of the credit guarantees. Governments can set a size cap for eligible borrowers and other targeted eligibility criteria so that scarce resources are focused on smaller-enterprise investments related to the adoption and generation of technologies. They also can set appropriate guarantee premium fees to lenders to discourage them from overusing this financing support instrument.

Matching grants and vouchers for new technology acquisition and consulting services to acquire needed skills and capabilities as well as R&D subsidies for technology genera-tion and adoption are typically the most common direct financial subsidy instruments.[44] As highlighted by Cirera and Maloney (2017), the diffusion of technologies to low- and middle-income countries represents an externality of historic proportions, providing a strong rationale for subsidies: in the long run, productivity improvements can account for half of gross domestic product growth (Easterly and Levine 2001), with adoption of technologies making up a sizable share. However, in practice, the impact on productivity of matching grants and nonreimbursable funds is mixed, though the intensity of R&D activities has typically increased.

R&D subsidies can be successful in stimulating R&D investments by start-ups and growing firms, fostering entrepreneurial activity, and improving SME productivity, yet evidence is still scarce—as is evidence from low- and middle-income countries on early-stage risk financing for start-ups (Cin, Kim, and Vonortas 2017). Those programs that have tended to focus on firm productivity and growth irrespective of firm size and have reached growing and exporting SMEs investing in new technologies have tended to yield more positive outcomes. Some programs appear to generate an impact on firm innovation only for younger firms that otherwise would not have been able to undertake the investments, in contrast to older firms that use the grants to substitute for private investments that they already were planning to undertake.[45]

Improved credit infrastructure and regulation

The improvement of credit infrastructure is a critical element of the regulatory financial sector framework to enable greater access to finance for investments in technology adoption and generation. In particular, private sector, market-oriented policies to reduce information asymmetries through the establishment and improvement of credit bureau coverage and the reform of secured transaction regimes can have a high impact on boosting the productivity and growth of enterprises. Better access to credit because of improved credit bureau coverage has a substantial positive impact on labor productivity and jobs growth of SMEs (Ghassibe, Appendino, and Mahmoudi 2019).

Widening the range of assets accepted as collateral by modernizing the legal frameworks for secured transactions and introducing digitalized movable asset registries, including by leveraging distributed ledger technologies, enables lenders to find effective means of recourse when hard collateral is not available.[46] In countries that introduced movable asset regimes and registries, the number of firms with access to finance increased by 10 percent on average, interest rates declined, and terms were extended, with stronger impacts for smaller and younger firms (Love, Martinez Pería, and Singh 2016).

More generally, regulatory and supervisory financial sector frameworks will need to be updated, both to support innovation in the use of DTs and associated data and to protect the needs and interests of customers. For example, providers of app-based, short-term, small-value loans in Kenya operated outside the regulatory perimeter between 2016 and 2019. Although usage expanded from 0.6 percent to 8.3 percent of adults who had financial access, many instances of irresponsible behavior took place (CBK 2019).

Regulators can become better digitally informed and experiment with the design of better regulations by using regulatory innovation hubs and sandboxes. Financial regulators and supervisors can also leverage DTs to improve market surveillance, enforce market conduct and consumer protection standards, and respond more effectively to complaints (World Bank 2021a). Importantly, data frameworks must ensure algorithmic transparency and accountability to reduce the chances that bias becomes hard-wired into AI decision models: if a data set does not include loan performance statistics from rural microenterprises run by owner-managers with low education levels, for instance, then an algorithm might continue to exclude this segment or might attribute loan performance to loan characteristics not reflective of the broader applicant pool.

In the area of consumer protection, awareness, knowledge, and skills about financial products and services by users can help them avoid risks such as overindebtedness, fraud, and cybersecurity abuses.[47] Governments need to complement other channels of learning by offering simple, actionable, and accessible financial education messages through digital channels. Finally, increased regional collaboration between national financial regulators and supervisors is essential to promote and address the increasing cross-border and cross-sector dimensions of financial services.

Designing effective policies and institutions

Promotion of market competition

A first principle of effective policy and institutional design is to ensure that business environment policies promote competition and efficient functioning across markets while facilitating associated economic and social adjustment. Level-playing-field competition across markets impels productivity for enterprise survival (Aghion, Antonin, and Bunel 2021; Syverson 2011).

In a dynamic setting, productivity is increased by adoption of better technologies and generation of new, more appropriate ones. By offering to successful suppliers the rewards from investment in using better technologies, competitive markets provide full incentives for this desirable dynamic behavior. By presenting no impediments to firms to enter markets, vie with each other, and expand to meet customer needs, competition undistorted by the granting of rents to privileged firms ensures that customers will be served by the suppliers best able to innovate and satisfy demands at the lowest possible cost.

It is therefore widely recognized that market competition weeds out inefficiency, encourages productivity and technological progress, and generally benefits society by providing a combination of goods and services (a) whose qualities and attributes are adapted to consumer demand, and (b) the supply of which uses up as small a quantity of resources as possible.[48] Competition also makes enterprise output and jobs expansion profitable by stimulating innovation-driven productivity gains.

Policies to promote market competition include strengthening the legal protection of commercial freedom, property rights, and contracts to preserve rewards from productive innovation. They also entail the *removal* of policies that constrain enterprise entry and growth (as well as exit if the execution of a business plan is not profitable). Overall, they include the introduction of a more activist supply-side competition policy emphasizing level-playing-field access to essential business services and other required local inputs, especially those vulnerable to monopolization and foreclosure.[49]

Coordination of complementary support

A second principle of effective policy and institutional design is coordination of complementary support activities. Coordination includes bundling of adoption of DTs and complementary technologies, acquisition of needed skills and capabilities, and financing support in ways that overcome obstacles to broader uptake of DTs while boosting coordination across various public support entities and between government and business. Coordination across different government and private bodies is required, for instance, for public investments in digital platforms providing spatial mapping including digital addresses for all geographic locations, geotagging of land records, and local weather mapping so that these are available as a set of common resource public goods.

One way to facilitate coordination and enhance public policy impact is to anchor government support programs in vertical industry value chains where public-private coordination problems can be solved through focused, industry-specific working groups, supported by a punctual execution plan and an effective delivery unit. These vertical industry value chain support programs, such as for specific agricultural products, should focus on solving coordination problems that arise. African countries' public support programs for businesses—for technology extension and firm capabilities with greater access to domestic and export markets, for entry and innovation promotion, for access to finance, and for the development and scaling-up of digital solutions across these areas—could benefit from being anchored in these value chains.

Efficient production by firms, in addition to private investments in adoption of better technologies, often requires highly specific public inputs, such as industry-specific laws, regulations, and permits; industry-specific skills, work practices, quality standards, and accreditation; and industry- and location-specific infrastructure along with the associated financing. Such public inputs are a form of positive coordination externality, benefiting all firms in the industry. Inputs are often required in bundles specific to the value chain and to the needs of specific types of producers, such as a combination of technology, skills training, financing, insurance, and access to markets for farms in specific horticulture value chains (box 2.3).

BOX 2.3

Public inputs to strengthen value chains in Senegal, Kenya, and Peru

Input bundling in Senegal and Kenya

A randomized control experiment examines how a new contracting arrangement affects the Senegal groundnut value chain. In partnership with two farming cooperatives in Senegal's groundnut basin, Deutschmann, Bernard, and Yameogo (2022) randomly offered micro-smallholder farmers across 40 villages a contract providing a bundle of credit to purchase

- *Quality-improving technology*—specifically the bio-control product Aflasafe SN-01, a new crop treatment to prevent aflatoxin from developing on crops (a product receiving regulatory approval and launched for commercial sale in 2019);
- *Training* on how to use the technology; and
- *Market access*, in the form of a guaranteed price premium conditional on quality certification.

The average treatment effect was 79 percentage points (uptake was 89 percent in villages where farmers received the contract offer relative to 10 percent in control villages). Farmers in high-risk areas were 49 percent more likely to comply with the strictest international standards. And treatment farmers increased total output sales to the cooperative by about 65 percent.

A related study in western Kenya examines the impact on smallholder farmers of the One Acre Fund's program that bundles skills and technology (training on improved farming practices), financing (input loans), and crop insurance. Relaxing multiple productivity constraints in these areas simultaneously caused statistically and economically significant increases of 26 percent in maize production and 16 percent in profits (Deutschmann et al. 2021).

Coordination of vertical and horizontal value chain support in Peru

Bundled inputs are typically underprovided in private markets without government intervention in the broader public interest. Their absence can prevent productivity growth, whereas their presence can enhance it. The example of Peru's "mesas ejecutivas" (MEs, or "executive tables" in English) makes a persuasive case for how such public-private

(continued)

BOX 2.3
Public inputs to strengthen value chains in Senegal, Kenya, and Peru *(continued)*

coordination problems can be solved. MEs are public-private working groups to identify and remove specific bottlenecks and add missing public inputs.

Between December 2014 and May 2016, Peru's Ministry of Production created eight MEs: six that were industry-specific or vertical (forestry, aquaculture, creative industries, textile, gastronomical, and agro-exports, in this order over time); and two that were cross-industry or horizontal (logistics and high-impact entrepreneurship).

The government helped address specific identified public inputs—such as help to comply with technical requirements for new export markets or to design an industry-specific training program—but it did not provide tax exemptions or subsidized credit. For example, the forestry ME obtained coordination between different public entities across line ministries and different levels of government to solve specific, jointly identified, public-good-type bottlenecks.

The forestry ME's achievements included the following:[a]

- A new law and regulation recognizing plantation trees as crops, removing the requirement of a permit to extract wood from plantations, and reducing the registration time of plantation properties from up to one year to three days
- A new protocol with the same timber resource standard at the national, subnational, and local government levels
- A process started by investors and reforestation companies to establish, for the first time, a business association that represents their interests
- Investments in Peru by some of the largest global forest funds

For effective implementation of such support, a time-bound action plan that is agreed upon within the value chain can be decisive, with clear goals that can be tracked on an easy-to-monitor dashboard by an effective delivery unit.[b]

a. See Ghezzi (2017), who emphasizes three main prerequisites for a successful ME: (a) a private sector capable of and interested in problem solving; (b) a public sector willing to participate and able to deliver; and (c) some convener very high up in government capable of inducing cooperation among the different stakeholders, resolving disputes, enacting regulations, and allocating budget.
b. See Sabel and Jordan (2015) for a detailed examination of the Performance Management and Delivery Unit (PEMANDU), an institutional innovation for making, monitoring, and revising ambitious plans for reform involving coordination between public and private actors and among government entities. Goals are translated into key performance indicators. Progress is monitored in a regular cycle of meetings across departments, agencies, and (at times) entities from the private sector or civil society. This monitoring reveals coordination problems or flaws in the initial goals, diagnoses their causes, and focuses efforts on solutions. If participants hoard information or reach a deadlock, disputes are "bumped up" to successively higher review bodies. If the deadlock continues, control of the situation passes to superior authorities, with results that may well make all participants worse off. This situation inflicts what the authors call a "penalty default" and incentivizes the avoidance of deadlocks.

Evidence-based contestability

A third principle of effective policy and institutional design is contestability of policies based on rigorous evidence. Policies should be designed with an explicit and adequate logical framework, stating the identification of market failures that the policy seeks to address and the expected impacts, based on a projection of expected benefits relative to costs. A transparent and clear objective for each policy is essential for an effective evaluation. The public should be informed how well policies work in achieving their objective and how much they cost. This information should constitute a critical input to periodic

Public Expenditure Reviews (PERs) that assess public programs supporting technology adoption and generation to, among other reasons, facilitate reallocation of scarce budget resources to more effective business support policies or toward other priorities of higher public interest.

Evaluations should ideally be included in the design of policies and support programs before they are launched to enable a contestable allocation of resources over time to the most effective and cost-efficient programs. The evaluations should include an analysis of the income incidence of the various programs to understand the extent to which specific policies and programs benefit lower-income people. Effective policies require strong design and implementation processes, with embedded learning mechanisms to facilitate continuous improvement of existing programs in the light of evidence. The design of effective institutional frameworks and processes should include periodic evaluation reviews as well as the creation of specialized evaluation departments in line ministries with the mandate of evaluating their portfolio of instruments.

Market-compatible incentives

Finally, effective business support policies must employ market-compatible incentives whenever possible. In cases where public policy is required to redress a market failure, including technology upgrading and training schemes, employing market-compatible incentives is likely to lead to better allocation of resources. For example, the marginal costs of business advisory support, extension, training, and technology support policies should be paid by the beneficiaries, such as through matching grants, even if through in-kind contributions for very low-income beneficiaries. And, as shown in the case of some training programs (O'Connell and Mation 2021), when the private sector is involved in designing the training priorities, the program shows better outcomes.[50] Matching grants, public-private dialogues, and benchmarking in exchange for provision of enterprise-level data are other examples of market-compatible business support incentives (box 2.4).

BOX 2.4

A job creation program in Senegal: Effective design for technological transformation

Senegal's Accelerating Competitiveness and Job Creation program focuses on improving the competitiveness of the private sector through enterprise technology upgrading for productivity and good jobs. It seeks to accomplish this goal through interventions at three levels:

1. *Enterprise level*—supporting access to technology and capabilities through matching grants, complemented by access to finance through partial credit guarantees and equity investments
2. *Value chain level*—fixing market failures along specific value chains, including by providing club goods
3. *Economywide level*—supporting underprovided complementary public infrastructure services

The four-year program is also a subset of the economic transformation and growth pillar of the Adjusted and Accelerated Priority Action Plan (PAP/AA) of the Senegalese government's Emergent Senegal Plan (Plan Sénégal Émergent, PSE).

(continued)

BOX 2.4
A job creation program in Senegal: Effective design for technological transformation *(continued)*

At its core, the program seeks to promote technological transformation for jobs by providing matching grants to micro, small, and medium enterprises to facilitate technology adoption, boost productivity, and expand output and jobs. At the enterprise level, the matching public subsidies seek to support adoption of digital and complementary technologies and capabilities related to general business functions (management practices including accounting, marketing, payments, and quality control) as well as sector-specific business functions in selected value chains (for example, modern irrigation systems and postharvest logistics for horticulture and other agricultural products, the manufacturing of selected pharmaceutical products, retail, tourism, and digital services). A special window is focused on microenterprises, including informal ones.

At the value chain level, a Competitiveness Task Force will conduct public-private dialogues to address inappropriate or missing regulations as well as market access and coordination bottlenecks specific to selected value chains (figure B2.4.1). The program seeks in parallel to address access to finance constraints facing micro, small, and medium enterprises in acquiring technologies. The mechanisms include a risk-sharing partial credit guarantee scheme for the banking sector to ease access to credit as well as a small and medium enterprise fund to directly provide equity and quasi-equity finance to eligible growing small and medium enterprises. The program also supports the structuring of public-private partnership projects that provide complementary public goods for specific value chains as well as economywide infrastructure services.

Finally, the Firm-level Adoption of Technology (FAT) survey index will be used before and after program interventions to measure both the extent of use and the intensive use of technologies as a result of program participation. Beneficiary enterprises will each fill out a FAT questionnaire as part of the initial screening. Doing so will enable enterprises to benchmark themselves against similar enterprises in their sector and size group. It also will facilitate the design of relevant business advisory and technology extension services.

FIGURE B2.4.1 Coordination of complementary support mechanisms tailored to specific value chains

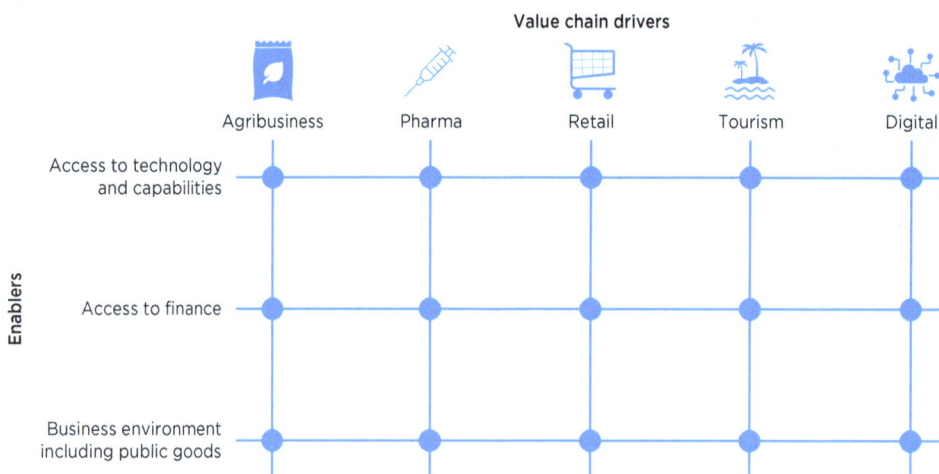

Source: World Bank 2021b.

Notes

1. FAT survey data used for this report were collected over 2019–21 in the following countries: 2021 data in Ghana (1,262 observations); 2020 data in Kenya (1,305 obs.); 2019–20 data in Malawi (482 obs.); 2019 data in Senegal (1,786 obs.); 2019 data in Ceará, one of the poorer states in Brazil's Northeast region (711 obs.); and 2019 data in Vietnam (1,499 obs.). The Senegal data allow for a disaggregation between formal and informal firms, with 78 percent of firms identified as informal (defined as those not using a prescribed accounting system). Brazil's Ceará state and Vietnam were selected for comparison because data about these new technology adoption measures were available only in these locations at the time of writing this report. Ceará has about 9 million inhabitants and was ranked in the lower half of Brazilian states in per capita income (18th out of 27) in 2019, according to the Brazilian Institute of Geography and Statistics (IBGE). See Cirera, Comin, and Cruz (2022).

2. The RIA work defines formal enterprises as those that have legally registered (a) at the national registrar general or country-level revenue authority; (b) at the local authority or municipality; or (c) both. Informal enterprises have neither type of registration. The RIA survey covers 3,325 observations during 2017–18. Although RIA also covers Rwanda and Uganda, the lack of sufficient data on variables of interest preclude the inclusion of those countries here.

3. Firm-level productivity is measured as nominal value added in US dollars divided by the number of employees. This relationship controls for country fixed effects, other firm-level observable variables, and dummies for the 12 sectors for which sector-specific technologies are available.

4. For instance, an average African enterprise whose technological sophistication index moves from 2 to 3 is associated with an increase in productivity of roughly 1 log point, from 13 to almost 14, whereas the same move from 2 to 3 for an average enterprise (based on data from all 10 available countries) is associated with an increase in productivity of less than 0.5 log points, from 10 to less than 10.5.

5. It is important to take into account the immediate up-front cost of technological upgrading, which must be compared with the potential benefits in productivity and jobs gains in response to an eventual increase in market demand.

6. Only in Senegal was it possible to draw a representative sample of informal firms. Thus, the "average" firm in Brazil, Ghana, Malawi, and Vietnam refers to an average of all formal firms, whereas the average in Senegal comprises both formal and informal firms. These associations with productivity level control for end-period firm size, formality status, sector, and region. See references to country-specific papers in Cirera, Comin, and Cruz (2022).

7. Although the point estimate of the association between technology use and job increases is higher for informal than formal Senegalese firms (12 percent versus 10 percent), the larger standard error for informal enterprises indicates that this 12 percent estimate is not statistically significantly different from zero at the 5 percent confidence level.

8. These jobs growth associations control for initial firm size, firm age, formality status, sector, and region, as well as for multinational company and export status. The share of chief executive officers and managers, professionals, and technicians to total workers is used as a proxy for higher-skilled workers; the share of clerks, production, and service workers is used as a proxy for lower-skilled workers. The difference in the share of higher-skilled workers between 2016 and 2018 is used as the dependent variable. (See references to country-specific FAT survey reports in Cirera, Comin, and Cruz 2022).

9. These estimates are based on cross-country regressions on a subset of the data summarized in Cirera, Comin, and Cruz (2022, figures 4.6 and 4.8).

10. Whether owners are "transformational" entrepreneurs is a proxy for their inherent aptitudes for productive entrepreneurship, based on their answers to the RIA survey question, "What was the main reason to start a business for you?" Transformational entrepreneurs are owners who responded, "My own business pays more than being employed." Such a response suggests that they have selected themselves as entrepreneurs because of the profit-making opportunity that owning a business provides. The remaining (subsistence) entrepreneurs answered either "To make additional money to my salary" or "Otherwise I would have been unemployed." These responses

suggest that entrepreneurship is a necessity or subsistence choice to supplement earnings or because no preferred wage job was available.

11. Large informal firms in West Africa differ from both formal and small informal firms. They tend to operate in import-export trade, domestic wholesale-retail, transportation, and construction. They typically begin as small operators with minimal education and become large owing to superior entrepreneurial ability and effort, along with assistance from ethnic and religious trading groups. Often, a single person controls most GBFs. See Benjamin and Mbaye (2012).

12. The top 20 countries globally in digital business density, in order, are Kenya, United States, Estonia, Israel, United Kingdom, India, Rwanda, New Zealand, Finland, Singapore, Sweden, Canada, Uganda, Cambodia, Iceland, South Africa, Ghana, Pakistan, China, and Bulgaria (according to the Digital Business Database, 2020, of the World Bank's Finance, Competitiveness & Innovation Global Practice).

13. The telecommunication subsector includes but is not limited to telecommunication service providers, telecommunication infrastructure developers, and internet connectivity services for both individual consumers and businesses.

14. Whereas digital-solution providers in telecommunication, fintech, and logistics tech directly support enterprise productivity upgrading, e-commerce enables all firms to procure and sell more efficiently, including by finding better matches. Health tech, in principle, helps all workers, employees, managers, and owners to stay healthy, prevent illness, and be more productive.

15. Regarding uptake, the gap between Sub-Saharan African countries and other low- and middle-income countries in terms of small firms' increased DT use (42.8 percent versus 48.7 percent) and the gap of 20.5 percent between small and large firms in Sub-Saharan Africa are the two comparisons that are highly statistically significantly different (at the 1 percent confidence level).

16. Regarding investments, the gap between Sub-Saharan Africa and other countries among small firms (19.0 percent versus 23.6 percent), medium firms (28.2 percent versus 33.0 percent), and large firms (38.7 percent versus 48.4 percent) as well as the gap between small and large firms in Sub-Saharan Africa of 19.7 percent are all highly statistically significantly different (at the 1 percent confidence level).

17. The "Business" category in the Google Play store includes video conferencing and collaboration apps such as Zoom, Microsoft Teams, and Google Hangout, as well as supply-side apps of well-known gig work platforms (for example, Uber and DoorDash); job search platforms; and ERP apps that help streamline parts of business operations including payroll, procurement, accounting, and so on.

18. A separate estimate of the causal effect of additional DT uptake on changes in sales using nearest-neighbor matching results in a total effect of 6.9 percentage points (Comin et al. 2022).

19. For a review of the theoretical and empirical literature on technology adoption and diffusion, see Cirera, Comin, and Cruz (2022), chapter 6. For adoption drivers of DTs including with network effects (like digital platforms), see Cusolito (2021). The digital lag among small and medium enterprises in Organisation for Economic Co-operation and Development (OECD) countries is attributed to similar factors, though with different relative emphases, including insufficient capital and missing complementary assets (ability to pay), lack of information and awareness, and skills gaps (willingness to use). See OECD (2021) and references therein.

20. The share of microenterprises citing lack of internet availability corresponds roughly with the average of 29 percent of people who lacked 3G+ coverage in 2018 across Sub-Saharan African countries (Atiyas and Dutz 2023). The lower share of enterprises lacking availability (20 percent) is to be expected from the RIA survey given that the sampled Enumeration Areas for microenterprises have largely focused on residential areas where coverage is expected to be higher. For a further explanation of Enumeration Areas in the RIA survey data, see Mothobi, Gillwald, and Aguera (2020).

21. Because elements of the business environment vary largely at the country level (data are not available to explore differential business environment effects across regions within countries), they are captured by country fixed effects and are not possible to disentangle from other country-level effects.

22. Reported results are marginal effects based on multinomial logit or probit regressions on enterprise characteristics, controlling for country fixed effects. Smartphone adoption is modeled as a multinomial logit regression with enterprise choice of either smartphone, 2G or 2.5G phone (without full internet functionality), or no phone, whereas computer adoption is modeled as a simple yes or no choice. FAT survey countries include Ghana, Kenya, and Senegal; RIA survey countries include Ghana, Kenya, Mozambique, Nigeria, Rwanda, Senegal, South Africa, and Tanzania. The findings are restricted to statistically significant associations and do not allow inferences to be made about causality.

23. The FAT survey did not ask about electricity use in Ghana. In the reported specification, it was assumed that all enterprises in Ghana have access to electricity.

24. The correlates for microenterprises are much lower than for larger firms because of the much lower average levels of schooling among microenterprise managers relative to those in larger firms.

25. Based on the FAT survey findings, technological sophistication is consistently higher for each country in the agriculture sector relative to manufacturing and services, as summarized by the average business sophistication index of the firm across all GBFs and the particular sector's SBFs. See Cirera, Comin, and Cruz (2022), figure 2.3.

26. That formal 5+worker firms are 22.7 percent more likely than informal ones to use computers is the largest conditional correlation across all variables. This comparison is largely relative to informal enterprises in Senegal, defined as those that do not use the approved accounting systems required for formal firms to file their taxes. The share of informal firms in the Ghana and Kenya sample is negligible.

27. When an enterprise has multiple owners, it is considered female-owned if at least 50 percent of owners are women.

28. Causal identification is based on distance of the enterprise from the backbone node used as an instrumental variable. Distance from the backbone is shown to be a predictor of internet access. And distance to the backbone is postulated to affect technology adoption only through the internet. All specifications control for region and sector fixed effects, and firm characteristics.

29. For a practical guide to policy makers in low- and middle-income countries to better formulate innovation policies including technology adoption and generation, see Cirera et al. (2020). It provides a rigorous typology of innovation policy instruments, including the types of institutional capabilities needed for governments to successfully implement these policy instruments in developing countries as well as evidence of policy impact.

30. More detailed information on the issues covered in this subsection are provided in Cirera, Comin, and Cruz (2022), chapter 7 (on policies to accelerate technology adoption).

31. Digital upgrading programs reviewed, including to increase firms' participation in digital platforms, are from Chile, Denmark, Korea, Malaysia, Singapore, Spain, and the United Kingdom.

32. In OECD countries, the use of government-funded TES programs targeting SMEs has expanded in recent decades. In OECD (2021), see box 1.6 and table 1.4.

33. One of the best-known networks of TCs is the Fraunhofer Society in Germany, a network of 69 applied research centers that work closely with industry and with other parts of the research sector. They are associated with the diffusion of Industry 4.0 technologies. A 1 percent increase in expenditures has been shown to result in 1.4 percentage points of higher growth in turnover and 0.7 percentage points in productivity (Comin et al. 2019).

34. Acemoglu and Restrepo (2021) show that 50–70 percent of the adverse wage structure dynamics in the United States between 1980 and 2016 is due to automation technologies. These dynamics are largely experienced by workers specializing in routine tasks in industries undergoing automation, with faster displacement of existing jobs relative to slower reinstatement of new jobs, and with new tasks largely more skill intensive. The negative effects on wages are concentrated in the bottom seven deciles of the wage distribution, worsening inequality. "Excessive automation" that displaces labor without creating sufficient new tasks and without significant productivity gains (with impacts on total factor productivity possibly even negative) is driven by global competition, business models linked to the growing size of big tech, labor market institutions that do not sufficiently promote worker interests, and net subsidies to physical capital (largely through the tax system).

35. Whether basic digital skills (how to use a smartphone, how to navigate the internet, and how to download apps and use them) must be separately taught before use, or whether the use of smartphones and specific associated apps can be designed to be so easy and intuitive to allow users to learn as they use them—if they are sufficiently attractive and of productive use—is an open question that could benefit from further research.

36. The positive lessons from renewable energy illustrate that a sizable redirection of technological change is possible, if supported by subsidies, a measurement framework, and changes in social norms and societal pressure (Acemoglu 2021a).

37. "Envelopment" occurs when a (private) digital platform enters another market by acquiring a company and combining its own functionality and data with the target's.

38. This subsection is inspired by and makes use of the framework and examples in chapter 4 of the World Bank's *World Development Report 2022* on enterprise financing (World Bank 2022).

39. The number of mobile money accounts in Sub-Saharan Africa exceeded 500 million in 2020 (GSMA 2021).

40. See Gambacorta et al. (2019) and Huang et al. (2020) on the recent experience of MYbank, an online bank serving MSMEs in China established by Ant Group (an affiliate of the Alibaba Group, formerly Ant Financial Services Group and Alipay). MYbank's credit underwriting uses ML to integrate payments and transactions data with other data from Alibaba Group's e-commerce platforms and Alipay's financial services. Roughly 80 percent of MYbank clients have fewer than 10 employees, and most have limited or no access to financing from traditional banks. MYbank has indicated in an interview that it leverages satellite imagery to estimate the crop production of micro and small farmers.

41. For more details about open banking regimes, see Plaitakis and Staschen (2020).

42. Credit guarantee schemes have been used extensively by governments in high-income and several low- and middle-income countries in response to the higher-risk COVID-19 environment. In 2020, public credit guarantee schemes amounted to an estimated 2 percent of global gross domestic product (Calice 2020). In Spain, for example, such schemes improved access to financing for MSMEs and imposed a smaller fiscal burden relative to government grants or direct lending (Corredera-Catalán, di Pietro, and Trujillo-Ponce 2021).

43. Principles to guide the good functioning of public partial credit guarantees include reducing political interference, encouraging private participation, and maintaining a certain amount of risk taking by lenders (World Bank and FIRST Initiative 2015).

44. See OECD (2021), table 1.4, for a list of financial support initiatives spanning grants, vouchers, and direct financial subsidies for preparing digital strategies and increasing the uptake and use of DTs, including cloud services, e-commerce, and teleworking across a range of countries including Argentina, Chile, Colombia, Israel, Hungary, Japan, Korea, Malaysia, Slovenia, and Türkiye. See OECD (2021), table 1.5, for skills development programs; table 1.6 for data governance and protection in SMEs; and table 1.8 for e-government and e-services for SMEs.

45. See the examples in the subsection on "Innovation, R&D and Adoption of Productivity-Enhancing Technologies" in World Bank (2021c). Howell (2017) found that, in China, production-based subsidies for technological upgrading improved innovation intensity but not productivity. This finding may indicate that specific funding of technology generation and adoption rather than general production will deliver better outcomes.

46. Modern collateral registries, including movable assets registries, can benefit from the use of DTs such as distributed ledger technologies (also known as blockchains) because they better enable lenders to track location collateral, monitor its use, and deactivate it to enforce repayment (World Bank 2020).

47. Over 50 percent of digital financial users in Kenya and Nigeria reportedly experienced fraud or attempted fraud since the COVID-19 pandemic began, according to recent surveys (Blackmon, Mazer, and Warren 2021).

48. Chinese import competition increased patenting, information technology adoption, and productivity by as much as 30 percent of the total increase in Europe in the late 1990s and early 2000s (Bloom, Draca, and Van Reenen 2016).

49. See Dutz, Ordover, and Willig (2000) on the need for public policies to foster productive entrepreneurship by protecting commercial freedom, property rights, and contracts and by preventing foreclosure and enabling access to essential business services and other required local inputs. This includes level-playing-field access to data and connectivity (information and communication technology, transportation, and logistics), electricity and financial services, sites for production and related land markets, professional business services, appropriately skilled labor, and needed institutional infrastructure.

50. O'Connell and Mation (2021) show that the employer-informed segment of Brazil's nationwide skills training program nearly doubled the short-term effect on trainees' jobs and earnings relative to the traditional program. The increased employment effects in the employer-informed program stem from trainees finding employment in large, high-growth firms located in low-growth municipalities. The results indicate that limited, structured input from the private sector appears to improve the alignment between skills trained and skill demand.

References

Acemoglu, Daron. 2021a. "Automation and the Inappropriateness of Technology." Slide presentation at the International Economic Association's Workshop on Digital Technologies: Limits and Opportunities for Economic Development, October 12.

Acemoglu, Daron. 2021b. "Harms of AI." Working Paper No. 29247, National Bureau of Economic Research, Cambridge, MA.

Acemoglu, Daron, and Pascual Restrepo. 2020. "The Wrong Kind of AI? Artificial Intelligence and the Future of Labour Demand." *Cambridge Journal of Regions, Economy and Society* 13 (1): 25–35.

Acemoglu, Daron, and Pascual Restrepo. 2021. "Tasks, Automation, and the Rise in US Wage Inequality." Working Paper No. 28920, National Bureau of Economic Research, Cambridge, MA.

Aghion, Philippe, Céline Antonin, and Simon Bunel. 2021. *The Power of Creative Destruction: Economic Upheaval and the Wealth of Nations.* Cambridge, MA: The Belknap Press of Harvard University Press.

Amosun, Adedoyin, and Deborah Unger. 2020. "Keeping African Goods Moving." *strategy+business*, August 26, 2020. https://www.strategy-business.com/article/Keeping-African-goods-moving.

Atiyas, İzak, and Mark A. Dutz. 2023. "Digital Technology Uses among Microenterprises: Why Is Productive Use So Low across Sub-Saharan Africa?" Policy Research Working Paper 10280, World Bank, Washington, DC.

Balbontin, R., Ana Paula Cusolito, and Xavier Cirera. 2021. "A Review of Digital Upgrading Programs." Unpublished manuscript, World Bank, Washington, DC.

Benjamin, Nancy, and Ahmadou Aly Mbaye. 2012. *The Informal Sector in Francophone Africa: Firm Size, Productivity and Institutions.* Washington, DC: World Bank.

Berkes, Enrico, Xavier Cirera, Diego Comin, Marcio Cruz, and Kyung Min Lee. Forthcoming. "Infrastructure, Productivity, and Technology Adoption." Background paper, World Bank, Washington, DC.

Blackmon, William, Rafe Mazer, and Shana Warren. 2021. "Consumer Protection in Digital Finance Surveys." Country-specific digital finance survey report, Innovations for Poverty Action, Washington, DC.

Bloom, Nicholas, Mirko Draca, and John Van Reenen. 2016. "Trade Induced Technical Change: The Impact of Chinese Imports on Innovation, IT and Productivity." *Review of Economic Studies* 83 (1): 87–117.

Calice, Pietro. 2020. "Boosting Credit: Public Guarantees Can Help Mitigate Risk during COVID-19." *Private Sector Development* (blog), May 28, 2020. https://blogs.worldbank.org/psd/boosting-credit-public-guarantees-can-help-mitigate-risk-during-covid-19.

CBK (Central Bank of Kenya). 2019. "2019 FinAccess Household Survey." Survey report, CBK, Nairobi.

Cin, Beom Cheol, Young Jun Kim, and Nicholas S. Vonortas. 2017. "The Impact of Public R&D Subsidy on Small Firm Productivity: Evidence from Korean SMEs." *Small Business Economics* 48 (2): 345–60.

Cirera, Xavier, Diego Comin, and Marcio Cruz. 2022. *Bridging the Technological Divide: Technology Adoption by Firms in Developing Countries*. Washington, DC: World Bank.

Cirera, Xavier, Diego Comin, Marcio Cruz, and Kyung Min Lee. 2021. "Anatomy of Technology in the Firm." Working Paper No. 28080 (Revised), National Bureau of Economic Research, Cambridge, MA.

Cirera, Xavier, Jaime Frías, Justin Hill, and Yanchao Li. 2020. *A Practitioner's Guide to Innovation Policy: Instruments to Build Firm Capabilities and Accelerate Technological Catch-Up in Developing Countries*. Washington, DC: World Bank.

Cirera, Xavier, and William F. Maloney. 2017. *The Innovation Paradox: Developing-Country Capabilities and the Unrealized Promise of Technological Catch-Up*. Washington, DC: World Bank.

Comin, Diego, Marcio Cruz, Xavier Cirera, Kyung Min Lee, and Jesica Torres. 2022. "Technology and Resilience." Working Paper No. 29644, National Bureau of Economic Research, Cambridge, MA.

Comin, Diego, Georg Licht, Maikel Pellens, and Torben Schubert. 2019. "Do Companies Benefit from Public Research Organizations? The Impact of the Fraunhofer Society in Germany." Discussion Paper 19-006, Centre for European Economic Research (ZEW), Mannheim, Germany.

Cornelli, Giulio, Jon Frost, Leonardo Gambacorta, Raghavendra Rau, Robert Wardrop, and Tania Ziegler. 2020. "Fintech and Big Tech Credit: A New Database." Working Paper No. 887, Bank for International Settlements, Basel, Switzerland.

Corredera-Catalán, Félix, Filippo di Pietro, and Antonio Trujillo-Ponce. 2021. "Post-COVID-19 SME Financing Constraints and the Credit Guarantee Scheme Solution in Spain." *Journal of Banking Regulation* 22 (3): 250–60.

Cusolito, Ana Paula. 2021. "The Economics of Technology Adoption." Unpublished manuscript, World Bank, Washington, DC.

Deutschmann, Joshua W., Tanguy Bernard, and Ouambi Yameogo. 2022. "Contracting and Quality Upgrading: Evidence from an Experiment in Senegal." Working paper, University of Chicago.

Deutschmann, Joshua W., Maya Duru, Kim Siegal, and Emilia Tjernström. 2021. "Can Smallholder Extension Transform African Agriculture?" Working Paper No. 26054, National Bureau of Economic Research, Cambridge, MA.

Diao, Xinshen, Mia Ellis, Margaret S. McMillan, and Dani Rodrik. 2021. "Africa's Manufacturing Puzzle: Evidence from Tanzanian and Ethiopian Firms." Working Paper No. 28344, National Bureau of Economic Research, Cambridge, MA.

Dutz, Mark A., Janusz Ordover, and Robert D. Willig. 2000. "Entrepreneurship, Access Policy and Economic Development: Lessons from Industrial Organization." *European Economic Review* 44 (4–6): 739–47.

Easterly, William, and Ross Levine. 2001. "What Have We Learned from a Decade of Empirical Research on Growth? It's Not Factor Accumulation: Stylized Facts and Growth Models." *World Bank Economic Review* 15 (2): 177–219.

Gambacorta, Leonardo, Yiping Huang, Han Qiu, and Jingyi Wang. 2019. "How Do Machine Learning and Non-Traditional Data Affect Credit Scoring? New Evidence from a Chinese Fintech Firm." BIS Working Papers No. 834, Bank for International Settlements, Basel, Switzerland.

Ghassibe, Mishel, Maximilliano Appendino, and Samir Elsadek Mahmoudi. 2019. "SME Financial Inclusion for Sustained Growth in the Middle East and Central Asia." Working Paper No. 2019/209, International Monetary Fund, Washington, DC.

Ghezzi, Piero. 2017. "Mesas Ejecutivas in Peru: Lessons for Productive Development Policies." *Global Policy* 8 (3): 369–80.

GSMA (Global System for Mobile Communications Association). 2021. "State of the Industry Report on Mobile Money 2021." GSMA, London.

Gubbins, Paul. 2019. "Digital Credit in Kenya: Facts and Figures from FinAccess 2019." Focus Note, Financial Sector Deepening Kenya (FSD Kenya), Nairobi.

Howell, Anthony. 2017. "Picking 'Winners' in China: Do Subsidies Matter for Indigenous Innovation and Firm Productivity?" *China Economic Review* 44: 154–65.

Huang, Yiping, Longmei Zhang, Zhenhua Li, Han Qiu, Tao Sun, and Xue Wang. 2020. "Fintech Credit Risk Assessment for SMEs: Evidence from China." Working Paper No. 2020/193, International Monetary Fund, Washington, DC.

Love, Inessa, María Soledad Martinez Pería, and Sandeep Singh. 2016. "Collateral Registries for Movable Assets: Does Their Introduction Spur Firms' Access to Bank Financing?" *Journal of Financial Services Research* 49 1–37.

Maylie, Devon. 2020. "Unsung Heroes: Truckers Keep Delivering, Thanks to Online Platform." *IFC Insights*, Issue 6 (Special Edition on COVID-19), March 31. International Finance Corporation, Washington, DC.

Mothobi, Onkokame, Alison Gillwald, and Pablo Aguera. 2020. "A Demand Side View of Informality and Financial Inclusion." Policy Paper No. 9, Series 5: After Access, Research ICT Africa, Cape Town, South Africa.

O'Connell, Stephen D., and Lucas F. Mation. 2021. "Tell Us What You Need: Matching Public Job Training to Local Skill Demand with Employers' Input." Unpublished manuscript.

OECD (Organisation for Economic Co-operation and Development). 2021. *The Digital Transformation of SMEs*. OECD Studies on SMEs and Entrepreneurship, Paris: OECD Publishing.

Plaitakis, Ariadne, and Stefan Staschen. 2020. "Open Banking: How to Design for Financial Inclusion." Working Paper, Consultative Group to Assist the Poor (CGAP), Washington, DC.

Ragoussis, Alexandros, and Jonathan David Timmis. 2022. "Global Transition Online." Policy Research Working Paper 9951, World Bank, Washington, DC.

Sabel, Charles F., and Luke Jordan. 2015. "Doing, Learning, Being: Some Lessons Learned from Malaysia's National Transformation Program." Report No. 96041, World Bank, Washington, DC.

Syverson, Chad. 2011. "What Determines Productivity?" *Journal of Economic Literature* 49 (2): 326–65.

World Bank. 2020. "Distributed Ledger Technology & Secured Transactions: Legal, Regulatory and Technological Perspectives." Guidance Notes Series - Note 1: Collateral Registry, Secured Transactions Law and Practice, World Bank, Washington, DC.

World Bank. 2021a. "The Next Wave of Suptech Innovation: Suptech Solutions for Market Conduct Supervision." Technical Note, World Bank, Washington, DC.

World Bank. 2021b. "Program Appraisal Document on a Proposed Credit in the Amount of EUR 106.6 Million (US$125.0 Million Equivalent) to the Republic of Senegal for a Senegal Jobs, Economic Transformation and Recovery Program." Report No. PAD4365, World Bank, Washington, DC.

World Bank. 2021c. "Strengthening World Bank SME-Support Interventions: Operational Guidance Document." Report No. 157949, World Bank, Washington, DC.

World Bank. 2022. *World Development Report 2022: Finance for an Equitable Recovery*. Washington, DC: World Bank.

World Bank and FIRST Initiative. 2015. "Principles for Public Credit Guarantee Schemes for SMEs." Report of the Task Force for the Design, Implementation and Evaluation of Public Credit Guarantee Schemes for Small and Medium Enterprises, Report No. 101769, World Bank, Washington, DC.

Zhu, Tingting Juni, Philip Grinsted, Hangyul Song, and Malathi Velamuri. 2022. "Digital Businesses in Developing Countries: New Insights for a Digital Development Pathway." Background paper, World Bank, Washington, DC.

CHAPTER 3

Households

Supporting Productive Use of DTs for Inclusive Economic Impact

Household internet use is low, uneven, but growing

Digital technologies (DTs) can help African governments to advance their poverty reduction and inclusion efforts across the continent, provided that more innovations in digital solutions address the constraints the poor face in using DTs productively. As chapter 1 showed, overall internet usage is deficient in low- and middle-income countries and even more so in Sub-Saharan Africa.[1] Two main factors limit internet use in the region: First, high-quality digital infrastructure supply is limited owing to a combination of market constraints and ineffective regulations. Second, and more important, there is a low demand for internet services and DTs offered over the internet, both in the extensive and intensive margins.

These factors create three gaps related to overall internet usage (World Bank 2021b):

1. *The availability gap:* lack of internet access due to a lack of infrastructure

2. *The uptake gap:* low demand for (or uptake of) internet services even when the services are available (the extensive margin)

3. *The consumption gap:* low data consumption or demand even among those who are connected to internet services (the intensive margin)

Chapter 4 discusses the first gap—the availability gap—and digital infrastructure challenges in Sub-Saharan Africa. This chapter focuses instead on the uptake and consumption gaps among households and individuals across Africa, emphasizing how internet uptake and consumption can benefit them through multiple channels—reducing the prices of goods and services, increasing productivity, and enhancing employment opportunities. With only 22 percent of the population connected to mobile broadband internet and the internet uptake gap of 74 percent (Atiyas and Dutz 2022), Sub-Saharan Africa could triple internet usage to 75 percent without any expansion in infrastructure. This projection indicates that the main challenge is the low *uptake* of internet services even when the infrastructure is available.

Growing usage with widening gaps between African subregions

Although individuals' use of internet services and internet-based DTs has grown tremendously across Sub-Saharan Africa over the past two decades—reaching 33 percent in 2020—this increase is faster in the Western and Central Africa subregions than in the

Eastern and Southern African subregions, widening the usage gap between these subregional groups (figure 3.1). For instance, the usage gap between these two Sub-Saharan African subregional groups increased from 0.8 percentage point in 2010 to 8 percentage points in 2020.

Looking at all four subregions within Sub-Saharan Africa shows an even wider range of differences. From lowest to highest, 21 percent of the population in Central Africa used the internet in 2020, 22 percent in Eastern Africa, 31 percent in Western Africa, and 33 percent in Southern Africa (figure 3.2).

FIGURE 3.1 **Internet usage, by subregion, Sub-Saharan Africa, 2000–20**

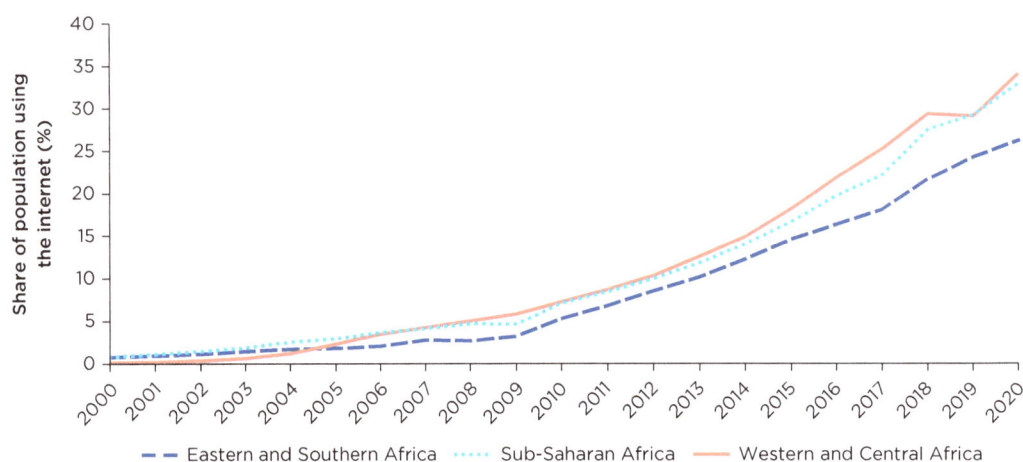

Source: World Bank, using data from World Development Indicators database.
Note: Internet "usage" is defined as the share of the total population using the internet, regardless of internet coverage. Subregions follow World Bank definitions.

FIGURE 3.2 **Wireless broadband and internet coverage, usage gaps, and coverage gaps, by subregion, Sub-Saharan Africa, 2020**

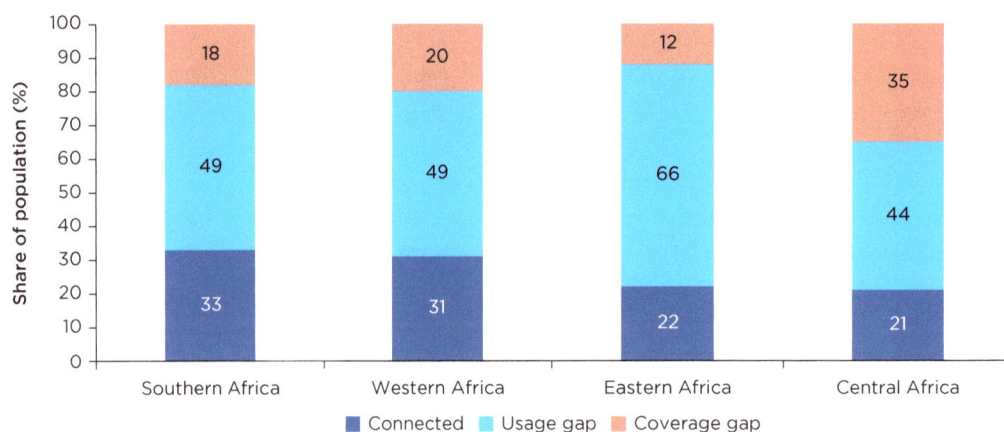

Source: Global System for Mobile Communications Association (GSMA) Intelligence, 2020 data, https://www.gsmaintelligence.com/data/.
Note: "Wireless broadband internet" refers to third- and fourth-generation (3G and 4G) mobile internet connections. Internet "usage" is defined as the share of the total population using the internet, regardless of internet coverage. Subregions follow World Bank definitions.

However, Eastern Africa has the highest usage gap—66 percent—which is 17 percentage points higher than that of Southern Africa (the subregion with the second-highest uptake gap) even though the two subregions have the same digital infrastructure coverage. These huge differences in the usage gap are likely due primarily to differences in internet affordability across countries in the subregions. The lowest uptake is present in populous countries such as the Democratic Republic of Congo, Ethiopia, and Tanzania (as further discussed in the section in this chapter titled "Understanding constraints to household internet use").

Gaps within African subregions

Within each Sub-Saharan Africa subregion, use of the internet varies across countries. For example, the relatively high internet penetration rate in Southern Africa is primarily driven by South Africa and Lesotho (figure 3.3).[2] Based on 2017–18 household survey data, South Africa has 53 percent of the population with internet usage, followed by Lesotho with a 32 percent internet usage rate. Internet usage in Eastern Africa was generally low, ranging from 9 percent in Rwanda to 27 percent in Kenya. In Western Africa, by contrast, Senegal, Nigeria, and Ghana had relatively high internet usage rates: 31 percent, 29 percent, and 28 percent, respectively.

FIGURE 3.3 Internet usage in 10 Sub-Saharan African countries, 2008, 2012, and 2018

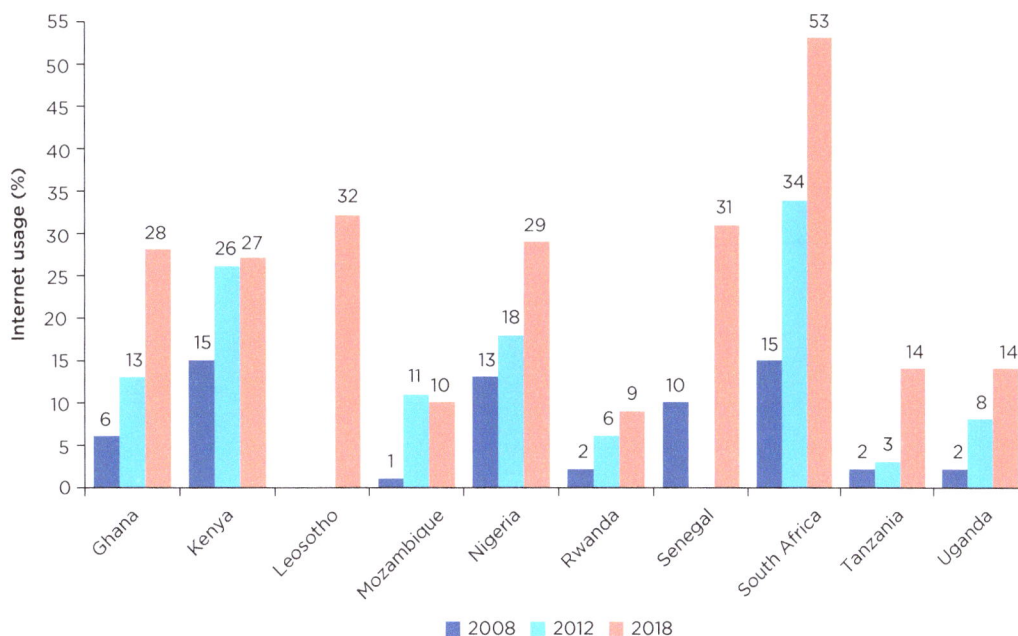

Source: Research ICT Africa (RIA) After Access Survey data, 2008, 2012, and 2018, adapted from Gillwald and Mothobi 2019, figure 10.
Note: The figure excludes 2008 and 2012 data for Lesotho and 2012 data for Senegal because they were not included in the RIA After Access surveys for those years. It also excludes Central African countries because of the lack of comparable data. Internet "usage" is defined as the share of the total population using the internet, regardless of internet coverage.

Gaps within African countries

The observed differences in internet usage within the Sub-Saharan Africa region extend to those within countries and are explained by several socioeconomic factors. There are also differences in internet access within countries along several dimensions (Atiyas and Doganoglu 2022; Rodríguez-Castelán et al. 2021).

Income. High-income deciles are more connected to the internet than those from lower-income deciles. Across nine surveyed Sub-Saharan African countries, internet uptake among the top 10 percent of the population in the income ladder is almost four times higher than among those in the bottom 40 percent (figure 3.4). And in South Africa, Gillwald and Mothobi (2019) find, all households in the top income bracket use the internet, whereas none in the bottom income bracket use the internet.

Area of residence. Twice as much of the population is connected to the internet in urban areas as in rural areas. Rural mobile internet usage in Sub-Saharan Africa in 2019 stood at 16 percent compared with 40 percent in urban areas, implying that rural individuals are 60 percent less likely to use the internet than their urban counterparts (Bahia and Delaporte 2020).

FIGURE 3.4 Correlation of household income with uptake of mobile services and mobile broadband internet, by income decile, selected Sub-Saharan African countries, 2017–18

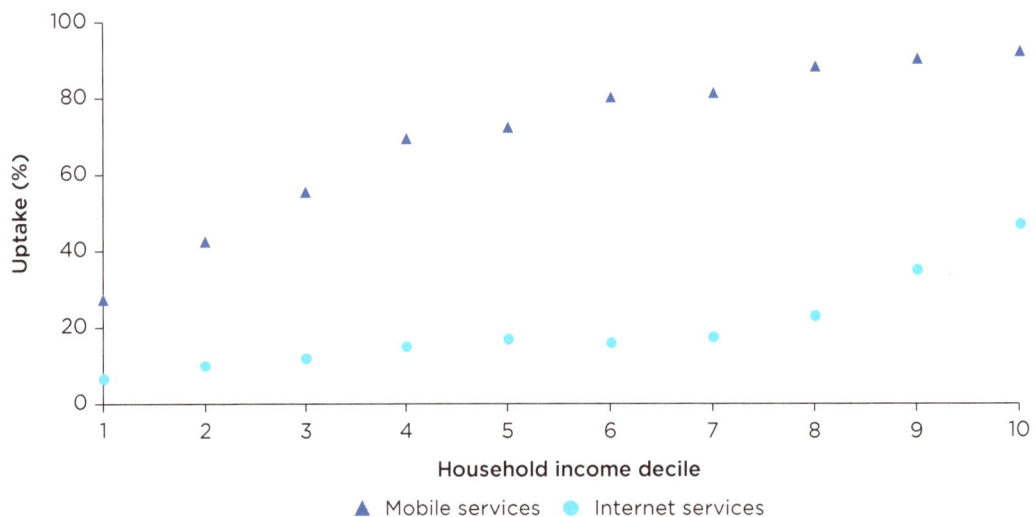

▲ Mobile services ● Internet services

Source: Adapted from Atiyas and Doganoglu 2022, based on Research ICT Africa (RIA) After Access 2017–18 household and individual country surveys.
Note: Internet "uptake" is defined as the share of the total population using the internet among the population with internet coverage. "Mobile services" include voice calls, short message service (SMS) and mobile internet connections (2G, 3G, and 4G), whereas "mobile broadband internet" refers to third- and fourth-generation (3G and 4G) internet connections. Surveys covered nine Sub-Saharan African countries: Ghana, Kenya, Mozambique, Nigeria, Rwanda, Senegal, South Africa, Tanzania, and Uganda (12,450 observations). Income deciles split the households' income distribution (for the entire sample of countries) into 10 equal parts; each income decile represents a percentage of the households (from 10 percent at decile 1 to 100 percent at decile 10) whose income is at or below that decile. Household income is expressed in US dollars corrected by purchasing power parity; index obtained from the World Development Indicators database.

Age. Internet usage is higher among young individuals (ages 15–34) than older people (ages 35–55+) (Gillwald and Mothobi 2019).

Education. There are disparities in internet usage between those with more education in general (secondary and above) and those without (or with lower) education (primary or less) (Gillwald and Mothobi 2019).

Gender. Finally, men have higher mobile broadband internet access than women. Only 6 percent of female-headed households have an active internet connection, compared with 10 percent of male-headed households (Mothobi and Gillwald 2021). Further, among those with smartphones, 17 percent and 11 percent of men and women, respectively, used the internet at least once a day in 2017 (Atiyas and Doganoglu 2022).

This gender gap in internet access has remained stagnant. In 2020, women in Sub-Saharan Africa were 37 percent less likely than men to use the internet (figure 3.5). The gender disparities in schooling, income, employment, and other complementary services, such as access to electricity, potentially explain this large gender gap in internet usage (Atiyas and Doganoglu 2022). Further, in certain countries, women may not have phones for cultural reasons, which may inhibit them from accessing mobile broadband internet even when such services are available.

FIGURE 3.5 **Gender gap in mobile internet usage, by region, all low- and middle-income countries, 2017–20**

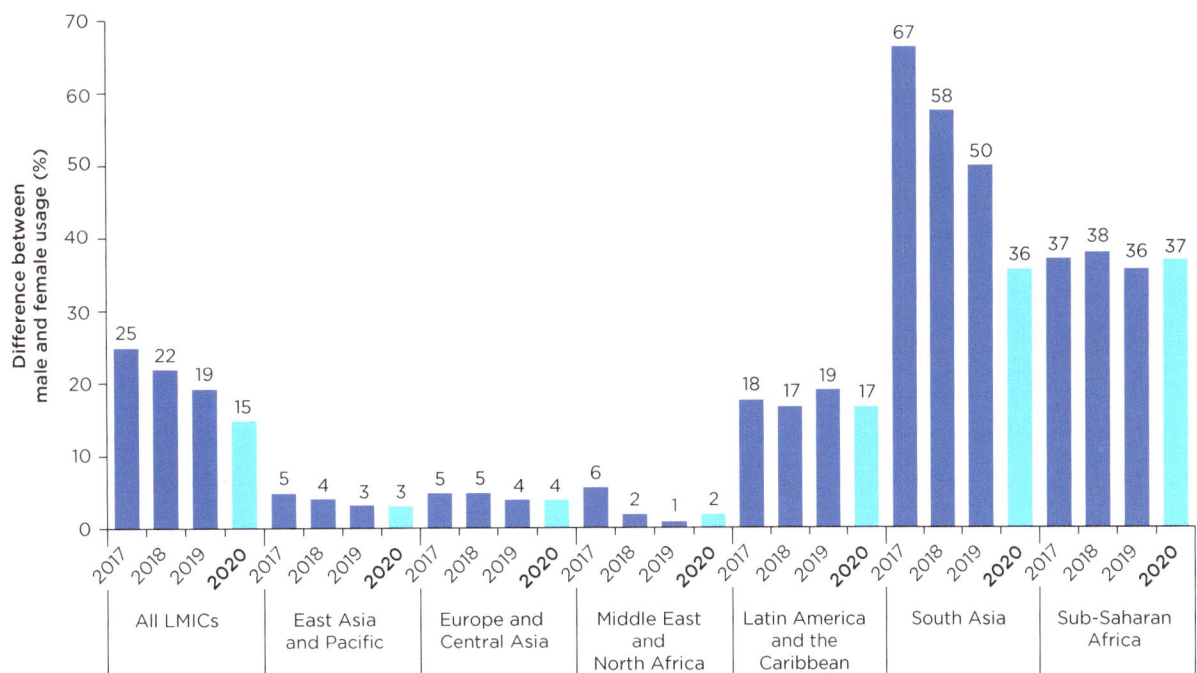

Source: Delaporte and Bahia 2021.
Note: "Gender gap" refers to how much less likely a woman is to use mobile internet than a man. The figure presents survey results and modeled data for adults of ages 18 and older. LMICs = low- and middle-income countries (according to World Bank income classifications).

Consumption gaps between Sub-Saharan Africa and other regions

Even among those connected to the internet, data consumption in Sub-Saharan Africa is lower than in other world regions. Figure 3.6 shows these inequalities in mobile data consumption as well as the consumption gap relative to benchmarks of basic and expanded data usage from *World Development Report 2021* (World Bank 2021b).

How much mobile data consumption is adequate for individuals' needs? Chen and Minges (2021) estimate that 660 megabytes per month per capita is an adequate data package to meet basic needs and services such as e-governance, online shopping, browsing news, educational information, and so on.[3] Even so, the authors acknowledge that such a package would not be enough for an individual to spend even an hour per day on social media (Chen and Minges 2021). Thus, a 1.5 gigabyte (GB) monthly bundle, as estimated by the International Telecommunication Union (ITU), is adopted as the basic needs data package in figure 3.6.

Chen and Minges (2021) also calculate that an expanded package—enabling an individual to meet basic data needs and services plus other entertainment services such as social media surfing and video streaming—would require a minimum of 6 GB per month per capita (also shown in figure 3.6).[4] The figure shows that mobile data consumption in Sub-Saharan Africa is almost 80 percent below that required to meet the daily basic needs and is just 5 percent of the minimum data package needed for the expanded use. Moreover, data consumption in the Middle East and North Africa region is almost 25 times larger than in Sub-Saharan Africa, and consumption in South Asia is about 3.7 times larger.

FIGURE 3.6 **Mobile data consumption per capita, by region, 2018**

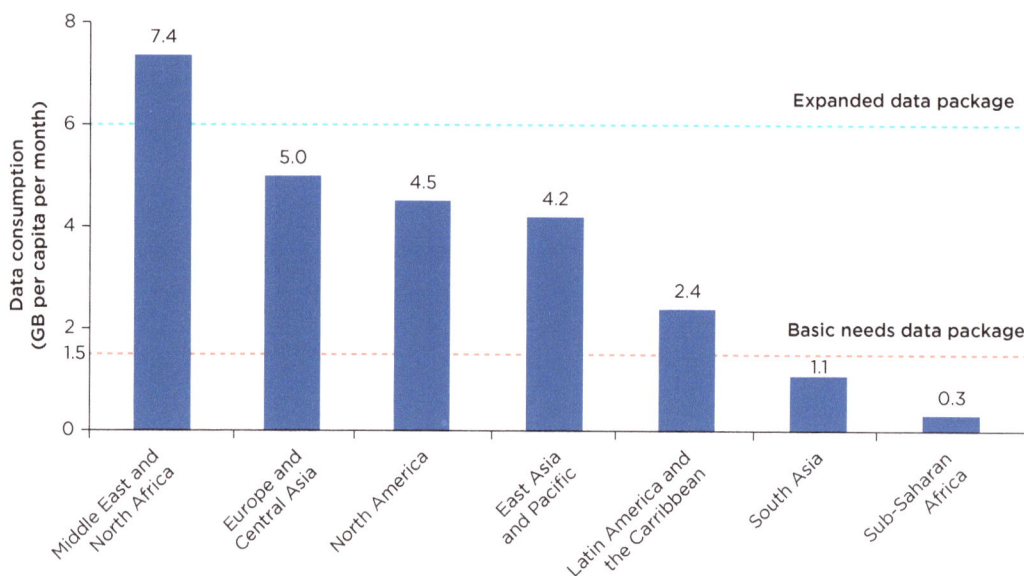

Source: Adaptation of World Bank 2021b, figure 5.6.
Note: Data for 2018. The "basic needs" data package refers to 1.5 gigabytes (GB) in monthly data per capita adequate to meet basic needs and services (estimated by the International Telecommunication Union). The "expanded" data package refers to 6 GB in monthly data adequate to meet basic data needs and services plus other entertainment services such as social media surfing and video streaming (estimated by Chen and Minges 2021). "North America" includes Bermuda, Canada, and the United States.

Usage gaps by country income level

Internet usage is low in Sub-Saharan Africa, especially in lower-income countries. The low internet usage in Sub-Saharan Africa relative to the rest of the world, as also highlighted in chapter 1 (figure 1.10, panel a), does not solely reflect lower income levels; other factors also play important roles.

Figure 3.7 plots internet usage conditional on countries' level of development, proxied by gross national income (GNI) per capita. It shows that most Sub-Saharan African countries are clustered in the low-income, low-internet-usage area (lower-left quadrant). However, among lower-middle-income countries (those between 7 and 8 log units or GNI per capita of US$1,096–US$2,981), the internet usage of a typical country in Sub-Saharan Africa is below that of other countries at the same level of development.

Moreover, as the region develops, its internet usage does not seem to catch up. The gap in internet usage between Sub-Saharan Africa and the rest of the world remains constant until GNI per capita passes 9.7 log units (or about US$16,318). This finding suggests that, without any interventions, Sub-Saharan Africa might reach universal internet access at a higher income level than the rest of the world. That is, it might take Sub-Saharan Africa longer to reach the universal access goal. As highlighted in chapter 1 (figure 1.10, panel b), Sub-Saharan Africa has internet usage of 22 percent and an uptake gap of about 74 percent. Thus, Sub-Saharan Africa can triple internet usage by addressing demand- and supply-side constraints without expanding coverage. Later, the section on understanding constraints to household internet use analyzes these factors more closely.

FIGURE 3.7 **Correlation between internet usage and GNI per capita, Sub-Saharan Africa and the rest of the world, 2019**

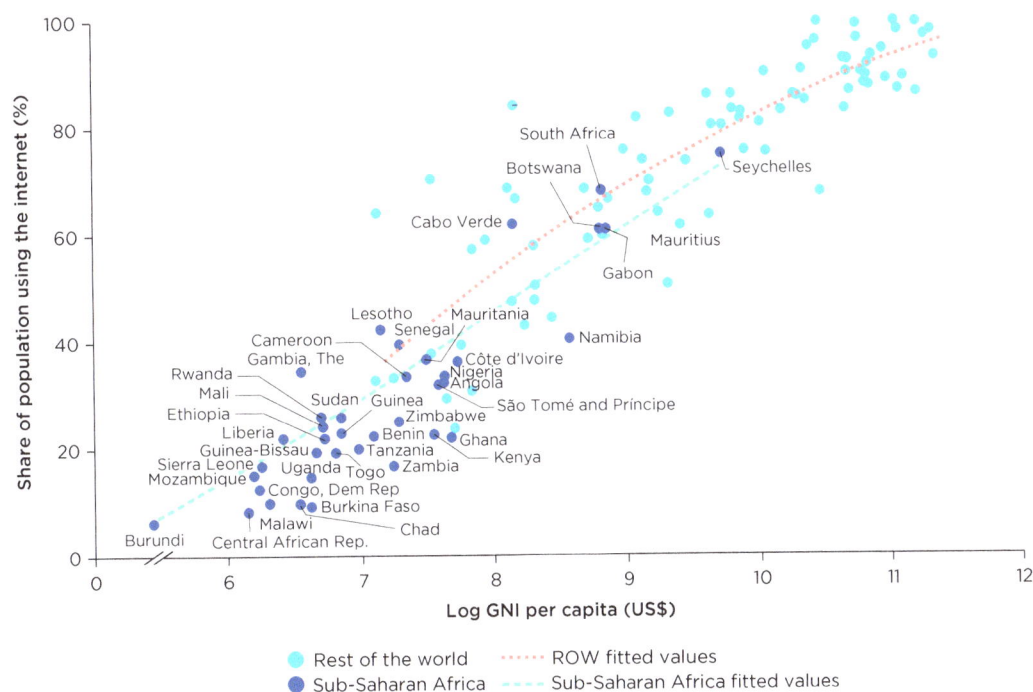

Source: Representation using 2019 data from the World Development Indicators database.
Note: GNI = gross national income; ROW = rest of the world.

The COVID-19 paradox: Increased internet usage but widened digital divides

The COVID-19 pandemic and the associated lockdowns have altered households' constraints to internet usage as internet access became more essential and have increased incentives for adoption. At the same time, the crisis reduced the average household income, making internet unaffordable for most individuals. The overall impact of COVID-19 on internet uptake and usage, therefore, depends on the tensions between increased need and affordability.

Incentives for adoption

Although internet access was already considered a basic need among higher-income and most urban residents with formal employment, the pandemic made it a necessity among the poor and rural households for several reasons:

- COVID-19 restrictions intensified the use of DTs to mediate effective communication among family members and friends.

- During containment, people needed internet service to access public services such as education.

- Many companies have been forced to adopt work-from-home policies facilitated by productivity and videoconferencing applications.

- The pandemic sparked an electronic government revival. Several governments, even those with little web presence in Africa, have increasingly adopted social media (Facebook, Twitter, WhatsApp, and so on) to communicate public health information (Bosman 2021; Chen and Minges 2021). This situation is likely to increase local content on the internet as well as internet uptake and consumption.

Another potential positive spillover from increased adoption is the emergence of new types of jobs. Even though the global emergency stimulated the growth of e-commerce in the region, most countries are unlikely to realize this potential because they lack the needed complementary infrastructure. China deliberately expanded internet access for productive use for many rural dwellers (see box 3.1, later in this chapter). Countries around the world have made similar policy choices to expand rural electrification and access to other key infrastructure services.

Constraints to adoption

Many households lost a significant share of their income temporarily or permanently because of the temporary or permanent shutdowns of businesses (Wieser et al. 2021; World Bank 2021a). In the wake of the pandemic, firms have been more likely to reduce hours of work and wages or furlough employees than to fire them (figure 3.8).

Even so, workers in Sub-Saharan Africa suffered more than those in low-income countries of other regions and in high-income countries. Sub-Saharan African firms are more likely to reduce hours of work and reduce wages than those in other non-high-income countries and high-income countries. For instance, the region's firms are 39 percent likely to reduce the employees' hours of work—a probability that is 12 percentage points and 22 percentage points higher than firms in other non-high-income countries and in high-income countries, respectively.

FIGURE 3.8 Probability of employment adjustments during COVID-19 pandemic by firms, by income group, Sub-Saharan Africa and the rest of the world, 2020/21

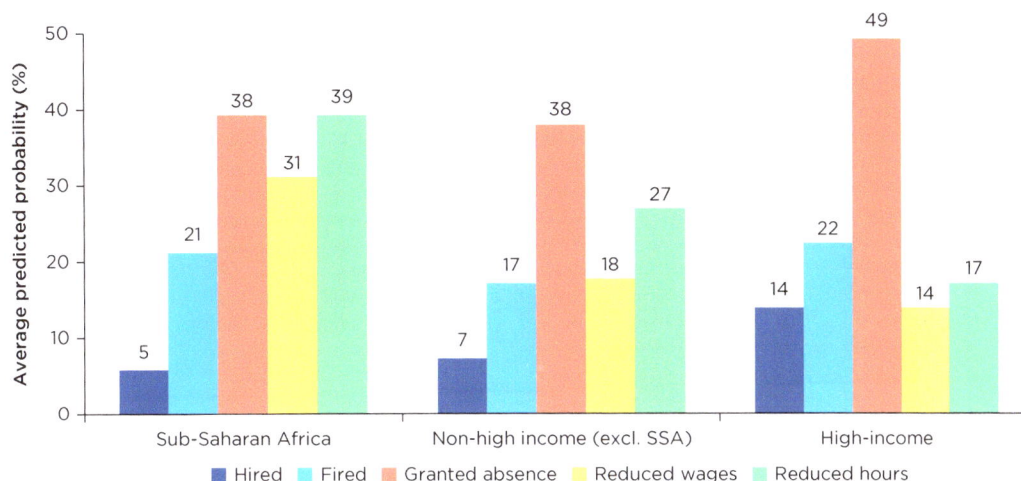

Source: World Bank, COVID-19 Business Pulse Surveys (BPS).
Note: Surveys of enterprises employing five or more full-time workers were implemented September 2020–February 2021. The chart presents average adjusted probabilities from probit regressions that control for region, size, and sector, as well as the timing of the survey. The regions in the regressions are Sub-Saharan Africa, non-high-income countries excluding Sub-Saharan Africa (SSA), and high-income countries (according to World Bank income classifications).

Further, between 56 percent and 87 percent of households in Sub-Saharan Africa experienced a fall in their incomes during the COVID-19 pandemic (Egger et al. 2021). The impact is likely concentrated among the poor and those working in the informal sector. In Ethiopia, for instance, 80 percent of those who could not afford to buy food after the onset of the pandemic cited less income as the main reason (Wieser et al. 2021).

COVID-19 fallout also contributed to higher food prices (Egger et al. 2021). The poor spend more on basic food items. Thus, with higher food prices, the poor spend even more of their income on basic food items, which limits demand for the internet despite the increased importance of internet use among the poor (figure 3.9). Even when they borrowed, households took loans mainly to buy food (World Bank 2021a). Urban residents felt the most impact, particularly the urban poor (Wieser et al. 2021).

The outcome: Widened digital divides

Consequently, the pandemic is likely to have increased the digital divide within and between countries in Sub-Saharan Africa—for households and enterprises alike. Within countries, the internet usage gap has potentially widened along several dimensions such as income, education, employment status, gender, age, and occupation, among others. On the extensive margin, internet demand in areas with third- or fourth-generation (3G or 4G) coverage has potentially dropped among the poor and the marginally poor given the lack of affordability. At the same time, as the internet becomes more of a necessity, demand is likely to have increased among high-income individuals and the young who were previously unconnected (Saka, Eichengreen, and Aksoy 2021).

FIGURE 3.9 **Changes in household expenditures during or after the COVID-19 outbreak, Kenya and Sierra Leone**

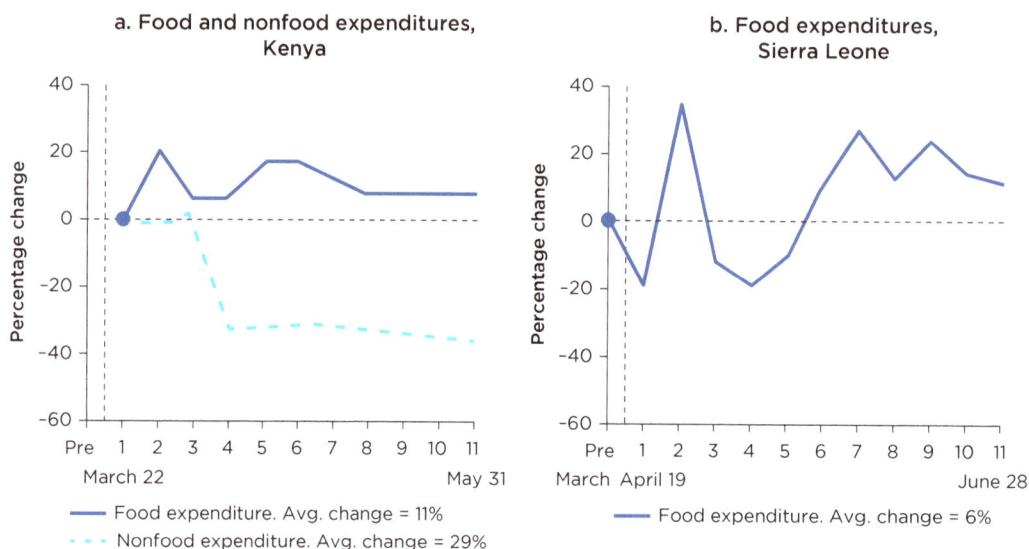

a. Food and nonfood expenditures, Kenya

b. Food expenditures, Sierra Leone

Food expenditure. Avg. change = 11%
Nonfood expenditure. Avg. change = 29%

Food expenditure. Avg. change = 6%

Source: Egger et al. 2021, figure 1.
Note: This figure shows the percentage difference from baseline for food and nonfood expenditures in rural Kenya and for food expenditures in Sierra Leone during the COVID-19 global pandemic relative to pre-COVID-19 (that is, before March 2020) or early COVID-19 levels. The pre-COVID-19 levels are from questions that recall data from March 2020. The post-COVID-19 levels are from questions that recall data from the prior 7 days and a combination (of prior 7 days for food and prior 2 weeks for nonfood expenditures in panel a). The weeks on the horizontal axis refer to the start of the recall period for each observation rather than the period during which the data were collected.

The gender gap in internet uptake and usage has increased too. During the crisis, women were more likely than men to lose jobs or incomes (Dang and Nguyen 2021). Therefore, the fall in nonfood expenditure (figure 3.9, panel a) is likely larger among females and in female-headed households than among males and male-headed families.

The poor and rural households are likely to have reduced consumption of the internet whereas the high income and the young are likely to have increased internet consumption, potentially worsening the usage gap in Sub-Saharan Africa. The increase in mobile data consumption is largely due to the increased use of social media and videoconferencing among high-income individuals. This interpretation is in line with the earlier results (shown in chapter 1, figure 1.10, panel b) showing that the internet uptake gap slightly increased in Sub-Saharan Africa between 2019 and 2021 while it declined in all other regions, which suggests either that the increase in digital infrastructure during that period was not matched by increased uptake or that for the same level of infrastructural availability uptake dropped.

Understanding constraints to household internet use

Why is internet adoption low among the general public, and what can be done about it? From the theoretical standpoint, people's willingness to pay for internet use requires that the cost be within their budget and that they derive sufficient benefits relative to their other competing needs and wants from use. The former speaks to affordability, the latter to important factors related to willingness to use, including information and skills.

Based on the evidence of potentially large and inclusive impacts observed in many African countries (as reported in chapter 1), the prime candidates to explain low internet usage should be a combination of (a) lack of information or knowledge about the returns to using internet, and (b) credit constraints—given that internet use would pay for itself. First, households may not possess enough information on internet use and education and skills to fully internalize the potential impact of internet use on their lives and livelihoods. The skills to process information and the skills to select and use appropriate apps for productive use are important in every aspect of consumer choice. Thus, the relatively low average literacy and, more broadly, low education and skills in many countries could make it hard to break the information gap and potentially lower the full impact on adopters.

Second, even if people become aware of the benefits, internet-enabled access devices and user fees may not be accessible at their income level. Disrupting credit constraints would be a key entry point, because internet access and use are presumably likely to pay for themselves if they are used to enhance productivity. However, many additional factors may affect households differently. This section examines the correlates of internet adoption and assesses a financially sustainable mechanism through which households, including those with low incomes, can adopt, use productively, benefit from, and pay for DTs.

Proximate drivers of adoption for better targeting

As noted earlier, internet adoption rates vary considerably both across countries and within Sub-Saharan African countries—with rural dwellers, women, poorer households, and those with fewer years of schooling lagging their urban, male, wealthier, and more educated counterparts. Each of these patterns provides additional explanations and policy levers for better targeting to encourage greater uptake of internet services.

Survey findings from West Africa

The latest harmonized household expenditure survey data from seven West African Economic and Monetary Union (WAEMU) countries point to several proximate determinants of adoption (figure 3.10): affordable availability (ability to pay); the price of mobile services and asset ownership; access to electricity; urban location; attractiveness (alternative modalities of access); and capabilities (tertiary education, youth, level of French language, sector of employment), in addition to socioeconomic factors (gender) (Rodríguez-Castelán et al. 2021).

That French, as one of the official languages in WAEMU countries, is associated with an increase in the probability of internet adoption highlights that literacy in the language in which official business is conducted is critical. In addition, determinants are often interrelated: the gender effect captures the compounded effect of education and income gaps, together with social norms. Nevertheless, many of the unconditional patterns in the data persist, such that there is lower adoption among women and rural dwellers relative to men and urban residents, respectively.

Although primary education is associated with no differential effect in the WAEMU findings, tertiary educational attainment is associated with 15 percentage points' more internet adoption on average. Access to electricity is associated with a 3-percentage-point differential increase in the adoption rate. This association underlines the

FIGURE 3.10 Association of factors with internet use, selected West African countries, 2018/19

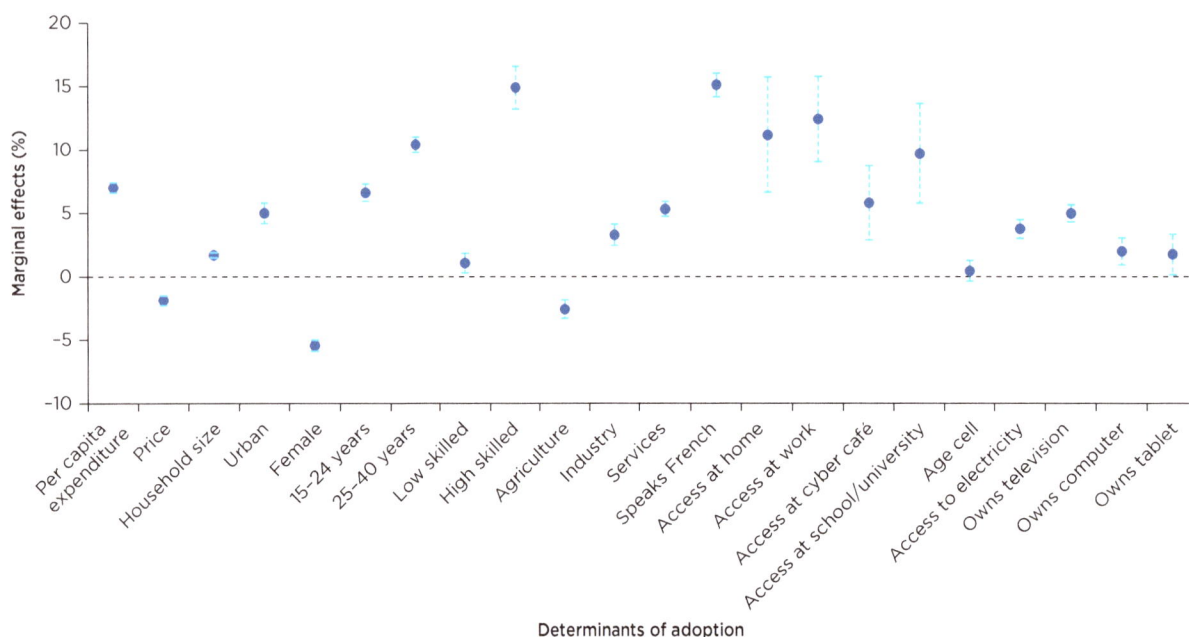

Determinants of adoption

Source: Rodríguez-Castelán et al. 2021.
Note: Data from harmonized household expenditure surveys in 2018/19 in seven West African countries: Benin, Côte d'Ivoire, Guinea-Bissau, Mali, Niger, Senegal, and Togo. Dark blue dots designate the point estimate and error bars the 95 percent confidence interval. Average marginal effects. Marginal effects for log per capita expenditure, price, and household size are calculated based on a one-unit increase in standard deviation, equivalent, respectively, to CFAF 36,400 (US$65) per capita per month, CFAF 2,000 (US$3.60) per month, and about four household members. The binary dependent variable is mobile internet access, which refers to individuals who access the internet through their mobile telephone devices. Price is obtained by calculating the median expenditure of prepaid mobile phone cards and airtime or data transfers among mobile internet users in each country's geographic area at which the survey is representative. This value is then computed as a share of total consumption at the same geographic level to adjust for the cost of living. This value is then attributed to each individual observed in the microdata. The age baseline dummy is 41+ years. The base variable across education categories is individuals with less than primary education. "Basic education" refers to those individuals with primary and secondary education, "secondary education" to those with less than tertiary but more than primary education, and "tertiary education" to those with tertiary education or more. The base category for "French" refers to national languages, other languages, and those who cannot read and write. Age of cell phone is the median value of time that the household has owned the device at the enumeration area level. The base variable across labor market sectors refers to inactive and unemployed. The agriculture sector includes jobs in crop yields, fisheries, and animal breeding. The industry sector includes extractive and other industries and public works/construction jobs. The services sector includes commerce, restaurants/hotels, transportation, communication, education, health, other and personal services jobs. Per capita expenditure; household size; access to electricity; and owning a computer, tablet, or television are household-level variables. All results are statistically significant, except for primary and secondary education, the median age of cell phone, and households that own a tablet.

importance of the role of complementary infrastructure in mobile internet adoption. Employment in the service sector is associated with an increase of about 5 percentage points in adoption, while working in agriculture decreases the likelihood of adoption by 3 percentage points.

The findings covering all seven countries mirror some variations observed across the continent. For example, household consumption and gender are more important in countries with higher internet penetration. In Senegal, the impact of household per capita expenditure is nearly double that of Benin. The likelihood that women in Côte d'Ivoire will not adopt mobile internet is more than twice as high (7 percentage points) as that of women in Niger (3 percentage points). In Côte d'Ivoire, individuals who can read and write in French—one of the region's main languages of digital content—are 23 percentage points more likely to adopt mobile broadband compared with only about 3 percentage points in Niger.

Of all the factors associated with differential adoption rates, affordability considerations are the common denominator. High pricing of internet services and economic well-being (proxied by consumption expenditures) are the two key constraints on mobile broadband adoption. An increase in household consumption—equivalent to CFAF 36,400 (about US$65) per capita per month—is associated with an increase in the probability of mobile internet adoption of 7 percentage points. Similarly, a reduction in the price of internet service by CFAF 2,000 (about US$3.60) per month associates with an increase of 2 percentage points in the likelihood of adoption.

Findings from a cross-regional sample

Another data source covering nine countries spanning Sub-Saharan Africa—including the largest countries with more dynamic markets, such as Ghana, Kenya, Nigeria, South Africa, Tanzania, and Uganda—points to qualitatively similar findings by assessing factors associated with households' adoption and use of mobile internet or data (figure 3.11). Adoption and use of mobile internet (designated as "mobile with data" in the figure) is defined as having a feature phone or a smartphone and using internet on a mobile phone or tablet at least once a day.

FIGURE 3.11 Correlates of internet adoption across nine Sub-Saharan African countries, 2017–18

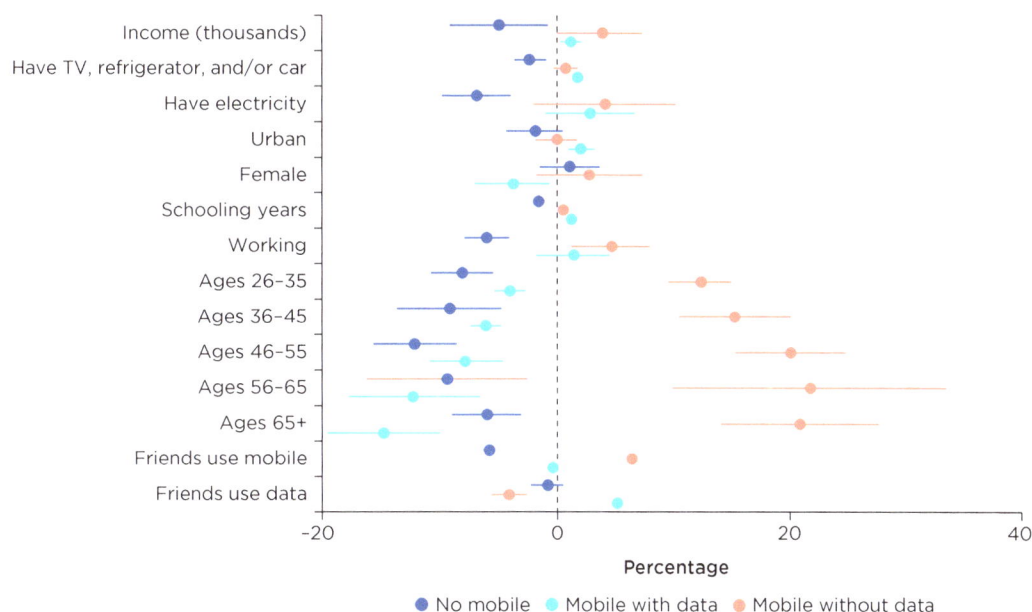

Source: Atiyas and Doganoglu 2022, based on Research ICT Africa (RIA) After Access 2017–18 household and Individual country surveys.
Note: The figure presents marginal effects regression results from a multinomial logit model of adoption using survey data from nine Sub-Saharan Africa countries: Ghana, Kenya, Mozambique, Nigeria, Rwanda, Senegal, South Africa, Tanzania, and Uganda (12,450 observations). Age categories are relative to ages 16–25. "Schooling years" are measured by number of years. Percentage changes refer to the likelihood of change in the variables on the y axis.

The data point to *affordable availability* (income and wealth, working, urban location); *attractiveness* (number of friends using data); and *capabilities* (schooling years, youth) in addition to socioeconomic factors (gender gaps). Having electricity reduces the probability of lacking a mobile phone but is not significantly associated with using mobile services with or without data. The network effect—that is, having friends using the internet—increases the value of using internet as an additional attractiveness factor. The probability of using mobile internet is negatively correlated with the number of friends using only second-generation (2G or 2.5G, not broadband capable) mobile phones and is positively correlated with the number of friends using mobile internet.

The low internet consumption among those using internet in Sub-Saharan Africa is also due to high mobile retail prices for data and technical constraints on network performance, another important set of components of affordable availability (figure 3.12). A large share of individuals in Sub-Saharan Africa countries—Ghana, Kenya, Mozambique, Nigeria, Rwanda, Senegal, South Africa, Tanzania, and Uganda—mention the cost of smartphones and internet services as the most important constraint against using mobile broadband internet (see also World Bank 2021b).

This finding is no surprise because mobile data in Sub-Saharan Africa is among the most expensive in the world, with 6 of the top 10 most expensive countries (for data) in the world found in the region and with only 1 of the top 10 cheapest countries in the world (Howdle 2021). The cost of a 1 GB data plan as a percentage of monthly gross domestic product (GDP) per capita is 4.2 percent, twice that in East Asia and Pacific (Bahia and Suardi 2019). However, internet service quality is not commensurate with costs. The download speed per US dollar per GB of internet (that is, the speed-price index) is the lowest in Sub-Saharan Africa, mainly because of the low quality of the internet connection (Kearney and Lipfert 2022).

FIGURE 3.12 **Constraints to internet usage in selected Sub-Saharan African countries, 2017–18**

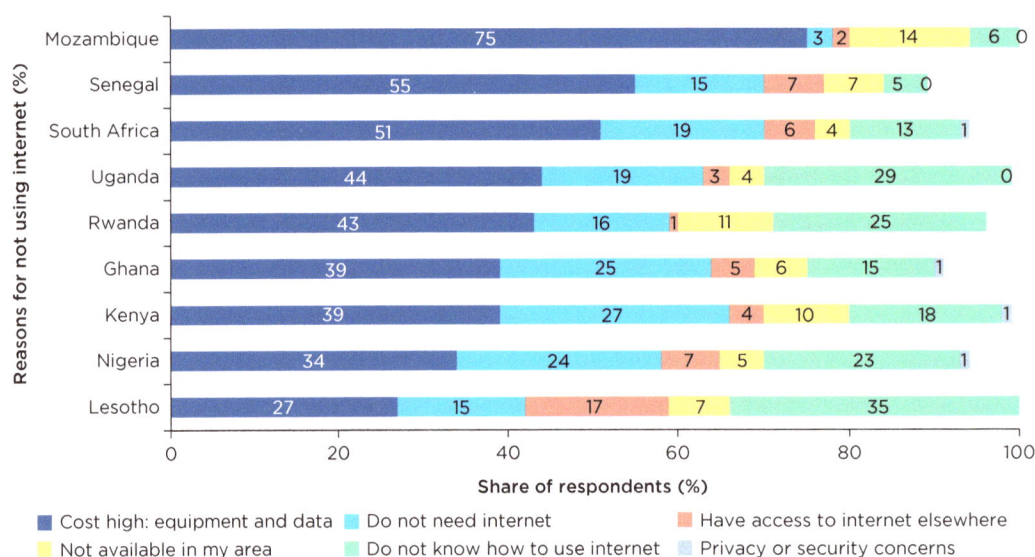

Source: Adapted from Gillwald and Mothobi 2019, using Research ICT Africa (RIA) After Access survey data, 2017–18.
Note: The figure presents survey results, across nine Sub-Saharan African countries, of respondents who do not use the internet, whether or not there is internet coverage where they live. Some bars do not total 100 due to missing data (that is, some respondents either declined to answer or responded "I don't know" to the question).

After the costs of equipment and mobile data, a significant proportion of individuals also mention that a top constraint is that they "do not know how to use internet," potentially indicating their lack of skills. Moreover, Ghana, Kenya, and Nigeria have relatively high shares of individuals citing "do not need internet" as the reason for not using the internet, which is potentially because of their limited information about the internet and its usefulness. Therefore, it is not surprising that, owing to these factors, Sub-Saharan Africa has the lowest data consumption globally—25 times less than that in the Middle East and North Africa (World Bank 2021b, figure 5.6). Therefore, addressing affordability, in general, is expected to significantly reduce the usage gap, thereby bridging the gap between the rich and the poor and improving the quality of mobile internet, among other factors (Bahia and Suardi 2019).

Quantitative global findings of uptake determinants

The significance of affordability to internet usage is further shown in figure 3.13, which presents an assessment of the relative quantitative importance of different factors associated with unique mobile internet usage across all available countries globally. All variables have been standardized, and the marginal effects of the variables are reported, showing by how many standard deviations mobile internet uptake changes when each associated variable increases by 1 standard deviation. Quantitatively the most important variable associated with internet uptake is GDP per capita as a proxy for average household affordability: a 1-standard-deviation increase in GDP per capita is associated with a 0.64 increase in the standard deviation of mobile internet uptake.

This finding aligns with the centrality of affordability for household mobile internet use. Next in terms of relative importance come (a) national education levels (average years of schooling adjusted by harmonized test scores as an indicator of quality) as a proxy for capabilities, and (b) access to electricity (as a percentage of the total population). In the case of skills, a 1-standard-deviation increase in learning-adjusted years of schooling is associated with a 0.25-standard-deviation increase in mobile internet uptake. A 1-standard-deviation increase in access to electricity is associated with a 0.16-standard-deviation increase in mobile internet uptake.

Finally comes national regulatory stance toward the mobile network operator industry on the supply side: a 1-standard-deviation decrease in the national Hirschman-Herfindahl (HHI) concentration index for providers of mobile internet services is associated with 0.11-standard-deviation increase in mobile internet uptake.[5] The findings also suggest that the level of data prices and national level of inequality are quantitatively less important—that is, not statistically significant as separate associates of internet uptake, when also controlling for average household income, average skills, access to electricity as a share of the population, and regulatory stance as reflected in the industry HHI level by country. Owing to data availability constraints, these findings are based on only one year (2018) of comparable national data across 137 countries. They should be interpreted as suggestive and complementary to the household-based data findings across Sub-Saharan African countries.

In light of these findings, the policy actions that may yield higher short-term direct impact should possibly target nonusers among the youth and urban dwellers with higher literacy and education levels—that is, if the objective is to more quickly lower uptake gaps. The network effect suggests that platforms that connect people will play a role in the growth of internet adoption. There may be an economic case to induce initial

FIGURE 3.13 Correlates of global mobile internet usage, 2018

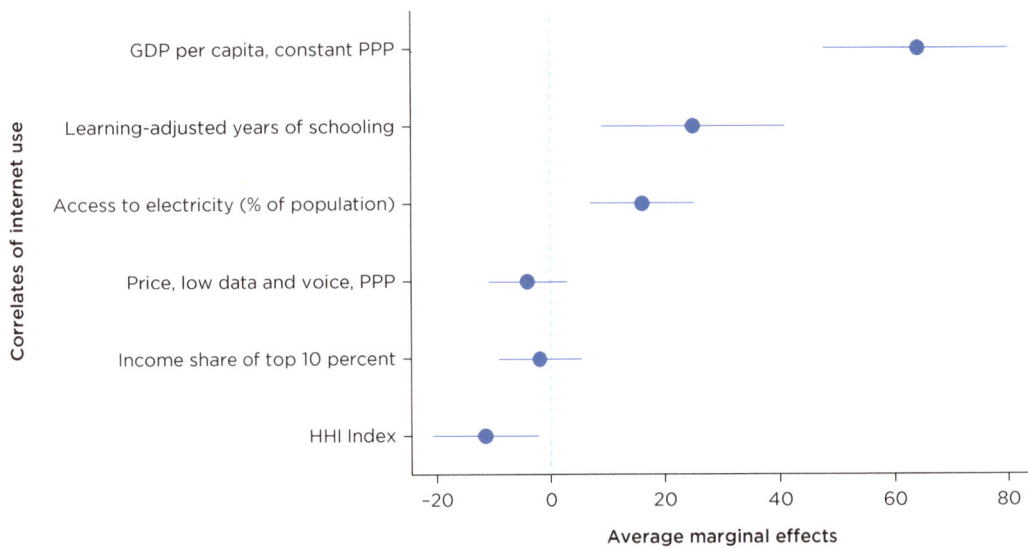

Source: Atiyas and Dutz 2022.
Note: Internet "usage" refers to a household or individual using the internet. Findings are based on only one year (2018) of comparable national data across 137 countries spanning all regions and income levels. Dots designate the point estimate; error bars represent the 95 percent confidence interval. Based on a regression covering 2018 and using standardized variables, equal to the original value minus the mean divided by the standard deviation. All regressors enter the regression equation in a linear fashion, except for gross domestic product (GDP) per capita (constant purchasing power parity [PPP]), for which a squared term is also used. The figure reports average marginal effects of the standardized variables—that is, how many standard deviations mobile internet uptake changes when each right-hand side variable increases by 1 standard deviation. HHI Index (Hirschman-Herfindahl concentration index) is based on TeleGeography data.

adopters who may serve as pioneers or role models for others for denser networks in social groupings like high schools, universities, and trade unions.

Internet adoption as a means to an end

Although over a dozen factors present a significant correlation with internet adoption, some of these factors have a common denominator, which indicates the overall economic status of the users and nonusers. For instance, access to electricity, television ownership, and per capita consumption are all related to the household's economic status. Therefore, in thinking about policies to raise adoption, it is essential to parse out symptoms and root causes of low adoption. In a context where over 40 percent of the continent lives below the extreme poverty line, it is reasonable to approach internet access primarily *as a means to an end* rather than *an end in itself*.

In examining how internet adoption can help enhance households' earnings and livelihoods—enabling them to pay for increased internet usage and a range of other purchases—one can view the constraints to adoption as complements entering a household's production function. The outcome of such a production function is not necessarily internet adoption but rather overall welfare or prosperity, which can be proxied through income. Low education and skills are associated with lower internet adoption. However, it may not be helpful to pursue a policy of raising the overall level of education and skills with the sole goal of raising internet adoption. Instead, education and skills should be viewed as other inputs that, together with internet use, can help some households earn more and raise their overall well-being. In that sense, internet access should be treated a priori within the broader set of other constraints households face. Thus, one should assess the extent to which the internet enters the household's production function, with higher earnings and improved livelihoods, and not internet access, being the main outcome.

Approaching internet access through the lens of its contribution to household earnings is vital because internet service remains expensive and out of reach for most individuals on the continent. First, the costs of smartphones, which constitute the first hurdle in internet access, are high for a typical household in Sub-Saharan Africa. Therefore, the use of smartphones, and thus internet uptake in Africa, is low and declining (figure 3.14, panel a). Second, internet costs are high, further limiting the intensity of internet usage. For instance, the average cost of the cheapest data plan—providing 1.5 GB of high-speed internet data (at least 256 kilobytes per second) over 30 days, a package needed for a few hours of basic daily use[6]—represents well over 19 percent of the income of two-thirds of the population living below the US$3.20 a day poverty line, and 32 percent of the income of the 40 percent below the global extreme poverty line of US$1.90 per day. Further, ITU benchmarked different regions of the world for the cost of 1.5 GB of 3G internet as a share of GNI and found that such a package costs over three times the median of 183 countries. The cost of internet as a share of national income (1.5 GB of data costs about 6.4 percent of GNI in Africa) is more than twice as expensive as the average in other low- and middle-income countries (figure 3.14, panel b). Additionally, internet access requires a considerable one-time expense to acquire a smartphone, which is out of reach for most. Thus, only a tiny fraction of the population possesses a smartphone on the continent (figure 3.14, panel a), limiting internet access. Access to the handset is essential.

The above discussion clearly shows that internet affordability is critical. However, although subsidizing household access and reducing smartphone prices may immediately increase internet uptake, such a strategy may not ultimately increase household income in the absence of other complementary interventions. The next subsection explains this logic using the experience of China, which addressed internet affordability partly by increasing households' productivity and thus incomes.

Making internet access impactful for the poor: China's experience

E-commerce may be one of the best facilitators of more inclusive benefits of digitalization because it comes with various related services, including the commercialization of new products that are otherwise not cost-effective to take to physical marketplaces and various delivery services. In addition, it significantly reduces transaction costs related to purchasing, sales, operating, and inventory management.

China has experienced rapid e-commerce development in the past two decades. The total amount of e-commerce sales increased tremendously from zero to US$750 billion between 2000 and 2016 (Liu et al. 2020). These sales make China the largest e-commerce market globally, with a global share of more than 40 percent (Liu et al. 2020). In 2021, China's e-commerce trade stood at US$1.3 trillion, almost twice the 2016 figure, and is projected to increase to US$2.0 trillion by 2025 (Buchholz 2021). Rural areas and poor people have not been left behind in this development process. Their inclusion is the

FIGURE 3.14 Smartphone versus feature phone adoption and affordability of data-only broadband internet prices, Africa and the rest of the world

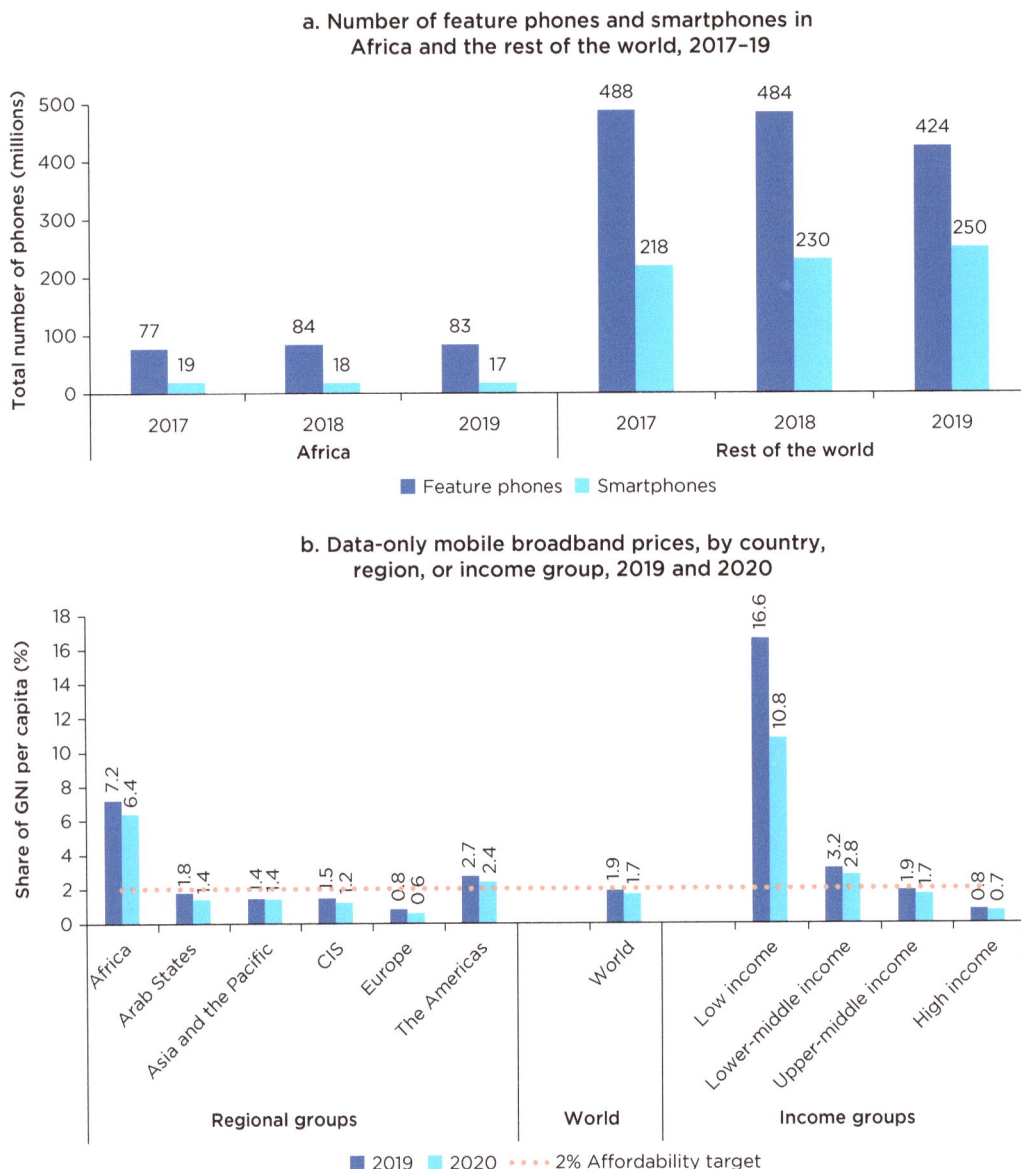

a. Number of feature phones and smartphones in
Africa and the rest of the world, 2017–19

Feature phones   Smartphones

b. Data-only mobile broadband prices, by country,
region, or income group, 2019 and 2020

2019   2020   ···· 2% Affordability target

Sources: Blimpo, Maruta, and Zeufack 2021 based on International Data Corporation data (panel a); International Telecommunication Union (ITU) and Alliance for Affordable Internet (A4AI) data, adapted from ITU (2021), figure 3 (panel b).

Note: In panel a, "feature phones" are mobile phones that can complete basic functions such as voice calls, text messaging, FM radio, and so on, typically with press-button-based inputs and a small nontouch display, but do not have all of the capabilities of a smartphone. Panel b shows the adoption and affordability of smartphones by world region and level of development, expressed as a percentage of monthly gross national income (GNI) per capita, 2019–20. Medians are based on 183 economies for which data were available for the two years. Countries are benchmarked according to the price of an entry-level data-only basket, defined as the cheapest data-only mobile broadband subscription available domestically, with a minimum of 1.5 gigabyte monthly data allowance and a technology of third-generation mobile communication technology or above. "2% affordability target" refers to the 2018 United Nations Broadband Commission for Sustainable Development set target of bringing prices for entry-level broadband services below 2 percent of monthly GNI per capita by 2025 (ITU 2021). Regional groups classification is from the ITU Telecommunication Development Sector, accessible on the websites of the ITU Telecommunication Development Bureau (https://www.itu.int/en/ITU-D/Statistics/Pages/definitions/regions.aspx). CIS = Commonwealth of Independent States.

result of careful long-term planning, which involves investing in critical infrastructure and complements such as electricity and education, which are vital to internet adoption and development in general. Many African countries' socioeconomic structures mirror China's a few decades ago, and some of the experiences from China can be adapted to tackle similar challenges.

Like Sub-Saharan Africa today, three decades ago, almost two-thirds of China's population lived below US$1.90 per day, and most of those poor people resided in rural areas. China adopted the strategy of pursuing analog complements to digital development. It undertook deliberate public policy measures so that rural areas, with a large share of the poorer population, were not left out of the economic transformation of digitalization.

The digitalization of China, including the rural areas, focused squarely on productive capabilities, without internet access being an end goal. It improved physical infrastructure, education and skills, and the business climate (World Bank and Alibaba Group 2019) as part of that effort. For example, in 2009, Chinese policies focused on developing the modern logistics industry; in 2014 and 2015, policies focused on reducing logistics costs and improving rural logistics systems, respectively (Liu et al. 2020). These measures increased the number of rural households that productively use the internet by participating in e-commerce in areas close to more developed areas of China. As a result, low-income rural households and those residing in eastern and central parts of China have diversified their incomes. Thus, improving rural broadband facilities, coupled with education and infrastructure such as roads development and electricity, helps increase internet adoption and its productive use among rural households, which subsequently increases income diversification (Leng et al. 2020). These efforts create a virtuous cycle whereby increased income levels increase internet uptake and consumption. The Taobao Villages illustrate such efforts (box 3.1).

Productive use requires intersectoral planning and coordination to invest in adequate complements in rural areas. In 2013, China launched the Broadband China Strategy to increase broadband networks nationwide, particularly in rural areas. Since 2013, the number of policies focused on rural internet provision has increased significantly in line with those focused on internet nationwide (Liu et al. 2020). Therefore, between 2010 and 2016, internet uptake in China increased by about 60 percent nationwide and in rural areas, respectively, from 457 million to 731 million users and from 125 million to 201 million users.

Internet use and e-commerce could not have picked up in China without key infrastructure such as electricity access. By 1990, although China's GDP per capita in purchasing power parity was less than half that of Nigeria, electricity access was already 90 percent in China—that is, near-universal access. This foundation, together with other infrastructural investments highlighted above, positioned rural areas to take advantage of the digital economy when the opportunity had arisen at the turn of the century. Access to reliable and affordable electricity is a key constraint that may threaten effective and inclusive digital development. Map 3.1 shows that greater access to reliable electricity is associated with greater internet access in Africa (Aviomoh et al., forthcoming).

Households' decisions to connect to the internet influence their electricity adoption decisions and vice versa, especially considering internet adoption for productive uses,

E-commerce for economic inclusion in China's Taobao Villages

China has taken deliberate measures to bridge the internet access gap and ensure that rural communities benefit too. Africans can learn from some of these measures as e-commerce gains ground but remains concentrated in cities. In rural China, online retail transactions increased by 153 percent, from ¥ 353 billion in 2015 to ¥ 895 billion in 2016, significantly higher than a growth rate of 26 percent for national online retail transactions. Africa can learn from the Taobao journey to support digital inclusion.

Taobao Villages, which by definition are groups of rural entrepreneurs selling their goods on Taobao, a Chinese shopping platform, generate more than ¥ 10 million in e-commerce and have more than 100 active online shops. All of the Taobao Villages have higher-level digital infrastructures, including access to the broadband internet and mobile network.

Furthermore, more than 50 percent of the people in these villages access the internet using smartphones, and Taobao households have higher levels of education. Rural Taobao plays an essential role in providing online services to the socially vunerable, including education, medical services, and travel. Taobao Village development has generated new job opportunities, such as graphic design, photography, express delivery services, goods storage, information technology technicians, and others in rural China.

It is also evident in Taobao Villages that e-commerce potentially contributes to inclusive jobs in rural China by lowering the required skill threshold, which allows less educated individuals to participate in trading activities and generate income. This, in turn, helps alleviate poverty and leads to the modernization of rural areas. The other aspect of Taobao Villages' inclusiveness is that women entrepreneurs make up half of all companies and start-ups. Well-functioning e-commerce requires developed infrastructure and logistics, skills, and entrepreneurship, and the encouragement of business environments is crucial. In Taobao Villages, massive investment in providing a wider range of e-commerce training helped to realize a higher level of e-commerce engagement and gains in rural China (see Luo and Niu 2019). In addition, return migrations from urban areas helped with several challenges, including reducing the skills gap.

Similarly, e-commerce is growing into an integral part of economic activity in almost all African countries, albeit mainly in cities now, and opening new opportunities to Africa. According to a 2018 United Nations Conference on Trade and Development report, the number of online buyers in Africa has increased by 18 percent annually since 2014. Furthermore, in 2017, about 21 million people shopped online in Africa, indicating huge potential for developing e-commerce (UNCTAD 2018). However, a wide range of obstacles to the fulfillment of this potential include infrastructure and logistics deficits and inadequate internet connectivity.

It may not be an easy task for African countries to adopt China's e-commerce model. Still, the spirit of planning and approaching internet access through the lens of productive use is an essential lesson. The success and promise of e-commerce in promoting rural development depend on various factors. It is crucial to identify promising local products, particularly agricultural products; to develop digital technologies and transportation infrastructures in rural areas; and to offer reliable e-commerce platforms with stable services so that villagers have equal opportunities to engage in entrepreneurship. Africa can learn and adapt from China's experience to make inclusion a reality in the digital space.

Source: Adapted from Blimpo, Maruta, and Zeufack 2021.

which inherently requires electricity access to power information technology (IT) equipment. Access to electricity is associated with more mobile telephony subscribers and higher smartphone ownership, which are key for internet uptake (Houngbonon, Mensah, and Traore 2022).

There is a robust correlation between electricity access and internet uptake at the national, subnational, and individual levels in 36 countries in Sub-Saharan Africa—in areas both with and without electricity coverage (Aviomoh et al., forthcoming). Notably, however, electricity penetration is lower than mobile phone penetration, showing that households value communications more than electricity, but there could be affordability and attractiveness issues that prevent internet use.

Greater digitalization increases the need for more reliable, abundant, and green electricity—not only to power digital devices but also as a key input to a wide range of modern productive economic activities. Additionally, the availability and reliability of electricity are key factors often associated with investments in data centers, a backbone infrastructure for effective digital development. Data centers consume significant

MAP 3.1 Shares of population with electricity and internet access, by country, Africa, 2017

a. Electricity access

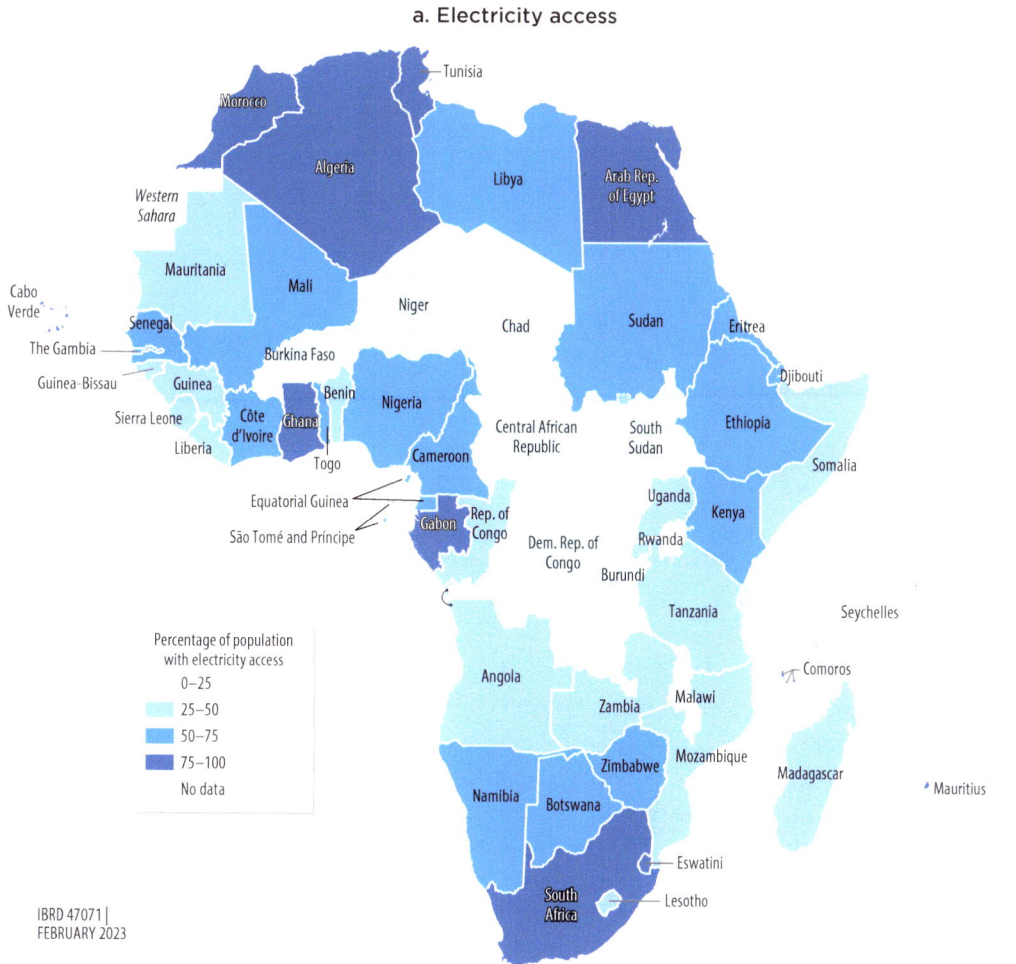

Percentage of population with electricity access
- 0–25
- 25–50
- 50–75
- 75–100
- No data

IBRD 47071 | FEBRUARY 2023

(continued)

Households

123

b. Internet access

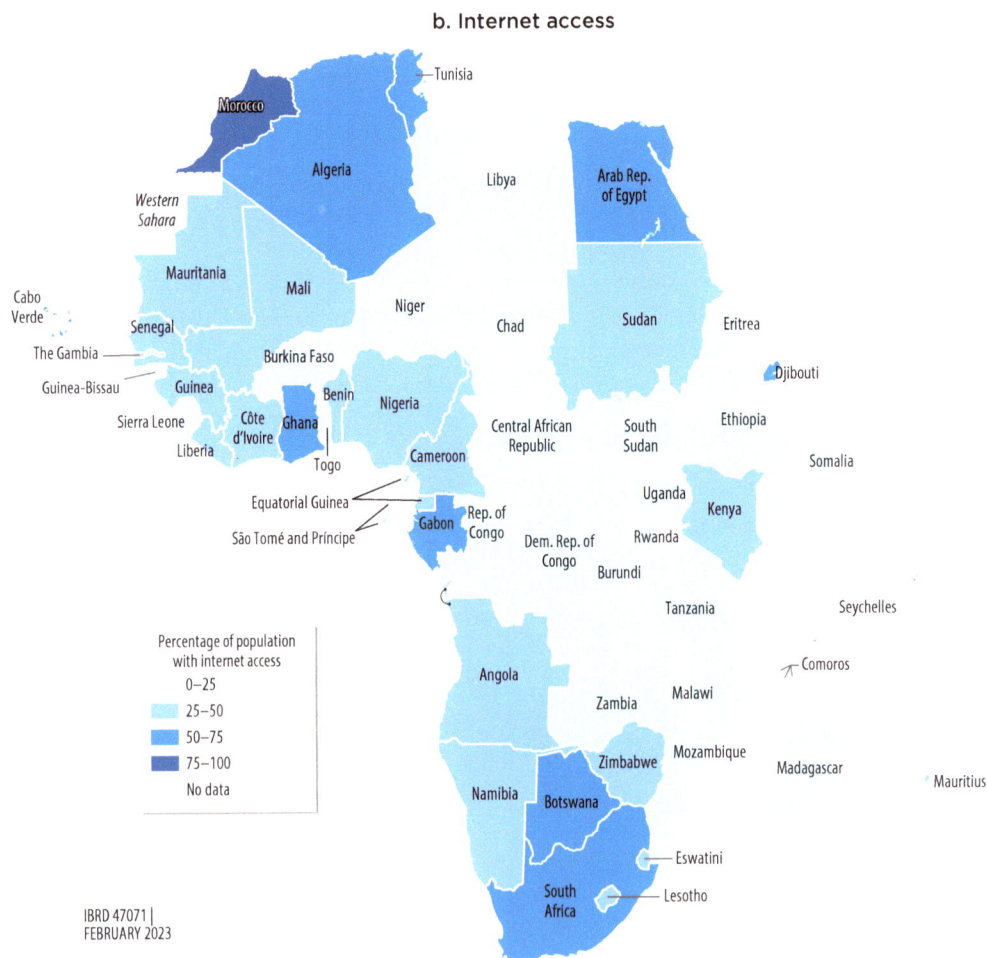

Percentage of population with internet access

- 0–25
- 25–50
- 50–75
- 75–100
- No data

IBRD 47071 |
FEBRUARY 2023

Sources: Panel a based on data from the World Bank (https://data.worldbank.org/indicator/EG.ELC.ACCS.ZS); panel b based on data from the International Telecommunication Union (https://www.itu.int/en/ITU-D/Statistics/Pages/stat/default.aspx).

Note: The maps in panels a and b show the shares of the population in each African country with electricity access and internet access, respectively. "Internet access" refers to fiber and mobile broadband (third- and fourth-generation mobile communication technology) internet access. Electricity access data are for 2020. Internet access data are latest available: 2014 (Libya), 2017 (the Comoros, the Republic of Congo, Equitorial Guinea, Eritrea, Eswatini, Niger, and Somalia), 2018 (Madagascar), 2019 (Côte d'Ivoire and Malawi), and 2020 (remaining countries).

amounts of electricity and can also serve as anchor customers to help improve utility sustainability in the region (box 3.2). Africa can benefit from green energy (wind, geo-thermal, solar, and hydroelectric) to offer greener digital infrastructure.

The significance of electricity access as a complement to internet usage in the house-hold production function has been highlighted in Sub-Saharan Africa. In Senegal and Tanzania, mobile broadband (3G) coverage increases household welfare (proxied by total per capita consumption), particularly for the high-skilled, the young, and those residing in urban areas that have relatively good infrastructure, including electricity (Bahia et al. 2020; Bahia et al. 2021;). Conditional on several different factors, including location, access to electricity is highly associated with internet usage (Atiyas and Doganoglu 2022; Rodríguez-Castelán et al. 2021). These results partly explain the

BOX 3.2
Reliable electricity and the digital economy

Digital technologies offer countries worldwide opportunities to diversify their economies, including expanding information and communication technology as a sector and increasing its use in enterprises. Among the core digital infrastructure elements are data centers. These facilities are a vital engine of the digital economy—storing data, hosting websites, and enabling cloud-based applications. Data centers are virtual factories that make productive use of electricity with measurable economic impacts on gross domestic product, employment, and government tax revenue.

Data centers consume considerable electricity in powering computer equipment and keeping it cool. In 2011, Google reported that it used 260 megawatts of electric power for its data centers, more than the 2014 installed capacity in 19 African countries. Data centers require high reliability to ensure the seamless, nonstop flow of data. Industry standards define reliability as ranging from 99.67 percent availability (with no more than 29 hours of interruption per year for Tier 1 data centers) to 99.995 percent reliability (with just 0.8 hour of interruption per year for the highest Tier 4 centers).

Most African nations would find it difficult to meet even Tier 1 reliability standards. Even the largest and most technologically advanced economies such as Nigeria and South Africa report significant challenges with the reliability of electricity supply. The standards also call for a guaranteed source of electrical backup that can power the center for at least half a day.

Source: Blimpo and Cosgrove-Davies 2019.

---

success of the Taobao Villages e-commerce model. In order to develop the Taobao Village model, China relied upon high electricity access and the abundance of high-skilled, young return migrants in rural areas (see box 3.1). As with that model, the positive welfare effects of internet access in Tanzania are transmitted through labor market outcomes—high labor force participation, wage employment, and nonfarm self-employment (Bahia et al. 2021).

To what extent is essential cross-sectoral coordination, induced by nexuses like the one between digital and energy infrastructure, accounted for in the design of infrastructure projects and policy? Aviomoh et al. (2021) examined 106 World Bank-approved infrastructure projects' Project Appraisal Documents (PADs) in Sub-Saharan Africa designated by the Digital Development and Energy and Extractives Global Practices between 2010 and 2020. The overall cross-sectoral coordination is not deep, but the Bank's Digital Development Global Practice's PADs are about 33 percent more likely to mention energy components in the design stage than their counterparts from the Energy and Extractives Global Practice. This discrepancy may not be surprising because the internet requires electricity to function, not the other way around. However, the synergy should be driven by the fact that the two are mutual complements for firms and household production functions. The cross-sectoral interventions can also generate more efficiency on the supply side, including possibilities for infrastructure sharing and helping to reduce cost.[7]

There are opportunities to increase internet access through better targeting, credit and payment facilities, and cost reduction to attract potential users at the margins of the various uptake constraints discussed in this section. However, these policy measures alone may not be enough to increase adoption substantially. The low average income levels and the high poverty levels in most countries, as well as hard-to-change constraints like adult literacy, stand in the way of universal adoption under business as usual. Without sufficient increases in household income, the uptake gap is unlikely to be closed fast enough in a way that is financially sustainable for both households and service providers.

The strategic question is, thus, how can countries close the internet uptake and usage gaps in an affordable and financially sustainable way for households and service providers? The answer to this question depends, on the one hand, on how increased internet uptake results in higher earnings. On the other hand, households are likely to take up and use the internet more as their income grows, irrespective of the source of income growth. It is therefore essential that productive use be an entry point and central to internet expansion strategies.

High informality and self-employment characterize much of the structure of most economies and the labor markets in most African countries (figure 3.15). The induced blurred line between a household and the firm offers an opportunity for productive use of DTs among households.

Enterprise and household internet uptake and use are then the same for most African households. Nearly 9 out of 10 workers in Sub-Saharan Africa are employed in informal labor markets, and over 70 percent of workers are informally self-employed—as high as 92 percent in Western Africa—often with unpaid family members. A key challenge for boosting the inclusive impact of DTs is to increase work-related uses so that households can learn as they work and run microenterprises, often at the household level, so that internet use enhances the productivity of these economic activities.

FIGURE 3.15 **Share of informal employment workers employed in the informal sector, formal sector, and households, excluding and including agriculture, by gender and subregion, Africa**

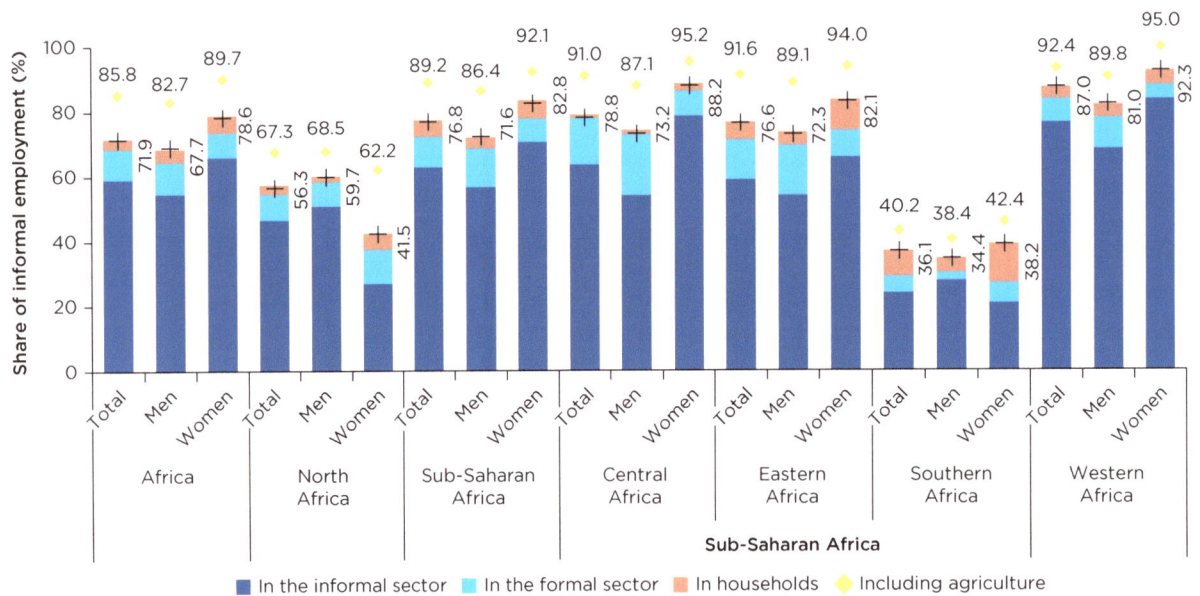

Source: ILO 2018.
Note: "Informal employment" is defined as as "all remunerative work (both self-employment and wage employment) that is not registered, regulated or protected by existing legal or regulatory frameworks, as well as nonrenumerative work undertaken in an income-producing enterprise" (ILO 2013). The percentages are of all workers of working age (15 years and older). "Africa" means Sub-Saharan Africa plus North Africa.

There are opportunities for DTs to make a difference in the informal sector, as reported in a recent assessment of Africa's "E-conomy" landscape (Google and IFC 2020). For example, in Nigeria, a distribution platform called TradeDepot relied heavily on DTs to improve supply chain management for informal retailers by enabling their connection with manufacturers. In 2018, the number of active retailers on the company's platforms jumped from 2,000 to 15,000. Services like TradeDepot have the potential to serve millions of retailers in Nigeria and across the continent.

Businesses in Africa's informal sector, which are often tightly linked to households, face many challenges that an internet economy can help alleviate significantly. Some of these benefits include reduction of transaction costs enabling access to finance, improved business practices, increased information about prices, and fewer intermediaries that often cut the profits for the poor. Therefore, DT interventions that aim to improve the productivity of microenterprises can help reduce the gender inequalities in internet access and income. About 79 percent of women in Africa and 95 percent in West Africa are self-employed in the informal sector.

A policy framework to transform use into inclusive impact

A policy framework centered around productive use requires a granular understanding of the role of DTs for microenterprises and informal self-employment. It is also essential to create an environment for the generation of productivity-enhancing DTs suited for the needs of poor people. Finally, because poor people, the self-employed, and other microenterprises often face multiple constraints, internet uptake alone may not be sufficient to enable its productive use by households. Thus, a better understanding of complementarities among various inputs for bundling services that include DTs is also essential. Therefore, careful consideration should be given to these context specificities as part of a "productive use of DTs" national strategy.

The "productive use" framework for closing the internet uptake gap

The dominant approach to closing the internet uptake gap depends on whether internet uptake is (a) *in itself a policy goal*, or (b) *a means to achieve a greater goal* of enhancing people's livelihood, greater productivity, and rising earnings. Figure 3.16 offers a framework to think about ways to close the internet uptake gap.

One approach is likely to drive faster uptake, albeit with weaker feedback and the possibility of financial unsustainability if internet access does not help concretely raise household earnings. The other approach views productivity gains and earnings as the main goal and assesses the internet's role in achieving such a goal. From that perspective, the ultimate goal is to create a virtuous cycle in which internet uptake enhances earning, feeding back into more use. Because uptake in itself may not be the goal, the pace of the closure of the uptake gap may be slower but financially sustainable.

Route 1. As such, under Route 1, the policy focuses mainly on addressing the symptomatic barriers to uptake, which involves implementing several interventions in concert:

- Increase digital skills to make it easy for individuals to use the internet.

- Provide information on the uses and value of using the internet.

- Provide credit and/or subsidies on smartphones and mobile broadband data to address the affordability constraint. Given the extent of poverty in Sub-Saharan Africa, however, this type of intervention will involve provision of large subsidies.

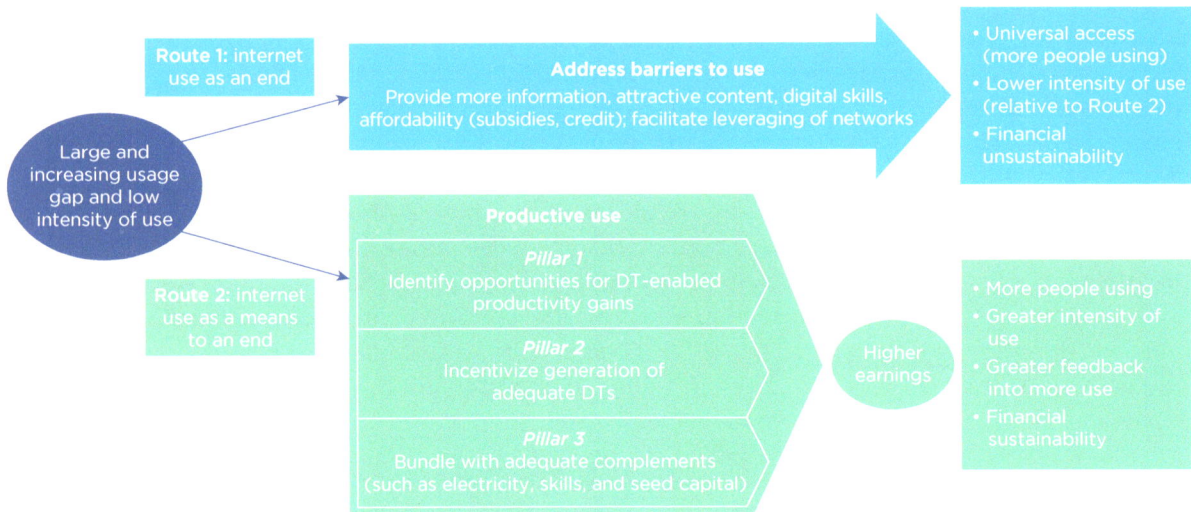

FIGURE 3.16 **A framework for closing the DT uptake gap and boosting DT users' welfare**

Source: Adapted from Blimpo and Cosgrove-Davies 2019.
Note: Internet "uptake" refers to use of the internet when there is internet coverage. DT = digital technology.

These interventions will contribute to achieving the universal access goal faster. Under this route, it is hoped that increased internet usage may lead to increased productivity, and this may happen to some households. However, without the presence of analog complements, the productive use and the feedback mechanism for further uptake are weaker under this route. Thus, this strategy is potentially financially unsustainable because it requires sustained provision of credit and/or subsidies for uptake.

Route 2. Alternately, under Route 2, internet uptake is seen as a means to an end—increasing household earnings and thus reducing poverty. The policy goal is to increase the productive use of the internet to increase household earnings and stimulate further internet uptake resulting from the increased ability to pay. Additionally, in this setting, facilating further and more intensive internet use for businesses and the nonpoor may be highly desirable for inclusion if it can help create jobs for the poor.

Productive use requires synergies among at least three types of interventions, under the three pillars in figure 3.16:

1. The first step, under pillar 1, is to identify those opportunities or economic activities by which DTs can be of greater use for increasing households' welfare. For instance, identify those economic activities that poorer households (and microenterprises) engage in, whereby the internet-supported technologies can enhance earnings.

2. The second step, under pillar 2, is to encourage the development of such apps. Doing so may involve, for example, the provision of incentives to firms and making advance market commitment policies for the development of low-skill-biased DTs.

3. The third and last step, pillar 3, is to bundle the interventions identified under pillars 1 and 2 with adequate complements, which may entail access to or increasing the quality of infrastructures such as electricity or road infrastructure. Therefore, the skill upgrading initiatives (emphasized under Route 1, for example) will emphasize increasing education or general skills (not necessarily DTs skills) to enable individuals to make informed choices generally and fully internalize the value of internet use.

Digital Africa

These policy interventions will lead to increased uptake of the internet for productive use, which will in turn lead to higher household earnings. With higher earnings, households can then afford increased broadband data and internet consumption as needed. Under this route, further internet usage leads to further increases in productivity and earnings, leading to further uptake. Route 2 is more context specific than Route 1 because it depends both on the market structure and on the availability (or lack thereof) of the complements.

Internet uptake as a means to an end: Understanding the three pillars of the productive use framework

Pillar 1: Understand the structure and composition of economic activities

The direct impact of DTs on households and microenterprises can vary significantly depending on the nature of the activity and the structure of related markets. For example, in agriculture that occupies a large share of the labor force, intermediaries play a crucial role in linking farmers to the market throughout Sub-Saharan Africa (Fafchamps, Gabre-Madhin, and Minten 2005). This situation has implications for whether DTs target and provide more help to the intermediaries or to the poorer farmers. For example, DTs can help small-scale farmers access timely information—including through voice in local languages—about the weather, prices of inputs, and agricultural practices.

On the one hand, the same DTs targeting only access to price information may not be relevant for farmers who lack the scale to take advantage of higher prices of their products in more-distant markets because of transportation costs. On the other hand, the same app may be essential for intermediaries who aggregate products from small-scale farmers for resale elsewhere. Productivity gains resulting from the latter may not enhance farmers' welfare without a pass-through of price-related benefits between intermediaries and farmers. For example, a significant pass-through to farmers occurred in Côte d'Ivoire when taxes were lowered on one side of the then-partitioned country on exporters of cocoa (Soumahoro 2017). And, when transportation costs were lowered for both traders and farmers in Sierra Leone through improved feeder roads, prices of agricultural products dropped (Casaburi, Glennerster, and Suri 2013).

Therefore, the DTs' welfare effect on the farmer remains ambiguous; it depends on how much input prices decrease because of DTs and the extent of production capacity constraints. Further, the potential welfare effects of price decreases (because of DTs) on the farmer also depend on whether households (small-scale farmers) are net consumers or net producers of the affected products (Porto 2020). All else equal, low product prices will increase welfare if households are net consumers (that is, their income share from the product is less than the budget share on the product) and vice versa.

DTs can also play a role in a range of economic activities in which poorer households are engaged, ranging from petty trade, street vendors, to microprocessors of food. As illustrated in the case of agriculture, the extent of the impact requires a context-specific understanding of an array of factors, including the following: Which economic activities are the poor or informal microentrepreneur households engaged in? What roles can different DTs (including different apps) play to solve problems linked to productivity gains in these activities? Are these DTs available and accessible? For instance, DTs that increase farm gate prices would result in welfare gains for informal small-scale farmers who are surplus producers of a particular crop—say, groundnuts (Porto 2020).

Pillar 2: Promote the development of DTs for households' productivity

A market-driven generation of digital solutions without any government intervention is likely to be high-skill-biased, addressing disproportionately the needs of those more educated and able to afford to acquire them and likely delaying the full benefit of DTs for the poor. An effective, inclusive "productive use" strategy of DTs may require altering the direction of technological change toward labor-augmenting rather than labor-replacing DTs that help managers and workers solve productivity-related problems and learn as they use them.

The generation of low-skill-biased DTs is an integral part of the strategy. It entails policies to incentivize start-up software developers' creation of apps that enable households' productive use and facilitate uptake of such apps. Considering that the adult illiteracy rate remains relatively high in many countries, applications with local language content through voice or visual illustration are more likely to serve a much larger share of the population. Policy makers should nurture a supportive environment enabling local entrepreneurs to generate these solutions from the bottom up (Blimpo et al. 2017).

Thousands of young Africans across the continent are working on new ideas and new products that may solve problems. Most of them will fail, a few will succeed, and some may be transformational. Many are already raising funding to the tune of millions of dollars owing to the market value of their ideas and products. Creating the condition for bottom-up initiatives to thrive requires much more attention from African governments than it has received.

Sometimes, all it takes is not to get in the way! African countries must embrace risk and abandon incrementalism to accelerate the transformational changes that their people deserve. Meaningful changes will occasionally come with unintended consequences—some positive, others negative. Taking risks means also being able first to observe and then to adapt the regulatory environment to new technologies. A flexible regulatory environment enables innovation by allowing new business models to be tested and innovations to be scaled. The same applies to the ease of access to finance by entrepreneurs. Finally, change will always face resistance. Many of the life-changing technologies we take for granted today faced stiff resistance at their outset, sometimes from unlikely sources. The government must play a critical role in ensuring that ideas clash in a constructive manner so that the best and socially desirable ones prevail (Juma 2016).

Pillar 3: Support bundles of complementary inputs for productive use

As discussed earlier, DTs are inputs in the production function of various modern economic activities, but so are many other inputs such as electricity, road infrastructure, skills, and access to credit. Understanding the complements needed to amplify the economic impact of internet use and how to best support them is essential to foster a more inclusive impact.

Some of the most recent interventions that make a difference in pulling households out of poverty in a sustained way are the graduation programs implemented in Ethiopia, Ghana, Honduras, India, Pakistan, and Peru (Banerjee et al. 2015). They constitute a multifaceted approach to addressing the constraints that poor people face. Although the interventions were under the umbrella of social protection programs, the principle of supporting bundles of complementary inputs for productive use applies more generally.

The rationale for such a program is grounded in the fact that poor people often face multiple constraints that are collectively but not individually binding. For example, in Senegal, a contracting arrangement with farmers in a groundnut farming cooperative bundled a contract providing certainty regarding price premiums with training and credit to help incentivize and support the purchase of a new quality-improving technology. The simultaneous relaxation of these three productivity constraints increased total output sales by recipient farmers to the cooperative by about 65 percent (Deutschmann, Bernard, and Yameogo 2020).

The same principle underpins some business models in the private sector with a strong social entrepreneurship component. The Senegalese dairy company Laiterie du Berger (LdB) is a good example at scale of this kind of bundling of complementary inputs. LdB helped organize disparate local herders into a cooperative of milk production for local yogurt manufacturing.[8] The company experienced significant growth over the years, thanks partly to the add-on services that LdB provides to herders in terms of animal feed inputs and skills to support proper sanitation and both quantity and quality upgrading of milk production.

DTs have been playing a significant role in these types of initiatives, helping to reduce various transaction costs, reduce information asymmetries, improve monitoring and credit allocation, and facilitate technology and skill transfers. The Smart Village program in Niger also offers an example of an intervention to increase not only the availability but also the productive use of DTs for financial access and as a complement to agriculture activities by vulnerable populations, including the rural population and women (box 3.3).

BOX 3.3

Smart Villages in Niger for inclusive availability and productive use

The Smart Villages program[a] implemented by the government of Niger with support from the World Bank provides an example of integrated supply and demand interventions for social inclusion. Both rural populations and women were targeted to boost the use of connectivity made available by the program.

This six-year initiative, started in October 2020, aims to improve digital connectivity as well as digital financial services in rural areas. Niger has a population of 24 million spread over 1.2 million square kilometers, mostly in the Sahara Desert. The low population density, especially in rural areas, coupled with the high security risk, makes it challenging for private sector players to invest in rural infrastructure, including digital and financial services. Through this US$100 million initiative, the government of Niger will improve rural broadband penetration from the current 12 percent to at least 25 percent and at the same time increase attractiveness of digital technologies focusing on financial services. Connectivity will enable the provision of digital financial services, with a current adoption rate of only 9 percent, and benefit 240,000 adults, prioritizing women-owned businesses and women farmers, allowing them to make and receive digital mobile payments for the first time.

As of January 2022, the program had started the first phase of deploying 150 digital centers to offer a wide range of digital services and digital literacy training to the rural population. This training aims at increasing familiarity with digital technologies and enhancing digital skills to boost productive use. In addition, the program will build 2,100 mobile connectivity sites in rural Niger based on a reverse-auction mechanism whereby telecom operators will receive a catalytic grant to extend their mobile coverage to rural areas without any connectivity.

a. For more information on this program, visit the World Bank's Smart Villages for Rural Growth and Digital Inclusion project web page: https://projects.worldbank.org/en/projects-operations/project-detail/P167543.

Expansion of DTs should therefore target necessary complements that are already in place or that can be provided in bundles where they are lacking. Not all barriers can be removed effectively and simultaneously, nor are all barriers in the form of complementary inputs. Although key constraints such as electricity access and access to credit are cross-cutting, others such as skills and technologies depend on local contexts. Additional work will be needed to identify the key complementary constraints in each specific context.

Conclusion

Internet usage by individuals and households is low in Africa. Given the extent of internet coverage, individual uptake can be more than doubled by addressing multiple constraints (such as education and skills, affordability, networks, and so on) that restrict households' uptake.

Moreover, internet and related DTs offer an opportunity for inclusive productivity gains. Early evidence from across African countries reports positive economic impacts associated with greater adoption and use of DTs. However, the adoption rate has remained low, with a large divide to the detriment of poorer, rural dwellers and the less educated population.

Many constraints stand in the way of internet adoption, leading to nearly half of the population having the services available but not using them. Demand-side considerations must be addressed alongside the supply constraint, and both are often intertwined. For instance, affordability, although in great part a demand issue, can be addressed by lower prices induced by efficiency gains on the supply side. Similarly, if low adoption is due to inadequate content or functionalities of the DT apps, the supply of sought-after content and attractive applications can help address the issue.

Given the current level and distribution of income in Africa, unless internet adoption and consumption help raise incomes to enable households to pay, the internet adoption gap is likely to persist. The high prevalence of informality and self-employment means there can be a thin line between a household and a microenterprise, which offers an entry point for households' productive use—with adequate complements such as electricity and the applications meeting households' needs. Thus, incentivizing the generation and adoption of DTs that address low-income households' productive needs should be given priority.

On the supply side, adequate and well-maintained infrastructure and related regulatory improvements to cut inefficiencies on the supply side so that cost-recovery prices are affordable to a much larger share of the population are essential to the future of digitalization of Sub-Saharan Africa. Chapter 4 examines the critical issues related to the foundational digital infrastructure.

Notes

1. "Internet usage" is a broad term that pertains to a combination of infrastructure coverage and uptake. "Usage" is defined as the share of the overall population using the internet, whether or not they have coverage, whereas "uptake" reflects the share of people *with* coverage who use the service.
2. See also chapter 1, figure 1.12. There are minor differences in internet access measured using Research ICT Africa (RIA) survey data (demand-side data) versus the Global System for Mobile Communications Association (GSMA) administrative data (supply-side data), partly because of the

prevalence of multiple SIM (subscriber identity module) cards per user. Nonetheless, the overall picture is similar.

3. This very conservative estimate is based on (a) an assessment of only six low- and lower-middle-income countries, with only one being a Sub-Saharan African country; and (b) a limited number of online services that exclude the streaming services that are critical for online teaching and learning.

4. A one-hour Zoom session requires about 500 megabytes of data (Chen and Minges 2021). Therefore, the 6 GB data package may not be enough in some settings, such as online education. The Alliance for Affordable Internet (A4AI) estimates that the basic needs bundle requires 1 GB of data. Still, because of the COVID-19 pandemic and the associated increase in data demand, A4AI is now calling for "meaningful connectivity" or unlimited data connectivity and consumption (A4AI 2020).

5. That the HHI is statistically significant but the mobile termination rates (MTRs) are not may both reflect both the lower number of observations in the case of MTR and suggest that regulatory actions and timing, including how they affect the nature and sequencing of entry, may be more important than policies specially focusing on MTRs. (MTRs refer to the prices operators pay to rivals for terminating a call that starts in their own network; high MTRs make it easier for operators to discriminate between off-net and on-net calls, creating a disadvantage against smaller operators and giving incumbent operators an important instrument to foreclose entry or expansion of new smaller rivals.)

6. Since 2018, ITU has used the 1.5GB mobile-broadband basket as the basic data basket—see ITU, "ICT Price Baskets (IPB)" data set, https://www.itu.int/en/ITU-D/Statistics/Dashboards/Pages /IPB.aspx.

7. Chapter 4 discusses the supply-side constraints more extensively.

8. For more information, see the LdB website, https://www.danonecommunities.com/la -laiterie-du-berger/.

References

A4AI (Alliance for Affordable Internet). 2020. "Covid-19 Shows We Need More Than Basic Internet Access — We Need Meaningful Connectivity." *Web Foundation* (blog), May 27, 2020. https:// webfoundation.org/2020/05/covid-19-shows-we-need-more-than-basic-internet-access-we-need -meaningful-connectivity/.

Atiyas, I., and T. Doganoglu. 2022. "Adoption of Mobile Services in Sub-Saharan Africa: An Exploration Using the Research Africa ICT Data Set." Unpublished manuscript.

Atiyas, İzak, and Mark A. Dutz. 2022. "Digitalization in MENA and Sub-Saharan Africa: A Comparative Analysis of Mobile Internet Uptake and Use in Sub-Saharan Africa and MENA Countries." Working Paper No. 1549, Economic Research Forum, Giza, Egypt.

Aviomoh, H. E., M. P. Blimpo, P. Dato, U. Ekhator-Mobayode, and J. Tei-Mensah. Forthcoming. "Electricity and Digital Development in Africa." Policy Research Working Paper, World Bank, Washington, DC.

Bahia, Kalvin, Pau Castells, Genaro Cruz, Takaaki Masaki, Xavier Pedrós, Tobias Pfutze, Carlos Rodríguez-Castelán, and Hernan Winkler. 2020. "The Welfare Effects of Mobile Broadband Internet: Evidence from Nigeria." Policy Research Working Paper 9230, World Bank, Washington, DC.

Bahia, K., P. Castells, T. Masaki, G. Cruz, C. Rodríguez-Castelán, and V. Sanfelice. 2021. "Mobile Broadband Internet, Poverty and Labor Outcomes in Tanzania." Policy Research Working Paper 9749, World Bank, Washington, DC.

Bahia, K., and A. Delaporte. 2020. *Connected Society: The State of Mobile Internet Connectivity 2020*. London: Global System for Mobile Communications Association (GSMA) Intelligence.

Bahia, K., and S. Suardi. 2019. *Connected Society: The State of Mobile Internet Connectivity 2019*. London: Global System for Mobile Communications Association (GSMA) Intelligence.

Banerjee, A., E. Duflo, N. Goldberg, D. Karlan, R. Osei, W. Parienté, J. Shapiro, B. Thuysbaert, and C. Udry. 2015. "A Multifaceted Program Causes Lasting Progress for the Very Poor: Evidence from Six Countries." *Science* 348 (6236): 1260799.

Blimpo, M. P., and M. Cosgrove-Davies. 2019. *Electricity Access in Sub-Saharan Africa: Uptake, Reliability, and Complementary Factors for Economic Impact.* Africa Development Forum Series. Washington, DC: World Bank.

Blimpo, M. P., A. Maruta, and A. Zeufack. 2021. "Africa Striving to Leapfrog: The Role of Win-Win Cooperation." Unpublished manuscript.

Blimpo, M. P., M. Minges, W. A. K. Kouame, T. T. Azomahou, E. K. K. Lartey, C. Meniago, M. M. Buitano, and A. G. Zeufack. 2017. *Leapfrogging: The Key to Africa's Development—From Constraints to Investment Opportunities.* Washington, DC: World Bank.

Bosman, I. 2021. "COVID-19 and E-Governance: Lessons from South Africa." Policy Insights 100, South African Institute of International Affairs. http://www.jstor.org/stable/resrep29596.

Buchholz, K. 2021. "These Are the World's Biggest E-Commerce Markets." Agenda article, September 8, World Economic Forum, Geneva.

Casaburi, L., R. Glennerster, and T. Suri. 2013. "Rural Roads and Intermediated Trade: Regression Discontinuity Evidence from Sierra Leone." *SSRN* 2161643. https://dx.doi.org/10.2139/ssrn.2161643.

Chen, R., and M. Minges. 2021. "Minimum Data Consumption: How Much Is Needed to Support Online Activities, and Is It Affordable?" Digital Development: Analytical Insights, Note 3, World Bank, Washington, DC. http://pubdocs.worldbank.org/en/742001611762098567/Analytical-Insights-Series-Jan-2021.pdf.

Dang, H. A. H., and C. V. Nguyen. 2021. "Gender Inequality during the COVID-19 Pandemic: Income, Expenditure, Savings, and Job Loss." *World Development* 140: 105296.

Delaporte, A., and K. Bahia. 2021. *Connected Society: The State of Mobile Internet Connectivity 2021.* London: Global System for Mobile Communications Association (GSMA) Intelligence.

Deutschmann, J. W., T. Bernard, and O. Yameogo. 2020. "Contracting and Quality Upgrading: Evidence from an Experiment in Senegal." Unpublished manuscript.

Egger, D., E. Miguel, S. S. Warren, A. Shenoy, E. Collins, D. Karlan, D. Parkerson, et al. 2021. "Falling Living Standards during the COVID-19 Crisis: Quantitative Evidence from Nine Developing Countries." *Science Advances* 7 (6): p.eabe0997.

Fafchamps, M., Gabre-Madhin, E., and B. Minten. 2005. "Increasing Returns and Market Efficiency in Agricultural Trade." *Journal of Development Economics* 78 (2): 406–42.

Gillwald, A., and O. Mothobi. 2019. "A Demand-Side View of Mobile Internet from 10 African Countries." Policy Paper No. 7; Series 5: After Access – Assessing Digital Inequality in Africa. Cape Town, Research ICT Africa. https://researchictafrica.net/wp/wp-content/uploads/2019/05/2019_After-Access_Africa-Comparative-report.pdf.

Google and IFC (International Financial Corporation). 2020. "E-conomy Africa 2020: Africa's $180 Billion Internet Economy Future." Report, Google and IFC, Washington, DC.

Houngbonon, G. V., J. T. Mensah, and N. Traore. 2022. "The Impact of Internet Access on Innovation and Entrepreneurship in Africa." Policy Research Working Paper 9945, World Bank, Washington, DC.

Howdle, D. 2021. "The Price of Mobile/Cellphone Data in 230 Countries in 2021 – Winners and Losers." *Mobile Data Pricing 2021* (blog), April 14, 2021. https://www.cable.co.uk/blogs/global-mobile-data-pricing-2021/.

ILO (International Labour Organization). 2013. *Measuring Informality: A Statistical Manual on the Informal Sector and Informal Employment.* Geneva: ILO.

ILO (International Labour Organization). 2018. *Women and Men in the Informal Economy: A Statistical Picture.* 3rd ed. Geneva: ILO.

ITU (International Telecommunication Union). 2021. "The Affordability of ICT Services 2020." Policy brief, ITU, Geneva. https://www.itu.int/en/ITU-D/Statistics/Documents/publications/prices2020/ITU_A4AI_Price_Briefing_2020.pdf.

Juma, C. 2016. *Innovation and Its Enemies: Why People Resist New Technologies*. New York: Oxford University Press.

Kearney, G., and F. Lipfert. 2022. "Mobile Data—The Price of Speed." *Speedcheck* (blog), August 25, 2022. https://www.speedcheck.org/price-of-speed-mobile-data-2021/.

Leng, C., W. Ma, J. Tang, and Z. Zhu. 2020. "ICT Adoption and Income Diversification among Rural Households in China." *Applied Economics* 52 (33): 3614–28.

Liu, M., Q. Zhang, S. Gao, and J. Huang. 2020. "The Spatial Aggregation of Rural E-Commerce in China: An Empirical Investigation into Taobao Villages." *Journal of Rural Studies* 80: 403–17.

Luo, X., and C. Niu. 2019. "E-Commerce Participation and Household Income Growth in Taobao Villages." Policy Research Working Paper 8811, World Bank, Washington, DC.

Mothobi, O., and A. Gillwald. 2021. "COVID-19 Compounds Historical Disparities and Extends the Digital Divide." Policy Brief No. 5/2021, Cape Town, Research ICT Africa. https://researchictafrica.net/publication/covid-19-compounds-historical-disparities-and-extends-the-digital-divide/.

Porto, G. 2020. "Digital Technologies and Poorer Households' Income Earning Choices in Sub-Saharan Africa: Analytical Framework and a Case Study for Senegal." Unpublished manuscript.

Rodríguez-Castelán, C., R. Granguillhome Ochoa, S. Lach, and T. Masaki. 2021. "Mobile Internet Adoption in West Africa." Policy Research Working Paper 9560, World Bank, Washington, DC.

Saka, O., B. Eichengreen, and C. G. Aksoy. 2021. "Epidemic Exposure, Fintech Adoption, and the Digital Divide." Working Paper No. w29006, National Bureau of Economic Research, Cambridge, MA.

Soumahoro, S. 2017. "Export Taxes and Consumption: Evidence from Côte d'Ivoire's de Facto Partition." *Economic Development and Cultural Change* 65 (3): 425–56.

UNCTAD (United Nations Conference on Trade and Development). 2018. "UNCTAD B2C E-commerce Index 2018—Focus on Africa." UNCTAD Technical Notes on ICT for Development No. 12, UNCTAD, Geneva.

Weiser, C., L. M. C. Sosa, A. A. Ambel, A. H. Tsegay, and O. Pimhidzai. 2021. "Evidence from High-Frequency Household Phone Surveys." Monitoring COVID-19 Impacts on Households in Ethiopia Report No. 8, March 2, Washington, DC, World Bank.

World Bank. 2021a. "Malawi COVID-19 Impact Monitoring, Round 8, April 2021." Brief presenting findings from the Living Standards Measurement Study (LSMS), World Bank, Washington, DC.

World Bank. 2021b. *World Development Report 2021: Data for Better Lives*. Washington, DC: World Bank.

World Bank and Alibaba Group. 2019. "E-Commerce Development: Experience from China. Overview." Report No. 143720, World Bank, Washington, DC.

CHAPTER 4

Digital and Data Infrastructure

Stimulating Greater Availability and Use through Policy and Regulatory Reforms

Market challenges of internet connectivity: Affordability, use, and quality

The previous chapters discussed the transformational effects that digital technologies (DTs) can have on enterprises and innovation, enabling better jobs for more people. For those effects to occur, adoption and intensive use of DTs by both enterprises and households are necessary. However, limited internet penetration, low data consumption, high prices, and poor quality of mobile internet services reflect the main market challenges in Africa. These market outcomes are largely the result of the lack of pro-competition market rules and adequate government interventions to incentivize competition and to facilitate the provision of affordable quality services, especially to segments with low purchasing power and where service provision is costly.

Although mobile broadband capable connections (third-generation and fourth-generation—3G and 4G, respectively) have grown rapidly—at an average annual rate of 30.2 percent between 2016 and 2022—the number of unique mobile internet subscribers has grown more slowly, at a 10.3 percent annual rate over the same period.[1] The availability of broadband connectivity (coverage) remains an issue for approximately 151 million citizens in Africa (146 million of whom are in Sub-Saharan Africa).[2]

Limited internet usage also persists. On average, unique mobile internet subscribers represent only 22 percent of Sub-Saharan Africa's population, with 34 countries having fewer than 25 unique mobile internet subscribers per 100 inhabitants in 2021. As mentioned in chapter 1 (figure 1.10, panel b), the uptake gap between availability and use has remained almost constant since 2010, and in 2021 Africa had the largest uptake gap (as a share of covered people) relative to other regions.

Furthermore, data traffic per capita remains low even relative to lower-middle-income countries in other regions (figure 4.1), with the lowest traffic originating in Western and Central Africa (0.6 gigabytes [GB] per capita per month). Even when accounting for gross domestic product per capita levels, per capita data traffic is lower than expected: most of the African countries were in the bottom-left quadrant in both 2018 and 2020 (figure 4.2).

Additionally, although prices have fallen over time, affordability remains a major issue for internet uptake. While Africa's simple average nominal prices (in US dollars) for 1 GB of data have fallen by 64 percent from 2015 to 2020,[3] two countries (Cabo Verde and the Seychelles) experienced price drops of less than 20 percent, and prices

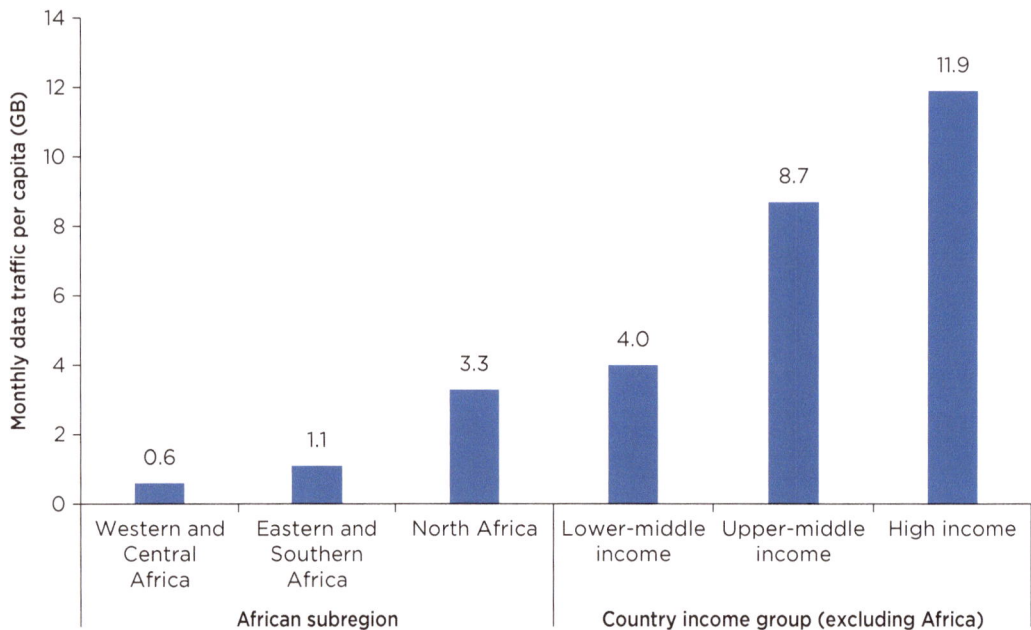

Source: TeleGeography 2020 market data.
Note: This graph shows the average mobile monthly data traffic per capita (number of gigabytes [GB] originating on networks within a given country) in Africa and across other countries by income group (excluding African countries) in 2020. The total sample includes 76 countries, of which 19 are in Africa.

even rose by up to 2 percent in six countries: Chad, Morocco, Gabon, Namibia, São Tomé and Principe, and Togo.

Prices for data have dropped significantly in Africa relative to gross national income (GNI) per capita (figure 4.3, panel a). However, they remain high as a percentage of monthly GNI per capita: the average cost of 2 GB as a share of GNI per capita was 7.2 percent in Africa (8.9 percent in Sub-Saharan Africa) in 2021 and more than 20 percent in Chad, the Central African Republic, Equatorial Guinea, and Zimbabwe (map 4.1). This cost is well above the goal of 1 GB for less than 2 percent of monthly GNI per capita set by the Broadband Commission for Sustainable Development.[4]

Moreover, device affordability is also a barrier (figure 4.3, panel b). For example, the prices of smartphones as a percentage of GNI per capita are higher in Western and Central Africa than in other regions' low- and middle-income countries. Low-use consumers, typically lower-income individuals or enterprise owner-managers, pay much higher prices per unit of data than higher-use, higher-income consumers (box 4.1).

Affordability is an issue for individuals and businesses. Data plans for small and medium enterprises are also more costly in Africa than in other regions, speeds are lower, and data allocations are more limiting, including lower allocations in mobile plans or lack of unmetered offers in fixed internet plans. In at least 11 Sub-Saharan African countries, operators do not have a standard offering that grants at least 25 megabits per second (Mbps) of download speed—the approximate speed needed for light web browsing and email for up to five workers and operating a point-of-service terminal (box 4.2).

FIGURE 4.2 Correlation between mobile data traffic per capita, 2020, and GDP, 2018

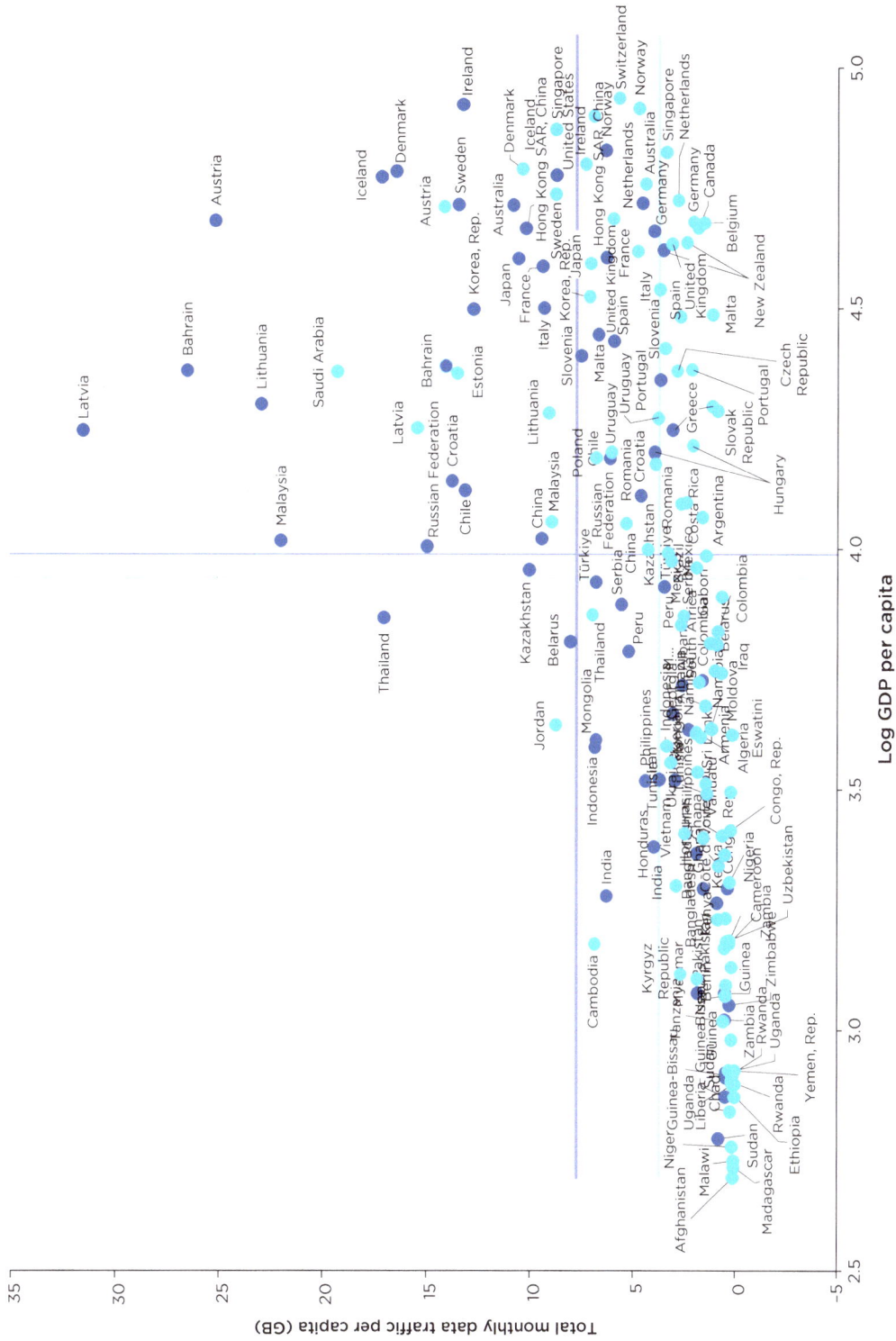

Sources: World Bank 2021e for 2018 data and TeleGeography 2020 market data.
Note: This graph shows mobile data traffic per capita (gigabytes [GB] per month) versus GDP per capita, for 2018 (light blue lines and dots) and 2020 (dark blue lines and dots).

FIGURE 4.3 **Average data and smartphone prices, by region, African subregion, and global country income group**

a. Average price of 1 GB of data, 2013–20

Legend:
- Sub-Saharan Africa
- Latin America and the Caribbean
- Canada and United States
- East Asia and Pacific
- South Asia
- Europe and Central Asia
- Middle East and North Africa

b. Average price of a smartphone, 2021

African subregion			Country income group (excluding Africa)		
Western and Central Africa	Eastern and Southern Africa	North Africa	Lower-middle income	Upper-middle income	High income
46.3	44.2	24.8	35.1	30.8	4.7

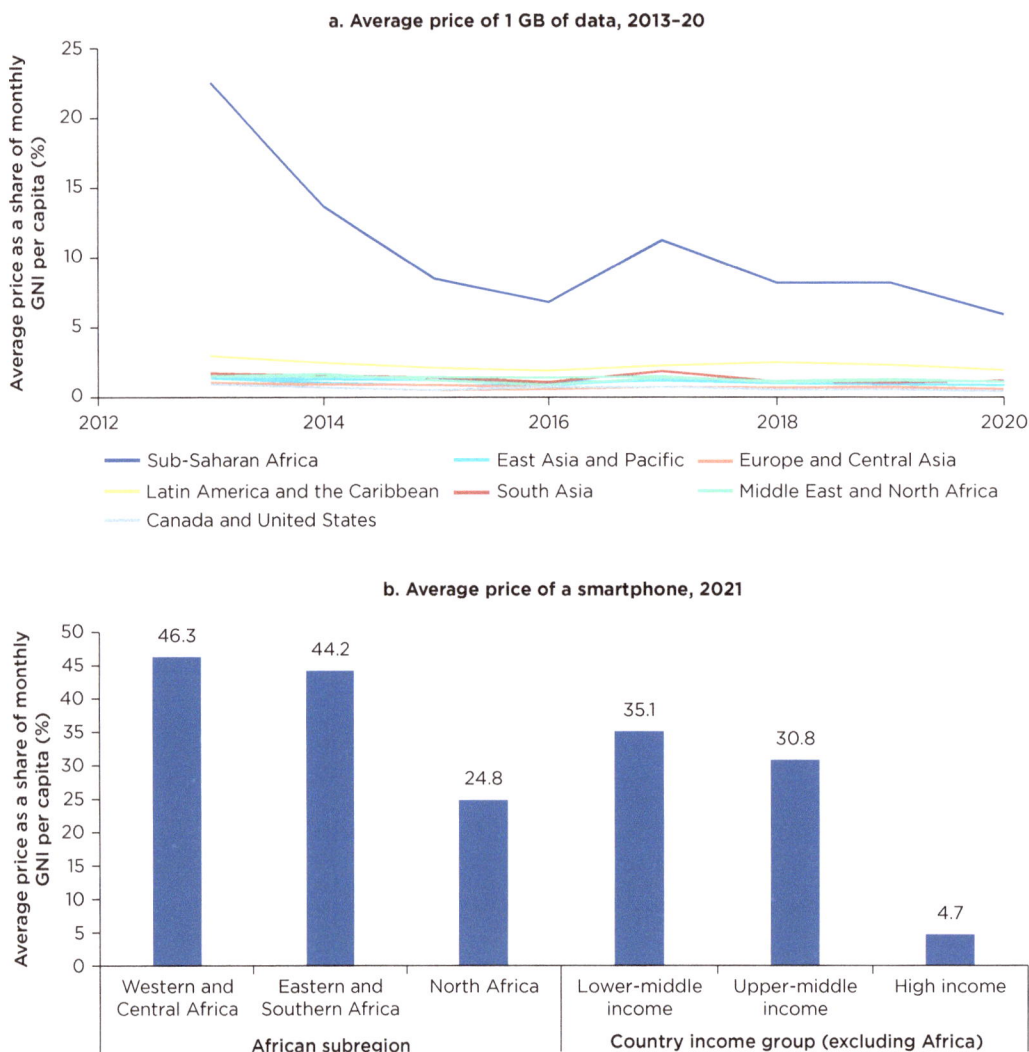

Sources: International Telecommunication Union (ITU), "ICT Prices" 2021 data set (https://www.itu.int/en/ITU-D /Statistics/Pages/ICTprices/default.aspx); Alliance for Affordable Internet (A4AI), "Device Pricing 2021" data set (https://a4ai.org/research/device-pricing-2021/).
Note: Panel a shows 1 GB from 2013 to 2016, 1.5 GB from 2017 to 2020, using World Bank country income classifications. Panel b shows average price of smartphones as percentage of monthly GNI per capita in Africa and across other countries by income group (excluding African countries) in 2021. GB = gigabyte; GNI = gross national income.

In 10 Sub-Saharan African countries, no packages with an unlimited data allowance were available. This lack affects the kind of content and digital technologies that can be offered online and limits consumer experience (for business and individuals), preventing demand from being pulled by online digital services, as it should be.

Low speed and high latency—that is, delays—have deep effects on the quality of service and user experience. Although the average download speed in Africa increased by more than five times between 2014 and 2021, it remains at only 23 Mbps,[5] below the 30 Mbps that is considered a low-speed broadband and the 78 Mbps available on average in high-income countries (figure 4.4, panel a). Eighteen Sub-Saharan Africa countries have average download speeds below 25 Mbps, and none has an average download speed above 100 Mbps.

MAP 4.1 Cost of a 2 GB data-only mobile broadband plan as a share of GNI per capita, by country, Africa, 2021

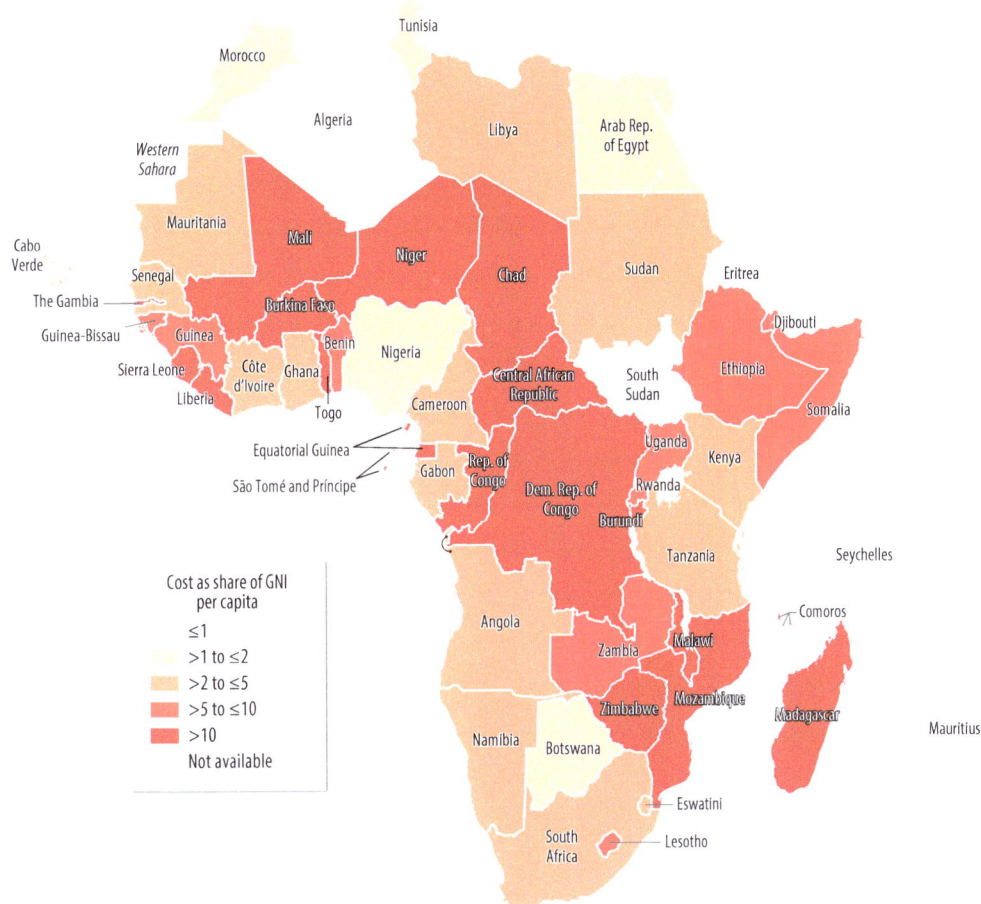

Source: International Telecommunication Union (ITU), "ICT Price Baskets (IPB)" 2021 data set (https://www.itu.int /en/ITU-D/Statistics/Dashboards/Pages/IPB.aspx).
Note: The map shows the total cost of a 2 gigabyte (GB) broadband plan—the data basket used for price comparison—expressed as a share of gross national income (GNI) per capita.

Faster 4G mobile technologies are often available in cities only, highlighting the gaps in broadband internet coverage between rural and urban areas (map 4.2). Furthermore, low latency—which is key for interactive applications and Industry 4.0— is still high (figure 4.4, panel b), reflecting limited data infrastructure in the region. Finally, although the cost-speed ratio in Africa has decreased in recent years, by 2021 it remained 50 percent higher than in Europe and 25 percent higher than in Asia and the Pacific (figure 4.4, panel c).

Where improvements in internet quality and speed occurred, they are unevenly distributed, with stark differences in download speeds within countries, regions, and even cities. Download speeds tend to be fastest in cities. For example, the median download speed of Vodacom South Africa is about 34 Mbps faster than the median download speed of the whole country. In other countries, this difference is smaller, but on average, cities show higher median download speeds than the rest of the country (Kechiche 2022).

Regressive broadband pricing constrains use by the poor

Regressive price discrimination strategies—including short expiration dates for data bundles and lower prices at specific times that are not suitable for productive use (nighttime and weekends)—undermine internet use by lower-income users. In countries like Gabon, prices per megabyte for low-consumption users are more than seven times those for high-consumption users. Analysis shows that these strategies are used by large and small operators alike.

Price discrimination by mobile operators leads to per unit discounts as data allowances increase, with higher unit prices for low-consumption users. Implied unit prices per megabyte for 100–300 megabytes of consumption are more than double the implied prices for 5–10 gigabytes in countries such as Gabon, South Africa, and Uganda, while discrimination is less pronounced in Sierra Leone (figure B4.1.1).

New pricing strategies and government interventions need to be tested to boost affordability for the poor. In the case of South Africa, the data market inquiry highlighted this issue; as a result, Vodacom and MTN agreed to reduce prices of plans with low data allowances. Targeted social tariffs could be used to reduce the prices for low-income users. However, the design of new pricing schemes should consider the context of mobile internet where consumption is at the individual and not the household level, and where the bundling of services, multidimensional product differentiation, and contestability are at play.

FIGURE B4.1.1 Comparison of absolute and implied prices of data plans, by vendor, selected African countries, 2021

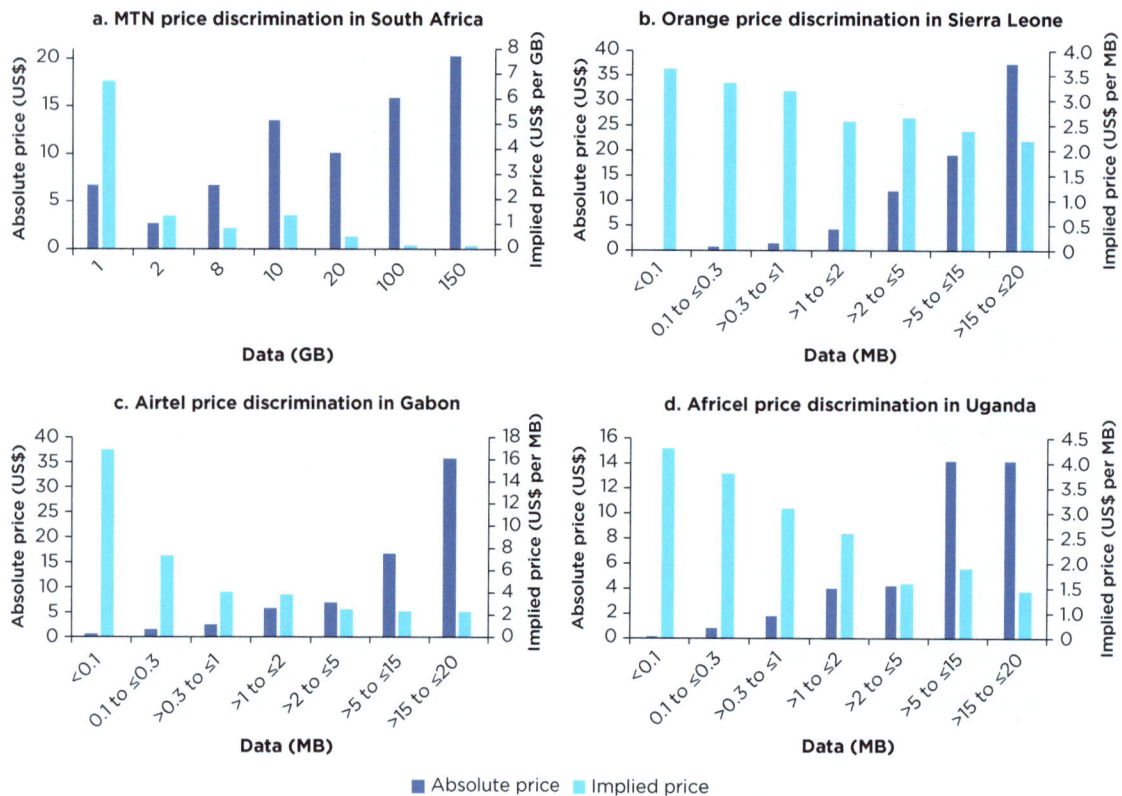

a. MTN price discrimination in South Africa

b. Orange price discrimination in Sierra Leone

c. Airtel price discrimination in Gabon

d. Africel price discrimination in Uganda

■ Absolute price ■ Implied price

Source: Operators' websites.
Note: The horizontal axis shows the amount of data included in a package in megabytes (MB) for Sierra Leone, Gabon, and Uganda and in gigabytes (GB) for South Africa. Data were collected in August–September 2021. "Absolute price" (left axis) is the nominal price of a data bundle. "Implied price" (right axis) results from dividing the absolute price by the amount of data units (MB or GB) included in a data bundle. Bars depict unweighted average prices within the data allowance range.

BOX 4.2
High broadband prices and limited offerings constrain data use by SMEs

The economic impact of digital adoption is potentially larger than past general purpose technologies such as railways and electricity (OECD 2008). Internet usage by small and medium enterprises (SMEs) is linked to increased productivity, internationalization processes, exporting activities, and cost reduction practices. Alas, internet adoption by SMEs remains limited in many low- and middle-income countries mostly owing to lack of infrastructure, affordable prices, and availability of adequate services. In Sub-Saharan Africa, SMEs connect to internet mostly through mobile plans or mobile products such as mobile Wi-Fi routers that generally offer lower speeds than fiber connections and include data caps.

To study the options available for SMEs across regions, information on the prices and characteristics of plans of fixed and mobile broadband services was collected for 70 low- and middle-income countries.[a] Data collection focused on packages that provide a speed and volume of data appropriate for an SME with one to five employees to use basic email, browse online, and download large files. This includes (a) fixed plans offering a download speed of at least 25 megabits per second (Mbps) and unlimited data use, and (b) mobile plans that include at least 10 gigabytes (GB) of total data per month. It is worth noting that higher speeds (25–50 Mbps) would be needed for SMEs to use online videoconferencing, manage basic e-commerce, take inventory, conduct logistics activities, and use point-of-sales terminals, as well as to access online backups.

Africa has the slowest and most expensive fixed internet business plans and fewer fixed business plans options. African countries also have the lowest data level and lowest speed for mobile business plans—with 35 Mbps of median download speed of fixed plans (compared with 40 Mbps in Asia and 43 Mbps in Latin America) and a median 133 GB of data included in mobile plans (compared with 150 GB in Asia and 164 GB in Latin America). Furthermore, offered speeds are below what would be needed to support online work, email, and videoconferencing by SMEs. Standard broadband business plans that offered at least 25 Mbps of speed were not available in 11 Sub-Saharan African countries (in addition to Afghanistan, Sri Lanka, and Uzbekistan), among the 70 low- and middle-income countries studied worldwide.

Most African countries have prices per GB and per Mbps of download speed that are above the world's averages (for both fixed and mobile plans). On average, Western and Central African countries have the most expensive mobile and fixed packages, the highest associated taxes, and the highest ratio of price to download speed of fixed plans (US$5 per Mbps). Eastern and Southern African countries have the highest average price per GB, and North Africa offers, on average, the least costly mobile and fixed plans on the continent. Africa's high prices per unit of speed and unit of data relative to other regions highlight affordability and quality issues for SMEs across the continent.

Source: Vergara-Cobos 2021, based on data collected by Tarifica.
a. Based on data collected by Tarifica from June and September 2020 from operators' websites. The plans compared here are only those profiled as adequate for SMEs to use and exclude uncontended leased lines. Chosen fixed plans were those that offer a download speed of at least 25 Mbps, and chosen mobile plans were those that include at least 10 GB of total data.

Even within cities, however, the distribution of fast internet is not equally distributed. Median download speeds can differ markedly between city districts (map 4.3).[6] Areas with very high download speeds of more than 50, 60, or even 80 Mpbs are often very close to those with speeds below the country average. For example, several areas in Abidjan and Accra have median download speeds slower than 7 Mbps and 5 Mpbs, whereas the overall medians for Côte d'Ivoire and Ghana are about 8.6 Mbps and 9.4 Mbps, respectively. Overall,

FIGURE 4.4 Internet speed, service quality, and average cost-speed ratio, by region

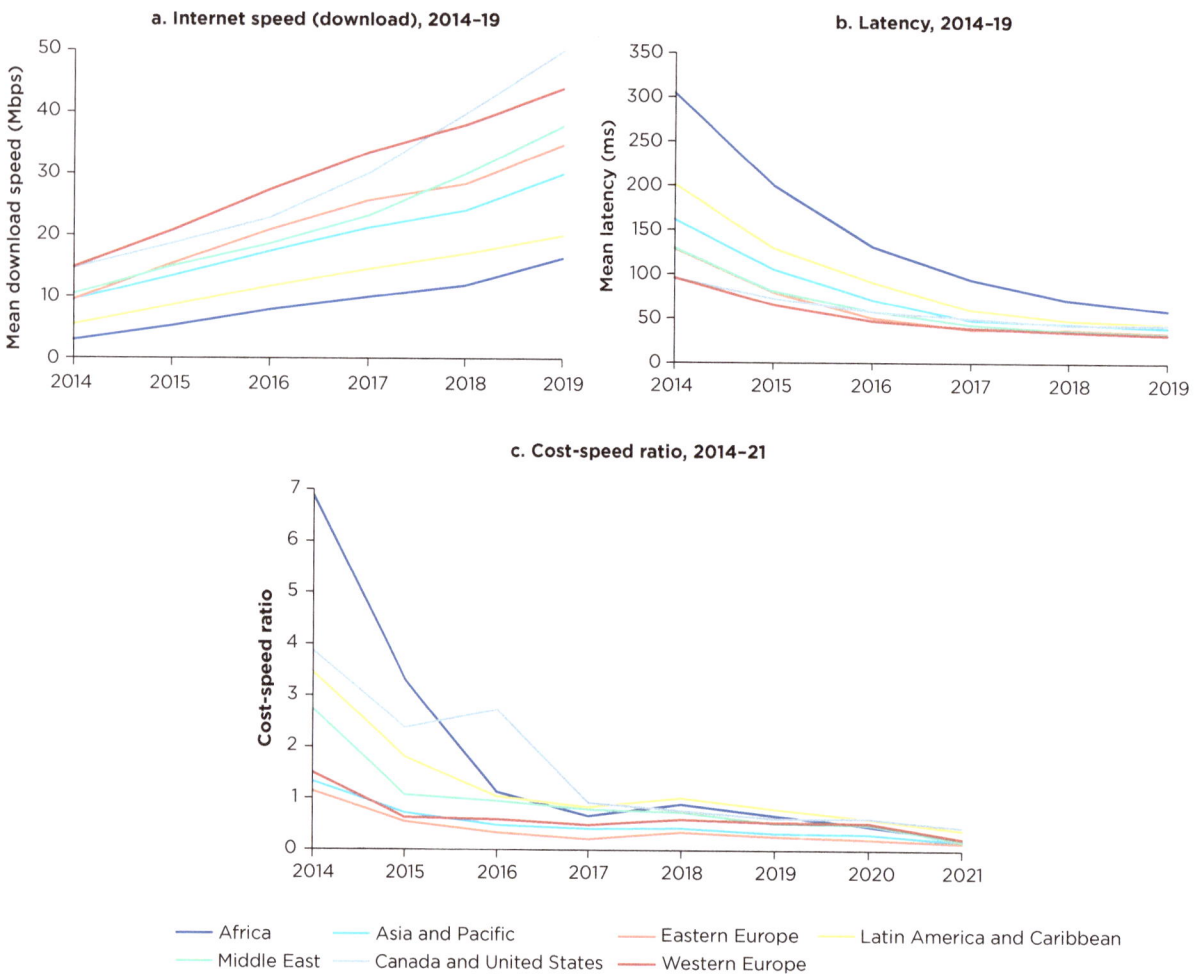

a. Internet speed (download), 2014–19

b. Latency, 2014–19

c. Cost-speed ratio, 2014–21

— Africa — Asia and Pacific — Eastern Europe — Latin America and Caribbean
— Middle East — Canada and United States — Western Europe

Sources: Based on data from Ookla's Speedtest Intelligence platform and International Telecommunication Union (ITU) data sets. *Note:* In panel b, "latency" refers to the transmission delay of a message, in milliseconds (ms). For panel c, "cost-speed ratio" is calculated as the ratio of (a) the cost of 2 gigabytes of data to (b) mean download speed, in megabits per second (Mbps). Panels use ITU regions.

among a group of large cities, within-city differences ranged from about 40 Mpbs in Lagos, Nigeria, to almost 80 Mbps in Abidjan, Côte d'Ivoire (map 4.3). This discrepancy shows that, despite improvements in connectivity infrastructure, large parts of the population might still be excluded from fast mobile internet—even in cities.

African countries need to achieve two main goals regarding digital infrastructure: (a) enhancing affordability to increase use, and (b) expanding availability to bridge the digital divide. The next two sections present challenges and policy recommendations in these areas. Depending on the relative importance of the use and availability gaps, governments can select the best combination among four main policy instruments (with overlaps): pro-competition regulation, cost-reducing regulation, regulation for rural coverage, and universal service rules (including targeted subsidies and price controls). Universal service policy can also support affordability if specially targeted to vulnerable market segments.

MAP 4.2 Shares of population with internet coverage (3G versus 4G), Democratic Republic of Congo, Nigeria, and Tanzania, 2021

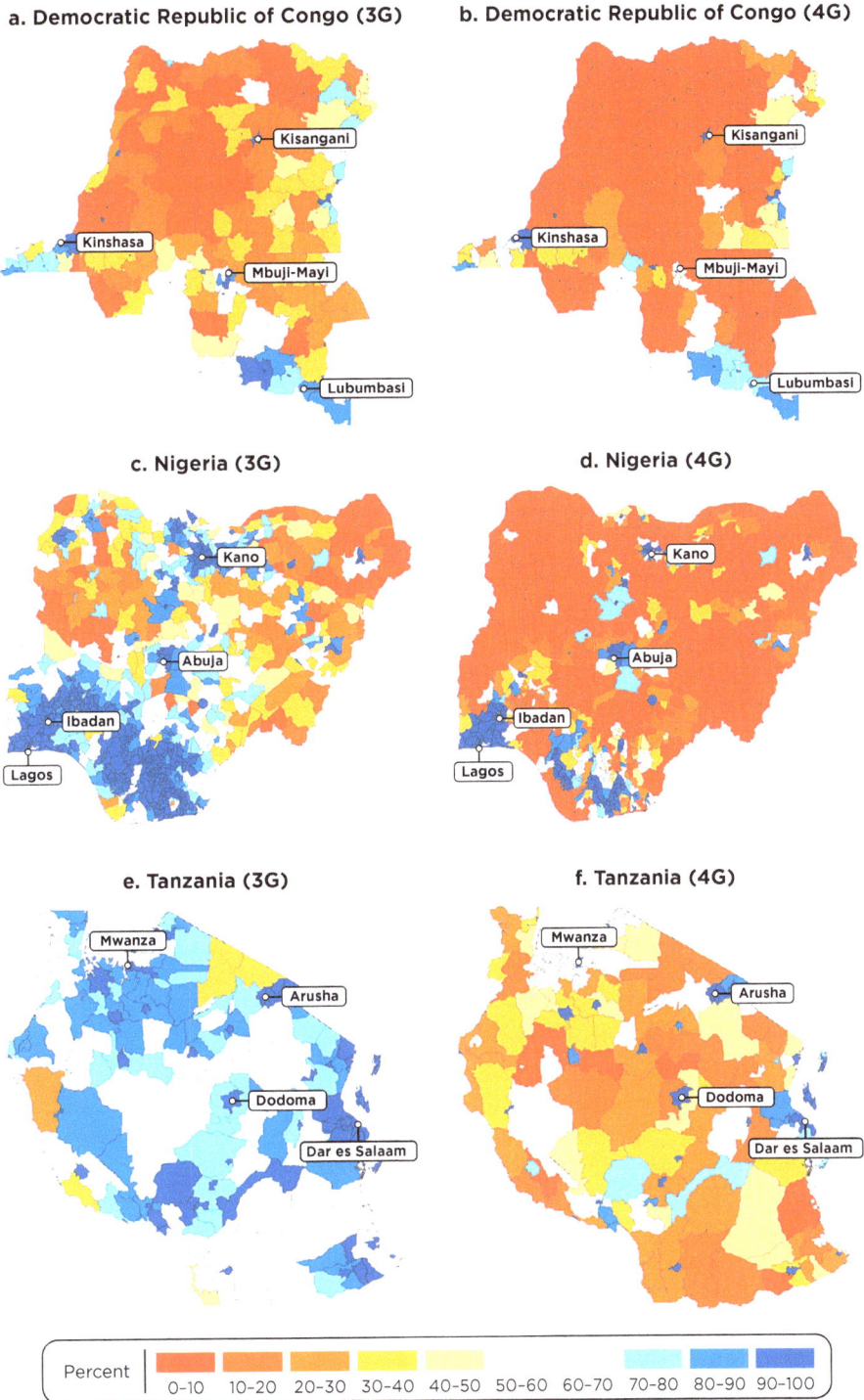

a. Democratic Republic of Congo (3G)

b. Democratic Republic of Congo (4G)

c. Nigeria (3G)

d. Nigeria (4G)

e. Tanzania (3G)

f. Tanzania (4G)

Percent | 0–10 10–20 20–30 30–40 40–50 50–60 60–70 70–80 80–90 90–100

Sources: World Bank 2022, based on Global System for Mobile Communications Association (GSMA) analysis of data from mobile operators, GSMA Intelligence platform, Facebook Connectivity Lab, Center for International Earth Science Information Network (CIESIN) household survey data, and Group on Earth Observations.
Note: Population coverage relates to total population. 3G = third-generation mobile communications technology; 4G = fourth-generation technology.

MAP 4.3 Mobile broadband download speeds, selected urban areas, Africa, 2020

a. Abidjan, Côte d'Ivoire

b. Accra, Ghana

c. Cairo, Egypt

d. Johannesburg, South Africa

e. Lagos, Nigeria

f. Nairobi, Kenya

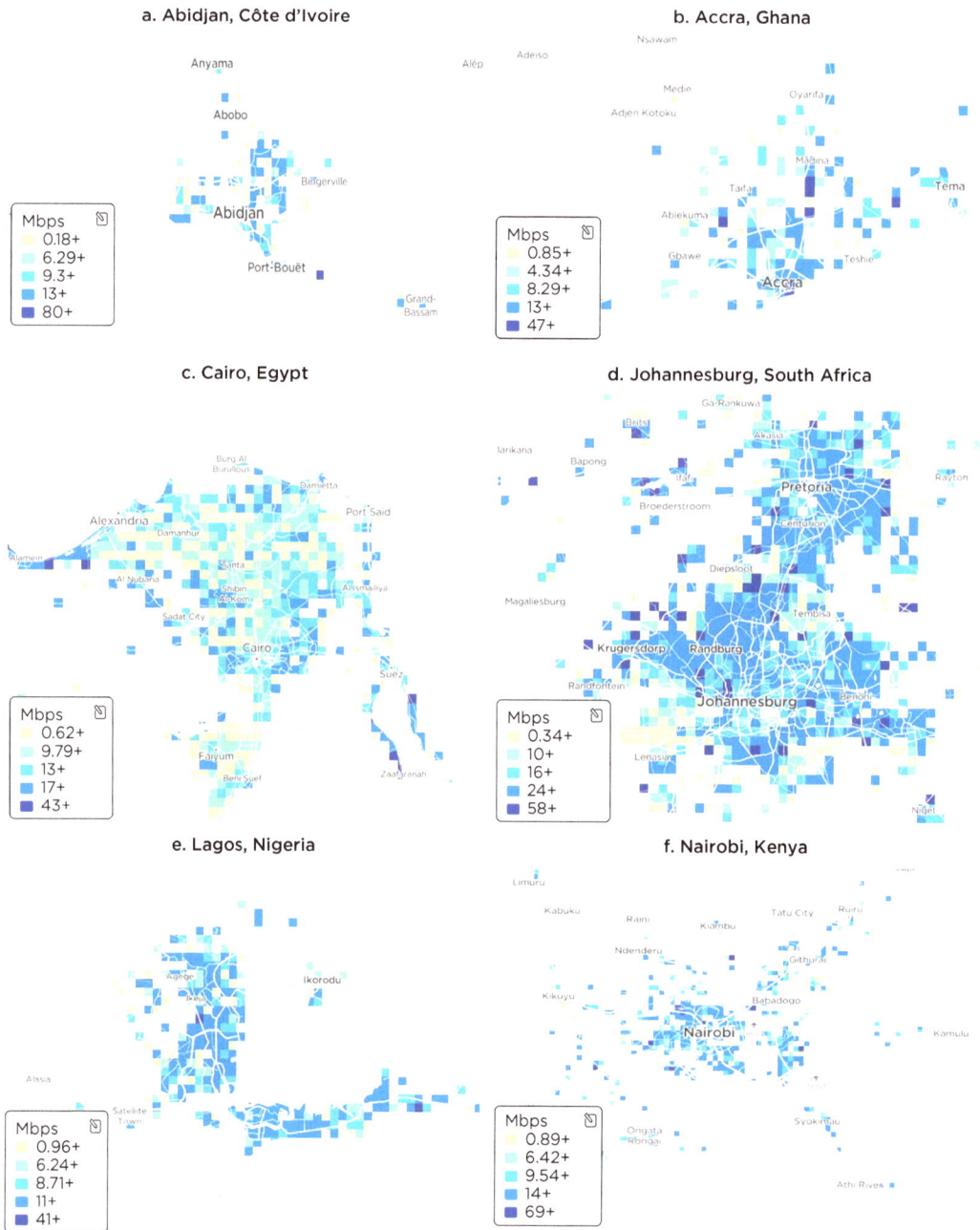

Source: Based on analysis of Ookla's Speedtest Intelligence data for June 2020, as of September 24, 2022.
Note: The maps show the median download speeds of mobile broadband for each area of about 70 square kilometers in June 2020. "Download speed" measures how quickly data can be pulled from a server on the internet to a device, measured in megabits per second (Mbps). Data are based on mobile samples, which vary in number by location.

The availability and usage of mobile broadband networks vary, underpinning the priorities for policy action to improve affordability and availability. On average, African countries have 3G or 4G population coverage of over 80 percent, but the level of use (unique mobile internet subscribers as percentage of the population) is only 26.4 percent on average, which is below the average in high-income countries–65.5 percent (figure 4.5).

FIGURE 4.5 Correlation between availability and use of mobile broadband-capable networks, by country, Africa, 2022

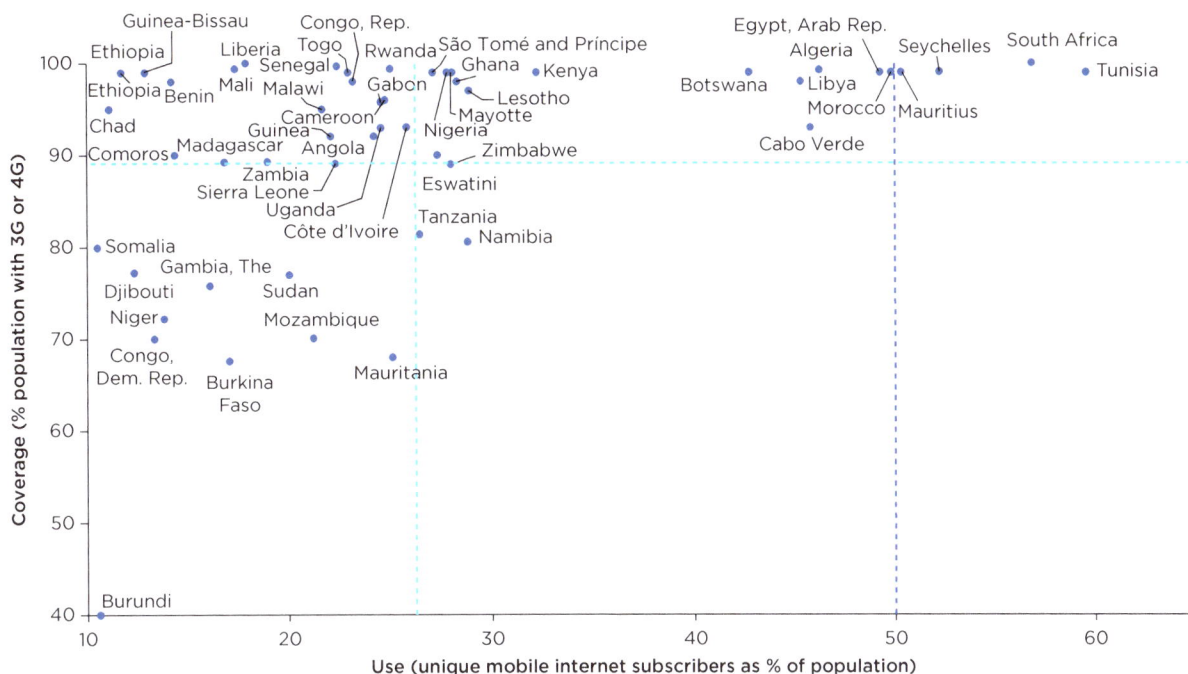

Source: Elaboration based on Global System for Mobile Communications Association (GSMA) data, accessed November 2022 through the GSMA Intelligence proprietary platform.
Note: Light blue dotted lines represent the averages of coverage and usage for Africa; the dark blue vertical line is a reference level capturing critical mass. The y-axis shows the average of each country's third-generation (3G) or fourth-generation (4G) mobile communications technology coverage of the population.

The literature suggests the existence of a critical mass for broadband diffusion at which the benefits become stronger (see Koutroumpis 2009), but most African countries are below that reference level (50 percent). Furthermore, almost 20 percent of Africa's rural population has no mobile broadband coverage, and only 62 percent of the rural population has access to a mobile broadband network, compared with 99 percent in urban areas (ITU 2021).

It is also worth noting that even 2G (second-generation) coverage varies across the countries, from being almost universal in Benin and Rwanda to being more limited in others such as the Democratic Republic of Congo (75 percent nationally and only 52 percent in rural areas). Furthermore, the usage gap is also considerable for voice and text mobile services supported by 2G. For example, in the Democratic Republic of Congo, mobile uptake in rural areas is less than 20 percent although coverage is 52 percent (World Bank 2022).

Affordability to increase use

Measures that support affordability of internet connectivity will help to increase uptake and use of DTs in Africa. As seen in chapters 2 and 3, affordability together with income levels determine the ability to pay, while capabilities determine the willingness to pay. Affordability policies should aim to promote competition in the provision of digital infrastructure and reduce operational costs using instruments that foster allocative and productive efficiency.

FIGURE 4.6 Effects of market concentration on affordability and 3G+4G+5G penetration

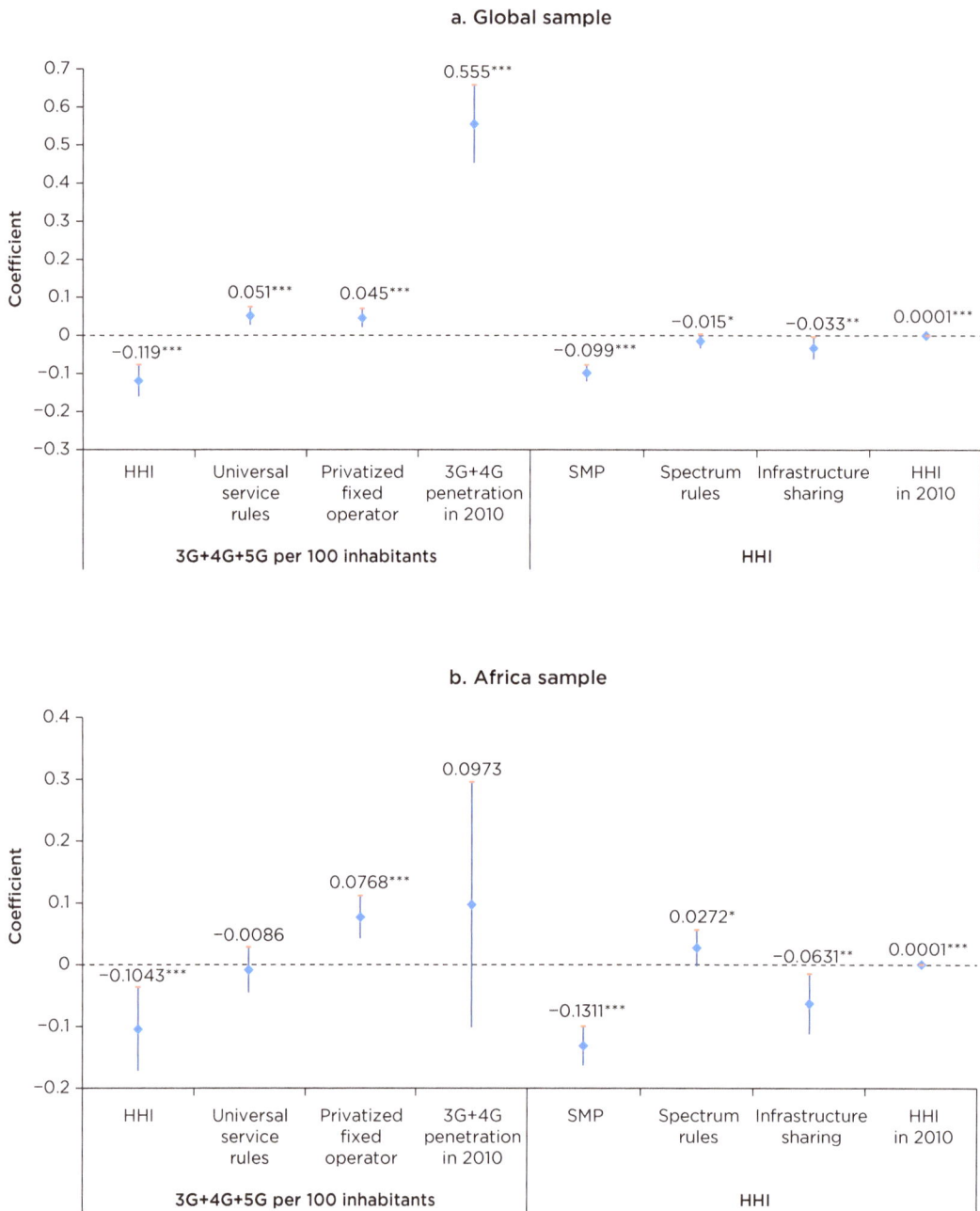

a. Global sample

b. Africa sample

Source: Aviomoh, Begazo, and Golla, forthcoming.
Note: Three-stage least squares model using country-level panel data for the period 2012–18, with the dependent variable for each equation noted at the bottom of the graphs. Total sample, 616 observations; Africa sample, 147 observations. Similar results when considering unique mobile internet subscribers' penetration instead of 3G+4G+5G (third- plus fourth- plus fifth-generation mobile communication technology) connections. Controls for electricity, schooling, urbanization, and population density are significant. Control for age of regulator is not significant. GB = gigabyte; HHI = Herfindahl Hirschman concentration index; SMP = regulation of operators with significant market power.
Significance level: * = 10 percent, ** = 5 percent, *** = 1 percent.

Digital Africa

Cross-country analysis for 2010–20 (Aviomoh, Begazo, and Golla, forthcoming) shows that market concentration (a proxy for weak competition) is linked to lower uptake (measured by unique mobile internet subscribers and 3G plus 4G subscriptions)—see figure 4.6. Pro-competition policies can affect ability to pay through more affordable data plans. They also can affect willingness to use through better quality of service that allows for more appealing digital applications and content. In a competitive environment, government interventions to reduce the cost of providing services—through the elimination of undue burdensome regulation and fees—should enable further reduction of prices to final users by providers.

Promoting competition along the digital infrastructure value chain

Competition and pro-competition measures have positive effects on market dynamics, including prices and quality. Pro-competition regulation reduces concentration, measured by the Herfindahl-Hirschman Index (HHI), and reduces prices without hurting quality, reducing investment, or reducing tax revenues (Faccio and Zingales 2017, using mobile telecommunications data from 148 countries). However, competition can both reduce prices and increase the incentive to invest, as has occurred in Rwanda (Björkegren 2020). Having a higher number of service providers in the mobile industry is associated with lower prices, and the presence of disruptive competitors affects the pricing strategies in mobile markets in favor of users (Ofcom 2016). Finally, competition can also influence technology upgrading and product offerings: having more competition speeds up the adoption of new technologies and increases the targeting of services (Seim and Viard 2011, using structural changes in the US telecommunications industry between 1996 and 1998).

Pro-competition interventions can also increase household welfare. Increasing competition in the telecommunications market can contribute to a reduction in the poverty headcount rate of between 0.02 and 0.82 percentage point (figure 4.7), and an increase in access to services of between 0.06 and 5.37 percentage points, even without considering labor participation effects.[7] Furthermore, regulation of mobile termination rates can benefit consumers significantly more than entry,[8] and high-income consumers and city dwellers could benefit more in terms of increased consumer surplus (Hawthorne and Grzybowski [2019] for South Africa). Moreover, delays in regulation that allow for or facilitate entry can drastically reduce social welfare (Björkegren [2020] for Rwanda).

However, market structures are not yet enabling competition across African digital infrastructure markets and key digital service markets. Lack of market competition broadly has been highlighted as a key challenge in most (54 percent) of the World Bank's Digital Economy for Africa Initiative (DE4A) country assessments in Eastern and Western Africa. Market outcomes such as high prices and low quality, as noted earlier, reflect that market structures along the value chain restrain competition, among other causes related to economies of scale and scope. Monopolies and duopolies still exist in many African countries (figure 4.8; see annex 4A for a regional overview). Many monopolies persist in key bottleneck markets such as international connectivity, which are necessary to exchange data with the world and use digital solutions that rely on cloud services. They also persist in domestic fixed networks, which are essential for backbone and backhaul to expand broadband beyond major urban areas and to deliver high-speed connections in urban and industrial areas.

FIGURE 4.7 **Reduction in the poverty headcount rate from simulated policies to increase telecommunications competition, selected Sub-Saharan African countries, 2015–18**

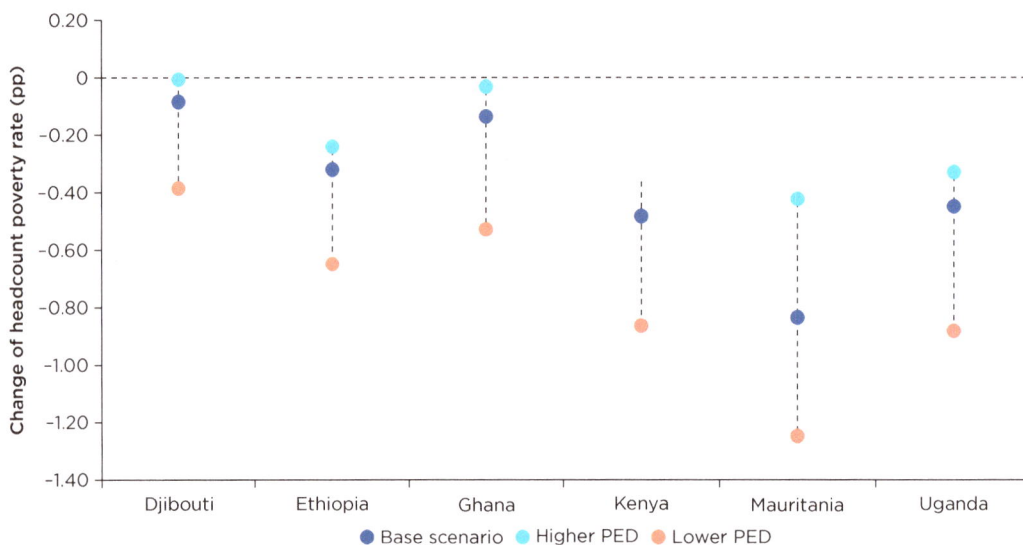

Source: Vergara-Cobos, Malasquez, and Granguillhome, forthcoming.
Note: The results shown in this graph come from simulating the effects of different pro-competition policies that are being applied in each country. For example, in the case of Ghana, the simulated policy is that in which the market share of the main competitor decreases from 65 percent to 49 percent. The results are sensitive to the price elasticity of demand (PED) assumed, so results are presented on a range of PED values. Point estimates are for elasticity scenarios. pp = percentage points.

The good news is that the level of supply and diversity of submarine cables and terrestrial fiber networks is increasing. However, in more than 25 countries, state-owned enterprises (SOEs)[9] remain as market players, giving them the potential to either thwart competition or enable private sector participation in linked markets if transparent, open, nondiscriminatory and cost-oriented access to facilities is provided.[10]

Market developments such as the operation of independent tower providers, mobile virtual network operators (MVNOs), and mobile money providers were expected to change the market structure and affect market dynamics positively, boosting competition. However, challenges have transformed this expected improved landscape. The appearance of monopolies and duopolies in the tower company market (for example, in Chad, Gabon, Uganda, and Zambia) still keep mobile passive infrastructure in few hands. Operation of MVNOs is much more limited than initially hoped for; it took almost two years for Equitel to be able to operate in Kenya as an MVNO.[11] Although 21 other African countries allow for MVNOs, none is operational to date.

As for mobile money operators, those that are vertically integrated have exacerbated market-concentrating network effects, resulting in sustained or strengthened market power by mobile network operators (MNOs).[12] Mobile money markets are now more concentrated than mobile retail markets—for example, in Kenya and Somalia. Concentration in data storage and cloud markets is lower than in infrastructure markets but still moderately or highly concentrated in 19 countries.[13] On the upside, market concentration[14] of digital solutions at the sector level is very low, and digital-solution business markets are dynamic with the entry of start-ups happening in 37 African countries (14 in Western and Central Africa, 17 in Eastern and Southern Africa, and 4 in North Africa).[15] The challenge is to prevent market power in digital infrastructure from limiting

FIGURE 4.8 Extent of competitive constraints in market structures across the digital value chain, 2021

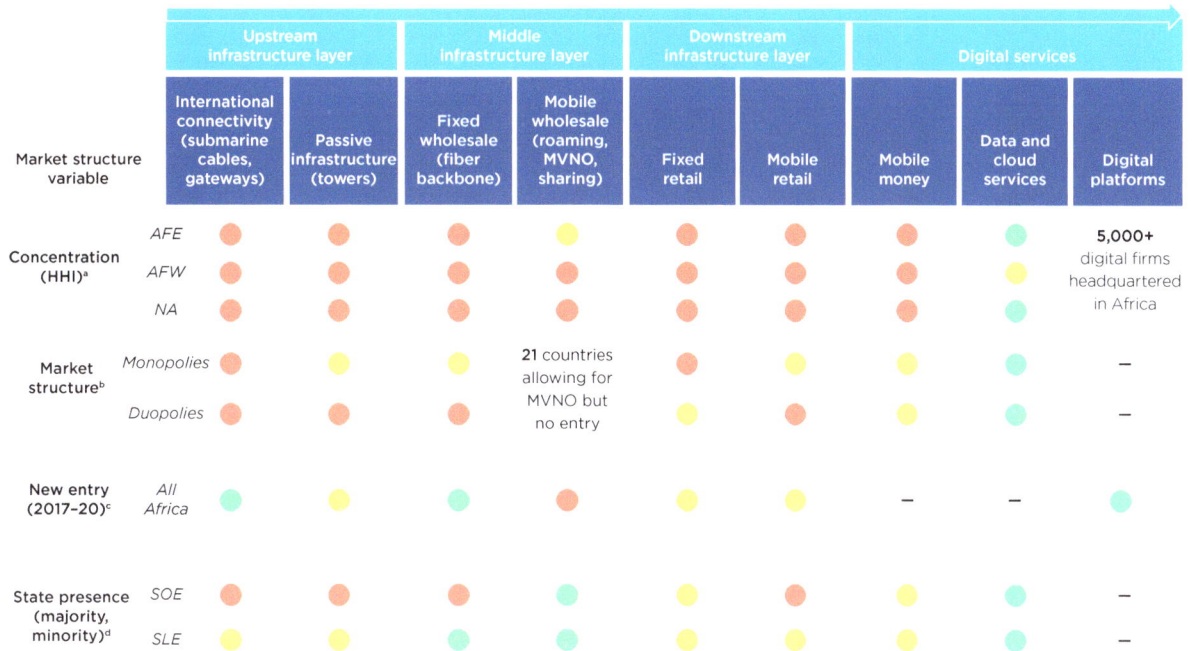

Market structure variable		Upstream infrastructure layer		Middle infrastructure layer		Downstream infrastructure layer		Digital services		
		International connectivity (submarine cables, gateways)	Passive infrastructure (towers)	Fixed wholesale (fiber backbone)	Mobile wholesale (roaming, MVNO, sharing)	Fixed retail	Mobile retail	Mobile money	Data and cloud services	Digital platforms
Concentration (HHI)[a]	AFE	orange	orange	orange	yellow	orange	orange	orange	green	5,000+ digital firms headquartered in Africa
	AFW	orange	orange	orange	orange	orange	orange	orange	yellow	
	NA	orange	orange	orange	orange	orange	orange	orange	green	
Market structure[b]	Monopolies	orange	yellow	yellow	21 countries allowing for MVNO but no entry	orange	yellow	yellow	green	—
	Duopolies	orange	orange	orange		yellow	orange	yellow	green	—
New entry (2017–20)[c]	All Africa	green	yellow	green	orange	yellow	yellow	—	—	green
State presence (majority, minority)[d]	SOE	orange	orange	orange	green	yellow	orange	yellow	green	—
	SLE	yellow	yellow	green	green	yellow	yellow	yellow	green	—

Source: World Bank, Africa Digital Market Players Database (internal), 2021, built on data from numerous sources, including TeleGeography, Global System for Mobile Communications Association (GSMA), Africa Bandwidth Maps, Afterfibre.org, Policytracker, TowerXchange, PeeringDB, and Xalam Analytics.

Note: Red circles represent higher risk to competition, on average; orange circles, medium risk; and green circles, lower risk. The sample covers 54 African countries for mobile retail, 38 for fixed retail, 52 for fiber backbone, 26 for telecommunications towers, 35 for submarine cables, 25 for data centers, and 15 for mobile money. AFE = Eastern and Southern Africa; AFW = Western and Central Africa; HHI = Herfindahl-Hirschman index (market concentration measure); MVNO = mobile virtual network operator; NA = North Africa; SLE = state as minority shareholder; SOE = majority or fully state-owned enterprise; — = not available.

a. A market with HHI of less than 1,500 is considered to have a competitive market structure, HHI of 1,500 to 2,500 is moderately concentrated, and an HHI of 2,500 or greater is highly concentrated.

b. In terms of monopolies and duopolies, less than 5 percent of countries are monopolies/duopolies = green, 5–20 percent of countries = orange, above 20 percent of countries = red.

c. For new entry, new entry in less than 5 percent of countries = red, in 5–20 percent of countries = orange, in more than 20 percent of countries = green.

d. SOE presence in less than 10 percent of countries = green, in 10–50 percent of countries = orange, and in more than 50 percent of countries = red.

competition in digital services or reducing their uptake given the high cost and low quality of the underlying internet services.

Vertical integration of dominant firms creates risks to competition along the value chain. Vertical integration in digital infrastructure is common given the existence of economies of scope and incentives to integrate to avoid holdup problems considering typical access issues with bottleneck infrastructure. In Africa, 81 percent of firms operate in three or more of the nine segments depicted in figure 4.8.

Aside from concentrated markets in the upstream, middle, and downstream layers, large market players in mobile retail and fiber networks are vertically integrated into other segments. Twenty-one operators with more than 40 percent market share in mobile retail are integrated into two other segments or more (mostly mobile money and tower infrastructure) (figure 4.9, panel a), while 17 large operators in fiber networks are present in two or more other segments (figure 4.9, panel b). Furthermore, for international connectivity, six (out of eight) monopolies in international gateways are vertically integrated

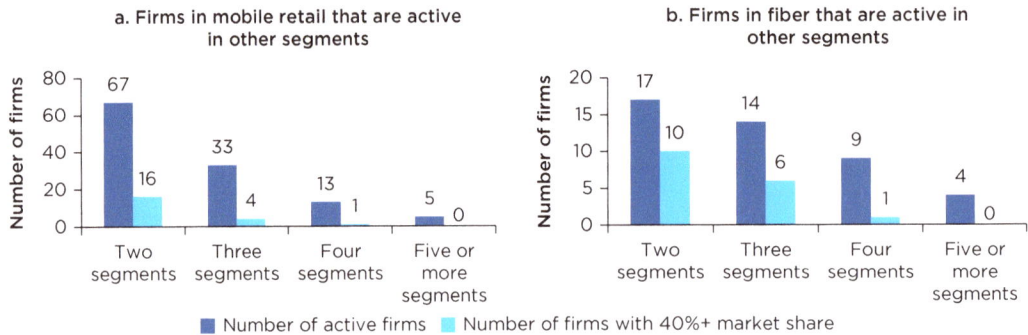

a. Firms in mobile retail that are active in other segments

b. Firms in fiber that are active in other segments

■ Number of active firms   ■ Number of firms with 40%+ market share

Source: World Bank, forthcoming.
Note: The charts show results among firms with a market share of 40 percent or more—a common threshold to presume dominance based on European Union case law. Total number of firms considered: 1,163 in 55 African countries. For the segments considered, see figure 4.8.

into fiber networks or fixed or mobile retail. Sixteen African countries have operators vertically integrated and holding over 40 percent market share in both mobile retail and fiber backbone.[16] This highlights the importance of introducing regulation of bottleneck markets to enable competition along the value chain.

SOEs are important players in digital infrastructure in Africa, especially in fiber backbone, yet weak governance could limit downstream competition. Governments have full or majority shareholdings in MNOs that account for more than 17 percent of all African mobile subscribers and minority shareholdings in MNOs that account for at least an additional 20 percent of mobile subscribers (figure 4.10, panel a). Additionally, 60 percent of telecommunication operators' fiber backbone network is fully or majority state owned (figure 4.10, panel b). Such ownership makes governments key players in allowing cost-oriented access to this infrastructure to enable downstream competitive markets; some countries such as Nigeria and Senegal are exploring this kind of intervention. If we consider fiber networks deployed in other network sectors such as electricity and transportation, this percentage increases. Furthermore, SOEs can affect the whole sector when they control essential infrastructure. From a sample of 37 state-owned or state-linked enterprises in 20 African countries, 15 are monopolies in at least one segment (such as international gateways, fixed retail, and fiber backbone).

Poor governance allows SOEs to continue operating even when they hinder fiscal positions. For example, in Angola, no fully or majority-owned SOEs paid dividends to the treasury, and some SOEs, including Angola Telecom, reported losses of over US$107 million (World Bank 2019b). Further, Comoros Telecom's debt, mainly to the China EXIM Bank, accounts for about 40 percent of the entire national debt of the country. There are issues not only with separation of policy-making and commercial activities but also with limited transparency and accountability: in Africa, only 17 percent of the 135 digital state-owned or state-linked enterprises with websites disclose financial information to the public (World Bank, forthcoming).

Monopolies in key international connectivity segments create bottlenecks between international submarine cable capacity and national broadband infrastructure. International internet capacity has increased significantly, including over 49 submarine cables landing in at least 37 coastal countries, facilitating connection of landlocked countries. It also includes

FIGURE 4.10 **Operators' shares of mobile subscribers and telecommunications fiber networks, by extent of state ownership and subregion, Africa, 2020**

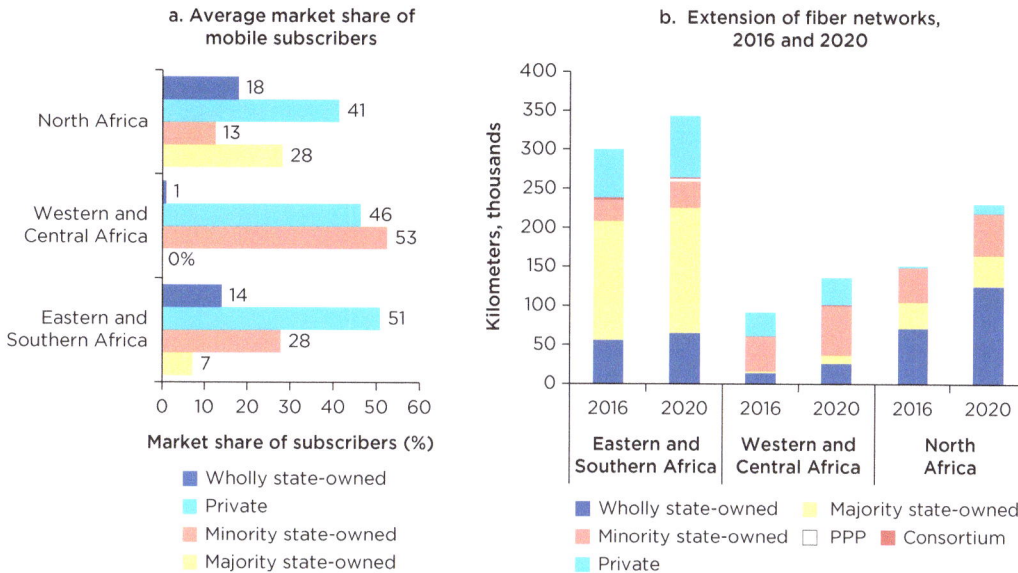

a. Average market share of mobile subscribers

b. Extension of fiber networks, 2016 and 2020

Source: World Bank, forthcoming, based on the World Bank's internal Africa Digital Infrastructure Market Players Database (panel a) and Hamilton Research's Africa Bandwidth Maps as of the fourth quarter of 2020 (panel b).
Note: PPP = public-private partnership; SOE = state-owned enterprise.

planned cables sponsored by content providers, such as 2Africa (Facebook) and Equiano (Google), promising unprecedented capacity in the next few years.[17]

Countries like the Arab Republic of Egypt, Ghana, Morocco, Nigeria, and South Africa have five or more cables, and 57 percent of the other coastal countries with cables have at least two. However, the number of landing stations relative to submarine cables—in several cases, owned and operated by incumbent SOEs—is limiting. Ghana and Nigeria have five and six cables, respectively, but only one landing station (figure 4.11). Furthermore, despite the push to liberalize international gateways, some countries retain a monopoly in access to international capacity in the hands of the incumbent or dominant player. For example, Côte d'Ivoire has four cables but only one landing station operated by Côte d'Ivoire Telecom and a monopoly in the international gateway. Algeria and Angola both have three landing stations with three and four cables, respectively, but also a monopoly in international gateways.

Effective pro-competition sectoral regulation is needed to boost competition and result in better market outcomes. Markets remain concentrated with limited entry (as shown in figure 4.8), mainly because of policies that either restrict entry and reinforce dominance or discourage rivalry based on a level playing field. Licensing, access to infrastructure, control of operators with significant market power, and spectrum management are critical for competition in domestic markets,[18] while rules on exclusivity and open access are vital for competition in international connectivity. General policies to empower consumers and protect them, as well as effective dispute resolution mechanisms for service providers, are essential complements. Tradability of spectrum licenses, mobile number portability, and openness to foreign entry have been found to be associated with lower concentration and reduced prices (Faccio and Zingales 2017). Similarly, lower mobile termination charges and international roaming price caps have

FIGURE 4.11 International internet capacity, proxied by submarine cables and landing stations, Africa, 2021

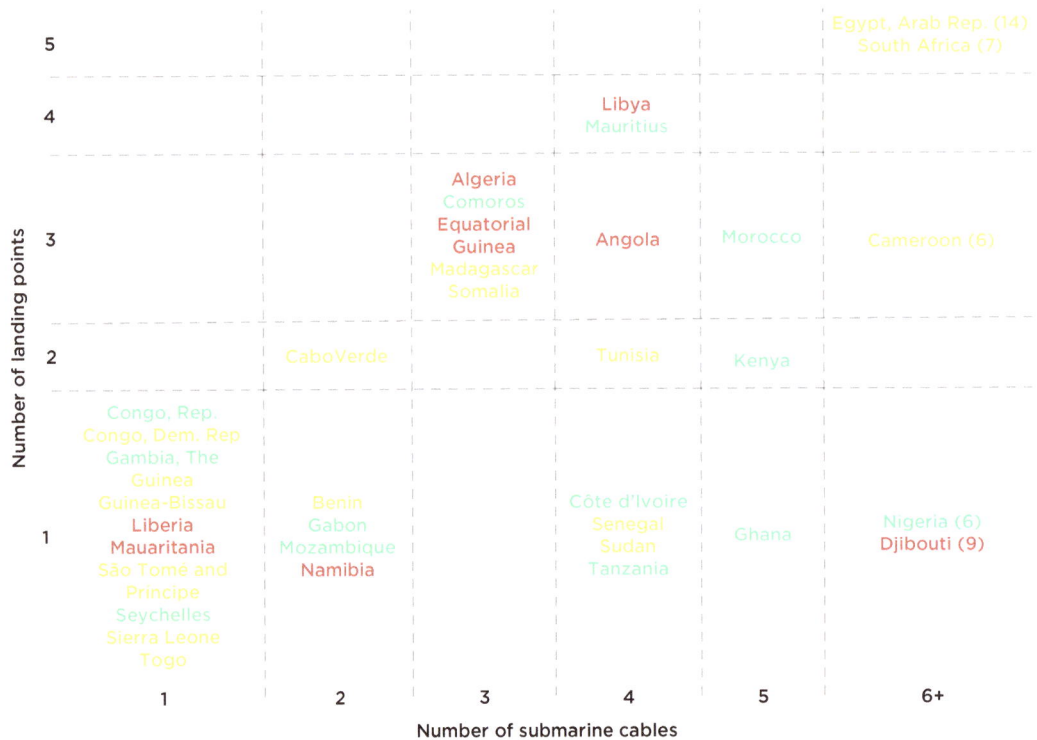

Source: World Bank, forthcoming, based on internal (World Bank Regulatory Watch Initiative, Phase 2), public (International Telecommunication Union's "Level of Competition in International Gateways"), and private proprietary (TeleGeography's Global Internet Geography) databases.
Note: Latest information available as of December 2021. Countries in red indicate monopoly in international gateway; in yellow, some extent of competition; and in green, free competition.

been found to be associated with a significant decline in quality-adjusted retail prices for both low-cost, noncommitment tariffs and classic contract tariffs with commitment (Nicolle, Grzybowski, and Zulehner 2018).

Regulation in Africa is not always well aligned with good international practices. On average, the attainment level of good practices is about 60 percent for five key areas: licensing, interconnection, regulation of operators with significant market power (SMP), spectrum management, and rules on international connectivity (figure 4.12).[19] The lowest attainment is on interconnection (49 percent on average), a key area for countries where voice and short message system (SMS) services are important. The next-lowest attainment is on international connectivity and spectrum management.[20] Regulations and implementation to allow for entry through licensing are the most aligned with good practices (65 percent on average). Inefficient or lacking laws and regulation were also named as key challenges to building a digital economy in 20 African countries and 10 African countries, respectively, as part of the DE4A country assessments, highlighting the need to improve laws and regulations and regulatory practices.

Interconnection services are essential to allow for competition. High mobile termination rates (MTRs) for calls and SMS messages can limit the ability of smaller service providers to cut their off-net rates to compete for subscribers, resulting in the creation of

FIGURE 4.12 **Alignment of digital infrastructure regulation with good international practice, selected African countries, 2020**

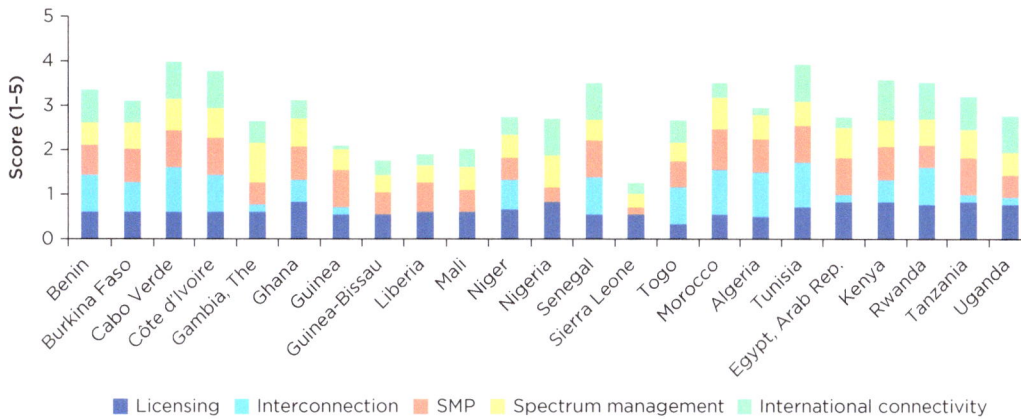

Source: Elaboration from World Bank's Regulatory Watch Initiative (RWI) Phase 2, 2021 (internal database).
Note: Information as of October 2020 covering 23 African countries in North, Western, and Eastern Africa. Full alignment with good practice = 1 for each of the five areas. "SMP" refers to regulation of operators with significant market power.

clubs that reinforce the market power of the largest service providers.[21] Given the importance of voice and SMS communications in Africa (representing more than 60 percent of operators' revenues), competition in these markets can determine consumer choice of MNOs for broadband internet. In South Africa, the reduction of MTRs in 2009–17 triggered a decline in both prepaid and quality-adjusted postpaid prices with on-net and off-net prices convergence (Hawthorne 2018). A first wave of MTR reductions was observed in Africa in 2009–13 followed by key price reductions (for example, in Kenya, Mozambique, South Africa, and Tanzania). Countries have recently launched MTR revisions and reduced MTRs considerably, such as in Kenya (CA 2021).

Implementing pro-competition rules through obligations on dominant operators can eliminate barriers to entry or expansion of service providers, provide cost-oriented access to infrastructure, and reduce consumer switching costs. However, only one out of the eight operators that have more than 65 percent market share (presumed to have SMP under EU standards) in mobile services is subject to obligations, with various challenges that affect implementation. For example, Kenya failed to impose obligations on Safaricom even after conducting a market analysis in 2016 (Piot, Bates, and Edmunson 2018), and South Africa has just issued draft regulations imposing conditions on two operators declared as having SMP (ICASA 2021) although issues were present for many years (Purfield et al. 2016). In Senegal, Sonatel gained SMP across 12 wholesale markets in 2014, yet the telecommunications law was not updated until 2018. Senegal's Telecommunications and Posts Regulatory Authority (ARTP) then imposed obligations to grant fair, transparent, and nondiscriminatory access to essential infrastructure.

Infrastructure sharing can allow smaller operators to expand their coverage and compete. Sharing of infrastructure includes either passive (towers and ducts) or active (fiber cables and radio access network) assets. Infrastructure sharing allows existing operators to give access to assets to smaller operators or new entrants. Roaming agreements are another way of granting access to infrastructure services. Regulation can ensure nondiscrimination, prevent unreasonable refusals to provide access, and facilitate agreements under reasonable cost and service conditions. Dispute resolution mechanisms are also key for agreement implementation.

Access to spectrum is also crucial to enter markets and to improve service offerings and competition. Concentrated spectrum reduces the likelihood of having competitive mobile markets. Pro-competition spectrum policy is, therefore, central to ensure enough spectrum to service providers through a transparent process. Mobile spectrum in African countries, especially in North Africa, is highly concentrated, more than in other regions (figure 4.13). High concentration of spectrum requires competition safeguards to allow for entry of new operators or expansion of smaller ones. However, pro-competition safeguards such as spectrum caps, set-asides, or bidding credits are rarely taken into consideration for spectrum management in Sub-Saharan Africa (Pop and Coelho 2021a).

For international connectivity, liberalization of cable landing stations and international gateways has not been completed, nor is access to monopoly facilities regulated across Africa. Some countries have liberalized cable landing stations and international gateways, at least on paper. However, implementation is lacking, resulting in a de facto monopoly such as in Togo, where Togo Telecom dominates in international capacity (World Bank 2021b). Furthermore, lack of regulation on IP (internet protocol) transit and cross-connect fees charged by dominant operators in international gateways can result in excessive costs for domestic internet service providers (ISPs) to access international submarine cable capacity. In some countries, procedures to grant licenses for cable landing stations and international gateways and permits for subsea infrastructure are unclear and unpredictable, and case-by-case analysis and engagement with various authorities are needed.

There are at least 54 telecom national regulatory authorities in Africa, with an average institutional age of 18 years as of 2020 for a sample of 43 countries, as well as new authorities, such as in Somalia (box 4.3). Their level of independence—measured by how the

FIGURE 4.13 Average spectrum concentration in 700/800 MHz bands, by region and African subregion, 2020

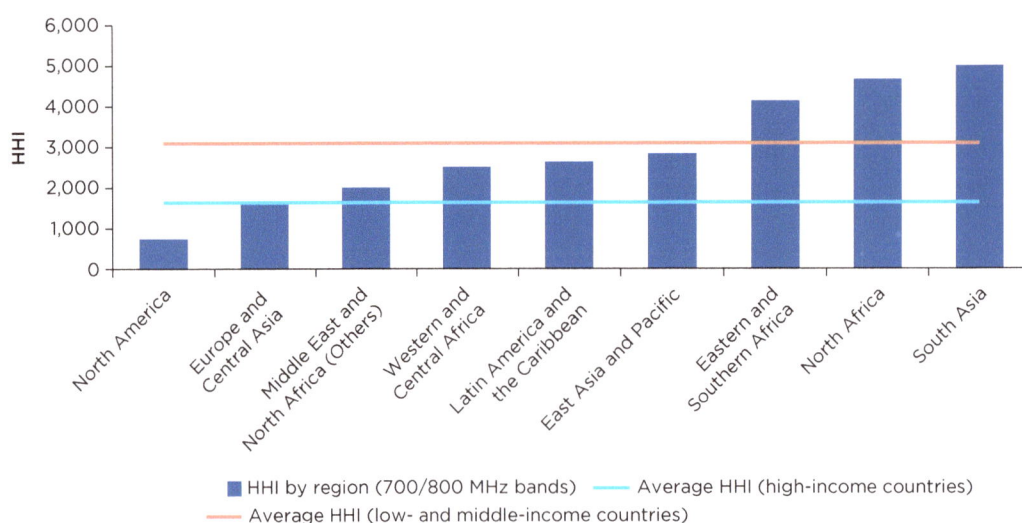

Sources: Elaboration based on Global System for Mobile Communications Association (GSMA), TeleGeography, and PolicyTracker Spectrum databases.
Note: HHI = Hirschman-Herfindahl (HHI) concentration index; MHz = megahertz.

Creating digital institutions in situations of fragility, conflict, and violence: Transforming the sector in Somalia

The digital infrastructure sector in Somalia has begun a transformation with the recent passing of the Communications Law. The functioning National Communications Authority (NCA) has created an increasingly stable environment fostering affordability and availability. International Telecommunication Union (ITU) data indicate that the price of a low-user basket of mobile services in Somalia—70 minutes of calls, 20 short message service (SMS) texts, and 500 megabytes (MB) of data—fell from US$15.40 in 2015 to US$3.70 in 2019, a 76 percent decrease. Although this is an industrywide trend, Somalia now has a more stable and predictable regulatory environment in which operators are more accountable. Somalia has leaped from the absolute bottom of the ITU Regulatory Tracker (with only 16 out of 100 points) to 63 points, which positions Somalia in the vicinity of regional peers with much more mature markets. However, in such a fragile environment, there is a long road ahead before the NCA emerges as a politically and financially independent regulator.

As a result of regulatory capacity building provided to the line ministry and the regulator, an initial set of regulations and guidelines on numbering, spectrum allocation, and interconnection was adopted. The Ministry of Communications and Technology also prepared a five-year information and communication technology policy, which provides a vision and a strategy in Somalia to guide investment in the sector. The repatriation of the country code top-level domain names for Somalia (.so) and the establishment of an internet exchange point (IXP) are also key developments helping to improve sector performance.

An improved institutional framework also increased the telecommunications sector's contribution to the public treasury. Before 2014, the sector was making no financial contribution to the treasury. In 2014, mobile operators began to contribute, albeit based on a negotiated agreement with the leading operators. By the end of 2020, a more transparent system for contributions was implemented, with most revenues collected from license fees. Strengthening the progressive establishment of the NCA as a strong and independent regulator will enable more significant contributions to be made to the national treasury in the future.

Source: World Bank 2021 project completion report, ICT Sector Support in Somalia Phase II (P152358).

president and the members are appointed and dismissed—varies. Some authorities fall under the supervision of the line ministry. Both the level of financing and the source of finance affect the possibility of making independent and solid technical decisions. An analysis of 23 African countries shows that only 9 have revenues coming from the sector, with budgets adopted by the authority (instead of allocated by parliament or the government) and publication of audited accounts. Regulators' ability to attract and retain technical staff is also a challenge given the competition for staff from the private sector. Transparent decision-making to set and enforce regulation is also important to create checks and balances. African countries vary on their alignment with good international practice regarding independence, financing, and transparency (figure 4.14).

Given the rapid pace of technological change, regulators are encouraged to have a more collaborative way of decision-making and analysis involving stakeholders and other regulators (such as competition, financial sector, and data protection authorities); revisit their powers to allow them to intervene when necessary; adjust their organizational structure; apply agile and experimental approaches (such as sandboxes or testbeds); and

FIGURE 4.14 **Alignment of telecommunications regulation with good international practice, selected African countries, 2020**

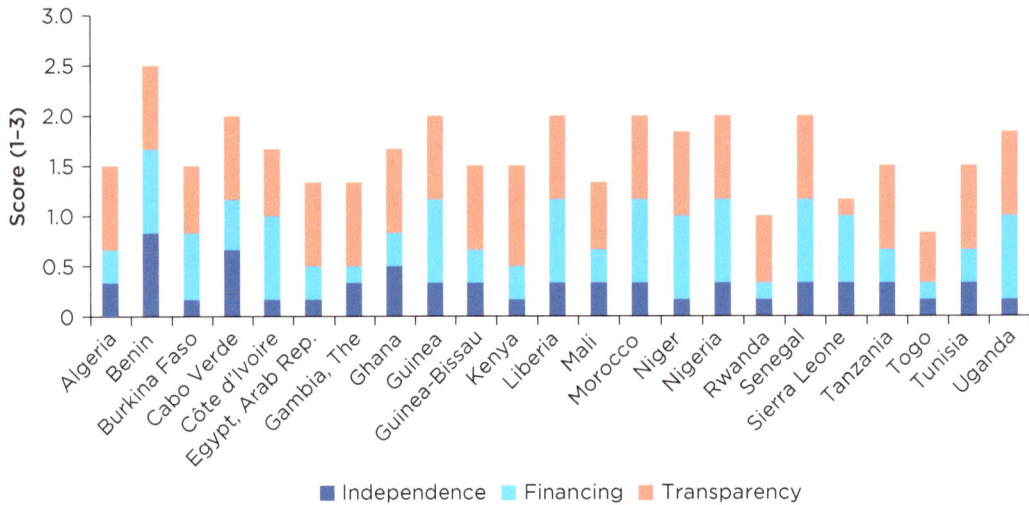

Source: Based on World Bank 2021b.
Note: Information as of October 2020 covering 23 African countries in Eastern, North, and Western Africa.

use digital data for more effective and responsive regulation (for example, to increase transparency on coverage and quality of service).[22]

Competition authorities can help shape the market through advocacy actions (market inquiries and recommendations to adopt pro-competition rules), remedies or settlements resulting from antitrust cases, and merger conditions.[23] In addition, decisions on anticompetitive practices can prevent or stop abuse of dominance or agreements among competitors that prevent entry or allow for exploitation.

When sectoral rules have gaps or implementation is lacking, operators have sometimes resorted to competition authorities. For example, interventions by the Competition Commission South Africa (CCSA) preempted regulatory changes on interconnection (Purfield et al. 2016), pro-competition features in spectrum management, and actions to curtail data prices. In 2017, the CCSA initiated a "Data Services Market Inquiry," studying high data prices and providing recommendations (CCSA 2019). Then, in 2020 the CCSA signed agreements with Vodacom and MTN to reduce data prices by 34 percent and zero-rate the price of data for certain websites (Bonakele 2020). The CCSA also analyzed mergers involving spectrum triggered by delays in clarifying spectrum policy and provided recommendations on the rules to award spectrum. Finally, in 2020, the Independent Communications Authority of South Africa (ICASA) set rules to award spectrum that integrated most of the CCSA's pro-competition recommendations, and it started a data market inquiry to set obligations on operators with SMP. The South Africa example shows the complementarity and mutually enforcing nature of actions by competition authorities and telecommunications regulators and thus the benefits of collaboration.

In another case, the Competition Authority of Kenya (CAK) intervened, settling abuse of dominance cases because of the exclusive contracts of the major MNO and mobile money operator with mobile money agents as well as exploitative and discriminatory practices in providing Unstructured Supplementary Service Data (USSD) services to financial service providers (Nkhonjera 2017; Ochieng 2014). CAK also analyzed mergers in the sector involving the transfer of spectrum and conducted a sector study of digital lending markets in Kenya (Nyawira 2020). In general, competition authorities can be an effective ally for digital infrastructure regulators, but only 36 African countries have adopted competition laws, and 26 have operational authorities (Pop and Coelho 2021b). Furthermore, low budgets[24] and a lack of institutional independence, particularly from the executive branch, limit their effectiveness (Nyman and Falco 2020).

Competition is critical to mobile internet adoption. In Ghana, the gains on mobile and mobile internet adoption from market-driven technological innovations and competition could be comparable to the gains from reducing taxes, together with technological innovations and active infrastructure sharing. Furthermore, increasing competition together with reducing taxes, spurring innovation, and active infrastructure sharing could allow for higher mobile and mobile internet adoption levels than might result from implementing all those policies along with infrastructure subsidies instead of with higher competition levels (figure 4.15, panel a). Similarly, technological innovation plus competition could result in larger gains in mobile internet adoption and 4G coverage than technological innovation plus active infrastructure sharing (figure 4.15, panel b).

Senegal offers a strong example of regulatory reforms that increase competition reinforced with measures to reduce operational costs and interventions to expand uptake. Pro-competition reforms allowed for entry of new operators in data infrastructure and

FIGURE 4.15 Projected mobile phone and internet adoption, by policy scenario, Ghana, 2030

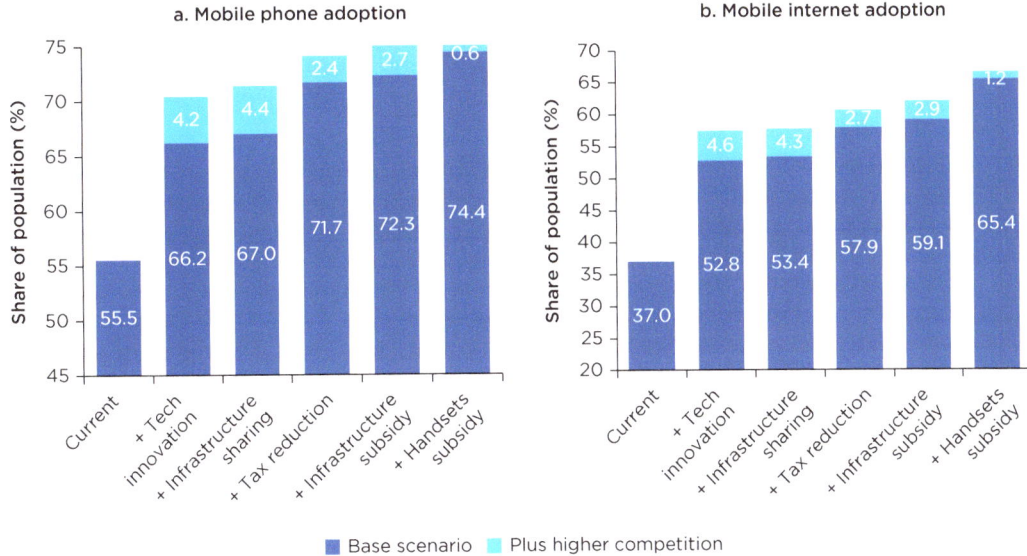

Source: Elaboration based on Global System for Mobile Communications Association (GSMA) model developed for World Bank 2022.
Note: Panel a shows a projection of mobile adoption by 2030 in Ghana, and panel b, a projection of mobile internet adoption. These graphs assume a base scenario (dark blue sections) of the current situation as well as additions of various types of regulatory policy development and implementation that could increase mobile adoption by 2030 in Ghana, such as technological innovation by mobile network operators, active infrastructure sharing, and industry-specific tax reduction. Moreover, it also shows what the extra gains in adoption will be if higher competition is enforced on top of the simulated scenarios (indicated by light blue sections). This "higher competition" scenario assumes a drop in the market share of the leading operator, MTN, from 58.1 percent to 40 percent, and a Herfindahl-Hirschman Index (HHI) price elasticity equal to 2.037 (Genakos, Valletti, and Verboven 2018).

expansion of a relatively smaller operator through access to spectrum (box 4.4). These reforms were complemented by interventions to reduce operational costs through the use of backbone infrastructure deployed by the government and changes in spectrum pricing. Senegal restructured the use of its Universal Service Fund to achieve greater availability. Now the government is deepening regulatory reforms and accompanying them with digitalization of government services and measures to support digital entrepreneurship to enhance the use of DTs.

BOX 4.4

Senegal's digital acceleration journey: The role of infrastructure regulatory reforms

The government of Senegal has implemented a wave of sectoral reforms to support digital infrastructure.[a] These reforms focused on increasing competition by further opening the telecommunications sector, including by facilitating the entry of three new internet service providers and attributing a second fourth-generation (4G) license to the country's second largest mobile network operator: Free Senegal (formerly Tigo). The government also helped to implement a public-private partnership for the management of the 4,050 kilometer public fiber optic network, currently operated by the State IT Agency (ADIE). Other measures included strengthening the sector regulation on dominant players, reducing spectrum fees, and restructuring and accelerating the use of the Universal Service Fund.[b]

As a result of these reforms, some sectoral indicators, such as the quality and price of internet subscriptions, have already improved. The average retail price of a megabit of data decreased by 50 percent since the entry of the three internet service providers, resulting in increased speed of internet offers and reduced installation times (from one month to five days), although the market share of the entrants reportedly remains limited, according to government statistics (less than 1 percent, amounting to only 3,500 subscribers by June 2020).

More recently, building on a range of analytical work and technical assistance engagements, including the Digital Economy for Africa (DE4A) Country Diagnostic of Senegal (World Bank 2019a), the Ministry of Digital Economy and Telecommunications and the Ministry of Finance and Budget are designing a new "Senegal Digital Economy Acceleration" program. The program, aimed at bridging the digital divide, is designed to (a) enhance an enabling legal, regulatory, and institutional environment for the digital economy; (b) drive digital inclusion through expanded digital infrastructure and improved digital skills; and (c) support digital transformation of the public sector by digitalizing selected public platforms and services.

In alignment with the World Bank's Maximizing Finance for Development principles, the program will support the expansion of the national fiber optic backbone network and completion of the last-mile connectivity in lagging areas with high poverty but also high economic potential. The project will support digital transformation of key government systems and services with a focus on taxes and customs as well as on the technical foundations for e-government services.

a. Some of these actions were supported by a series of World Bank Development Policy Financing (DPF) operations: the Senegal First, Second, and Third Multi-Sectoral Structural Reform DPF Projects (P159023, P164525, and P170366, respectively); and the First Equitable and Resilient Recovery in Senegal DPF (P172723).
b. This Fund is a public treasury account financed by a one-time allocation of 5 percent of the financial contribution paid by operators following a license allocation and by an annual contribution from license holders of an amount equivalent to 0.75 percent of their turnover (excluding taxes and net of interconnection costs).

Enabling operational cost reductions through regulation

Given the low ability to pay for internet connectivity and the higher cost of operation relative to other regions, the regulatory environment in African countries must help reduce operational costs. Policies to help achieve this include the following:

- *Spectrum policy:* technology neutrality in spectrum assignments and availability of spectrum at reasonable fees

- *Management of state-owned fiber backbone and passive infrastructure management:* cost-based, nondiscriminatory, timely, and high-quality access

- *Infrastructure sharing:* rules to facilitate commercial agreements for infrastructure sharing with competition safeguards

- *Updated taxation policy:* phasing out undue excise taxes, value added tax overcharges, or excessively high import duties

Spectrum policy. Government can use spectrum policy more effectively to reduce operational costs. The level of assigned spectrum in Africa is relatively low, constraining the deployment of new and more cost-effective technologies (figure 4.16, panel a). Furthermore, so-called digital dividend spectrum, released as part of the transition from analog to digital television, is yet to be assigned and used in some countries (such as Ghana and South Africa).

Median up-front spectrum fees in Africa are four times higher than in high-income countries and twice as high as the global median (Pedros et al. 2020). Simulations of the impact of spectrum fees on 5G network deployment show that high spectrum fees could increase private costs by up to 30 percent in Kenya or Senegal (Oughton et al. 2022).[25] Furthermore,

FIGURE 4.16 **Spectrum holdings and spectrum management quality, Africa, 2020**

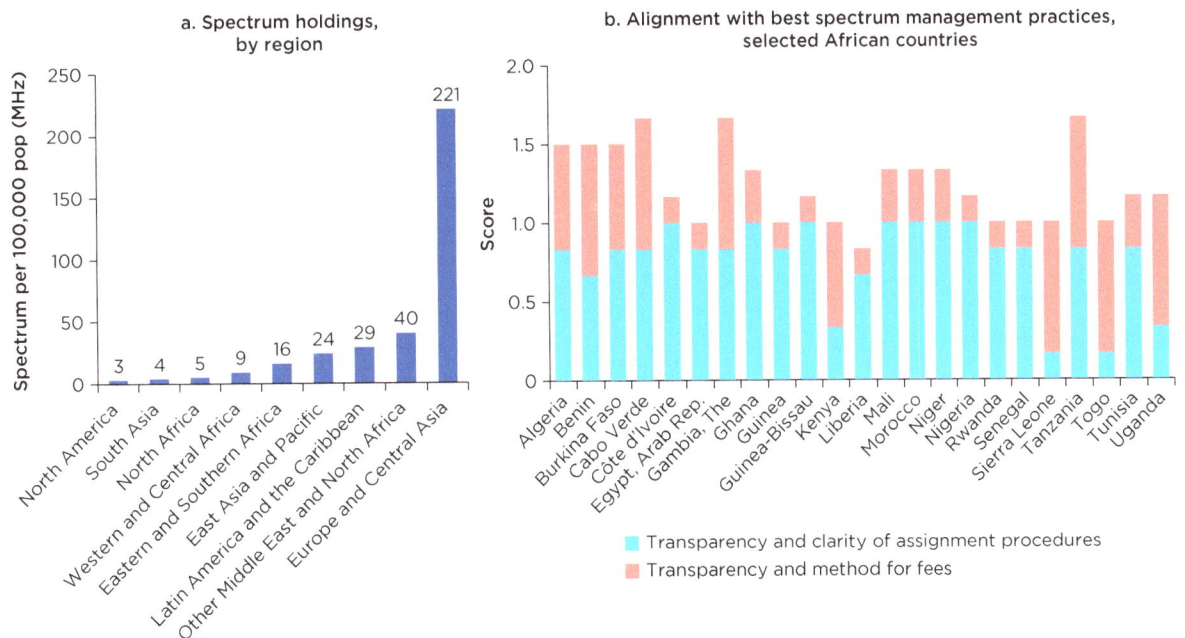

a. Spectrum holdings, by region

b. Alignment with best spectrum management practices, selected African countries

Source: TeleGeography and Spectrum PolicyTracker databases (2020 data); World Bank 2021b, based on internal 2020 Regulatory Watch Initiative (RWI) data.
Note: In panel b, full alignment with best practice gives a score of 1 for each transparency category, for a total possible score of 2. MHz = megahertz.

transparency and clarity in the procedures to assign spectrum are critical, as well as transparency and clear methods for setting fees, to allow for efficient use of spectrum. Attainment of these good practices is low in Africa, except in a few countries (figure 4.16, panel b).

Infrastructure sharing and management. Infrastructure sharing and access to essential infrastructure are key to facilitating downstream competition and reducing deployment costs. Yet, although many countries mandate or encourage infrastructure sharing, some challenges undermine its successful implementation, including lack of regulatory capacity, weak mechanisms for dispute resolution, incentives to keep first-mover advantage in coverage, lack of trust, and technological issues, among others (Arakpogun et al. 2020).

Additionally, lack of regulation concerning access to fiber backbone limits the ability to access this key infrastructure. Some 60 percent of fiber in Africa is controlled by SOEs or operators with state shareholdings. But, in most cases, conditions to access these networks (such as nondiscrimination and reasonable price) are not regulated, and the service standard is not appropriate for other operators to rely on these networks. Countries such as Burkina Faso, Nigeria, and Senegal are exploring initiatives to use SOE backbone infrastructure more effectively. Access to passive infrastructure presents similar challenges. Tower companies play an important role in network deployment and passive infrastructure sharing, particularly to reduce capital and operational costs.

For mobile services, passive sharing strategies (for example, of towers) exhibit substantial savings—of 26–44 percent for 30 GB per month per user of capacity and 18–34 percent for 10 GB per month (Oughton 2022). Yet several implementation challenges exist—including regulatory, trust, or technological issues (Arakpogun et al. 2020).

It is worth highlighting that, in some cases, mandatory infrastructure sharing to reduce infrastructure deployment costs can also impose barriers to expansion. For example, in Benin and Niger, operators must get authorization from regulators to deploy fiber infrastructure, and requests can be denied if they are thought to duplicate or compete with the existing incumbent's infrastructure. Similarly, "dig once" policies can sometimes result in barriers to competition. Therefore, a balanced implementation of infrastructure sharing policies is important to preserve the benefits of infrastructure competition.

Updated taxation policy. Aligning tax policy with good practices can drive gains in both availability and use. African countries apply a wide range of tax surcharges and parafiscal fees on telecommunications services:

- *Excise taxes:* for example, 17 percent percent in Tanzania, 18 percent in Zambia, and others present in nine other countries

- *Registration fees for new phones:* for example, US$7.00 per year for 3G or 4G handsets in the Democratic Republic of Congo

- *Charges on incoming international calls:* for example, US$0.16 per minute in Niger, and others present in at least four other countries

- *Import duties for handsets:* for example, 12 percent in North Africa and 10 percent in Western and Central Africa, compared with approximately 2 percent in Eastern and Southern Africa, on average

Sector-specific taxes and fees can reach up to 31 percent (in Guinea) versus 4 percent in Europe or Latin America (Pedros et al. 2020). The average effective taxation rate for telecom in Africa has been found to be greater than for gold mining (Rota-Graziosi and Sawadogo 2022).[26] About US$1 in additional taxes typically requires a countervailing

US$1 in subsidies to reduce costs again to cover rural areas, without considering government administration cost (Oughton 2022).

In this context, tax reforms to phase out excessive taxes could foster mobile internet adoption, as examples from Benin and the Democratic Republic of Congo show (figure 4.17). Furthermore, shifting government taxes on internet-enabled devices to usage taxes could increase household welfare by at least 26 percent (Björkegren 2020). Such reforms could go in hand with realignment of taxation toward sectors that generate negative externalities, for example considering climate impact, or expanding the tax base for value added tax by taxing goods and services delivered online—instead of penalizing sectors with positive externalities such as digital connectivity—and taking advantage of expanded online transactions to improve tax administration. The good news is that some countries are revisiting sectoral taxation and other have started reducing taxes. In January 2022, for example, Chad eliminated import duties on digital devices. These measures coupled with pro-competition interventions would result in tax reductions passed on to consumers.

Taxes on digital services have been introduced as well, with limited effectiveness in raising tax collections but adversely affecting DT affordability and use. Some countries impose taxes on use of digital platforms (for example, US$0.055 social media tax per day in Uganda) as well as taxes on mobile payments (present, for example, in Cameroon, the Democratic Republic of Congo, Ghana, Kenya, Malawi, Tanzania, and Uganda).

Given the alternatives to digital mobile payments, taxes only discourage financial inclusion, especially for low-income people. For example, when Uganda introduced a social media tax in 2018 to reduce the time citizens spent online and to reduce the spread of false information, it failed to generate significant revenue—reaching less than

FIGURE 4.17 Projected impact of sector-specific tax reductions on mobile and internet adoption, Benin and the Democratic Republic of Congo, 2030

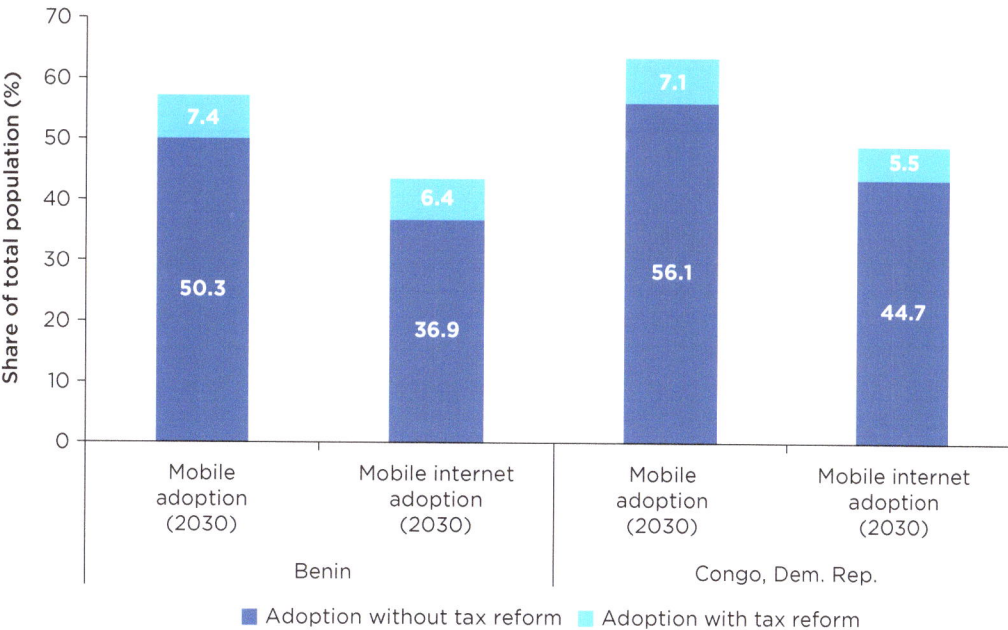

Source: World Bank 2022, based on Global System for Mobile Communications Association (GSMA) analysis of data from mobile operators, GSMA Intelligence platform, Center for International Earth Science Information Network (CIESIN), and Group on Earth Observations.
Note: Existing coverage is calculated based on site data provided between the fourth quarter of 2018 and the first quarter of 2020. Coverage may have increased since the data collection was completed.

Digital and Data Infrastructure

20 percent of the target, mainly because of tax avoidance (for example, through virtual private networks) and administrative difficulties (Kavuma et al. 2020). In the same country, following the 1 percent tax on mobile money transactions in 2018, the average volume of business transactions fell by 24 percent and the value of person-to-person transactions by more than 36 percent as consumers opted for alternatives (AFI 2021).

Taxation of digital services is a hot topic globally, and countries have adopted various approaches as global discussions take place to agree on a system that is more effective and equitable (box 4.5).

BOX 4.5
The evolving taxation of digital services

As the digital economy grows, governments are struggling to fully share its value through tax revenue mobilization and at the same time create an enabling environment for the use and development of digital technologies. Taxation policy must consider (a) how to create a level playing field between digital and analog businesses; (b) how to adapt indirect tax—such as value added tax (VAT) or goods and services tax (GST)—rules and administration to tax goods and services sold online by digital business (especially by digital intermediation platforms without national presence); and (c) how to adapt direct tax (such as corporate income tax) rules to account for intangible value created in countries where digital businesses do not have physical presence (World Bank 2021e).

Expansion of indirect taxation to digital goods and services

There has been progress in adapting indirect taxation rules to create a level playing field between goods and services acquired online and those purchased in a traditional manner. Indeed, indirect taxation of the digital economy is internationally accepted: the Organisation for Economic Co-operation and Development has issued international guidelines and other materials related to the VAT and GST, and countries are increasingly expanding the scope of indirect taxes (VAT or GST) to digital supplies. By 2021, more than 80 countries, 10 in Sub-Saharan Africa, have successfully introduced consumption taxes on digitally provided goods and services.

Additional efforts are also being invested in developing mechanisms for the effective collection of VAT or GST when the supplier is not located in the jurisdiction of taxation (the market jurisdiction) as well as in defining the role of digital platforms in the collection of VAT or GST on online sales. Moreover, business-to-consumer digital transactions involve an additional layer of complexity for tax administration purposes, because nonresident digital suppliers or tax agents (digital platforms) are responsible for collecting the VAT or GST from users and for remitting the taxes collected to the tax administrations of market jurisdictions where those users are located.

When designing indirect taxes (VAT or GST), countries must also avoid unnecessary distortions and double taxation issues that could emerge from the cross-border aspect. Economic analysis and country experiences show that implementing an effective and efficient VAT on the digital economy would have a significant positive impact not only on revenue collection but also on competition (digital versus traditional trade) and equity (given the consumption patterns, the distribution of the tax burden would be progressive).

Challenges in direct taxation of digital businesses

Tax authorities face higher challenges in collecting revenues from profits generated by digital business (such as digital platforms) that offer services without physical presence

(continued)

and can shift tax liabilities across international borders (World Bank 2021e). These challenges have been exacerbated by increasing digitalization because of the COVID-19 pandemic in a context of tight fiscal constraints. The current debate centers on whether the countries where users are located are entitled to tax the value that users contribute to digital businesses that are tax-resident abroad. Such tax claims are intimately linked to both the notion of permanent establishment (taxable presence) and the notion of source taxation (taxable source of income).

A multilateral approach would be useful, but progress has been slow as part of the Group of Twenty and Organisation for Economic Co-operation and Development Inclusive Framework, and some countries have started implementing measures to tax income from digital services. The political agreement reached in October 2021 could accelerate the implementation of a multilateral approach, although the proposal under development is still too complex for low-capacity countries to adopt.

Of the 141 jurisdictions included in the Inclusive Framework, 23 are African, and all except for Kenya and Nigeria approved the statement providing a framework for reforming international tax rules that would apply to the largest and more profitable multinational enterprises (about 100). In Africa, Kenya, Nigeria, Sierra Leone, Tunisia, and Zimbabwe have implemented alternative tax measures aiming at taxing digital companies, whereas others such as South Africa are waiting for a global solution.

Furthermore, the African Tax Administration Forum published a "Suggested Approach to Drafting Digital Services Tax Legislation" in 2020 to provide guidance to members that are considering the implementation of a digital service tax (DST). That forum highlights the importance of avoiding negative effects of DSTs on digital sector growth in African countries, particularly start-ups and small and medium enterprises, and recommends considering a robust de minimis threshold, to ensure the DST targets only established and profitable digital businesses (ATAF 2020). The forum also suggests considering a commitment to repeal DSTs once an international solution is agreed in the Inclusive Framework.

Sources: Cebreiro-Gómez et al. 2021; Lucas-Mas and Junquera-Varela 2021; World Bank 2021e.

In addition to taxes, telecommunications services are subject to other fees and contributions that are not common practice and unduly increase the regulatory burden on the sector. For instance, some countries have platforms in place that monitor international or domestic traffic to check overall revenues and contrast those with operators' declarations. These systems are costly. For example, Ghana's build-operate-transfer (BOT) contract with a revenue assurance company reportedly considers commitments to pay annual fees of US$1.5 million for the management of the system and an investment cost of US$90 million. Nonetheless, technical analysis showing the effectiveness of this kind of system is lacking, such as actual correlation between volumes of tracked traffic and value of additional declared revenues. These platforms are usually financed by introducing additional parafiscal fees (on international or domestic calls), which further distorts the market (especially because the collection of these fees is not always transparent). This kind of system is present in Burundi, the Comoros, and Niger. For example, Burundi introduced this system in 2015, granting an exclusive license to service company ITS to manage international incoming traffic and receive 50 percent of taxes on this traffic (US$0.16 per minute), with a fixed minimum payment. The introduction of the requirement for operators to route international traffic through ITS led to a decline of 60 percent in incoming international traffic in the first 15 months,[27] meaning that, after payment of the agreed minimum to ITS, the license generated negative revenue for the government.

Availability to reduce digital divides

In addition to improving affordability—through competition and cost reductions induced by regulation—for those families and businesses that enjoy mobile internet coverage, countries should seek to increase coverage to bridge the digital divide. Lack of network coverage has been identified as a key issue in 18 of 28 DE4A country assessments,[28] highlighting the relevance of efforts to increase coverage. Although most urban areas have or are expected to have 3G or 4G coverage by 2025, most of the uncovered populations will be in sparsely populated areas with lower levels of socioeconomic development—for example, in the north of Ghana and outside of the western regions of Sierra Leone.

Bridging the geographical divide requires both supply and demand interventions. For commercially unviable areas, a package of regulatory policies is a first step to expand coverage and uptake. A second step is considering the implementation of complementary interventions in a way that minimizes market distortions: more effective supply subsidies or targeted demand subsidies and demand-boosting programs.

Regulatory policies to expand coverage and uptake

Rural coverage regulatory policies can focus on reducing the costs of infrastructure deployment and operation in rural areas and incentivizing network rollout, including through spectrum policies. Given the frequencies used for 4G, coverage by one base station can be greater than for 3G. On average, 4G is 10–57 percent less expensive than 3G when using either a wireless or fiber backhaul to deliver 10 GB of data per month per user, or 20–47 percent less costly for 30 GB per month per user (figure 4.18). This suggests a motive for "leapfrogging" in an environment that is without spectrum constraints and has enough demand uptake. Unfortunately, there are demand barriers that constrain the possibility of leapfrogging, such as the availability of affordable smartphones[29] and awareness of broadband internet's potential uses.[30]

Facilitating deployment of more efficient technologies through technology neutrality, releasing spectrum, and allowing testing of new technologies (granting spectrum for trials) can help facilitate technology upgrading and open the possibility of leapfrogging to increase coverage. Looking toward the future, the adoption of spectrum sharing arrangements for subnational or rural networks could be explored especially for 4G and 5G—for example, following the approach taken in New Zealand (RSM, n.d.), the United Kingdom (Ofcom 2019), or the United States (FCC 2020). Complementarily, pricing and licensing rules for wireless backhaul should be adjusted to facilitate the use of this technology especially for rural areas.

In some countries, mobile broadband coverage can be increased by ensuring availability of sub-1 GHz (less than 1 gigahertz) spectrum. Having sufficient coverage in sub-1 GHz bands is important in rural areas to reduce the number of required sites. Not all operators have access to sub-1 GHz spectrum for 4G—sometimes for commercial reasons but also because governments haven't assigned all available spectrum or

FIGURE 4.18 **Costs of universal mobile broadband and potential rural coverage, Africa and selected countries**

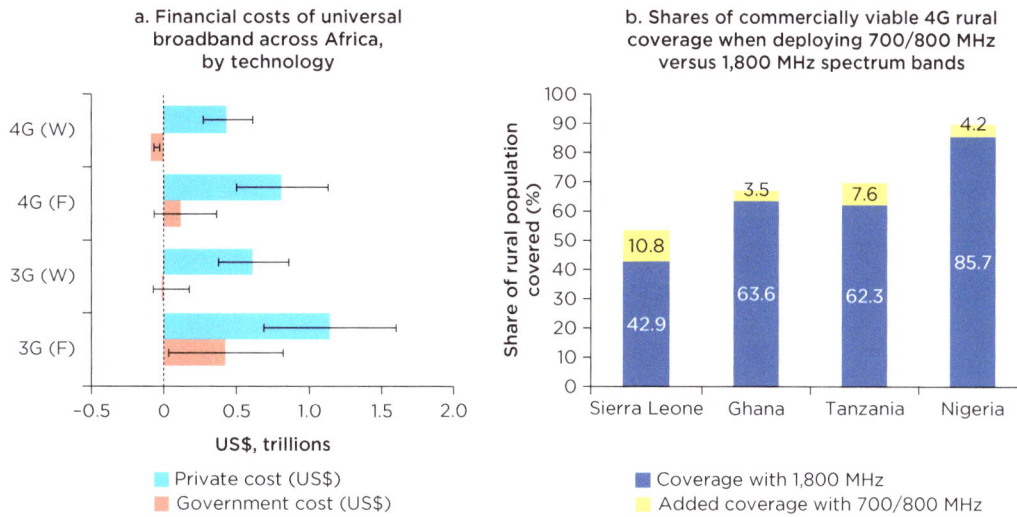

a. Financial costs of universal broadband across Africa, by technology

b. Shares of commercially viable 4G rural coverage when deploying 700/800 MHz versus 1,800 MHz spectrum bands

Private cost (US$)
Government cost (US$)

Coverage with 1,800 MHz
Added coverage with 700/800 MHz

Source: Oughton 2022 (panel a); Global System for Mobile Communications Association (GSMA) based on site data provided between 2018 Q4 and 2020 Q1 (panel b).
Note: Panel a is based on a capacity target of 10 gigabytes (GB) per month per user, with results obtained by calculating the mean financial cost per user by population decile for a sample of countries and then estimating the cost for connecting all users across Africa. Values reported represent the net present value for 2020–30. The estimates are broken down by both the private and government cost composition. "Private cost" refers to private investment, and "Government cost" to government or public investment through supply subsidies. As seen in the graph, the cheapest option is using fourth-generation (4G) technology with a wireless backhaul, at about US$0.4 trillion for the baseline adoption scenario. Interval bars (in red) reflect estimates for low- and high-cost scenarios. Panel b shows estimates of 4G coverage in rural areas that would be viable for an operator by 2025 based on a 3G/4G supply and demand analysis for both brownfield and greenfield sites. Where sub-1 GHz spectrum bands—that is, 700/800 MHz bands—are used, the population covered for each site will be higher than that when higher-frequency bands (1,800 Mhz) are used. The model considers the costs of upgrading to 4G-based coverage and determines whether the site upgrade is financially viable to generate a positive return, given expected demand and average revenue per user. F = fixed network; GHz = gigahertz; MHz = megahertz; W = wireless network.

have charged high fees that discourage the use of certain bands. To give operators the flexibility to introduce new, more efficient technologies, it is important to both (a) complete migration to release digital dividends in sub-1 GHz spectrum, and (b) ensure technology neutrality. Lack of predictability on the release and conditions for the use of sub-1 GHz for 4G deployment limits the possibilities to use this technology to reach rural areas or increase availability of faster internet connectivity in urban areas. This has been the case in South Africa, where the regulator has faced many delays in completing the auction for sub-1 GHz spectrum, and digital migration of broadcasters from the 700 MHz and 800 MHz bands has not been completed.

Promoting infrastructure sharing can also help increase reach in unserved areas.[31] Sharing of passive infrastructure is relatively more common in Africa, with 44 percent of towers owned by tower companies ("towercos"), but active sharing and roaming agreements are used less. Infrastructure sharing can enable increased competition and consumer choice in areas where multiple networks are not commercially sustainable owing to a lack of demand. It can also reduce investment needs, thus freeing capital to roll out infrastructure in less attractive (but still profitable) locations instead of duplicating infrastructure in places where there is already another provider. Nonetheless, infrastructure sharing can soften competition, highlighting the importance of protecting competition.

Geospatial analysis conducted for Benin and Tanzania shows how active infrastructure sharing would allow for broader coverage of rural populations relative to passive infrastructure sharing—by 9 additional percentage points for Benin and by 22 additional percentage points for Tanzania considering 4G and three networks (World Bank 2022). A shared rural network (SRN) that allows for radio access network (RAN) sharing only in rural areas (for example, like the one implemented in the United Kingdom)[32] also provides efficiencies, preserving infrastructure competition in urban and suburban areas, with a saving against the baseline (without infrastructure sharing)[33] of 11–47 percent for 10 GB per month and 18–52 percent for 30 GB per month per user for the six countries included in the analysis (figure 4.19).

FIGURE 4.19 **Cost of universal broadband with infrastructure sharing, selected Sub-Saharan African countries**

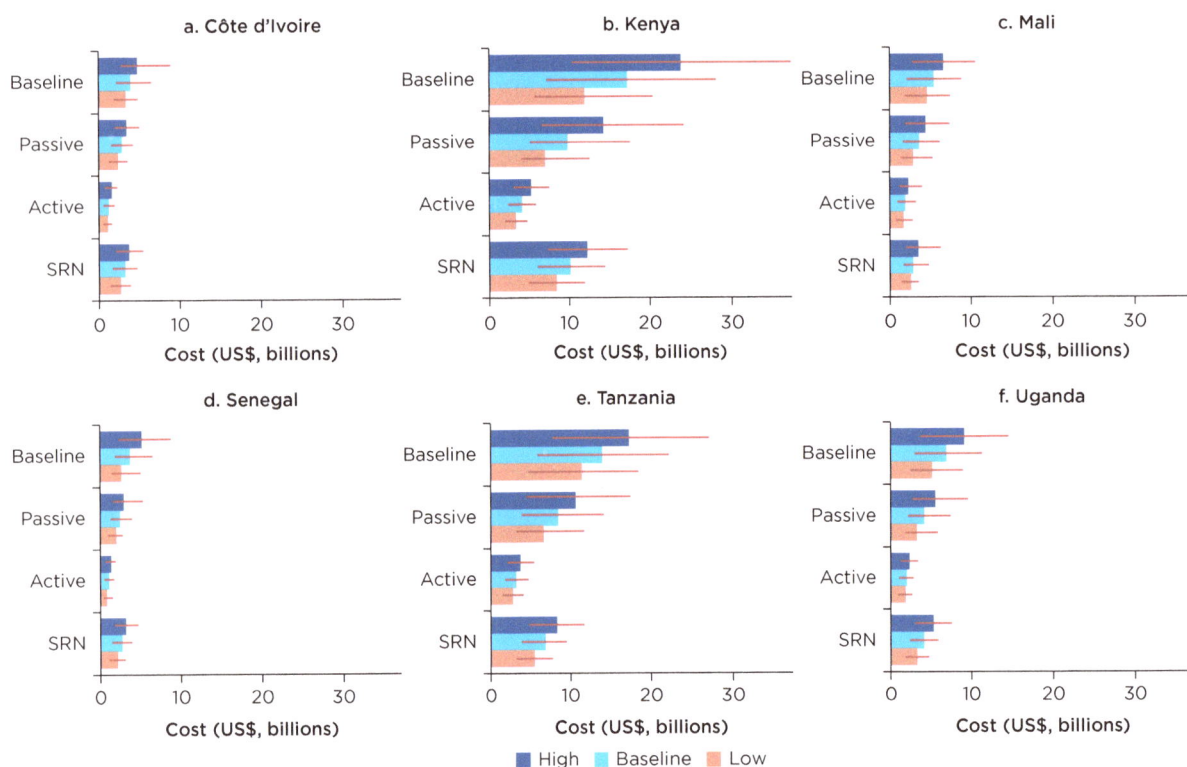

Source: Oughton 2022.

Note: The figure shows the financial cost savings possible from infrastructure sharing strategies under the low, baseline, and high adoption scenarios at 10 Mbps capacity per user target, using 4G and microwave technologies (for 30 GB per month per user). Financial cost is the net present value sum of private cost (investment and operational costs) and public subsidies to reach universal broadband coverage over a 10-year period. The model sets a threshold of 10 percent of profit margin and assumes that the additional profit is reinvested to expand coverage. In the "baseline," each MNO builds its own network to serve its market share with no sharing taking place. Interval bars reflect estimates of "high" and "low" cost scenarios. "Passive sharing" refers to sharing of the physical mast and energy supply; "active sharing" to sharing of the radio access network [RAN] including site, mast, base transceiver station, backhaul, and base station controllers); and "SRN" to a shared rural network. GB = gigabyte; Mbps = megabits per second; MNO = mobile network operator.

Policy intervention is needed to make infrastructure sharing a viable option. An enabling environment for private co-investments and sharing arrangements is needed—including increased transparency on the characteristics of available infrastructure, predictability on permits and evaluation of agreements between partners, and clarity on competition safeguards to preserve rivalry. This environment would enable co-investments for fiber connectivity such as the co-investment by Liquid Telecom and Facebook in the Democratic Republic of Congo (Thomas 2021). Complementary measures—including access to state-owned fiber backbones and passive infrastructure at affordable prices, together with assured quality of service—are key to reducing operational and investment costs. This is particularly important in the 27 countries (22 in Sub-Saharan Africa) where SOEs control more than 40 percent of the fiber network.[34]

Establishing coverage obligations to reach rural areas is another policy alternative. Simulations for six African countries (Côte d'Ivoire, Kenya, Mali, Senegal, Tanzania, and Uganda) show that, if coverage obligations were established that resulted in a maximum profit margin of 10 percent by site, 60–100 percent of the population could be covered by a 4G network, with wireless backhaul delivering 30 GB per month at peak time, without the need for government subsidies (Oughton 2022).

Finally, having licensing and spectrum frameworks that allow for testing and deployment of different technologies for rural areas is important to minimize costs. Wireless technologies are more cost-effective than fixed networks, but wireless infrastructure costs can be prohibitive in rural areas, particularly radio equipment, civil engineering for passive infrastructure (towers), energy supply, and transmission links. The industry has provided innovations in all these areas: alternative radio equipment, lighter towers, optimized transmission and new technologies (including laser), and alternative sources of energy (solar) (box 4.6). Furthermore, new business models that offer rural connectivity as a service have expanded, reducing the costs for operators such as Africa Mobile Networks and iSAT Africa. Availability of unlicensed spectrum (for example, for Wi-Fi 6)[35] and adoption of rules that allow for television "white space" solutions can also allow for a wide array of alternative technologies for last-mile connectivity.

BOX 4.6
Alternative technologies for covering rural and remote areas *(continued)*

Large-area coverage in rural and remote areas could also be achieved with the use of a tethered aerostat carrying payloads. Given its lift powered by a buoyant gas, one of its main advantages is that it can be easily moved between locations. Moreover, depending on the altitude and size of the aerostat, it could replace multiple small or macro sites, needing a single-site backhaul. However, given its nature, it is unreliable in harsh weather conditions such as under high-speed winds. A similar alternative for covering wide areas is stratospheric balloons that can reach high altitudes at relatively low costs. This technology has been tested, but Google stopped the deployment of its Loon project.

Alternative low-cost solutions include modular microwave backhaul solutions; low Earth orbit (LEO, orbiting 500–2,000 kilometers from Earth); and medium Earth orbit (MEO) constellations (altitude of 2,000–36,000 kilometers). Satellite internet constellations constitute artificial satellites capable of providing low-latency and high-bandwidth internet. Their development as networks is still some years ahead but, in the case of LEO, they may become competitive with terrestrial options if the three main LEO constellations remain under specific user densities (Osoro and Oughton 2021). Amazon's Project Kuiper is an example of a long-term LEO constellation initiative that seeks to provide high-speed, low-latency broadband services to underserved areas.

In Africa, a form of wireless optical communications is being tested to connect the remote areas separated by the Congo River (Erkmen 2021). The wireless optical communications links of Project Taara consist of a system that points at and tracks each other, finding optical alignment and creating a high-bandwidth connection. Although the technology has limitations such as reliability under environmental changes, it could be a "close-to" solution for those who are completely unconnected.

Complementary interventions to support demand and supply

Regulatory reforms will significantly increase connectivity, but coverage and uptake gaps will persist unless both supply and demand support programs are implemented. Applying policy reforms to release spectrum, facilitate infrastructure sharing, and reduce tax overcharges, accompanied by strong universal coverage obligations, will drive significant gains in coverage and adoption (figure 4.20). Moreover, these policy reforms can save 10–20 percent of the cost required to achieved near-universal 4G coverage in the analyzed countries, resulting in over US$200 million in savings for governments across the countries included in the analysis (World Bank 2022).[36]

Boosting competition in the sector will expand adoption further, as simulations for Ghana have shown (see figure 4.15). However, in some areas—and especially for low-income households and small, informal firms—uptake will be limited, necessitating complementary policies on both demand (such as digital skills and awareness about the benefits of DTs) and supply (such as competitive prices) as well as broader socioeconomic policies to enhance willingness to use and pay for digital services.

Both private and government costs for universal broadband coverage are high in some areas, making universal targets difficult to achieve (map 4.4). Coverage obligations that allow for MNO cross-subsidies would need to be complemented by government subsidies for universal coverage (for example, backbone, backhaul, sites) to reduce digital divides.

FIGURE 4.20 **Projected broadband internet coverage, coverage gaps, and usage under baseline and policy reform scenarios, selected African countries, by 2030**

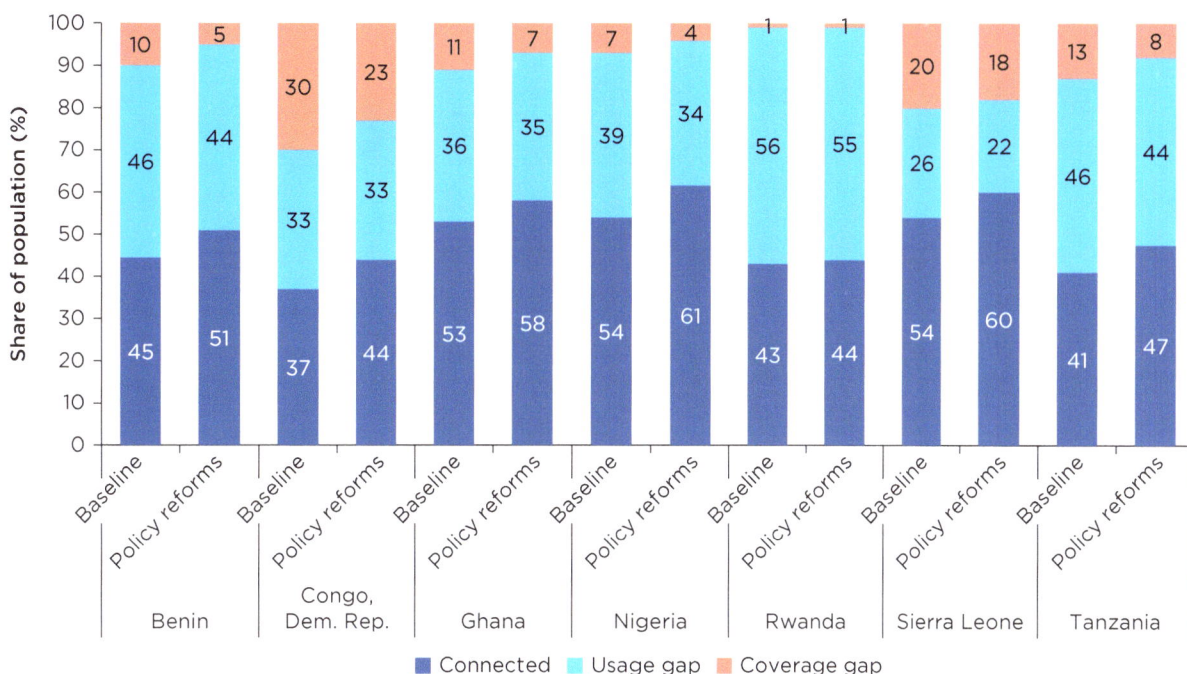

Source: World Bank 2022, based on Global System for Mobile Communications Association (GSMA) estimations.
Note: "Usage gap" refers to the share of the population who have broadband internet coverage but do not use it. "Coverage gap" refers to lack of broadband internet coverage. "Policy reforms" include only sub-1 gigahertz (GHz) spectrum release and reduced tax overcharges. They do not account for policies to promote competition or facilitate infrastructure sharing.

Coverage obligations can be included in competitive spectrum awards; alternatively, the costs of extending infrastructure to uncovered areas can be deducted from spectrum fees resulting from auctions (as in Colombia), or co-investments by operators and the government under infrastructure sharing agreements can take place (as in the SRN in the United Kingdom).

In uncovered areas, supply subsidies could help increase uptake, but they must be complemented by demand-side interventions such as programs that increase digital skills and others that increase the perceived value of using DTs. Based on an analysis of seven Sub-Saharan African countries, even if 4G universal infrastructure were subsidized to expand availability, mobile internet adoption would increase by only 1–3 percentage points because demand would remain limited. If potential 4G uptake increased to 40 percent in uncovered areas owing to demand-side policies, then 4G coverage would reach the same levels that would be achieved with a pure supply subsidy (World Bank 2022).

Common policies that could boost demand include device subsidies and loan guarantees for devices. Experience with device subsidies has been mixed given issues related to targeting, reselling of devices, and willingness to pay for data. An analysis of handset subsidies in 2008 in rural Rwanda shows that benefits accrued mostly to urban users and that vouchers to early adopters in rural areas could have been more effective (Björkegren and Karaca 2022).

MAP 4.4 Estimated government cost per user for 4G (wireless) universal broadband, Africa, net present value for 2020–30

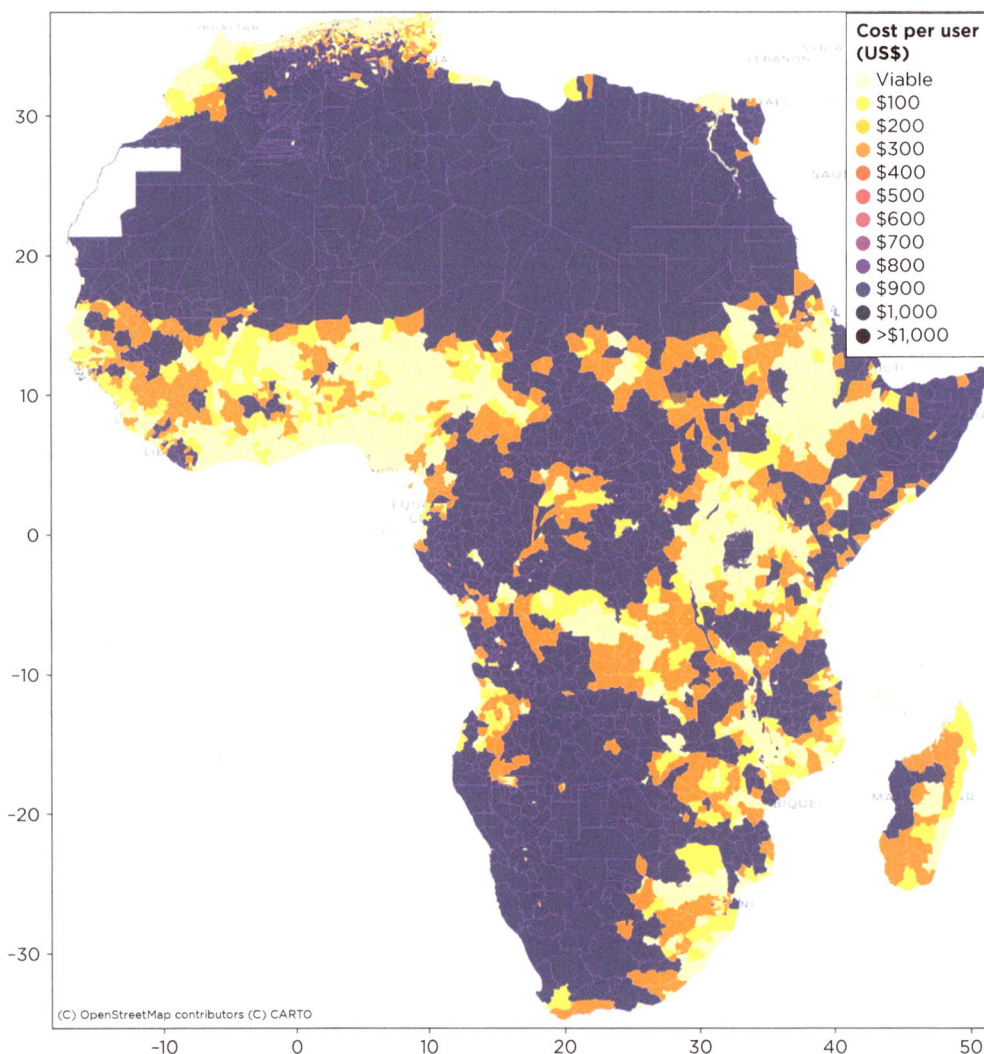

Source: Oughton 2022; used with the permission of OpenStreetMap (CC BY-SA 2.0).
Note: Estimates of government costs (US$ per user) are for fourth-generation (4G) networks with microwave backhaul to provide universal broadband with a 30 gigabyte per month capacity per user at a 10-year net present value. In the legend, "viable" refers to areas that will not require financial contributions by governments.

The magnitudes of the effects of handset interventions vary: in a randomized controlled trial in Tanzania, giving a smartphone had effects on consumption that were three times higher than those from handing people a basic phone and 3.6 times higher than a cash grant (Roessler et al. 2021). However, a high turnover of devices can reduce the sustainability of those effects: in the Tanzanian experiment, only 34 percent of women retained the granted smartphones after 13 months. Other business models are focused on financing devices that could be supported through government guarantees or funds to extend the repayment period.

Targeting of demand support programs and monitoring are important for effectiveness. Big data analytics of geospatial information, consumption, and infrastructure availability, among others, could be useful to target vulnerable households or users with greater potential for spillovers. Furthermore, mobile payments consumption data could be used by operators or other players for credit rating to grant loans for smartphones. Other alternatives to enhance device affordability include eliminating import duties for devices and components, removing the value added tax on lower-cost smartphones (such as in Colombia), and supporting secondhand phone markets.

Interventions to reduce prices for low-income consumers can also boost demand. In South Africa, the agreements reached between the Competition Commission and Vodacome and MTN (as result of the market inquiry that identified high per unit of data prices for low-use consumers) would enable price reductions for low-use internet plans and also grant free access to certain content. Other countries such as Colombia,[37] the United Kingdom,[38] and the United States[39] have targeted price reductions of internet services at low-income or vulnerable consumers. Others have proposed providing free access to data services on 2G to allow users to experiment with using the internet, albeit at lower speed (Song 2016).

Operators have also implemented programs with reduced prices for internet and complements for low-income groups, with varying results. As part of its approval of the Comcast-NBCU merger in 2011, the US Federal Communications Commission (FCC) required Comcast to introduce a low-income broadband program, "Internet Essentials (IE)." As a result, broadband adoption by eligible households—those with school-age children eligible for free or reduced-price school lunches—increased more in areas where Comcast provided broadband internet service (Rosston and Wallsten 2020). Zou (2021) studied the effects of the same low-income broadband program and found that participants exhibited higher employment rates, earnings, and increased internet adoption while participating in the IE program.

Another initiative that subsidized internet access in rural and remote areas of Peru was found to increase internet usage and ownership of cell phones, with stronger and more widespread effects on cell phone ownership (Guerrero Barreto and Ritter Burga 2014). The study also shows results in terms of increased employment of educated, single, and young individuals as well as higher prices for farmers' produce.

Governments have funded programs to connect schools and public internet kiosks to boost internet uptake, and there is evidence supporting spillover effects from access to the internet at school. Goolsbee and Guryan (2006) studied a California program to subsidize internet access in schools and found no significant effects on student performance. However, Belo, Ferreira, and Telang (2016) studied the effect of internet use by children at school on internet adoption at home and spillover effects from neighboring households equipped with a broadband connection in Portugal. They found positive causal effects, especially when children use the internet intensively at school.

Demand-side intervention discussion for ultrafast broadband adoption underscores the importance of access at the office, school, or public libraries (Bourreau, Feasey, and Hoernig 2017). A positive correlation between the number of libraries with broadband access and broadband adoption by households was found only for rural counties in the United States, but no causal link was found (Whitacre and Rhinesmith 2015). Finally, using survey data on 134,000 individuals between 2009 and 2014 in South Africa, Hawthorne and Grzybowski (2019) found that having a computer and access to an internet connection at work or school are more important than reducing mobile data prices by 10 percent in driving broadband penetration.

Interventions to increase willingness to use (for example, digital literacy and greater awareness of benefits brought by DTs) have been piloted as well. In Rwanda, the government launched the Digital Ambassadors program, which trained and deployed 50 young Rwandans in five districts to train about 17,000 people in the use of digital services and the potential of digital tools from late 2017 to mid 2018. An initial evaluation showed the program's effectiveness in enhancing digital skills and confidence to use DTs, increasing awareness and uptake of e-services, and boosting daily use of DTs (DOT 2019). Lessons learned in the pilot phase include increasing community outreach, supporting local content, strengthening links with other programs, and using alternative instruction approaches, among others (World Bank 2021c). In Nigeria, the Kaduna state government supported digital skills and entrepreneurship through training on the use of digital services, such as online work platforms and job matching. The program has reported success in generating increased earnings for participants (World Bank 2019c).

Interventions to increase internet use can be funded by a universal service fund (USF), cross-subsidies by operators responding to regulation or agreements, or budgets from other sectors or general budget. USFs are legally mandated contributions from operators (industry levies) to fund projects directed to increase access to telecommunication services and, ultimately, close the digital divide (Bleeker 2019). Some countries also have universal service obligations (USOs) together with—or instead of—USFs, and in these cases, operators are mandated to offer special service packages for low-income consumers (as in France, the United Kingdom, and the United States) or expand connectivity in certain areas (Ajibulu and Nyman 2019).

In Africa, most governments have established USFs. However, various studies indicate that, with a few exceptions, USFs have not been successful. For example, GSMA (2014) and A4AI (2018) report that most of these funds have not even been used. This failure has been due to poor policy formulation, inadequate stakeholder engagement, lack of accountability, low fund disbursement rates, inaccurate data, ineffective plans to deploy broadband in rural areas, and political influence (Arakpogun, Wanjiru, and Whalley 2017; Bleeker 2019). However Ghana, Lesotho, Nigeria, Rwanda, Tanzania, and Uganda have successfully implemented USFs (Arakpogun, Wanjiru, and Whalley 2017).

Although both supply and demand subsidies could be funded by USFs, many challenges must be addressed for them to be effective. USFs can limit efficient use of resources: if based on revenues, USFs leave capital unemployed that could otherwise be productively invested, which can distort pricing decisions and lower economic efficiency. As of 2020, Benin's USF had not disbursed any funding, disbursements were up to only 5 percent in Tunisia in 2020, and 2.5 percent of the funds collected in Senegal are allocated to telecommunications and 97.5 percent to the Energy Support Fund (Niesten and Begazo 2021). An estimated US$408 million was not disbursed across all 37 African countries with USFs (A4AI 2018).

Other governance issues that affect the functioning of USFs include the absence of reporting. As of 2020, only 13 out of 23 African countries have USFs that disburse and publish data on collection and use (World Bank 2021b). Furthermore, in many countries, only current operators can access funds, which reduces the possibility of entry into rural markets including support to community-based networks.

USFs and related policies should be reoriented to address use issues through robust policies. First, it is critical to improve the operation of USFs, including transparency and accountability. Alternative options, such as a "play or pay" scheme whereby operators take coverage obligations or reduce prices (social tariffs) instead of USF contributions, could be considered (ITU and World Bank 2020). Demand-side interventions should consider the specific objective for a given population, depending on that population's ability and willingness to use (figure 4.21). The introduction of regulations and programs to create subsidized social or low-cost data plans—with low "friends and family" tariffs to boost network effects and targeted vouchers for data services—can be complemented by using the USF to facilitate device financing or access to devices. For those with low willingness to use given limited awareness and exposure, the USF could fund programs to pull demand, such as schools' connectivity and public access hot spots. The cost of connecting research and education institutions in Africa is estimated at US$52 billion in 2021–25 (Melhem et al. 2021). Capacity building and programs to allow for productive use of internet are other options to boost uptake and use.

In summary, policy reforms to enhance digital connectivity depend on promoting competition, enabling operational cost reductions for service provision, and reforming universal service with more effective institutions (figure 4.22). Regulatory reforms should be considered first and complemented when needed with targeted supply and demand support programs. Government support programs, including subsidies in some cases, are generally justified because of the positive spillover effects of DT use on jobs and productivity (see chapter 1) and for social objectives of equity and inclusion (Clarke and Wallsten 2002). The private sector also has an important role to play

FIGURE 4.21 Polices to increase internet usage, by extent of user groups' ability to pay and willingness to use

	Effective pro-competition rules and cost-reducing rules to boost affordability	
(high)+	Targeted demand-side subsidies such as • Social tariffs or lifeline plan, vouchers for data discounts; and • Subsidies or financing for smartphones or other devices	• Regulations to facilitate availability (coverage) in users' locations • No need for public funds (supply or demand subsidies)
Willingness to use internet		
(low)–	• Exposure to internet services and digital services (in schools, public institutions, and public hot spots and through generation of "killer apps" catering to low-income groups) to increase willingness to use (capabilities and attractiveness) • Social plans with reduced tariffs for friends and family to increase affordability	• Exposure to internet services and digital services (in schools and public institutions and through generation of "killer apps" catering to digital-illiterate and vulnerable groups) to increase willingness to use (capabilities and attractiveness) • Programs with financial incentives to upgrade and improve user experience (financing for smartphones, laptops) • Limited justification for supply-side subsidies
	(low)– Ability to pay for internet **(high)+**	

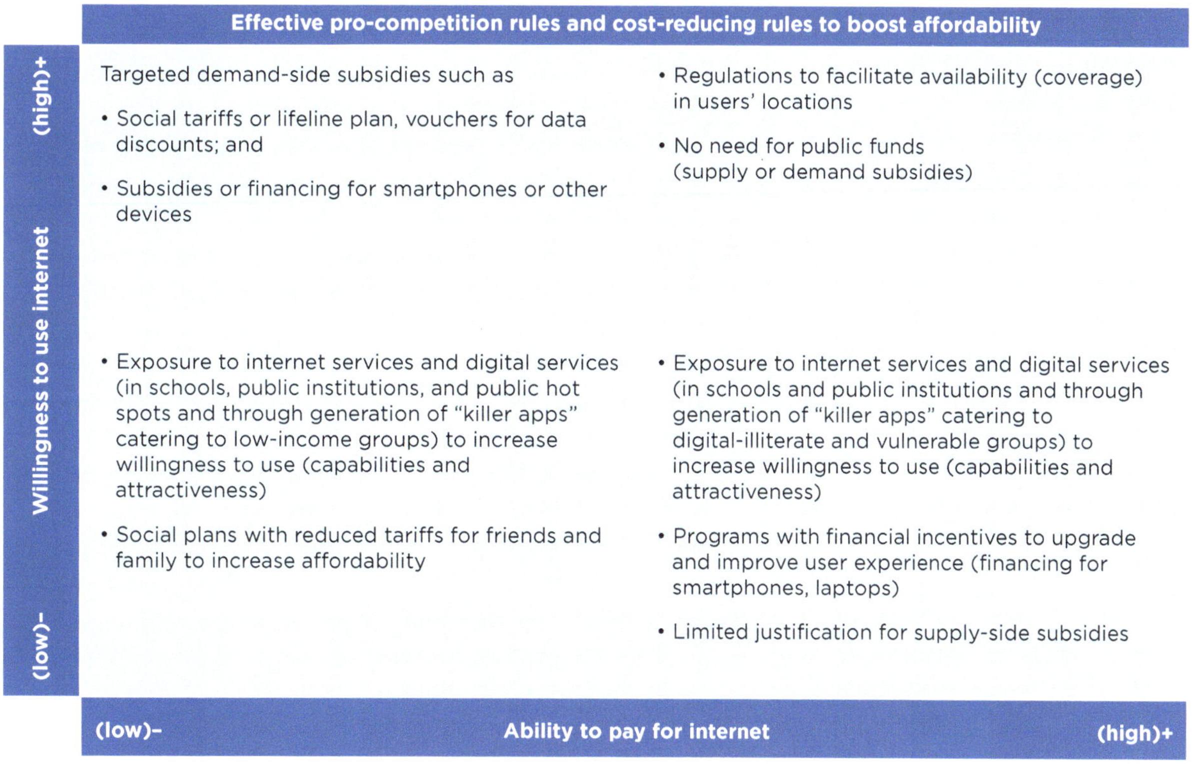

Source: Elaboration adapted from Bourreau, Feasey, and Hoernig 2017.

FIGURE 4.22 Summary of proposed policy reforms for affordable internet availability

Goal	Policy area	Topic	Emerging sector ———————————————→ Transitioning sector		
Affordability	Market entry and effective competition	Licensing and ex ante regulation of dominance	Entry liberalization (unified license); elimination of monopolies (for example, international gateway)	Rule to allow ISPs to deploy infrastructure, elimination of VoIP restrictions	SMP rules, SMP designation and remedies; control of license transfers and mergers
		Access and infrastructure sharing	Interconnection rules (cost-based, nondiscrimination, effective dispute resolution)	Infrastructure sharing (cost-based, nondiscrimination, transparent, dispute resolution) Intersector infrastructure sharing, rights of way, licensing for passive infrastructure operations	Rules for co-investment and wholesale-only networks to deploy high-capacity networks; database of available public and private infrastructure
	Cost reductions	Spectrum management	Spectrum policy; published national spectrum frequency register	Spectrum rules: allocation, methods for assignment, pricing, sharing/transfer/lease, license conditions	5G spectrum allocation and assignment; unlicensed spectrum or dynamic spectrum access
		SOE, state assets, and PPP	SOE open to private shareholding; SOE restructuring	Open access to state fiber networks (energy); SOE transparency and accountability	PPP for open access fiber network, government connectivity projects (such as high education networks)
Availability	Subsidiary government interventions to complement markets	Sectoral taxes and contributions	Elimination of sector-specific (excise) taxes on telecom services	Revision of taxes on digital services; rules to set cost-oriented regulatory fees	National framework to harmonize subnational fees for infrastructure deployment
		Universal access or service	USF creation; transparent and more effective USFs focusing on availability of demand-responsive services and use	Redefinition of USF scope (digital services in sectors to pull demand) and payment modality (CAPEX versus contribution)	Focus on use and upgrading: new, targeted demand-side support; pricing rules for vulnerable groups
		Climate mitigation and adaptation	Mandatory emergency preparedness plans	Policy for resilient and green design, construction and operation of ICT infrastructure	E-waste management; incentives for energy efficiency and green ICT (standards, targets)
	Institutions and regulatory governance	Effective and transparent regulation	Overarching ICT law; independent and accountable regulator	Transparency of telecom regulator financials and decisions; collaborative policy making	Digital Economy strategy; interinstitutional collaboration; use of digital data for better regulation

Source: Adapted from Aviomoh, Begazo, and Golla, forthcoming.
Note: The figure presents a nonexhaustive list of policies. An "emerging sector" refers to a digital sector where the digital economy is still emerging and internet use is low. A "transitioning sector" refers to a digital sector transitioning toward universal internet use. 5G = fifth-generation mobile communications technology; CAPEX = capital expediture; ICT = information and communication technology; ISP = internet service provider; PPP = public-private partnership; SOE = state-owned enterprise; SMP = [operator with] significant market power; USF = universal service fund; VoIP = voice over internet protocol.

to co-finance and innovate on mechanisms to expand availability and uptake, as highlighted by the Broadband Commission (Gallegos et al. 2019). A shift from a top-down investment-driven policy to a user-centered demand-driven policy to address the digital divide is necessary. However, further research and experimentation are needed to identify the most effective policy mix to boost internet uptake for DT use in the context of each country in Africa.

Data infrastructure and regulation for affordability and willingness to use

Availability of attractive DTs is affected by the operation of data infrastructure and the characteristics of data regulation. Data infrastructure allows digital entrepreneurs to develop and launch DTs through the use of cloud computing and storage services. At the same time, greater availability of data infrastructure improves the consumer experience of DT users, facilitating uptake. Similarly, data regulation can enable the use and reuse of data to produce and operate more attractive DTs while also establishing safeguards for greater trust and willingness to use DTs.

Data infrastructure is critical to improve the affordability and quality of service, and it can allow for local exchange of internet traffic and more direct access to global content—through mirror servers, faster web performance through content delivery networks, cloud on-ramps from data centers to access global cloud computing, and edge servers that bring computation and data storage closer to the sources and users. Availability of this infrastructure can reduce latency and international bandwidth consumption, resulting in better service quality and lower data transmission costs.[40] Furthermore, edge computing and easy access to cloud computing can help develop and access digital solutions that respond to Africa's needs—solutions such as the Internet of Things for precision agriculture, smart logistics and manufacturing, or more reliable e-government services. Africa has a vibrant data center sector aiming at offering more capacity and better services to support the use of DTs, but an enabling and predictable environment is still needed to speed up expansion, upgrading, and innovation.

Data infrastructure in Africa has expanded considerably, and some countries have moved from supporting basic internet traffic exchange to data centers with direct access to cloud computing services. There are about 64 internet exchange points (IXPs) in Africa[41]—only 8.5 percent of all IXPs globally—although Africa accounts for 27.7 percent of countries[42] and 17.5 percent of the global population. Sub-Saharan Africa has only 0.1 data center per 1 million people, compared with 0.5 per million in the world and 3.1 per million in North America (figure 4.23, panel a). The low concentration of data centers (figure 4.22, panel a) and IXPs (figure 4.23, panel b) is associated with low download speeds and high latency, as well as higher costs and usage of international data (Aviomoh et al. 2021).

Srinivasan, Comini, and Minges (2021) characterize the level of data infrastructure development across four stages based on information about existence of IXPs, diversity of participants in IXPs, presence of large content providers, existence of colocation data centers, and cloud providers. They find that higher numbers of data centers are associated with lower latency and data prices. Only Ghana, Kenya, Morocco, Nigeria, and South Africa have reached the highest stage; and only Kenya, Nigeria, and South Africa have direct access to cloud computing through national data centers (map 4.5).

There are significant economies of scale in the provision of data storage and processing; therefore, the aggregation and operation of data centers that serve the region, combined with domestic and international infrastructure, are vital. For data traffic to flow, operators need greater clarity on licensing to bring foreign traffic, exchange it, and deliver it to other countries, as well as access to reliable regional and international connectivity.

As noted earlier, various restrictions of international connectivity still exist. Data policies on cross-border data flows also affect the possibility of aggregating regional demand, and the existence of different rules and different legal concepts across countries increases

FIGURE 4.23 **Characteristics of data infrastructure, 2020**

a. Density of data centers, by download speed

b. Density of IXPs, by latency

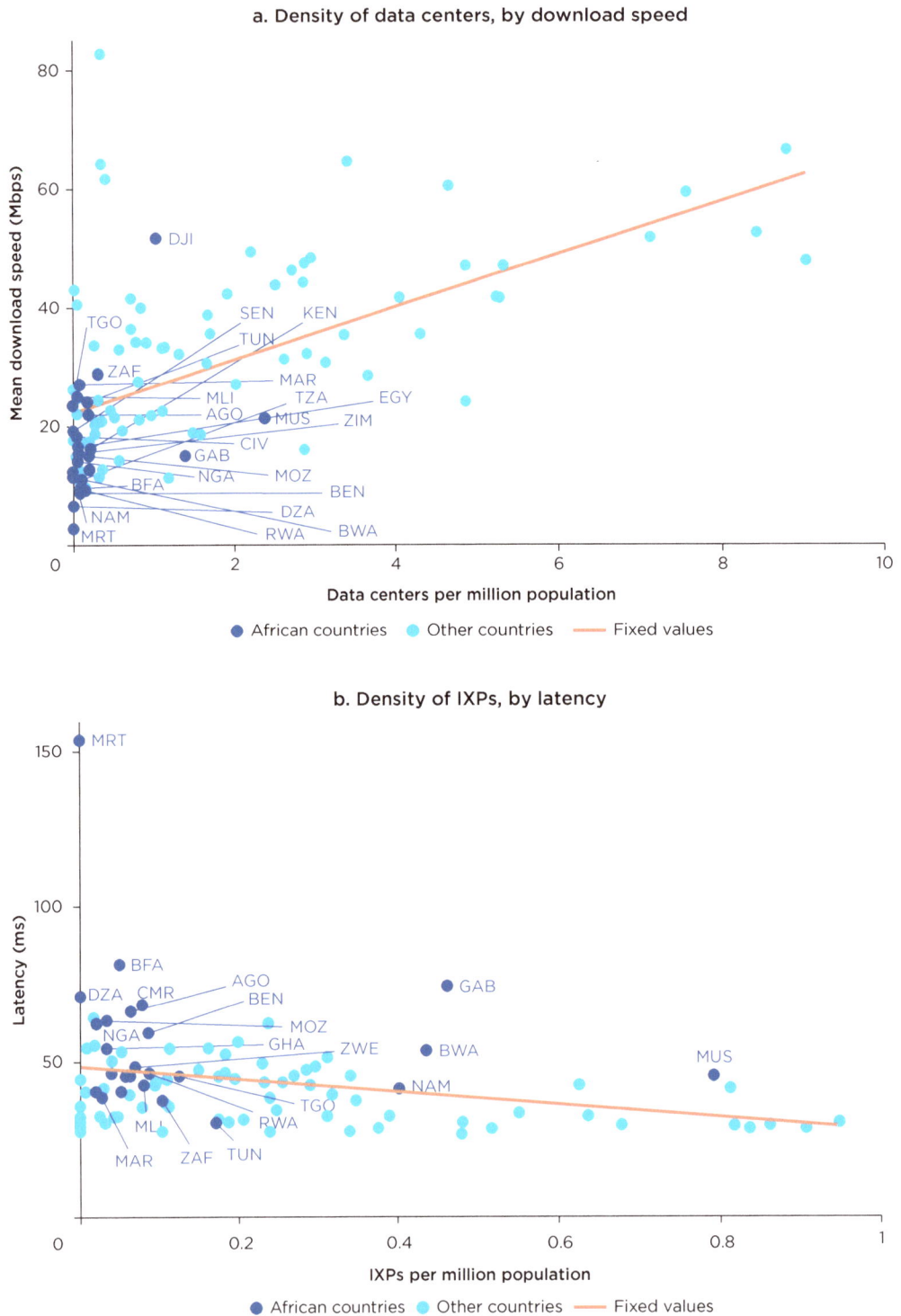

Source: Elaboration of Aviomoh et al. 2021, based on data from World Development Indicators database; Ookla Speedtest Intelligence (panel a); and the World Development Indicators database and Data Center Map (https:// www.datacentermap.com) (panel b).
Note: African countries (dark blue dots) are designated by ISO alpha-3 code. "Latency" (panel b) refers to the transmission delay of a message, in milliseconds (ms). IXP = internet exchange point; Mbps = megabits per second.

MAP 4.5 **Stage on Africa's data infrastructure ladder, by country, 2020**

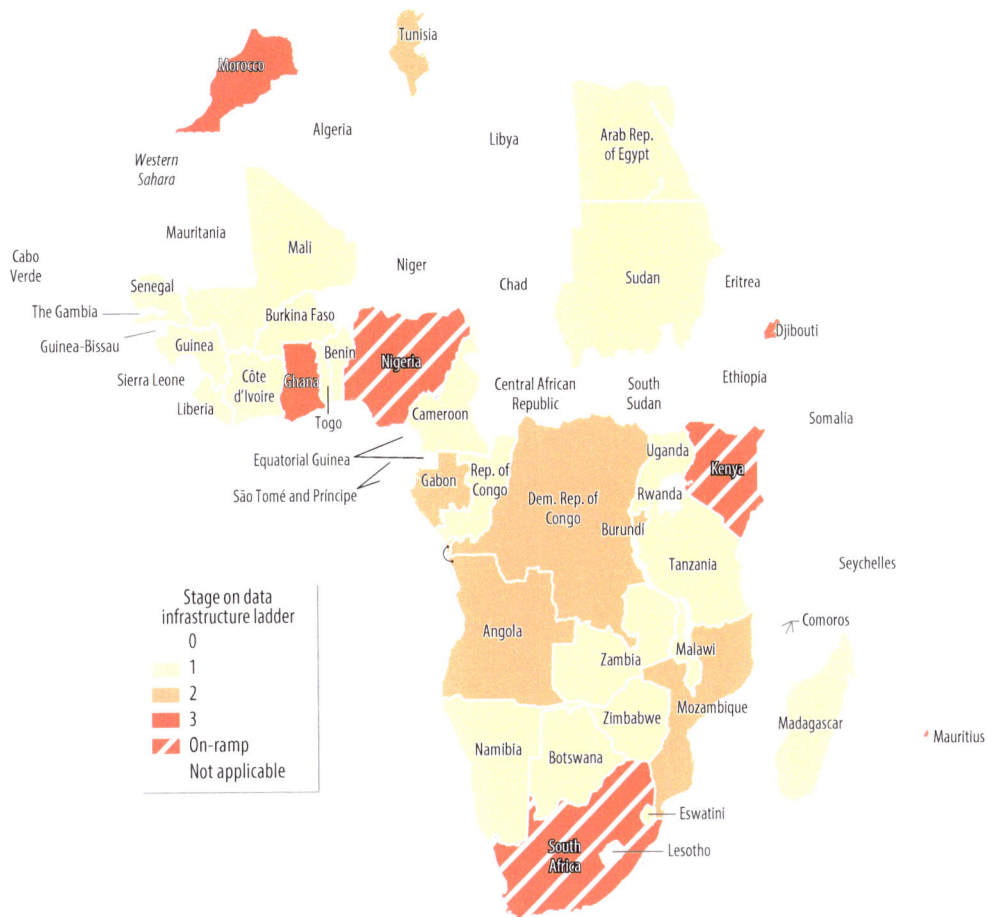

Source: World Bank, based on data from World Bank 2021e, Packet Clearing House (PCH), and PeeringDB (https://www.peeringdb.com/).
Note: Stage 0 = no internet exchange point (IXP); 1 = IXP for domestic internet service providers; 2 = IXP with major content providers; 3 = IXP + colocation data centers; on-ramp = direct connection to cloud provider.

regulatory burdens. Of the African countries surveyed for the *World Development Report 2021* (World Bank 2021e), half (13 countries) have adopted an "adequacy approach" (preauthorized safeguards) that allows data transfers to countries that guarantee an equivalent level of data protection. The remainder adopt either an "accountability approach" (holding the controller responsible for ensuring that the recipient complies with the relevant personal data protection laws) or an "authorization approach" whereby the authorities can allow transfers if the controller ensures the data are protected through contractual clauses or internal rules (Chen, Daza, and Begazo Gomez 2021).

In some countries, certain data must be stored in the country (for example, telecommunications subscriber and consumer data in Nigeria), whereas others allow for data transfer with a copy stored in the country (as in South Africa's draft National Data and Cloud Policy). The need for coordination and interoperability within Africa is glaring, and some initiatives such as the African Union (AU) Data Policy Framework, the African Network of Data Protection Authorities, and the Smart Africa Data Protection Program have started working on this.

Furthermore, issues with the operation and upgrading of data facilities must be further tackled and safeguards put in place to prevent market distortions. Governments have been proactive in facilitating the creation of IXPs,[43] but updated interventions are necessary to facilitate IXP growth and upgrading into more advanced data facilities. These updates include reassessing the governance of IXPs and enhancing technical and financial capacity as well as allowing non-ISPs (such as government institutions, financial service providers, foreign content providers, and others) to exchange traffic (Aviomoh et al. 2021).

The optimal functioning of data infrastructure depends on energy reliability and availability, especially for air conditioning—a challenge in many African countries where power outages, uneven power flow, and high energy prices are still constraints. Finally, policies to ensure neutral colocation data centers to favor a level playing field and reduce the switching costs for users are also important to preserve competitive dynamics. Such policies would help allay concerns about vertically integrated firms leveraging their market power in digital (telecom) infrastructure or global digital services into data storage and computing services and preventing users from switching between alternative data centers and computing providers. To this end, strong antitrust frameworks are important as well as competition safeguards in the design of public investment initiatives in data infrastructure and minimum standards on data protection and security for data centers to facilitate switching.

Appropriate data regulation and institutions are essential to create a trusted environment that incentivizes willingness to use DTs (through safeguards) and a business environment in which data are used to offer fit-for-purpose digital solutions (through enablers). "Safeguards" are regulations oriented toward promoting a safe online environment, minimizing risks, and limiting potential harms. They come in the form of cybersecurity, personal data protection, online consumer protection, regulation of unfair trade practices, and ways of ensuring appropriate use of artificial intelligence (AI). "Enablers," by contrast, are regulatory initiatives that facilitate the use and reuse of data, promoting interaction between different actors and lowering the cost of processing and sharing data. They include policies related to data as well as to antitrust and intellectual property.

As of April 2021, 25 African countries had introduced general data protection legislation, whereas cybersecurity or cybercrime frameworks are still in the early stages of development. These two areas are key to ensure trust in digital transactions. Most African countries have implemented regulatory strategies to prevent cybercrime, by criminalizing the unauthorized damage, deletion, deterioration, alteration, or suppression of personal data. Nonetheless, African countries have fallen behind regarding cybersecurity regulation. Increasing cybersecurity requirements for data processors or controllers and for automated processing of personal data, together with a national cybersecurity strategy, will allow for a more cohesive and strengthened online realm.

Data protection regulation is more advanced than cybersecurity in African countries, although more innovative solutions are yet to be implemented. According to the Global Data Regulation Diagnostic (GDRD),[44] only 15 out of 27 African countries are still not quite halfway toward good data regulation frameworks for safeguards (figure 4.24)—including limitations on storage, use of algorithmic decision-making, privacy by design,[45] and cybersecurity for data processing.

Enablers for data can play a prominent role in helping develop more attractive and skill-appropriate digital solutions and allow for DT use across various industries, but African countries are even farther from good practice in this area. Regarding enabling rules related to reuse of public and private data such as open data, access to information, data portability, e-commerce, digital signature, and digital identification (ID), only 8 of the 27 countries achieved at least 40 percent of good practice (figure 4.24). This highlights the need to create a better environment for the use and reuse of data to generate more economic value for African citizens. For instance, digital ID systems can facilitate electronic Know Your Customer (eKYC) requirements bolstering the financial technology industry; e-commerce laws can facilitate digital platforms for the exchange of goods; and open data can enable industry-specific solutions (such as in agriculture).

However, only 3 of the 27 African countries included in the GDRD allow private sector service providers to digitally verify or authenticate the identity of a person against data stored in the ID system, and half of the African countries analyzed do not have open data legislation or an open data policy applicable across the entire public sector.

FIGURE 4.24 Attainment of good practice in enablers and safeguards of data use and reuse, selected African countries, 2020

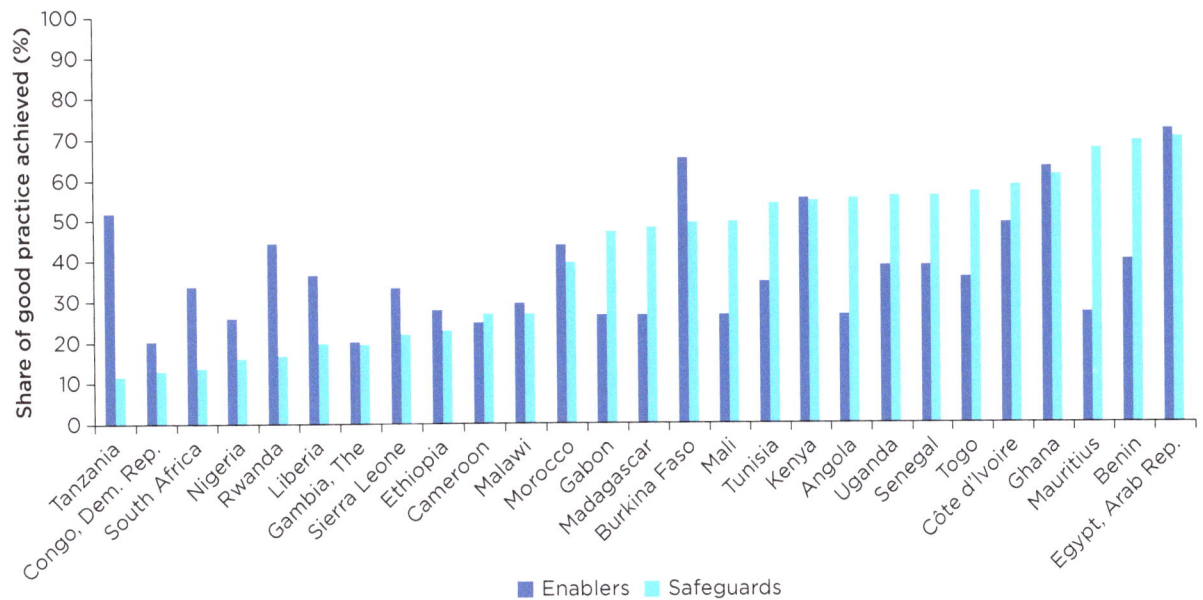

Source: World Bank, using data from World Bank 2021e, chapter 6.
Note: Data collected as of July 2020. A score of 100 = good practice. As defined by Chen (2021), "safeguards" refer to regulations promoting a safe online environment, minimizing risks, and limiting potential harms (as through cybersecurity, personal data protection, online consumer protection, regulation of unfair trade practices, and appropriate use of artificial intelligence); "enablers" refer to regulations facilitating the use and reuse of data, promoting interaction between different actors, and lowering the cost of processing and sharing data (such as policies related to data as well as antitrust and intellectual property).

Furthermore, data portability can give more options to consumers, borrowers, and small sellers on digital platforms. However, in more than 85 percent of the African countries studied in the GDRD, individuals do not have the right to request that their data be transferred to another service provider. Considering only the rules on the books, Sub-Saharan African countries are distant from high-income countries and good practice on enabling use of public intent data and private intent data and cross-border flows (figure 4.25), but they perform well regarding enablers for e-commerce.

Regulation of cross-border data flows varies greatly from one country to another. Although cross-border transfers can allow for the use of cloud computing to develop apps by local start-ups as well as the viability of regional data infrastructure, there is a global trend to adopt cross-border data flow restrictions (Cory and Dascoli 2021), and Africa is no exception. Three main approaches to data transfers can be identified: a limited transfer model, a conditional transfer model, and an open transfer model (World Bank 2021e). These approaches range from more restrictive ones (which require data to be stored in the country of origin) to more open frameworks (where data can be transferred with almost no requirements).

These differences are also present among African countries. For example, Kenya has adopted a limited transfer model that requires government approval to ensure that the laws in the country to which the data are transferred are equivalent and that the transfer

FIGURE 4.25 **Distance from good practice in data regulation across country income groups, Sub-Saharan Africa relative to global income groups, 2020**

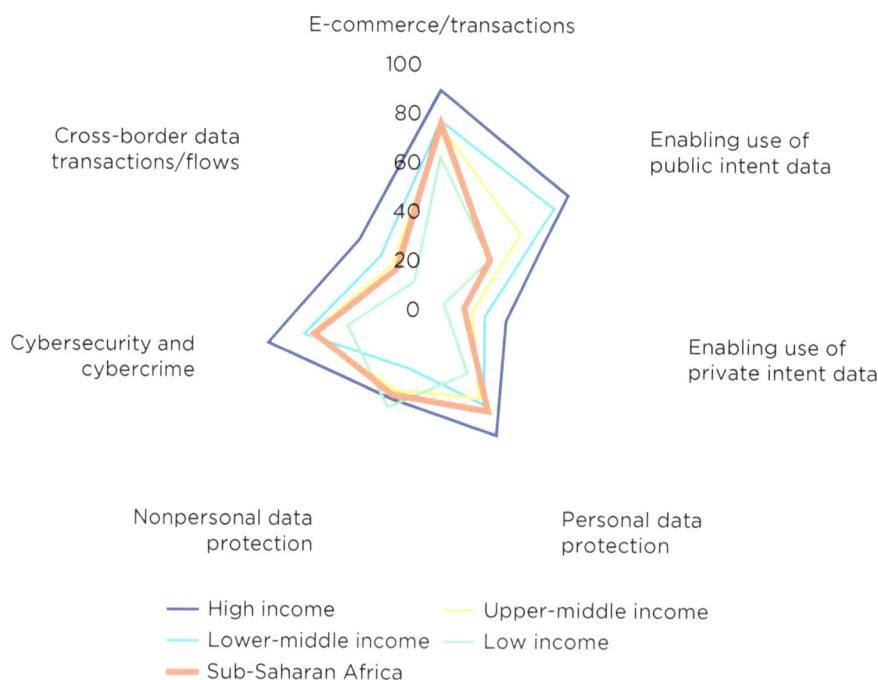

Source: Chen, Daza, and Begazo Gomez 2021.
Note: The radar diagram represents data from 24 Sub-Saharan African countries out of a global country sample of 80, with information collected as of June 2020. It displays performance (from 0 to 100 percent) as the distance from "good practice" (100 percent) in seven regulatory areas.

is necessary. In Ghana, the controller is responsible for ensuring that the recipient will comply with the regulation without government approval. Limiting cross-border data flow restrictions to circumstances when it is necessary to protect consumer privacy and essential security interests, facilitating data portability and access, and developing interoperable rules across the African continent would create a more fecund environment for DTs.

With the development of data hubs, the increased rate of internet penetration, and advances in machine learning, AI has emerged worldwide as a way of finding innovative development solutions (World Bank 2021a) and has the potential to lower the cost of entry for entrepreneurs, create new business models, improve health diagnoses, expand access to credit and financial services, and improve the entire logistics chain (IFC 2020). Still, the development and productive use of such technologies remain heavily concentrated in high-income countries. Apart from Egypt, Mauritius, South Africa, and Tunisia, African countries rank lower than the world average in the Oxford Government AI Readiness Index (Shearer, Stirling, and Pasquarelli 2020). Infrastructure limitations together with inconsistent national strategies act as barriers to AI. Ensuring a predictable environment to develop and use AI solutions in a safe and transparent manner will be crucial, especially in sectors such as finance.

The development of a data governance culture is also key. Doing so requires counting on technical, independent, and accountable institutions to adopt an agile regulation approach that favors DT innovation while enforcing safeguards. As of September 2021, only 13 out of 30 Smart Africa member countries had an independent data protection authority, in 8 countries a ministry was overseeing data protection, and the rest had no such authority (Sense Strategy 2021).

Furthermore, there is a need to increase awareness of citizens and business regarding protection, cybersecurity, consumer rights, and the benefits of using data-based solutions. Interviews with legal professionals in selected African countries highlight implementation challenges, such as limited awareness by businesses, lack of enforcement and compliance, burdensome or unclear procedures, and limited resources at data protection entities. In the case of cybersecurity, out of 44 African countries surveyed by the International Telecommunication Union in 2019, only 13 countries had a national Computer Emergency Response Team (CERT) with information security experts who protect, detect, and respond to cybersecurity incidents, and 14 had a National Cyber Security Centre (NCSC) that provides cybersecurity guidance and support (ITU 2021). Issues of technical capacity and equipment are also a challenge in African countries.

On the upside, countries have started deploying integrated strategies to enhance data protection and cybersecurity while initiatives proceed to expand the uptake of DTs. In Rwanda, the government is carrying out a digital acceleration program for (a) digital access and inclusion, (b) digital public service delivery, and (c) digital innovation and entrepreneurship, including support for more effective data protection and cybersecurity policies, regulations, institutions, and enforcement.[46]

As DTs play an ever-larger role in everyday life, cyber risks continue to grow. These risks affect the confidentiality, availability, and integrity of information (Cebula and Young 2010). The World Economic Forum's Global Risks Report categorizes cyber risks in the top three positions in terms of the likelihood of their occurrence among major global risks, following behind natural disasters and extreme weather events, and in the sixth position in terms of severity of their impacts on victims (WEF 2018, 3). In its annual survey to monitor existing and emerging risks that may affect the global financial system, the Depository Trust and Clearing Corporation (DTCC) ranked cyber risk as the number one threat (DTCC 2022), as shown in figure 4.26.

The ramping up of DT applications following the emergence of COVID-19 has amplified preexisting risks. There has been an upsurge in the reports of digital threats and malicious cyber activities across Africa, ranging from public infrastructure sabotage, espionage, and organized crime resulting in losses from digital fraud to illicit financial flows and national security breaches (Allen 2021). Financial industries have been exposed to cyber threats such as phishing and malware attacks (Bhasin 2007; Leukfeldt, Kleemans, and Stol 2017), ransomware attacks (Ren et al. 2020), and stealing and manipulating data as well as identities. The health sector experienced cyberattacks in the midst of the pandemic (Khan, Brohi, and Zaman 2020), including a cyberattack at a South African hospital (Walker 2020). Often, ransoms are paid before restoring functionality of the computer systems in these institutions. Cyber threats are considered worrisome, particularly for small businesses with scarce means to acquire and implement cybersecurity protection tools (Sulayman et al. 2012). A lack of structured cybersecurity policies and capacity for response to threats could potentially heighten users' vulnerability to cybercrime in the face of the increasing use of DTs.

Addressing vulnerabilities to cyberattacks and data breaches in Africa requires a greater commitment to data governance by various stakeholders. This includes, among others, deploying technologies and infrastructure to detect and mitigate cybercrime, supported by large-scale investments to strengthen cybersecurity capacities to protect the cyberspace of each country. Technology-based approaches for addressing cybersecurity include intrusion detection software, an application that monitors a network for malicious activity to detect attempted or successful unauthorized access; anomaly-based

FIGURE 4.26 **Perceived threats to financial markets, 2021**

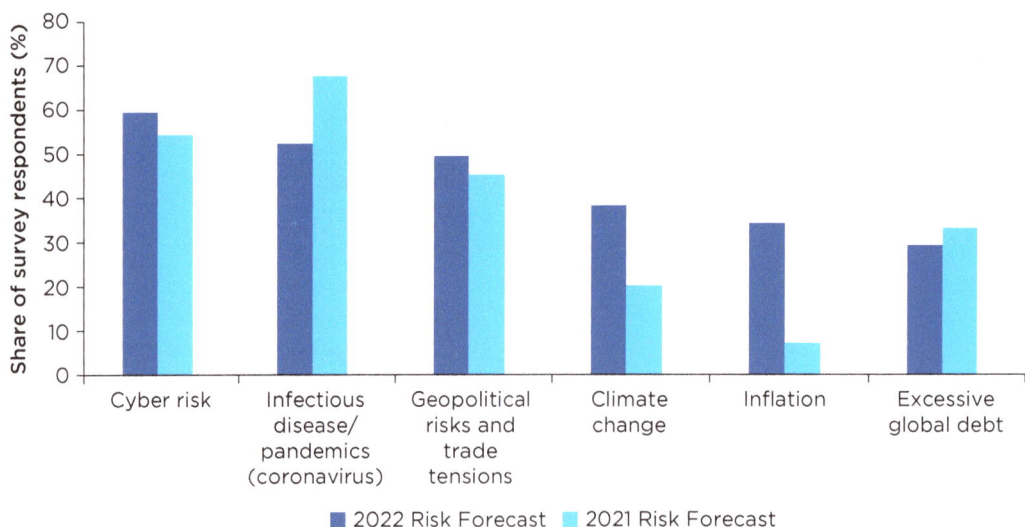

Source: DTCC 2022.
Note: Figure shows the top systemic risks to the broader economy identified by respondents to the annual Systemic Risk Barometer Survey conducted by the Depository Trust and Clearing Corporation (DTCC). The 2022 Risk Forecast reflects results from the survey conducted in the fourth quarter of 2021. The 2021 Risk Forecast reflects results from the survey conducted in the fourth quarter of 2020.

intrusion detection software, deployed to detect and flag deviations from normal usage behavior and help to protect against malicious attacks; and signature-based detection, used mainly to identify known threats that attempt to exploit application software or a system (Kabanda, Tanner, and Kent 2018).

Cooperation is also required for addressing cybercrime across all stakeholders including government, business, and civil organizations as well as among countries because of the lack of boundaries in cyberspace (ITU 2021). Cross-country cooperation is essential on cyber policies and the legal enforcement to strengthen cybersecurity strategies. In addition, restructuring of education curricula to equip students to understand cybersecurity is crucial. Furthermore, developing and retaining cybersecurity experts is essential: Irons and Ophoff (2016) propose the development of digital forensics skills in South Africa through university programs for cybersecurity.

There are concerns across Africa regarding misuse of data by governments for political motives, including through surveillance and increased misinformation, which adversely affect social cohesion. Government misuse of DTs could also allow widespread digital infringement of individual freedoms to surreptitiously track political opposition, suppress political dissidents, restrict free speech, and peddle misinformation during elections. For example, some African civil society organizations have raised concerns over possible breaches of privacy and digital rights (Woodhams 2020). In Africa, as elsewhere, DTs have enabled citizens to open civic spaces online but have also enabled governments to close online civic spaces through digital surveillance, disinformation, internet shutdowns, or arrest for online speech, among others (Roberts 2021).

Besides increasing political risks, techniques such as internet shutdowns can generate negative effects on economic activities. According to Netblock, among African countries recently exposed to shutdowns, the cost of one day of shutdown ranges from US$0.48 million in Liberia to US$8.30 million in Ethiopia.[47]

The debates around privacy, digital infringements, and access are couched in terms of a trade-off between individual human rights and national security. The strengthening of institutional quality in Africa is crucial because technological advances in the absence of countervailing institutional checks and balances could further expose citizens to surveillance and repression. Precise rules on cybercrime and content regulation, as well as constraints on government surveillance and disinformation, would be needed to prevent misuse for political reasons. More rigorous evidence and effective policy responses are needed to ensure that the downside risks of new technologies are managed and do not prevent the positive effects of broader uptake and use to be realized.

Looking ahead: Regional integration and climate transition

In the medium term, regional integration for connectivity, data, and online markets is a must to expand markets and deliver DT solutions to African business and citizens, as recognized in the AU's "Digital Transformation Strategy for Africa (2020–2030)" (AU 2020). Reaching this target requires a supportive enabling environment at both national and regional levels (figure 4.27). Regional frameworks by supranational blocs can enable cross-border harmonization of policy, legal, and regulatory frameworks. Policy reforms for cross-border infrastructure and data ecosystems can provide foundations to deliver digital services. Finally, country-level reforms, effective regulation, and investments under a harmonized transparency and accountability framework can ensure that benefits are delivered to consumers, business, and governments.

FIGURE 4.27 **Regional digital market layers and target outcomes**

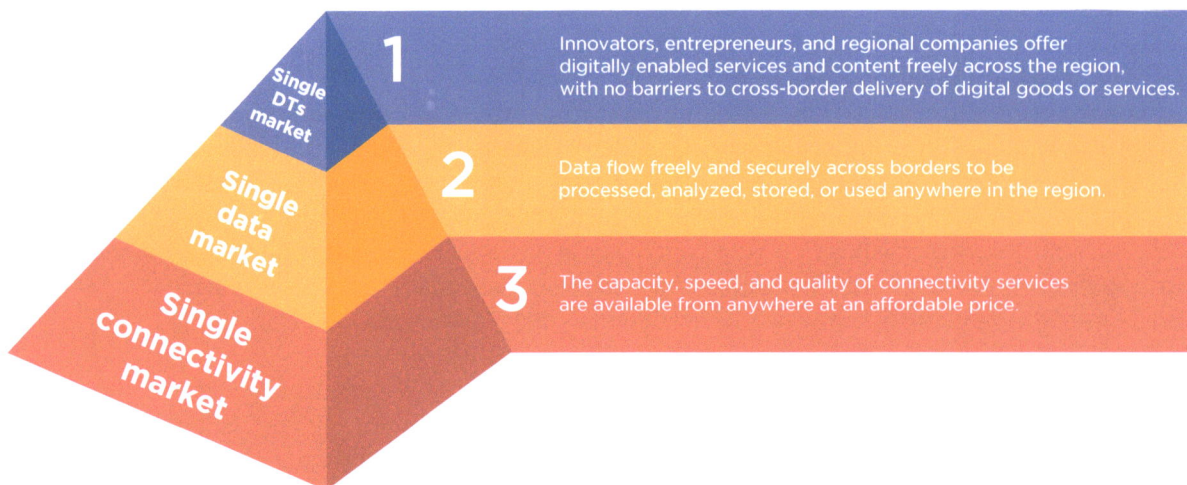

1 Innovators, entrepreneurs, and regional companies offer digitally enabled services and content freely across the region, with no barriers to cross-border delivery of digital goods or services.

2 Data flow freely and securely across borders to be processed, analyzed, stored, or used anywhere in the region.

3 The capacity, speed, and quality of connectivity services are available from anywhere at an affordable price.

Single DTs market

Single data market

Single connectivity market

Source: Adapted from Torgusson et al. 2018.
Note: DTs = digital technologies.

Digital regional integration for telecommunications services is occurring in selected pockets in Africa. For example, the East Africa One Network Area has facilitated roaming in this region. The initiative was launched in January 2015 and, to date, Kenya, Rwanda, South Sudan, and Uganda have capped international mobile roaming tariffs, and Tanzania confirmed its participation. The Economic Community of West African States (ECOWAS) launched a similar initiative, but implementation has been more limited.

The implementation of regional frameworks, such as in Western Africa, has also delivered benefits at the country level: in Cabo Verde, the implementation of an ECOWAS directive stipulating conditions for accessing landing stations for international submarine fiber optic cables allowed for colocation at the submarine cable landing station, resulting in lower prices for international connectivity.[48] And multicountry initiatives have bought international bandwidth capacity, such as the bulk purchase of wholesale submarine and satellite internet bandwidth spearheaded by the Smart Africa Alliance of 32 African countries.

The convergence of national regulatory frameworks is more limited regarding licensing, spectrum policy, or subsidies for digital connectivity. In particular, DE4A assessments for Eastern Africa recommend regional harmonized rate caps for cross-border traffic, elimination of roaming surcharges, and establishment of additional links to neighboring countries. For Western Africa, there is significant scope to strengthen the physical fiber interconnection of networks, enable traffic exchanges on a regional level, and ensure industry-friendly pricing and transport capacity over transnational fiber links.

In the data policy space, regional blocs have taken steps to facilitate regional integration and harmonization, but a binding mechanism is not in place. Mechanisms for interoperability across national frameworks are needed. ECOWAS adopted a regional Data Protection Act in 2010 compelling member states to establish national data protection laws. As of April 2021, five member states either had no legislation or were trying to adopt legislation. The AU's Convention on Cyber Security and Personal Data Protection (also known as the Malabo Convention) was adopted in 2014, but it falls short of the 15-member requirement to enforce. In February 2022, the AU adopted a comprehensive data policy framework to guide member states. The Southern Africa Development Community (SADC) released a model law in 2013. Since 2016, the African Network of Data Protection Authorities (RAPDP) has been a forum for exchange on personal data protection. These efforts face deep challenges stemming from diverse country contexts and multiplicity of subregional blocs.

In practice, regional frameworks can be a vehicle to deepen integration by supporting national-level actions. To facilitate the uptake and more intensive use of DTs in Africa, regional policies can address various, traditionally national policy areas including digital infrastructure, enablers for digital markets, digital skills, and e-government services (figure 4.28). The long-term goal of a truly integrated market would allow

- Spectrum auctions to cut across states (as in the United States);

- Harmonized regulation to control dominant operators, boost expansion of high-speed internet, and enable start-ups and enterprises to easily switch data centers and cloud computing providers within the region (as in the European Union); and

- Logistics and transportation digital platforms to operate seamlessly across borders.

FIGURE 4.28 **National-level actions to facilitate deeper regional integration of digital connectivity, data, and markets**

Policy area	Topic	Emerging sector		Transitioning sector
Digital infrastructure	Integrated regional digital infrastructure markets	Rules on roaming and termination rates for international calls, roaming for data, prices for cross-border transportation within regional blocs	Rules to allow for cross-border infrastructure deployment and regional exchange points, harmonized framework for licensing	Coordination/harmonization of spectrum management and ex ante pro-competition regulation
	Institutions and regulatory governance	National policy on regional harmonization (network of regulators/technical working groups)	Clear delineation of mandates for national vs. supranational regulation; more effective national adoption	Harmonized policy and coordinated rules on sector taxation and parafiscal fees
Data policy	Trust in online markets/ e-transactions	Interoperabillity of rules for e-signature, e-contracts, e-commerce	Convergence of rules to protect consumers (transparency of online intermediation services and redress)	Common rules to facilitate switching of data centers/cloud computing providers across countries
	Data protection	Regional policy, national rules that allow for cross-border data flows while safeguarding personal data	Regional interoperability of national laws for data protection (portability, access, consent, sharing)	Adoption of regional/global conventions for harmonization
	Cybersecurity	National policy/strategy on regional harmonization on cybercrime and cybersecurity	Harmonized laws on cybercrime and cybersecurity to allow for cross-border collaboration	Framework for cross-border coordination of CERTs/SOCs; adoption of global/regional agreements on cybersecurity
Digital services enablers	Foundational ID	Agreement to recognize IDs in another country	Rules to facilitate cross-border ID verification	Interoperable ID systems
	Digital financial services	Harmonized USSD regulation (pricing, QoS, nondiscrimination)	Regional integration of payment systems (including emoney)	Interoperability for mobile money/ mobile payments
	Digital skills	Harmonized certification standards for ICT programs		MRA for ICT professionals
	Public digtal platforms	Coordination of national digitalization strategies across countries and sectors		Interoperability of government e-services especially for cross-border trade movement of persons, digital businesses

Source: World Bank.
Note: The figure presents a nonexhaustive list of policies. An "emerging sector" refers to a digital sector where the digital economy is still emerging and internet use is low. A "transitioning sector" refers to a digital sector transitioning toward universal internet use. CERT = computer emergency response team; ICT = information and communication technology; ID = identification; MRA = mutual recognition agreement; QoS = quality of service; SOC = security operations center; USSD = Unstructured Supplementary Service Data.

Inspirational estimates can provide insight into the magnitude of productivity and jobs benefits that could be achieved from integrated continental connectivity, data, and DT markets and from testing fuller integration across two or three neighboring countries. It would be a remarkable achievement if Africa could show the rest of the world how large these benefits of full continental integration could be.

DTs can also play an innovative role in greening economies and ensuring sustainability in the face of climate change. As Africa expands its digital infrastructure and increases the use of DTs, it can benefit from more climate-friendly infrastructure as well as data-driven green sectoral solutions (figure 4.29). DTs can enable and accelerate pro-green initiatives and the transformation of consumption and production patterns across sectors—particularly in energy, transportation, and agriculture.[49]

DTs can be used in the sectors that are the primary generators of greenhouse gas (GHG) emissions—for example, smart grids for electricity, intelligent transportation systems, smart logistics, and agriculture practices that reduce GHG emissions and other pollutants. Through tracing, DTs can enable a shift in consumption patterns in key GHG-emitting sectors. DTs also can monitor air and water pollution and optimize energy use to minimize impact on the environment and adopt circular approaches to reduce waste. In addition, DTs are critical to adaptation for preparedness and response to climate change, increasing the resilience of economic activities, social protection systems, and other government services. Finally, start-ups and digital business models have developed innovative solutions to help citizens and firms reduce their carbon footprint and optimize the use of energy. Expanding the use of DTs to sustain greener economies will require foundational digital and data infrastructure as well as robust frameworks for safeguards.

Digital and data infrastructure must become more environmentally sustainable by building on the symbiotic relationship with electricity to facilitate mitigation. Although energy use always involves a trade-off against provided capacity per user, digital infrastructure requires additional sources of energy, especially to reach rural or remote areas. This offers the possibility of replacing diesel with solar power. New business models are already emerging in Africa: TESCOs (telecommunications energy services companies) manage 11.6 percent of sites (March 2021), with market potential forecast to reach about 60,000 sites across the Middle East and Africa by 2025 (TowerXchange 2021).

FIGURE 4.29 **Contributions to green outcomes from digital and data infrastructure**

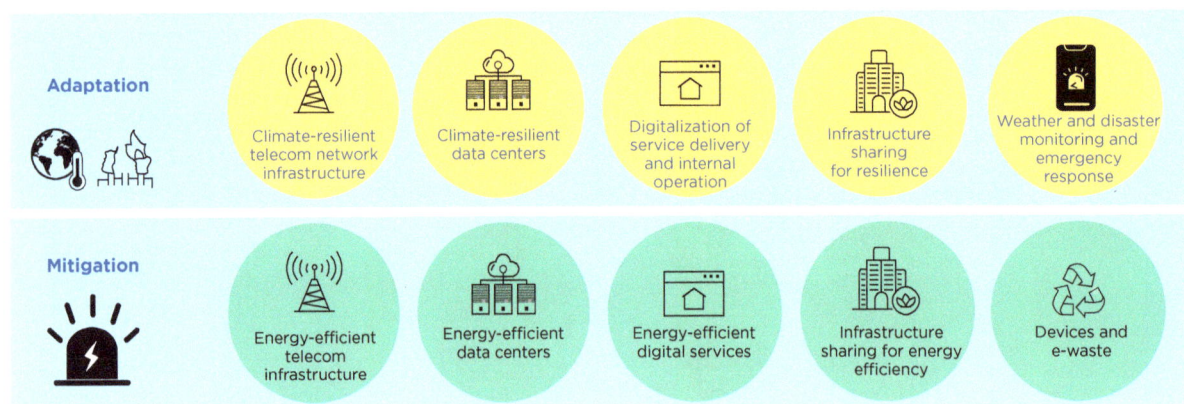

Adaptation

Climate-resilient telecom network infrastructure

Climate-resilient data centers

Digitalization of service delivery and internal operation

Infrastructure sharing for resilience

Weather and disaster monitoring and emergency response

Mitigation

Energy-efficient telecom infrastructure

Energy-efficient data centers

Energy-efficient digital services

Infrastructure sharing for energy efficiency

Devices and e-waste

Source: World Bank's Digital Development Global Practice.

Data centers require reliable electricity to function and support the use of digital applications. Clean energy sources (potentially generated on-site) and energy savings (for example, innovative cooling techniques) will be needed to complement the anticipated growth in data centers in the region. Data centers are expected to require at least 1,000 megawatts to meet demand in Africa over the next decade (Xalam Analytics and ADCA 2021).

Furthermore, new technologies can make digital infrastructure more energy efficient, thereby contributing to green goals. Fiber-optic cable, for example, is 85 percent more energy efficient than copper wires; 4G can be more than 50 times more energy efficient than 2G, and larger data centers are more energy efficient (World Bank 2021e). Various organizations have set net zero targets and strategies to guide pro-environment actions in the sector.[50] However, the increasing use of electronics also generates e-waste and emissions,[51] requiring frameworks to allow for a functioning e-waste management system and to address current constraints—lack of policies, awareness, and infrastructure (Maphosa and Maphosa 2020).

E-waste contains both valuable minerals that have an economic value that can be recovered as well as highly dangerous substances that can be hazardous to the physical environment and human health. The mining of minerals for the growing global consumption of electronic devices generates indirect effects on emissions along the digital value chain. Among the 15 most important producing countries of the seven key minerals for information and communication technology worldwide,[52] 5 countries are in Africa. Therefore, Africa needs support for lower carbon emissions technologies for its mining industry, including in the Democratic Republic of Congo, Ethiopia, Madagascar, and Nigeria (Onianwa 2021).

Summary of key findings for more inclusive use

In sum, to increase availability and use of affordable internet and other DTs, it is critical that policies focus on the following:

- Increased competition by enabling entry and access to spectrum as well as to infrastructure, and more effective regulation of dominant operators

- Operational cost reductions through spectrum policy that enables more efficient technologies, infrastructure sharing, or co-investments, including access to SOE backbone infrastructure, and elimination of excise taxes

- Updated universal service support for low-income people, using both supply- and demand-side interventions through regulation and public financial support

- A nurturing environment for data infrastructure, including IXPs, data centers, and cloud computing that support local digital businesses through better quality and lower data prices

- Improved data regulation to expand availability of new pro-poor and pro-productivity DTs; enable digital business models (through rules for data access, sharing and cross-border data flows); and increase trust in DT use (through safeguards such as data protection, cybersecurity, and consumer protection)

A long-term vision will require thinking big in terms of regional integration as well as thinking green, so digital and energy infrastructure coexist in a symbiotic relationship for greater environmental sustainability.

Decisions on priority interventions will depend on the country situation. The relative importance of the coverage gaps and the uptake gaps (figure 4.5) can inform decisions on the most important policy goal. Government interventions should consider the dynamics of the private sector, institutional capacity for implementation, and public resources available, as well as expected effects of interventions. Simulations conducted for selected African countries show positive effects of the main regulatory proposals to achieve availability of affordable internet and other DTs. Table 4.1 summarizes these proposals and effects.

TABLE 4.1 Summary policy recommendations and simulated effects of selected measures

Goal	Topic	Simulation of potential effects for selected countries
Affordability of internet	Pro-competition rules: • Open licensing and elimination of monopolies particularly in international connectivity • Regulation of dominant operators • Access to essential infrastructure • Spectrum assignment • Synergies between telecommunications regulators and competition authorities Cost-reducing regulation: • Spectrum availability (digital dividend from broadcast migration) • Regulated access to SOE backbone infrastructure and cross-sectoral infrastructure sharing • Minimization of excise taxes on telecommunicatons services and rationalization of sectoral fees	• Once pro-competition policies are implemented, they can help decrease poverty headcount rates by 0.02–0.82 percent and increase access to services by 0.06–5.37 percentage points. • Increasing competition—together with reducing sector-specific taxes, technological innovation, and active infrastructure sharing—could allow for higher mobile and mobile internet adoption levels than implementing all those policies with infrastructure subsidies and without higher competition levels. • Policy reforms that include releases of sub-1 GHz spectrum and reduction of tax overcharges could reduce the 2030 estimated broadband coverage gap by 2–7 percentage points. • Technological innovation together with infrastructure sharing and tax reduction could add 5.0 percentage points in mobile phone adoption and 4.5 points in mobile internet adoption relative to policies that include only technological innovation and infrastructure sharing. • About US\$1 in additional taxes must be compensated with US\$1 in subsidies to cover rural areas. • Aligning tax policy with best practice principles and removing distortionary sector-specific taxes that are applied solely to the mobile sector can raise mobile internet adoption by 6 percentage points (based on data from Benin and the Democratic Republic of Congo). • Cost-reducing policy reforms (spectrum, infrastructure sharing, and taxation) can save 10–20 percent of the cost required to achieve near-universal coverage, which meant US\$204 million savings for governments across six analyzed countries.

(continued)

Goal	Topic	Simulation of potential effects for selected countries
Availability of affordable internet	More effective universal service policy: • Improved governance and effectiveness of USFs • Allow for "pay or play" by operators • Introduce coverage obligations	• A single SRN that allows for RAN sharing only in rural areas provides efficiencies, preserving infrastructure competition in urban and suburban areas, with a saving against the baseline (without infrastructure sharing) of 21–56 percent for 10 Mbps and 12–48 percent for 2 Mbps per user. • If coverage obligations are established resulting in a maximum profit margin of 10 percent by site, 30–100 percent of the population could be covered by a 4G network with wireless backhaul delivering 30 GB per month without need of government subsidies.
	Demand-side interventions: • *Affordability:* social plans, targeted vouchers, subsidies for devices, financing for devices • *Attractiveness and usability:* digital training programs, familiarity with DTs via public access, schools, and social digital transfers	• Even if 4G universal infrastructure is subsidized, mobile internet adoption would increase by only 1–3 percentage points because demand would remain limited. If 4G uptake increased to 40 percent in uncovered areas owing to demand-side policies, then 4G coverage would reach the same levels that would be achieved with a pure supply subsidy.
Availability of attractive DTs	Data infrastructure: • Support IXPs' progression into more advanced data centers Data policy: • Clarify data policies to safeguard users and enable development of DTs • Implement data rules effectively • Achieve regional harmonization or interoperability of frameworks to create single regional data and DTs markets	• More accessible data storage and cloud computing services to develop and use productivity-enhancing DTs • Higher trust for broader use of DTs, increased use and reuse of data, and reduced losses from cyberattacks • Stronger digital entrepreneurship • More integrated regional data and DT markets
Cross-cutting	• Regional harmonization and interoperability for integrated digital infrastructure markets, digital data markets, and DTs • Greener digital and data infrastructure using more sustainable energy sources • Mainstreaming of DTs across sectors to support use of data for climate transition	• More variety of DTs and increased trade • Lower environmental impact and greater energy cost savings

Source: World Bank.
Note: 4G = fourth-generation mobile telecommunications technology; DT = digital technology; GB = gigabyte; GHz = gigahertz; IXP = internet exchange point; Mbps = megabits per second; RAN = radio access network; SOE = state-owned enterprise; SRN = shared rural network; USF = universal service fund.

Annex 4A Supplemental data

TABLE 4A.1 Simplified digital value chain and market characteristics, by subregion, Africa, 2020

Indicator	Subregion	International connectivity	Passive infrastructure (towers)	Fixed wholesale	Mobile wholesale	Fixed retail	Mobile retail	Mobile money	Data and cloud services	Digital platforms
Concentration (HHI)	AFE	5,591	4,638	6,656	38[a]	4,904	4,476	5,334	1,596	5,000 digital firms headquartered in Africa
	AFW	7,820	3,474	6,089	9[a]	6,882	4,288	4,789	2,782	0
	NA	3,732	3,482	7,471	3[a]	6,046	3,941	NA	1,470	0
Market structure: monopolies	AFE	1	2	3	—	4	2	1	0	0
	AFW	4	0	1	—	5	0	1	0	0
	NA	3	0	1	—	2	1	0	0	0
Market structure: duopolies	AFE	2[b]	5	2	—	3	8	1	0	0
	AFW	8[b]	2	5	—	3	3	0	0	0
	NA	2[b]	0	2	—	0	0	0	0	—
New entry	AFE	10 investments in cables or upgrades since 2016	3	12	11	4	3	17	0	—
	AFW		3	6	10	5	1	24	0	—
	NA		0	5	2	0	1	4	0	—
SOE presence	AFE	12	11	22	1	17	23	13	4	—
	AFW	14	6	22	0	15	20	10	2	—
	NA	6	4	6	1	6	6	3	2	—

Sources: World Bank's Africa Digital Market Players Database (internal) 2021, built on numerous (11+) data sources including TeleGeography, Global System for Mobile Communications Association (GSMA), Africa Bandwidth Maps, Afterfibre.org, Policytracker, TowerXchange, PeeringDB, and Xalam Analytics.

Note: AFE = Eastern and Southern Africa; AFW = Western and Central Africa; HHI = Hirschman–Herfindahl market concentration index; NA = North Africa; SOE = state-owned enterprise; — = not available.

a. Refers to the number of active mobile virtual network operators.

b. Refers to the number of countries with partial competition in international connectivity as reported by the International Telecommunication Union.

Notes

1. All mobile internet subscriber statistics are from Global System for Mobile Communications Association (GSMA) data, accessed in November 2022 through the GSMA Intelligence proprietary data platform.
2. This number of Africans lacking broadband connectivity coverage was calculated using GSMA statistics on population (1.38 billion by September 2021) and 3G network coverage by population by 2021 (89.1 percent), accessed in November 2022 through the GSMA Intelligence proprietary data platform.
3. Data prices for 2015–20 in Africa are from Research ICT Africa Mobile Pricing (RAMP) data, https://researchictafrica.net/research-ict-africa-ramp-index-2/.
4. See "2025 Targets: Connecting the Other Half" of the Broadband Commission for Sustainable Development, https://www.broadbandcommission.org/broadband-targets/.
5. Estimated average download speed is from World Bank staff analysis of Ookla Speedtest Intelligence June 2021 data.
6. Download speed data are June 2020 data from the Ookla's Speedtest Intelligence platform.
7. This finding is based on simulations for nine diverse African countries by Vergara-Cobos, Malasquez, and Granguillhome (forthcoming). Estimations assume feasible reductions in mobile retail market concentration for each country.
8. For example, a study in Rwanda using monthly panel data from telecommunications companies two and a half years before and after implementing mobile termination rate regulations found that introducing reductions in interconnection rates in Rwanda reduced overall mobile retail prices for end consumers (Nshunguyinka, Shema, and Saint 2021).
9. SOEs are here defined as any corporate entity recognized by national law as an enterprise and in which the national or subnational government exercises ownership, including joint stock companies, limited liability companies, and partnerships limited by shares. Statutory corporations, with their legal personality established through specific legislation, should be considered SOEs if their purpose and activities are of a largely economic nature (that is, the entity operates in a market for goods or services that could, in theory, be provided by a private company). For the statistics presented in this report, "SOE" includes entities in which the state holds 50 percent or more of shares. Entities in which the state holds less than 50 percent are considered state-linked enterprises.
10. Background papers for this report provide more in-depth analysis on (a) the role of SOEs in the digital economy in Africa (Pop and Connon, forthcoming); and on (b) governance of digital SOEs in Africa (Jaupart and Begazo, forthcoming).
11. Equitel received a license in 2014 and started operations in 2015 (Equity 2019) but received significant pushback relating to the deployment of its "thin SIM [subscriber identity module]" and license awarded by the regulator (*Business Daily Africa* 2015; Wainaina 2016). Aside from Finserve (Equitel), which has managed to grow over the years (Chitavi, Cohen, and Hagist 2021), two other MVNOs were awarded the licenses in 2014 but barely took off (Mumo 2017).
12. Although vertical integration can be justified in terms of efficiency gains through economies of scale and scope, it can lead to competition risks in the absence of adequate regulation or remedies.
13. These figures refer to the market shares of cloud hosting providers among websites with an African country domain across 34 countries. An HHI of 1,500–2,500 indicates moderately concentrated markets and an HHI of over 2,500, highly concentrated markets ("Cloud Hosting Usage Distribution in the Top 1 Million Sites: Statistics for Websites using Cloud Hosting Providers," BuiltWith data [accessed April 2021], https://trends.builtwith.com/hosting/cloud-hosting).
14. "Market concentration" measures the extent to which market shares are concentrated between firms in a market. Measures of market concentration are often used to proxy competition on the market. High market concentration may give rise to market power, which refers to a situation in which a firm is able to raise and prevail prices above a level that would prevail under competition.

15. These figures refer to the number of new companies founded (headquarters) in a country since 2017. This analysis is based on Pitchbook's 2020 data on investments in digital business and preliminary analysis based on Apptopia data on mobile apps.

16. A 40 percent market share is a common threshold to presume dominance, based on European Union (EU) case law. Competition laws in selected African countries have more stringent thresholds, of 25–30 percent (for example, in Botswana, the Arab Republic of Egypt, and Zambia), whereas others have looser thresholds of 40–50 percent market share (Kenya, Namibia, and South Africa) to define dominance. See World Bank Group and Africa Competition Forum (2016) and Pop and Coelho (2021b) for more details on dominance definitions in Africa.

17. However, cable projects owned by content providers also pose risks to markets, such as potential negative impacts on competition and difficulties regarding taxation.

18. Mobile number portability regulation that allows for affordable and seamless switching of service providers can also be relevant to boost competition in mobile retail services (Mothobi 2020).

19. Good practices in "licensing" include no limitation on the number of licenses, authorized services, or technology for service providers or infrastructure providers as well as a transparent licensing process. Good "interconnection" practice includes publication of a detailed reference interconnection offer. Regulation of operators with SMP refers to market analysis and designation of operator with SMP. In "spectrum management," good practice refers to the clarity and transparency of procedures to award spectrum licenses and set spectrum fees. Rules on international connectivity would include liberalization of international gateways and access to international connectivity infrastructures.

20. For a discussion on spectrum and competition in West Africa, including a conceptual framework on how to limit spectrum scarcity, see Pop and Coelho (2020).

21. MTRs, also called interconnection rates, refer to the amount that network A must pay to network B to connect a call or send an SMS from a subscriber on A to a subscriber on B.

22. See, for example, actions by the French regulator (ARCEP) presented in OECD (2020).

23. For a discussion of antitrust enforcement and advocacy activities of competition authorities in digital markets, see Pop and Coelho (2021b). In addition, for an overview of competition authorities in Africa and their enforcement activities across a range of sectors, see World Bank Group and African Competition Forum (2016).

24. Only Kenya, Malawi, and South Africa are funded at the same level as the EU and the US, accounting for income levels (Nyman and Falco 2020).

25. This estimate is for a 5G nonstandalone network with 200 Mbps of capacity.

26. The taxation study included 25 African countries: Algeria, Angola, Benin, Burkina Faso, Cameroon, Chad, Côte d'Ivoire, the Democratic Republic of Congo, the Arab Republic of Egypt, Ethiopia, Kenya, Gabon, Ghana, Guinea, Madagascar, Mali, Morocco, Niger, Nigeria, Senegal, Sierra Leone, South Africa, Tanzania, Tunisia, and Zambia.

27. The "missing" traffic was most likely routed via the internet, or through so-called SIM boxes that make incoming international traffic "look" like local calls.

28. For the DE4A assessments, see the country diagnostics on the World Bank's DE4A website, https://www.worldbank.org/en/programs/all-africa-digital-transformation/country-diagnostics.

29. For example, estimated smartphone adoption (the number of SIM cards used in smartphones, divided by the average number of SIM cards per unique subscriber) for a sample of seven countries (Benin, the Democratic Republic of Congo, Ghana, Nigeria, Rwanda, Sierra Leone, and Tanzania) ranges from about 15 percent in Tanzania to almost 40 percent in Ghana based on 2020 data from the GSMA Intelligence platform. Furthermore, there is an important rural-urban gap in smartphone ownership. In Nigeria and Tanzania, adults living in rural areas are about 35 percent less likely to own a smartphone than those living in urban areas according to estimates based on the GSMA Intelligence Consumer Survey (2020 for Nigeria and 2018 for Tanzania) (World Bank 2022).

30. In Benin, the Democratic Republic of Congo, Rwanda, and Sierra Leone, most mobile internet users (55–70 percent) do not connect with 3G or 4G technology even though mobile broadband coverage is widespread. For a sample of six mobile operators in Africa, revenues coming from

2G services (voice and SMS/USSD applications) are 58–77 percent, showing the limited importance of data to determine commercial viability (World Bank 2022).

31. Mobile infrastructure sharing can be broadly classified into (a) *passive sharing* (sharing of the physical mast and energy supply); (b) *active sharing* (sharing of the radio access network [RAN] including site, mast, base transceiver station, backhaul, and base station controllers); and (c) *roaming* (when a mobile subscriber uses the network of another operator).

32. From the Mobile UK web page, "About the Shared Rural Network," https://www.mobileuk.org /shared-rural-network; see also Alpha Wireless (2021).

33. In the baseline, each MNO builds its own network to serve its market share with no sharing taking place.

34. Sub-Saharan African countries where SOEs control more than 40 percent of the fiber network include Algeria, Angola, Botswana, Cabo Verde, Cameroon, Chad, the Comoros, the Democratic Republic of Congo, Djibouti, Egypt, Equatorial Guinea, Eritrea, Eswatini, Ethiopia, The Gambia, Libya, Namibia, Niger, South Africa, Tunisia, and Zimbabwe.

35. Wi-Fi 6 is the sixth generation of Wi-Fi technologies that offers a significant improvement in speeds and latency. For more information, see the Intel web page, "What Is Wi-Fi 6?" https://www .intel.com/content/www/us/en/gaming/ resources/wifi-6.html.

36. The savings would be US$204 million for six countries (Benin, the Democratic Republic of Congo, Ghana, Nigeria, Sierra Leone, and Tanzania) given that 4G coverage is already near-universal in Rwanda.

37. The "Internet Movil Social para la Gente" plan and the "Vive Digital para la Gente" plan provide subsidized data plans for low-income and remotely located households (OECD 2019).

38. See information on the conditions on low-cost tariffs imposed on British Telecom and Kingston Communications as part of their designation as universal service providers for broadband (Ofcom 2020).

39. For more information, see "Lifeline Program for Low-Income Consumers" on the Federal Communications Commission website: https://www.fcc.gov/general/lifeline-program-low-income -consumers.

40. In Latin America, expenses on international bandwidth (US$ billion per year) could fall by one-third because of the use of IXPs (Agudelo et al. 2014, as cited in World Bank 2021c).

41. According to the PeeringDB (https://www.peeringdb.com/) database (as of September 16, 2021), there are 63 IXPs in Africa (62 in Sub-Saharan Africa and 1 in Egypt) out of 738 worldwide. As of December 2020, the African IXP Association (AFIX) reported 52 member IXPs in 35 African countries, including one IXP in Tunisia.

42. According to the United Nations, there are 54 countries in Africa and 195 countries overall.

43. For example, the African Internet Exchange System (AXIS) project established 15 new IXPs in African economies in 2012–17.

44. The GDRD is an underlying database that was developed for *World Development Report 2021* (World Bank 2021e).

45. "Privacy by design" is a concept that integrates privacy into the creation and operation of new devices, information technology systems, networked infrastructure, and even corporate policies.

46. For more details about this program, see World Bank (2021c, 2021d) and the Bank's Digital Acceleration Project for Rwanda site (accessed February 13, 2023), https://projects.worldbank.org /en/projects-operations/project-detail/P173373.

47. The cost of one day of shutdown is based on 2020 data using Netblock's estimation tool: https://netblocks.org/cost/.

48. The price drop is reported by the regulator (the Multisectoral Regulatory Agency for the Economy, ARME). This reform was supported by the Second State-owned Enterprises and Fiscal Management Development Policy Financing with the objective to improve competition and ensure an open and nondiscriminatory access regime in the international bandwidth. In October 2019, the government of Cabo Verde adopted a decree (Regulamento C/REG.06/06/12 sobre as condiçoes terrestres de cabos submarinos) implementing ECOWAS directives.

49. The Global e-Sustainability Initiative found that increased use of information and communication technology (ICT) solutions can enable a 20 percent reduction of global carbon dioxide emissions by 2030, equivalent to 12.08 gigatons of GHG emissions (GeSI and Deloitte 2019).

50. See International Telecommunication Union Recommendation ITU-T L.1471, which seeks to guide ICT organizations in clarifying the meaning of net zero in the context of the ICT sector and setting net zero targets and strategies. It also identifies actions that would lead the sector toward net zero.

51. E-waste includes mobile phones, computer equipment, televisions, electronic boards, chips, and data storage waste, among others. The amount of e-waste generated worldwide was estimated to be greater than 53.6 million metric tons, averaging 7.3 kilograms per capita in 2019 (Forti et al. 2020). Africa's contribution to e-waste amounted to 2.9 million metric tons, with an average of 2.5 kilograms per capita in 2019. The vast majority of e-waste goes into landfills, while a lower proportion ends up in recycling and incineration.

52. The seven key minerals for ICT are gallium, germanium, indium, rare earth elements (such as praseodymium, neodymium, dysprosium, and so on), selenium, tantalum, and tellurium.

References

A4AI (Alliance for Affordable Internet). 2018. "Universal Service and Access Funds: An Untapped Resource to Close the Gender Digital Divide." World Wide Web Foundation. http://webfoundation.org/docs/2018/03/Using-USAFs-to-Close-the-Gender-Digital-Divide-in-Africa.pdf.

AFI (Alliance for Financial Inclusion). 2021. "Regulatory Approaches to Digital Payments Transaction Costs in Sustaining Financial Inclusion in Africa." Special Report of the African Financial Inclusion Policy Initiative, AFI, Kuala Lumpur, Malaysia.

Agudelo, Mauricio, Raul Katz, Ernesto Flores-Roux, Maria Cristina Duarte Botero, Fernando Callorda, and Taylor Berry. 2014. *Expansión de infraestructura regional para la interconexión de tráfico de internet en América Latina.* Caracas, Republica Bolivariana de Venezuela: Development Bank of Latin America.

Ajibulu, Ade, and Sara Nyman. 2019. "Affordability of Mobile Data Services." Policy note of the Competitiveness for Investment in South Africa program, financed by the Multi-Country Investment Climate Program of the International Finance Corporation, World Bank Group, Washington, DC.

Allen, Nathaniel. 2021. "Africa's Evolving Cyber Threats." Spotlight article, January 19, Africa Center for Strategic Studies, Washington, DC.

Alpha Wireless. 2021. "What Other Countries Can Learn from the UK's Shared Rural Network." *Insights Blog*, January 4, 2021. https://alphawireless.com/what-other-countries-can-learn-from-the-uks-shared-rural-network/.

Arakpogun, Emmanuel Ogiemwonyi, Ziad Elsahn, Richard B. Nyuur, and Femi Olan. 2020. "Threading the Needle of the Digital Divide in Africa: The Barriers and Mitigations of Infrastructure Sharing." *Technological Forecasting and Social Change* 161: 120263.

Arakpogun, Emmanuel Ogiemwonyi, Roseline Wanjiru, and Jason Whalley. 2017. "Impediments to the Implementation of Universal Service Funds in Africa: A Cross-Country Comparative Analysis." *Telecommunications Policy* 41 (7–8): 617–30.

ATAF (African Tax Administration Forum). 2020. "Suggested Approach to Drafting Digital Services Tax Legislation." Guidance publication, ATAF, Pretoria, South Africa.

AU (African Union). 2020. "The Digital Transformation Strategy for Africa (2020–2030)." Strategy document, AU, Addis Ababa, Ethiopia.

Aviomoh, Henry, Tania Begazo, and Anne Golla. Forthcoming. "Review of 'Getting Connected: Market Structure, Regulation, and Internet Access in Africa and the Rest of the World.'" World Bank, Washington, DC.

Aviomoh, Henry, Moussa P. Blimpo, Woubet Kassa, and Michael Minges. 2021. "Data Infrastructure in Africa: The Missing Middle Mile." Unpublished manuscript, World Bank, Washington, DC.

Belo, Rodrigo, Pedro Ferreira, and Rahul Telang. 2016. "Spillovers from Wiring Schools with Broadband: The Critical Role of Children." *Management Science* 62 (12): 3450–71.

Bhasin, Madan. 2007. "Mitigating Cyber Threats to Banking Industry." *Chartered Accountant* 50 (10): 1618–24.

Björkegren, Daniel. 2020. "Competition in Network Industries: Evidence from the Rwandan Mobile Phone Network." Working Paper, Orlando Bravo Center for Economic Research, Brown University, Providence, RI.

Björkegren, Daniel, and Burak Ceyhun Karaca. 2022. "Network Adoption Subsidies: A Digital Evaluation of a Rural Mobile Phone Program in Rwanda." *Journal of Development Economics* 154: 102762.

Bleeker, Amelia. 2019. "Using Universal Service Funds to Increase Access to Technology for Persons with Disabilities in the Caribbean." Studies and Perspectives Series No. 79, ECLAC Subregional Headquarters for the Caribbean, Economic Commission for Latin America and the Caribbean, Santiago, Chile.

Bonakele, Tembinkosi. 2020. "Economic Inclusion Requires Digital Inclusion." Remarks by the commissioner in *Competition News* 65 (March), Competition Commission South Africa, Pretoria. http://www.compcom.co.za/wp-content/uploads/2020/12/CompCom-Newsletter-March-2020 .pdf.

Bourreau, Marc, Richard Feasey, and Steffen Hoernig. 2017. "Demand-Side Policies to Accelerate the Transition to Ultrafast Broadband." Project report, Centre on Regulation in Europe (CERRE), Brussels.

Business Daily Africa. 2015. "Court Boosts Roll-Out of Equity's Thin SIM." *Business Daily Africa*, June 26, 2015.

CA (Communications Authority of Kenya). 2021. "Revision of Mobile Termination Rates (MTRs) and Fixed Termination Rates (FTRs) Proposal." Proposal document, CA, Nairobi, Kenya. https://ca.go .ke/wp-content/uploads/2021/07/Proposal-to-Revise-MTR-and-FTR-2021-.pdf.

Cebula, James J., and Lisa R. Young. 2010. "A Taxonomy of Operational Cyber Security Risks." Technical Note CMU/SEI-2010-TN-028, Software Engineering Institute, Carnegie-Mellon University, Pittsburgh.

Cebreiro-Gómez, Ana, Colin Clavey, Marcello Estevão, Jonathan Leigh-Pemberton, and Benjamin Stewart. 2021. *"Digital Services Tax: Country Practice and Technical Challenges."* Report No. 167859, World Bank, Washington, DC.

Chen, Rong. 2021. "Mapping Data Governance Legal Frameworks Around the World: Findings from the Global Data Regulation Diagnostic." Policy Research Working Paper 9615, World Bank, Washington, DC.

Chen, Rong, Lillyana Daza, and Tania Priscilla Begazo Gomez. 2021. "Regulating Digital Data in Africa." Unpublished manuscript, World Bank, Washington, DC.

Chitavi, Mike, Lauren Cohen, and Spencer C. N. Hagist. 2021. "Kenya Is Becoming a Global Hub of FinTech Innovation." *Harvard Business Review*, February 18, 2021. https://hbr.org/2021/02 /kenya-is-becoming-a-global-hub-of-fintech-innovation.

Clarke, George R. G., and Scott J. Wallsten. 2002. "Universal(ly Bad) Service: Providing Infrastructure to Urban and Poor Urban Consumers." Policy Research Working Paper 2868, World Bank, Washington, DC.

CCSA (Competition Commission South Africa). 2019. "Data Services Market Inquiry: Final Report." Inquiry report, Competition Commission South Africa, Pretoria.

Cory, Nigel, and Luke Dascoli. 2021. "How Barriers to Cross-Border Data Flows Are Spreading Globally, What They Cost, and How to Address Them." Report, Information Technology and Innovation Foundation, Washington, DC.

DOT (Digital Opportunity Trust). 2019. "Digital Ambassador Program Proof of Concept: Final Evaluation." Report, DOT, Ottawa, Canada.

DTCC (Depository Trust and Clearing Corporation). 2022. "Systemic Risk Barometer Survey: 2022 Risk Forecast." Annual survey report, DTCC, New York.

Equity (Equity Group Holdings). 2019. "Equitel's Mobile Commerce Payments Continue to Drive Growth for the Operator." Press release, October 17, 2019. https://equitygroupholdings.com /equitels-mobile-commerce-payments-continue-to-drive-growth-for-the-operator/.

Erkmen, Baris. 2021. "Beaming Broadband across the Congo River." *The X Blog*, September 16, 2021. https://x.company/blog/posts/taara-beaming-broadband-across-congo/.

Faccio, Mara, and Luigi Zingales. 2017. "Political Determinants of Competition in the Mobile Telecommunication Industry." Working Paper No. 23041, National Bureau of Economic Research, Cambridge, MA.

FCC (Federal Communications Commission). 2020. "Auction of Priority Access Licenses for the 3550–3650 MHz Band." Public Notice FCC 20-18, March 2, FCC, Washington, DC. https://docs.fcc.gov/public/attachments/FCC-20-18A1.pdf.

Forti, Vanessa, Cornelis Peter Baldé, Ruediger Kuehr, and Garam Bel. 2020. *The Global E-Waste Monitor 2020: Quantities, Flows and the Circular Economy Potential*. Bonn, Geneva, and Rotterdam: United Nations University/United Nations Institute for Training and Research, International Telecommunication Union, and International Solid Waste Association.

Gallegos, Doyle, Lucine Munkyung Park, Ane Morales Elorriaga, Rokuhei Fordyce Fukui, Timothy John Charles Kelly, Je Myung Ryu, and Natalija Gelvanovska-Garcia. 2019. "Connecting Africa Through Broadband: A Strategy for Doubling Connectivity by 2021 and Reaching Universal Access by 2030." Report, Broadband Commission for Sustainable Development of the International Telecommunication Union (ITU), Geneva; and United Nations Educational, Scientific and Cultural Organization (UNESCO), New York.

Genakos, Christos, Tommaso Valletti, and and Frank Verboven. 2018. "Evaluating Market Consolidation in Mobile Communications." *Economic Policy* 33 (93): 45–100.

GeSI (Global Enabling Sustainability Initiative) and Deloitte. 2019. "Digital with Purpose: Delivering a SMARTer2030." Summary report, GeSI, Brussels.

Goolsbee, Austan, and Jonathan Guryan. 2006. "The Impact of Internet Subsidies in Public Schools." *Review of Economics and Statistics* 88 (2): 336–47.

GSMA (Global System for Mobile Communications Association). 2014. "Sub-Saharan Africa – Universal Service Fund Study." Report prepared by Ladcomm Corporation for GSMA, London.

Guerrero Barreto, María Eugenia, and Patricia I. Ritter Burga. 2014. "The Effect of Internet and Cell Phones on Employment and Agricultural Production In Rural Villages in Peru." Undergraduate thesis in economics, Faculty of Economics and Business, University of Piura, Peru.

Hawthorne, Ryan. 2018. "The Effects of Lower Mobile Termination Rates in South Africa." *Telecommunications Policy* 42 (5): 374–85.

Hawthorne, Ryan, and Lukasz Grzybowski. 2019. "Narrowing the 'Digital Divide': The Role of Complementarities between Fixed and Mobile Data in South Africa." Working Paper No. 7711, Center for Economic Studies and ifo Institute (CESifo), Munich.

ICASA (Independent Communications Authority of South Africa). 2021. "Draft Mobile Broadband Services Regulations Pursuant to Section 67(4) of the Electronic Communications Act No. 36 of 2005." *Government Gazette Staatskorerant* 669 (44337): 3–59.

IFC (International Finance Corporation). 2020. "Artificial Intelligence in Emerging Markets: Opportunities, Trends, and Emerging Business Models." Report No. 156840, IFC, Washington, DC.

Irons, Alastair, and Jacques Ophoff. 2016. "Aspects of Digital Forensics in South Africa." *Interdisciplinary Journal of Information, Knowledge, and Management* 11: 273–83.

ITU (International Telecommunication Union). 2021. *Global Cybersecurity Index 2020: Measuring Commitment to Cybersecurity*. Geneva: ITU.

ITU (International Telecommunication Union) and World Bank. 2020. *Digital Regulation Handbook*. Geneva: ITU and World Bank.

Jaupart, Pascal, and Tania Begazo. Forthcoming. "Corporate Governance and Transparency of State-Owned and State-Linked Digital Enterprises in Africa." Background paper for *Digital Africa: Technological Transformation for Jobs*, World Bank, Washington, DC.

Kabanda, Salah, Maureen Tanner, and Cameron Kent. 2018. "Exploring SME Cybersecurity Practices in Developing Countries." *Journal of Organizational Computing and Electronic Commerce* 28 (3): 269–82.

Kavuma, Susan Namirembe, Christine Byaruhanga, Nicholas Musoke, Patrick Loke, Michael Noble, and Gemma Wright. 2020. *An Analysis of the Distributional Impact of Excise Duty in Uganda Using a Tax-Benefit Microsimulation Model.* Helsinki: United Nations University World Institute for Development Economics Research (UNU-WIDER).

Kechiche, Sylwia. 2022. "MTN Performed Best among Operator Groups in Sub-Saharan Africa." Ookla Insights, September 19, 2022. https://www.ookla.com/articles/mobile-perfrormance-mtn-airtel -orange-vodacom-sub-saharan-africa-q3-2022.

Khan, Navid Ali, Sarfraz Nawaz Brohi, and Noor Zaman. 2020. "Ten Deadly Cyber Security Threats Amid COVID-19 Pandemic." TechRxiv. Preprint. doi:10.36227/techrxiv.12278792.v1.

Koutroumpis, Pantelis. 2009. "The Economic Impact of Broadband on Growth: A Simultaneous Approach." *Telecommunications Policy* 33 (9): 471–85.

Leukfeldt, Eric Rutger, Edward R. Kleemans, and Wouter P. Stol. 2017. "Cybercriminal Networks, Social Ties and Online Forums: Social Ties versus Digital Ties within Phishing and Malware Networks." *British Journal of Criminology* 57 (3): 704–22.

Lucas-Mas, Cristian Óliver, and Raúl Félix Junquera-Varela. 2021. *Tax Theory Applied to the Digital Economy: A Proposal for a Digital Data Tax and a Global Internet Tax Agency.* Washington, DC: World Bank.

Maphosa, Vusumuzi, and Mfowabo Maphosa. 2020. "E-Waste Management in Sub-Saharan Africa: A Systematic Literature Review." *Cogent Business & Management* 7 (1): 1814503. doi:10.1080/233119 75.2020.1814503.

Melhem, Samia, Tim Kelly, Lucine Munkyung Park, Charles Pierre Marie Hurpy, and Sajitha Bashir. 2021. "Feasibility Study to Connect all African Higher Education Institutions to High-Speed Internet." Report No. 161742, World Bank, Washington, DC.

Mothobi, Onkokame. 2020. "The Impact of Mobile Number Portability on Demand Price Elasticities in Sub-Saharan African Countries." *Review of Network Economics* 19 (4): 249–68.

Mumo, Muthoki. 2017. "Airtel Kenya Earns Sh309m from Leasing Out Network to Third Parties." *Business Daily Africa*, September 1, 2017. https://www.businessdailyafrica.com/bd/corporate /companies/airtel-kenya-earns-sh309m-from-leasing-out-network-to-third-parties--2167346.

Nicolle, Ambre, Lukasz Grzybowski, and Christine Zulehner. 2018. "Impact of Competition, Investment, and Regulation on Prices of Mobile Services: Evidence from France." *Economic Inquiry* 56 (2): 1322–45.

Niesten, Hannelore, and Tania Begazo. 2021. "Taxing Digital Connectivity in Africa." Unpublished paper, World Bank, Washington, DC.

Nkhonjera, Maria. 2017. "Competition Authority of Kenya (CAK) Rules on USSD Pricing." *CCRED Quarterly Review* (blog), April 12, 2017. https://www.competition.org.za/ccred-blog-competition -review/2017/4/12/competition-authority-of-kenya-cak-rules-on-ussd-pricing.

Nshunguyinka, Alexandre, Obed Shema, and Martin Saint. 2021. "An Econometric Analysis of the Effects of Mobile Termination Rates on the Telecom Services Market in a Developing Country: Evidence from Microdata." Paper presented at TPRC48: The 48th Research Conference on Communication, Information and Internet Policy (virtual), February 17–19. doi:10.2139 /ssrn.3749687.

Nyawira, Susan. 2020. "Competition Authority of Kenya Seeks to Regulate Vast Digital Lending Sector." *Star*, February 24, 2020. https://www.the-star.co.ke/business/kenya/2020-02-24 -competition-authority-of-kenya-seeks-to-regulate-vast-digital-lending-sector/.

Nyman, Sara, and Guilherme Falco. 2020. "Institutional Design for Independent and Efficient Competition Authorities." Unpublished manuscript, World Bank, Washington, DC.

Ochieng, Lilian. 2014. "CAK Orders Safaricom to Open Up M-Pesa." *Nation*, July 27, 2014. https:// nation.africa/kenya/business/cak-orders-safaricom-to-open-up-m-pesa-1009260.

OECD (Organisation for Economic Co-operation and Development). 2008. "Broadband and the Economy." Ministerial background report DSTI/ICCP/IC(2007)3/FINAL for the OECD Ministerial Meeting in Seoul, Republic of Korea, June 17–18.

OECD (Organisation for Economic Co-operation and Development). 2019. *OECD Reviews of Digital Transformation: Going Digital in Colombia.* Paris: OECD.

OECD (Organisation for Economic Co-operation and Development). 2020. *Shaping the Future of Regulators: The Impact of Emerging Technologies on Economic Regulators.* Paris: OECD Publishing.

Ofcom (Office of Communications). 2016. "Communications Market Report 2016." Research document, Ofcom, London.

Ofcom (Office of Communications). 2019. "Local Access Licence." Guidance document, Ofcom, London.

Ofcom (Office of Communications). 2020. "Universal Service Conditions and Directions." Document, Ofcom, London.

Onianwa, Percy. 2021. "Towards Achieving Net Zero in the ICT Sector: Africa's Priorities for Environmentally Sound Management of E-Waste." Presentation at the Sustainable Digital Transformation in Africa webinar, International Telecommunication Union (virtual), September 28.

Osoro, Ogutu B., and Edward J. Oughton. 2021. "A Techno-Economic Framework for Satellite Networks Applied to Low Earth Orbit Constellations: Assessing Starlink, OneWeb and Kuiper." *IEEE Access* 9: 141611–141625. doi:10.1109/ACCESS.2021.3119634.

Oughton, Edward J. 2022. "Policy Options for Broadband Infrastructure Strategies: A Simulation Model for Affordable Universal Broadband in Africa." Policy Research Working Paper 10263, World Bank, Washington, DC.

Oughton, Edward J., Niccolò Comini, Vivien Foster, and Jim W. Hall. 2022. "Policy Choices Can Help Keep 4G and 5G Universal Broadband Affordable." *Technological Forecasting and Social Change* 176: 121409. doi:10.1016/j.techfore.2021.121409.

Pedros, Xavier, Kalvin Bahia, Pau Castells, and Dennisa Nichiforov-Chuang. 2020. "Effective Spectrum Pricing in Africa: How Successful Awards Can Help Drive Mobile Connectivity." Report, Global System for Mobile Communications Association (GSMA), London.

Piot, Stéphane, Philip Bates, and Kerron Edmunson. 2018. "Telecommunication Competition Market Study in Kenya." Presentation to stakeholders and members of the public, Analysys Mason, London, February 20.

Pop, Georgiana, and Gonçalo Coelho. 2020. "Getting the Competition Game Right in Mobile Communications and Radio Spectrum in West Africa: An Assessment of Regulatory Restrictions to Competition." Policy note, World Bank, Washington, DC.

Pop, Georgiana, and Gonçalo Coelho. 2021a. "Competition Across the Radio Spectrum in West Africa: Regional and National Aspects." Competition Policy International, January 6, 2021. https://www.competitionpolicyinternational.com/competition-across-the-radio-spectrum-in-west-africa-regional-and-national-aspects/.

Pop, Georgiana, and Gonçalo Coelho. 2021b. "Competition Policy in Digital Markets in Africa." Unpublished manuscript, World Bank, Washington, DC.

Pop, Georgiana, and Davida Connon. Forthcoming. "State-Owned Enterprises in Digital Infrastructure and Downstream Digital Markets in Africa." Background note, World Bank, Washington, DC.

Purfield, Mary Catriona, Marek Hanusch, Yashvir Algu, Tania Priscilla Begazo Gomez, Martha Martinez Licetti, and Sara Nyman. 2016. "South Africa Economic Update: Promoting Faster Growth and Poverty Alleviation through Competition." *South Africa Economic Update, 8th Edition*, World Bank, Washington, DC.

Ren, Amos Loh Yee, Chong Tze Liang, Im Jun Hyug, Sarfraz Nawaz Broh, and N. Z. Jhanjhi. 2020. "A Three-Level Ransomware Detection and Prevention Mechanism." *EAI Endorsed Transactions on Energy Web* 7 (26): e6.

Roberts, Tony, ed. 2021. *Digital Rights in Closing Civic Space: Lessons from Ten African Countries.* Brighton, UK: Institute of Development Studies.

Roessler, Philip, Peter Carroll, Flora Myamba, Cornel Jahari, Blandina Kilama, and Daniel Nielson. 2021. "The Economic Impact of Mobile Phone Ownership: Results from a Randomized Controlled Trial in Tanzania." Working Paper Series 2021-05, Centre for the Study of African Economies, University of Oxford.

Rosston, Gregory L., and Scott J. Wallsten. 2020. "Increasing Low-Income Broadband Adoption through Private Incentives." *Telecommunications Policy* 44 (9): 102020. doi:10.1016/j.telpol.2020.102020.

Rota-Graziosi, Gregoire, and Fayçal Sawadogo. 2022. "The Tax Burden on Mobile Network Operators in Africa." *Telecommunications Policy* 46 (5): 102293. doi:10.1016/j.telpol.2021.102293.

RSM (Radio Spectrum Management). n.d. "Managed Spectrum Park Licences." Ministry of Business, Innovation & Employment, New Zealand Government, Wellington. https://www.rsm.govt.nz /licensing/licences-you-must-pay-for/managed-spectrum-park-licences/.

Seim, Katja, and Brian Viard. 2011. "The Effect of Market Structure on Cellular Technology Adoption and Pricing." *American Economic Journal: Microeconomics* 3 (2): 221–51.

Sense Strategy. 2021. "Data Protection in Africa." Unpublished report prepared for Smart Africa.

Shearer, Eleanor, Richard Stirling, and Walter Pasquarelli. 2020. "Government AI Readiness Index 2020." Report, Oxford Insights, Malvern, UK.

Song, Steve. 2016. "What If Everyone Had Free 2G Mobile Internet Access?" *ICTworks* (blog), January 6, 2016. https://www.ictworks.org/what-if-everyone-had-free-2g-mobile-internet -access/#.Y_qvaS-B3zh.

Srinivasan, Sharada, Niccolò Comini, and Michael Minges. 2021. "The Importance of National Data Infrastructure for Low and Middle-Income Countries." Paper presented at TPRC49: The 49th Research Conference on Communication, Information and Internet Policy (virtual), September 22–24.

Sulayman, Muhammad, Cathy Urquhart, Emilia Mendes, and Stefan Seidel. 2012. "Software Process Improvement Success Factors for Small and Medium Web Companies: A Qualitative Study." *Information and Software Technology* 54 (5): 479–500.

Thomas, David. 2021. "Facebook and Liquid Technologies Plan 2000km Fibre Network from DRC to Rwanda." *African Business*, July 5, 2021. https://african.business/2021/07/technology-information /facebook-and-liquid-technologies-partner-on-2000km-drc-fibre-network/.

Tiwari, Abhishek. 2020. "SuperCell: Reaching New Heights for Wider Connectivity." *Engineering at Meta* (blog), December 3, 2020. https://engineering.fb.com/2020/12/03/connectivity/ supercell-reaching-new-heights-for-wider-connectivity/.

Torgusson, Casey, Cecilia Paradi-Guilford, Isabella Hayward, Ivan Gonzalez Berenguer Pena, Edgardo Sepulveda, Michael Kende, Richard Morgan, Neil Grandal, and David Abecassis. 2018. "A Single Digital Market for East Africa: Presenting a Vision, Strategic Framework, Implementation Roadmap and Impact Assessment." Report No. 136699, World Bank, Washington, DC.

TowerXchange. 2021. "TowerXchange 31, 05/21." TowerXchange, London. https://www.towerxchange .com/Publications/TowerXchange-31-05-21.

Vergara-Cobos, Estefania. 2021. "High Broadband Prices and Limited Offerings Constraining Data Use by SMEs." Unpublished background note, World Bank, Washington, DC.

Vergara-Cobos, Estefania, Eduardo Malasquez, and Rogelio Granguillhome. Forthcoming. "Competition, Mobile Telecommunication, and Welfare: A Multicountry Analysis in Africa." Unpublished manuscript, World Bank, Washington, DC.

Wainaina, Eric. 2016. "Equitel Wins Case Challenging Awarding of Its MNVO Licence." *Techweez*, January 8, 2016. https://techweez.com/2016/01/08/equitel-mnvo-licence-case/.

Walker, James. 2020. "South African Healthcare Provider Hit by Cyber-Attack." *Daily Swig*, June 9, 2020. https://portswigger.net/daily-swig/south-african-healthcare-provider-hit-by-cyber-attack.

WEF (World Economic Forum). 2018. *The Global Risks Report 2018, 13th Edition*. Geneva: WEF.

Whitacre, Brian, and Colin Rhinesmith. 2015. "Public Libraries and Residential Broadband Adoption: Do More Computers Lead to Higher Rates?" *Government Information Quarterly* 32 (2): 164–71.

Woodhams, Samuel. 2020. "Huawei Says Its Surveillance Tech Will Keep African Cities Safe but Activists Worry It'll Be Misused." *Quartz Africa*, March 20, 2020. https://qz.com/africa /1822312/huaweis-surveillance-tech-in-africa-worries-activists.

World Bank. 2019a. "Digital Economy for Africa (DE4A): Country Diagnostic of Senegal." Digital Development Partnership report, World Bank, Washington, DC.

World Bank. 2019b. "Financial Performance, Corporate Governance and Reform of State-Owned Enterprises in Angola." Report No. AUS0000911, World Bank, Washington, DC.

World Bank. 2019c. "Nigeria Digital Economy Diagnostic Report." Report of the Digital Economy for Africa (DE4A) Initiative, World Bank, Washington, DC.

World Bank. 2021a. "Harnessing Artificial Intelligence for Development in the Post-COVID-19 Era: A Review of National AI Strategies and Policies." Analytical Insights Note 4, World Bank, Washington, DC.

World Bank. 2021b. "Regulatory Watch Initiative (RWI) Phase 2: Thorough Legal, Regulatory and Competitive Analyses of Issues Related to Licensing, OTTs, International Gateways, Spectrum Management and Regulatory Governance." Internal report, World Bank, Washington, DC.

World Bank. 2021c. "Rwanda Digital Acceleration Project (P173373) Project Information Document (PID)." Report No. PIDA29659, World Bank, Washington, DC.

World Bank. 2021d. "World Bank Provides $100 Million to Accelerate Rwanda's Digital Transformation." Press release, December 1, 2021. https://www.worldbank.org/en/news/press -release/2021/12/01/world-bank-provides-100-million-to-accelerate-rwanda-s-digital -transformation.

World Bank. 2021e. *World Development Report 2021: Data for Better Lives.* Washington, DC: World Bank.

World Bank. 2022. "Using Geospatial Analysis to Overhaul Mobile Connectivity Policies: How to Expand Mobile Internet Coverage and Adoption in Sub-Saharan Africa." Report No. 169437, World Bank, Washington, DC.

World Bank. Forthcoming. "Regulating the Digital Economy in Africa: Managing Old and New Risks to Economic Governance for Inclusive Opportunities." Report, World Bank, Washington, DC.

World Bank Group and African Competition Forum. 2016. "Breaking Down Barriers: Unlocking Africa's Potential through Vigorous Competition Policy." Report No. 106717, World Bank, Nairobi, Kenya.

Xalam Analytics and ADCA (Africa Data Centres Association). 2021. "Growing Africa's Data Center Ecosystem: An Assessment of Utility Requirements." White paper, ADCA, Abidjan, Côte d'Ivoire.

Zou, George W. 2021. "Wired and Hired: Employment Effects of Subsidized Broadband Internet for Low-Income Americans." *American Economic Journal: Economic Policy* 13 (3): 447–82.

www.ingramcontent.com/pod-product-compliance
Lightning Source LLC
Chambersburg PA
CBHW050906210326
41597CB00002B/41